AF782379

PNAS
www.pnas.org
Rs. 2108/-
21/4/18

Economic Pc
2C

GOING FOR GROWTH

OECD

This work is published on the responsibility of the Secretary-General of the OECD. The opinions expressed and arguments employed herein do not necessarily reflect the official views of the Organisation or of the governments of its member countries.

This document and any map included herein are without prejudice to the status of or sovereignty over any territory, to the delimitation of international frontiers and boundaries and to the name of any territory, city or area.

Please cite this publication as:
OECD (2012), *Economic Policy Reforms 2012: Going for Growth*, OECD Publishing.
http://dx.doi.org/10.1787/growth-2012-en

ISBN 978-92-64-16825-1 (print)
ISBN 978-92-64-16844-2 (PDF)

Annual: Economic Policy Reforms
ISSN 1813-2715 (print)
ISSN 1813-2723 (online)

The statistical data for Israel are supplied by and under the responsibility of the relevant Israeli authorities. The use of such data by the OECD is without prejudice to the status of the Golan Heights, East Jerusalem and Israeli settlements in the West Bank under the terms of international law.

Corrigenda to OECD publications may be found on line at: *www.oecd.org/publishing/corrigenda*.

© OECD 2012

You can copy, download or print OECD content for your own use, and you can include excerpts from OECD publications, databases and multimedia products in your own documents, presentations, blogs, websites and teaching materials, provided that suitable acknowledgement of OECD as source and copyright owner is given. All requests for public or commercial use and translation rights should be submitted to *rights@oecd.org*. Requests for permission to photocopy portions of this material for public or commercial use shall be addressed directly to the Copyright Clearance Center (CCC) at *info@copyright.com* or the Centre français d'exploitation du droit de copie (CFC) at *contact@cfcopies.com*.

Going for Growth was launched in 2005 as a new form of structural surveillance complementing the OECD's long-standing country and sector-specific surveys. In line with the OECD's 1960 founding Convention, the aim is to help promote vigorous sustainable economic growth and improve the well-being of OECD citizens.

This surveillance is based on a systematic and in-depth analysis of structural policies and their outcomes across OECD members, relying on a set of internationally comparable and regularly updated policy indicators with a well-established link to performance. Using these indicators, alongside the expertise of OECD committees and staff, policy priorities and recommendations are derived for each member and, starting from the 2011 edition, six key non-member economies with which the OECD works closely (Brazil, China, India, Indonesia, Russia and South Africa). From one issue to the next, *Going for Growth* follows up on these recommendations and priorities evolve, not least as a result of governments taking action on the identified policy priorities.

Underpinning this type of benchmarking is the observation that drawing lessons from mutual success and failure is a powerful avenue for progress. While allowance should be made for genuine differences in social preferences across OECD members, the uniqueness of national circumstances should not serve to justify inefficient policies.

In gauging performance, the focus is on GDP per capita, productivity and employment. As highlighted in the past and again in this issue, this leaves out some important dimensions of well-being. For this reason, *Going for Growth* regularly features thematic chapters dedicated to these other dimensions, and increasingly looks at the side effects of growth-enhancing priorities on other government policy objectives.

Going for Growth is the fruit of a joint effort across a large number of OECD Departments.

www.oecd.org/economics/goingforgrowth

Editorial

Struggling with the Crisis: Structural Reforms Can Make the Difference

The uncertainty surrounding world economic prospects for the coming year and beyond is unusually high. This is largely because the course economic policies will take in major OECD economies remains unclear. Worst-case outcomes can be forestalled provided monetary policy remains very supportive, sovereign debt and banking sector problems in the euro area are contained, and excessive fiscal tightening is avoided where there is room to proceed gradually, not least in the United States. But even then unemployment would stay high through 2013, there would be no prospect of recovering the output foregone with the crisis, and public budgets would remain on unsustainable paths across most of the OECD. Even under a more optimistic scenario, underpinned by a decisive resolution of the crisis in the euro area, the need to work off the divergence in cost competitiveness among member countries could still produce economic and political headwinds. On the other hand, failing to address such divergence would keep in place the fundamental imbalances that have led to the current crisis. More generally, growth needs to be lifted in most advanced economies and made more sustainable in most emerging markets.

The structural reform priorities we have identified in Going for Growth are key to addressing these issues in OECD and non-OECD countries. In separate work we carried out as part of the G20 Mutual Assessment Process, we estimated that a broad and ambitious reform agenda could raise annual GDP growth by as much as one per cent on average across the OECD over the next ten years. In the BRIICS, product market liberalisation could deliver sizeable gains as well, both in terms of growth and global rebalancing. Productivity-enhancing reforms, not least a reduction in entry barriers in product markets, can go some way towards restoring the external competitiveness of those European countries hit by the sovereign debt crisis, provided complementary labour market reforms ensure wage moderation. More generally, growth-enhancing structural reforms should be an essential part of the policy action needed to put the euro area on a sustainable path.

Some of our Going for Growth recommendations would also mitigate risks that higher unemployment turns structural. In particular, sheltering active labour market policies from ongoing fiscal consolidation efforts – and indeed strengthening them where possible – would help job seekers find new jobs more quickly and ensure that those at risk of discouragement remain attached to the labour market. And in economies that experience renewed economic set-backs, it will be important to build on the lessons from the crisis in terms of what works to cushion the labour market impact of adverse economic shocks, such as making use of short-time working schemes and, more broadly, of state-contingent policies.

The good news is that governments are now acting more forcefully on the structural front than they did before or in the early stages of the crisis. This year's edition of Going for Growth provides a unique and detailed review of the policy measures taken by each country since the start of the crisis in 2007. This stocktaking exercise shows that the pace of structural reform has clearly accelerated over the past two years. Even more encouraging, this acceleration has also taken place where it is most needed, not least in some of the most affected euro area countries.

One often voiced and legitimate concern is that structural reforms could initially deepen the slump. The truth is that economic theory is thin and empirical evidence virtually non-existent on the short-term effects of reforms. Our new research, gathered in a special chapter, fills some of this gap and delivers an optimistic message: fears that reforms may depress economic activity in the short run are overblown. Indeed among the wide range of reforms we looked at, none was found to have had systematic adverse short-term effects in the past, while many quickly stimulated output and employment. At the same time, our analysis suggests that some labour market reforms can indeed be temporarily detrimental if implemented in bad times. Where possible, these should wait until the labour market improves decisively, and be preceded by product and financial market reforms. Another important implication of our analysis is that a comprehensive reform package is necessary to alleviate the adverse short-term effects of some reforms while contributing to kick-start the economy, especially through investment induced by stronger product market competition. In any event, effective communication and consensus building are of the essence to foster the confidence households need to take advantage of reform-driven income gains.

Another legitimate concern is that reforms may harm the least well-off. Income inequality was already on the rise in most OECD countries before the crisis, and it has likely risen further in its aftermath. It is also a major issue in the BRIICS. Two special chapters in this report yield encouraging lessons regarding what reforms do to inequality both in the long term and in the wake of macroeconomic shocks like financial crises. We find that several reforms, notably enhancing the quality and equity of secondary education, liberalising product markets and making employment protection legislation more uniform across workers, appear to have favourable growth and distributive impacts. Some tax reforms can also be beneficial on both grounds. Starting with a drastic cut in tax expenditures would seem especially warranted at the current juncture, not least since it would also help fiscal consolidation. Now not all growth-friendly reforms would yield such double or triple dividends, of course. In particular, it remains challenging to design tax and transfer systems in ways that are conducive to both higher growth and lower inequality. For one, the experience of some Nordic countries shows that it can be done. And again, broad reform packages including win-win policies could deliver on both goals.

As mentioned at the outset, the global economy could take different paths in the coming months depending on the decisiveness and effectiveness of policy action. While this requires appropriate and possibly bold contributions by macroeconomic policies, structural reforms are necessary both to accelerate the exit from the deep phase of the crisis, especially in some regions, and to make longer term growth stronger, more sustainable, and possibly less unequal.

Pier Carlo Padoan
Deputy Secretray-General and
Chief Economist, OECD

Table of contents

This book has...

StatLinks

A service that delivers Excel® files from the printed page!

Look for the *StatLinks* at the bottom right-hand corner of the tables or graphs in this book. To download the matching Excel® spreadsheet, just type the link into your Internet browser, starting with the ***http://dx.doi.org*** prefix.
If you're reading the PDF e-book edition, and your PC is connected to the Internet, simply click on the link. You'll find *StatLinks* appearing in more OECD books.

ISO Codes

The codes for country names and currencies used in this volume are those attributed to them by the International Organization for Standardization (ISO).

Country code	Country name	Currency code
AUS	Australia	AUD
AUT	Austria	EUR
BEL	Belgium	EUR
BRA	Brazil	BRL
CAN	Canada	CAD
CHE	Switzerland	CHF
CHL	Chile	CLP
CHN	China	CNY
CZE	Czech Republic	CZK
DEU	Germany	EUR
DNK	Denmark	DKK
ESP	Spain	EUR
EST	Estonia	EUR
FIN	Finland	EUR
FRA	France	EUR
GBR	United Kingdom	GBP
GRC	Greece	EUR
HUN	Hungary	HUF
IDN	Indonesia	IDR
IND	India	INR
IRL	Ireland	EUR
ISL	Iceland	ISK
ISR	Israel	ILS
ITA	Italy	EUR
JPN	Japan	JPY
KOR	Republic of Korea	KRW
LUX	Luxembourg	EUR
MEX	Mexico	MXN
NLD	Netherlands	EUR
NOR	Norway	NOK
NZL	New Zealand	NZD
POL	Poland	PLN
PRT	Portugal	EUR
RUS	Russian Federation	RUB
SVK	Slovak Republic	SKK
SVN	Slovenia	EUR
SWE	Sweden	SEK
TUR	Turkey	TRL
USA	United States	UDS
ZAF	South Africa	ZAR

Economic Policy Reforms 2012: Going for Growth
Going for Growth
© OECD 2012

Executive summary

Structural reform priorities to boost real incomes have been identified by the OECD through the *Going for Growth* analysis since 2005 for each OECD country and, starting with the 2011 edition, the BRIICS – Brazil, China, India, Indonesia, Russia and South Africa, key non-member countries with which the OECD works closely. This process provides a tool for governments to reflect on policy reforms that affect their residents' long-term living standards. *Going for Growth* analysis has been used in the Mutual Assessment Process of the G20 since the 2008 Pittsburgh Summit.

This new edition of *Going for Growth* assesses progress that countries have made on structural reforms since the start of the crisis, covering the whole period 2007-11. The crisis has delivered new policy challenges and lessons, but it has also made the necessity of many *Going for Growth* priorities more apparent. The main reform patterns that emerge over the years since the start of the crisis, which are summed up in an overview chapter (Chapter 1) and described in greater detail in individual country notes (Chapter 2), are as follows:

- The pace of reform, as measured by the responsiveness of countries to reform priorities identified in previous issues of *Going for Growth*, was greater overall after than before the crisis.
- The pace and the nature of reforms have varied markedly throughout the distinct phases of the crisis, however. The 2008 recession at first slowed down structural reforms in OECD countries, with the main preoccupations being the pressing need to stabilise aggregate demand and provide income support to the unemployed. As the need for medium-term fiscal consolidation became more pressing, reforms were implemented in policy areas which could help assist the fiscal adjustment process, such as retirement schemes, welfare systems and public sector reforms.
- The crisis and ensuing sluggish recovery have acted as a catalyst for structural reforms especially in OECD countries where reforms were most needed. Lower-income OECD countries, which are generally in greater need of reform, and those countries that saw unemployment rise most during the crisis, have acted more on their relevant *Going for Growth* priorities.
- The need to consolidate public finances and the financial pressure arising from mushrooming sovereign debt have given another impetus to reform since 2009, contrasting with past evidence that fiscal tightening tends to hold back reforms. In particular, the most recent phase of the crisis has seen an acceleration of politically sensitive reforms designed to help lift potential growth, regain price competitiveness and restore fiscal sustainability in countries affected by the European debt crisis.

- The impact of the crisis was both milder and shorter in the BRIICS, but it also made more apparent the necessity of measures that could deliver more inclusive growth. All emerging economies covered here have implemented policies aimed at enhancing the quality and inclusiveness of their education systems, but less has been done to address other important priorities, such as the reduction of barriers to foreign direct investment and the enhancement of the rule of law.
- Given what has been done in recent years, priority should be given to policies that can boost jobs in the context of ongoing fiscal consolidation:
  - Effective active labour market policies aimed at retraining displaced workers and encouraging return to work can reduce unemployment persistence. There is a case for sheltering such policies from fiscal consolidation efforts, and for complementing them with unemployment benefit reforms once recovery in labour market demand is solid. In particular, crisis-related increases in benefit levels and/or duration could be gradually phased out while some of the recent extensions in the coverage of unemployment benefits could be made permanent.
  - Growth-friendly tax reforms could help strengthen the jobs content of a recovery, while also helping fiscal consolidation insofar as they are implemented in a way that raises tax revenue. These include removing tax expenditures and shifting the tax burden towards tax bases that are less harmful to employment and growth, such as immovable property, consumption and environmental taxes.
  - Product market reforms are a priority for many OECD countries – in particular in Europe, and could have fairly rapid effects on growth, especially if implemented in certain sheltered sectors such as retail trade and professional services where the potential to quickly create jobs is rather high.
  - In economies that experience renewed economic slack, it will be important that the policy response draws on the lessons from the crisis as to what works in terms of cushioning the labour market impact of weak activity, such as making use of short-time working schemes.

While the crisis has made the necessity of structural reforms more apparent and provided an impetus to action, concerns have been raised that some of them could be detrimental in the short term, for instance if they further weaken aggregate demand. Drawing on 30 years of reform experiences across OECD countries, Chapter 4 sheds light on the short-term impact of structural reforms. It provides a number of policy lessons on how to design the current reform agenda in ways that would help kick-start the recovery:

- Concerns about possible negative short-term effects of structural reforms seem exaggerated. Some structural reforms appear to boost growth fairly quickly, while usually very few if any have short-term costs.
- The benefits from reforms often take time – typically several years – to fully materialise, however.
- Also, cyclical conditions matter for the short-term effects of reforms. There is some evidence that in "bad times", certain labour market reforms (of unemployment benefit systems and job protection in particular) can make the economic situation temporarily worse. In still depressed economies and unless current policies are clearly seen as aberrant, it may be preferable therefore that such reforms be carried out only once the labour market shows clear signs of recovery.

- A well designed package of labour and product market reforms would deliver the largest gains and alleviate the transitional costs of certain individual reforms – for instance, liberalising product markets alongside job protection or unemployment benefit reforms can mitigate possible real wage declines associated with the latter.
- The short-term impact of structural reforms will be stronger if an effective communication strategy and a strong and well-regulated banking sector foster confidence and induce households and firms to spend against future reform-driven income gains.

The recognition of widening income gaps within most OECD countries over the past decades has highlighted concerns that structural reforms – and therefore some of the *Going for Growth* priorities – may increase income inequality. Such concerns have gained further prominence in the context of the crisis, particularly in countries where current reform action is being driven primarily by fiscal consolidation objectives. Chapter 5 examines complementarities and trade-offs between reducing inequality and promoting economic growth:

- Many structural reforms entail a double dividend as they reduce income inequality while at the same time boosting long-run GDP per capita. Examples include facilitating the accumulation of human capital notably at the secondary level, improving the efficiency and the equity of education, reducing labour market dualism, promoting the integration of immigrants and fostering female labour market participation. Reducing tax expenditures along with reducing marginal tax rates also typically contributes to both goals.
- By contrast, other reforms may entail a trade-off between growth and income distribution objectives. For instance, shifting the tax mix away from labour and corporate income taxes towards consumption taxes improves incentives to work, save and invest, but can undermine equity. However, cash transfers targeted to lower incomes can be used to ease this trade off.

The distribution of income is not only shaped by long-term trends like changes in policies and institutions, technological change or globalisation, but is also affected, sometimes durably, by macroeconomic shocks such as the recent financial crisis. Based on empirical analysis for 40 OECD and BRIICS countries over 30 years, Chapter 6 explores the distributive effects of macroeconomic shocks on both income and employment, and the role of policies and institutions in shaping them. The Chapter identifies who gains and loses, and sheds light on the articulation between risk-sharing and growth objectives:

- Incomes of the poor and jobs of the young have in general been most affected in bad times, although they have also risen more strongly in good times. In the case of past financial crises, both high-income households and the poor have been hurt more severely than middle classes.
- Reforms that can improve risk sharing while also benefiting growth and jobs, not least by facilitating the reallocation of labour across the economy, include liberalising product markets, removing barriers to trade and FDI and lowering high taxes on labour.
- Many social protection programmes appear to have mitigated the job or income losses of vulnerable groups in the wake of past shocks, but since such schemes can come at a cost in terms of jobs and income particular care is needed in designing them. This is especially the case for generous unemployment benefits, high minimum wages and strict job protection.

- Countries can be classified in four groups, depending on the extent to which their policy settings provide social protection and facilitate labour reallocation. Most countries of continental Europe provide income risk sharing primarily *via* social protection programmes, while English-speaking and Asian OECD countries rely mainly on reallocation-facilitating institutions. Nordic countries tend to have both, while in emerging countries neither class of institutions are developed. An effective policy mix to deliver on both risk-sharing and growth objectives combines reallocation-facilitating institutions – which always benefit both goals – and a well-designed social protection system – *i.e.* one that achieves a given insurance objective at minimum cost.

PART I

Taking stock of structural policies in OECD countries and the BRIICS

Economic Policy Reforms 2012
Going for Growth
© OECD 2012

PART I

Chapter 1

Structural reforms in times of crisis

The crisis has raised new policy challenges, but it has also made the necessity of structural reforms more apparent. This initial chapter of Going for Growth *assesses progress that countries have made in structural reforms since the start of the crisis, covering the whole period 2007-11.*

The key political economy lesson emerging from the analysis is that the crisis and ensuing recession have acted as a catalyst for structural reforms, especially in OECD countries where reforms were most needed. In particular, the depth of the labour market crisis has provided an impetus for structural reforms aimed at raising labour utilisation. The need to consolidate public finances and the financial pressure arising from mushrooming sovereign debt have given another impetus to reform, with a clear acceleration of politically sensitive reforms designed to help lift potential growth, regain price competitiveness and restore fiscal sustainability, especially in some euro area countries.

Going forward, priority should be given to boosting jobs in the context of ongoing fiscal consolidation. For now, there is a clear case for sheltering activation policies aimed at retraining displaced workers and encouraging return to work from fiscal consolidation efforts. And in countries that experience renewed economic set-backs it will be important to build on the lessons from the financial crisis in terms of policies that can help cushion the labour market and social impact of weak activity, such as making use of short-time working schemes. Tax reforms, not least a reduction in tax expenditures and a shift in the tax burden away from labour, could help kick-start the jobs recovery and assist fiscal consolidation. Product market reforms could also boost short-term growth, especially if implemented in sheltered sectors where the potential to quickly create jobs is relatively high, such as retail trade and professional services.

Summary and conclusions

Going for Growth reports have been published by the OECD every year since 2005. The *Going for Growth* analysis identifies five structural reform priorities to boost real income for each OECD country, for the European Union as a whole, and starting with the 2011 edition, the BRIICS – Brazil, China, India, Indonesia, Russia and South Africa – key non-member countries with which the OECD works closely. This process provides a tool for governments to reflect on "structural" policy reforms that affect their residents' long-term living standards. Structural policy reforms are central to the mission of the OECD, and the *Going for Growth* analysis has been used in the Mutual Assessment Process of the G20 since the 2008 Pittsburgh Summit.

The methodology used identifies policy recommendations based on their ability to improve long-term material living standards through higher productivity and labour utilisation. The reference performance measure in this regard is gross domestic product (GDP) per capita, given its contemporaneous availability and relatively broad coverage and despite its various drawbacks.[1] Policy priorities have been mainly concentrated on labour and product market policies, education, health, innovation, housing policies, the efficiency of public sectors, and tax systems. Five policy priorities were first identified in 2005, which were then reassessed in the 2007, 2009 and 2011 editions based on both observed progress in reform and new evidence. The intervening editions of *Going for Growth* have reviewed progress made on previous priorities.

This paper provides a broad overview of the progress that countries have made in structural reforms since the start of the crisis, covering the whole period 2007-11. This crisis has raised new structural policy challenges, such as reviving economies and consolidating public finances in a way that also fosters sustainable long-term growth. At the same time, it has also made the necessity of reforms such as those identified in *Going for Growth* more apparent – for example pension reforms that would boost labour utilisation while addressing fiscal sustainability concerns. The five-year retrospective allows identifying reform patterns throughout the various phases of the crisis, from which political economy lessons can be drawn. As a tool for structural surveillance, this analysis aims primarily at taking stock of reforms carried out in areas that had been previously identified as priorities in *Going for Growth*. At the same time, however, the crisis induced timely policy action to support the economy and especially the labour market,[2] including in structural areas which were not previously covered by *Going for Growth*, and it therefore delivered relevant policy lessons to amend and broaden the surveillance exercise. Against this background, this chapter covers major labour market policies and interventions implemented in the crisis context, including when those were *not* identified as *Going for Growth* priorities.

The main reform patterns that emerge over the years since the start of the crisis are as follows:

- The responsiveness of countries to OECD reform recommendations featured in *Going for Growth* was greater overall after than before the crisis. However, the pace and the nature of reforms have varied markedly throughout the distinct phases of the crisis.

The 2008 recession first slowed down structural reforms in OECD countries, due to the pressing need to stabilise aggregate demand and provide income support to the unemployed. As the need for medium-term fiscal consolidation became more pressing, reforms were implemented in policy areas which could help assist the fiscal adjustment process. This was the case with respect to both labour-utilisation (retirement schemes and welfare systems) and labour-productivity (public sector reforms and privatisation programmes)-enhancing areas.

- The crisis and ensuing recession have acted as a catalyst for structural reforms especially in OECD countries where reforms were most needed. In contrast to what was observed before the crisis, lower-income OECD countries, which are generally in greater need of reform, have acted more on priorities identified in *Going for Growth* than their higher-income counterparts. Likewise, there has been a strong correlation between the depth of the labour market crisis and subsequent reforms, *i.e.* those countries that saw unemployment rise most during the crisis have taken more measures along the *Going for Growth* labour utilisation-enhancing priorities.
- The need to consolidate public finances and the financial pressure arising from mushrooming sovereign debt have given another impetus to reform most recently, contrasting with past evidence that fiscal easing usually accompanies and facilitates reforms. Indeed, there is a strong cross-country correlation between the intensity of ongoing fiscal consolidation efforts and responsiveness to *Going for Growth* priorities over the period 2010-11. This pattern is driven mostly by the actions taken in countries affected by the European debt crisis. Indeed, the most recent phase of the crisis has seen an acceleration of politically sensitive reforms designed to help lift potential growth, regain price competitiveness and restore fiscal sustainability, especially in some euro area countries.
- Countries have sought to raise labour utilisation especially by cutting labour taxes, delaying effective retirement ages, reforming disability schemes and strengthening active labour market policies (ALMPs). At the onset of the recession, most OECD countries sought to improve the safety net for job losers by boosting unemployment benefit generosity and expanding coverage to new groups of workers. At the same time, more than two-thirds of OECD countries raised resources for job-search assistance and training programmes in order to facilitate re-employment and re-deployment. To stimulate labour demand, work-sharing arrangements were introduced or expanded in two-thirds of OECD countries, labour taxes were cut and new job or hiring subsidy schemes were introduced, often targeting marginal job seekers such as youth, older workers, or the long-term unemployed. Some temporary measures were subsequently phased out, and difficult labour market reforms were implemented in the areas of retirement schemes, job protection, minimum wages and wage bargaining systems, especially in the context of the European debt crisis.
- Regarding priorities aimed at boosting labour productivity, countries have been especially active in improving the design of their innovation policies and reforming their education systems, while much less progress has been achieved towards reducing agricultural policy support and removing barriers to foreign direct investment. The need to deliver both higher growth and credible fiscal consolidation in many OECD countries has also provided additional impetus for growth-friendly tax reforms that reduce impediments to work and invest.

- The impact of the crisis was both milder and shorter in the BRIICS, but it also made more apparent the necessity of some of the structural reforms recommended in *Going for Growth*, in particular the need in several cases to expand social protection systems in order to support workers in times of crisis and – in a longer-term perspective – achieve more equitable and sustainable growth.[3] Policy responsiveness to *Going for Growth* priorities has been mixed since early 2011, when policy recommendations to the BRIICS were made for the first time. All emerging economies have implemented policies aimed at enhancing the quality and inclusiveness of their education systems, which is a key challenge these countries face to achieve higher living standards. Helped by their generally more sustainable fiscal situations along with their higher growth prospects, most large emerging countries continued investing in physical infrastructure, another specific *Going for Growth* priority in a number of them. By contrast, less has been done to address other important productivity-enhancing priorities, such as the reduction of barriers to entrepreneurship and foreign direct investment and the enhancement of the rule of law and of governance systems.
- Given what has been done in recent years, priority should be given to action that can boost jobs in the context of ongoing fiscal consolidation:
  - At the current juncture, there is a need to reduce the risk of unemployment persistence in a number of OECD countries, which can be achieved through effective ALMPs aimed at retraining displaced workers and encouraging return to work – in this regard there is a case for sheltering public spending on such activation from fiscal consolidation efforts. Once recovery in labour market demand is solid, ALMPs should be accompanied by unemployment benefit reforms with a view to enhancing work incentives.
  - Growth-friendly tax reforms could strengthen the jobs content of a recovery, while also helping fiscal consolidation insofar as they are implemented in a way that raises tax revenue. These include removing tax expenditures and shifting the tax burden towards tax bases that are less harmful to employment and growth, such as immovable property, consumption and environmental taxes.
  - Product market reforms are a priority for many OECD countries – in particular in Europe, and could boost short-term growth, especially if implemented in certain sheltered sectors such as retail trade and professional services where the potential to quickly create jobs is rather high. By lifting productivity and potential growth, such reforms would also have beneficial effects on debt dynamics and fiscal sustainability.
  - Concerns that reforms may entail short-term economic losses before their benefits start to materialise seem to be overdone. New empirical evidence provided in Chapter 4 suggests that some structural reforms may fairly quickly boost growth while very few if any have short-term costs in general. However, some reforms can be temporarily detrimental in "bad" times, which may be a concern at the present time. For instance, the pay-off from unemployment benefit and job protection reforms appears to be less when the economy is depressed, suggesting these should probably wait until the economic situation improves decisively.
  - In economies that experience renewed economic slack, it will be important that the policy response draws on the lessons from the crisis as to what works in terms of cushioning labour market and social outcomes, such as making use of short-time working schemes.

Growth performance and policy priorities in OECD countries and the BRIICS

Understanding differences in GDP per capita across countries

Structural reforms recommended in *Going for Growth* are aimed at improving living standards by raising either labour productivity, or labour utilisation or both. Labour resource utilisation is measured as the total number of hours worked per capita, while labour productivity is measured as GDP per hour worked. The policy priorities (see Table 1.1) were identified by mapping performance weaknesses (*e.g.* low labour productivity) against policy deficiencies (*e.g.* high barriers to product markets), using internationally comparable indicators.[4]

Table 1.1. **Share of *Going for Growth* policy recommendations by subject area**

Per cent

Going for Growth edition	2007	2009	2011	2011			
	Pre-enlargement OECD			OECD in 2011	Upper-income OECD[1]	Lower-income OECD[2]	BRIICS
Productivity							
Product market regulation	25	25	24	26	20	32	33
Agriculture	5	5	5	4	6	2	0
Human capital	14	15	15	15	13	16	17
Other policy areas	15	14	18	17	16	16	30
Total	*59*	*58*	*61*	*61*	*54*	*67*	*80*
Labour utilisation							
Average and marginal taxation on labour income	7	8	8	8	11	4	0
Social benefits	20	17	17	17	21	12	7
Labour market regulation and collective wage agreements	12	13	11	11	8	14	10
Other policy areas	2	3	3	2	6	4	3
Total	*41*	*42*	*39*	*39*	*46*	*33*	*20*
Overall (%)	100	100	100	100	100	100	100
Overall (*number of priorities*)	155	155	155	175	11	90	30

1. Upper-income OECD includes countries with per capita GDP levels above the median.
2. Lower-income OECD includes countries with per capita GDP levels below the median.

Source: OECD (2007), *Economic Policy Reforms 2007: Going for Growth*, OECD Publishing; OECD (2009), *Economic Policy Reforms 2011: Going for Growth*, OECD Publishing; OECD (2011), *Economic Policy Reforms 2011: Going for Growth*, OECD Publishing.

Looking at broad indicators of performance, OECD countries' patterns of labour utilisation and productivity have remained quite stable despite the depth of the crisis (Figure 1.1, Panel A). Some exceptions stand out though, reflecting large differences across OECD member countries in the magnitude of the decline in output and the way labour markets responded to it. For instance, Ireland experienced a major decline in GDP per capita as a result of the crisis, which turned the positive income gap with respect to the upper-half of the OECD into a negative one. There was also a substantial reduction in the United States' lead in labour utilisation over the crisis period, reflecting a large increase in unemployment and a significant decline in labour force participation. The impact of the crisis has been both milder and shorter in the BRIICS countries. This has allowed them to continue to converge rapidly with OECD GDP per capita levels, mostly thanks to rising labour productivity. Nevertheless, for almost all the BRIICS, income is still 60%-90% lower than the upper half of OECD countries, mainly owing to labour productivity shortfalls. In this respect they are similar to the lower-income OECD countries. Low labour resource utilisation is also a particularly large challenge in South Africa (Figure 1.1, Panel B).

Figure 1.1. **Factors behind income variations: OECD and BRIICS countries, 2007 and 2010**

A. OECD countries

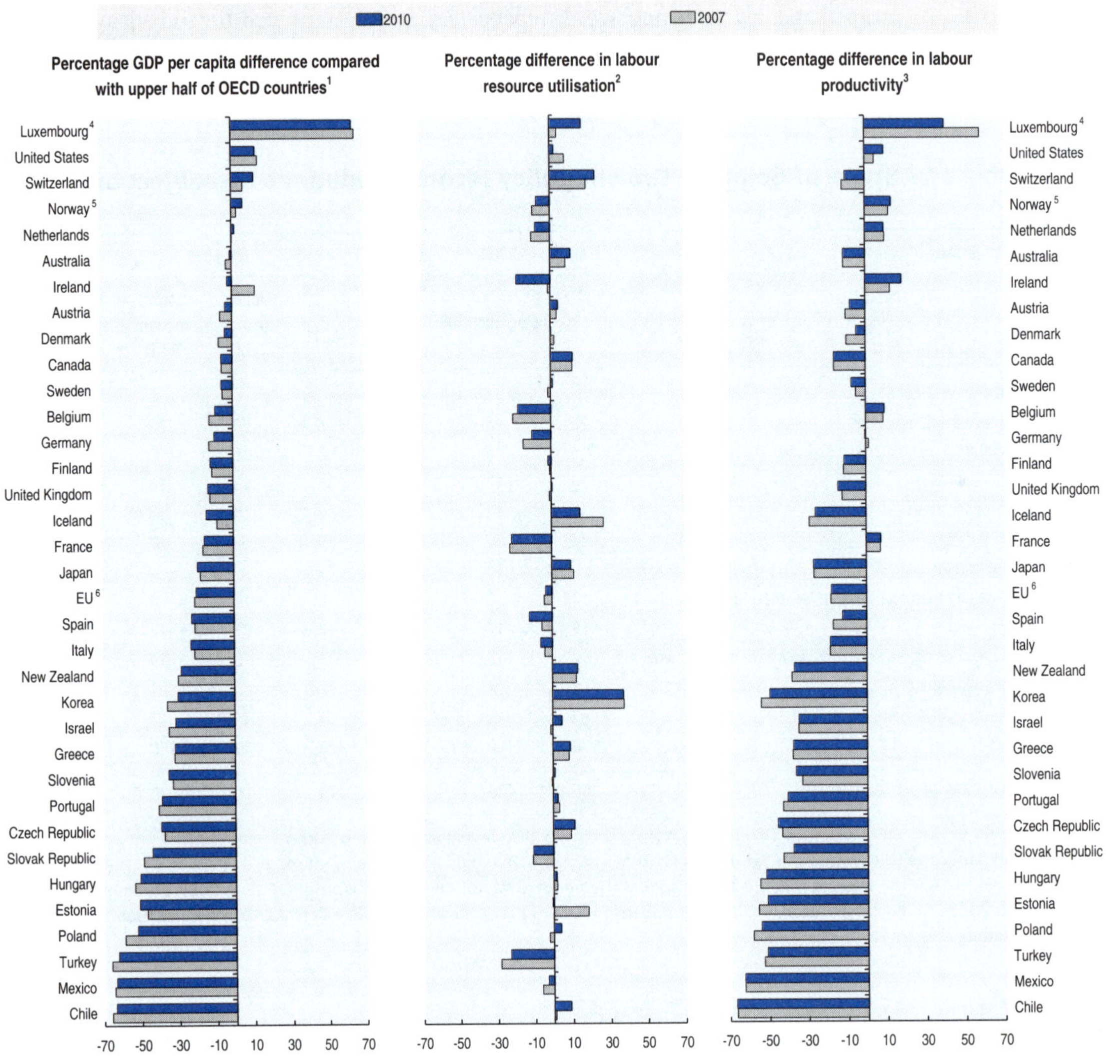

1. Compared to the average of the 17 OECD countries with highest GDP per capita in 2007 and 2010, based on 2007 and 2010 purchasing power parities (PPPs). The sum of the percentage difference in labour resource utilisation and labour productivity do not add up exactly to the GDP per capita difference since the decomposition is multiplicative.
2. Labour resource utilisation is measured as the total number of hours worked per capita.
3. Labour productivity is measured as GDP per hour worked.
4. In the case of Luxembourg, the population is augmented by the number of cross-border workers in order to take into account their contribution to GDP.
5. Data refer to GDP for mainland Norway which excludes petroleum production and shipping. While total GDP overestimates the sustainable income potential, mainland GDP slightly underestimates it since returns on the financial assets held by the petroleum fund abroad are not included.
6. The EU category brings together countries that are members of both the European Union and the OECD. These are the EU15 countries plus the Czech Republic, Estonia, Hungary, Poland, the Slovak Republic and Slovenia.

Source: OECD National Accounts Statistics *(Database)*; OECD (2011), *OECD Economic Outlook No. 90: Statistics and Projections (Database)*; OECD *Employment Outlook* (*Database*).

StatLink http://dx.doi.org/10.1787/888932564844

Figure 1.1. **Factors behind income variations: OECD and BRIICS countries, 2007 and 2010** *(cont.)*

B. BRIICS countries *vis-à-vis* the OECD (using headcount productivity data)

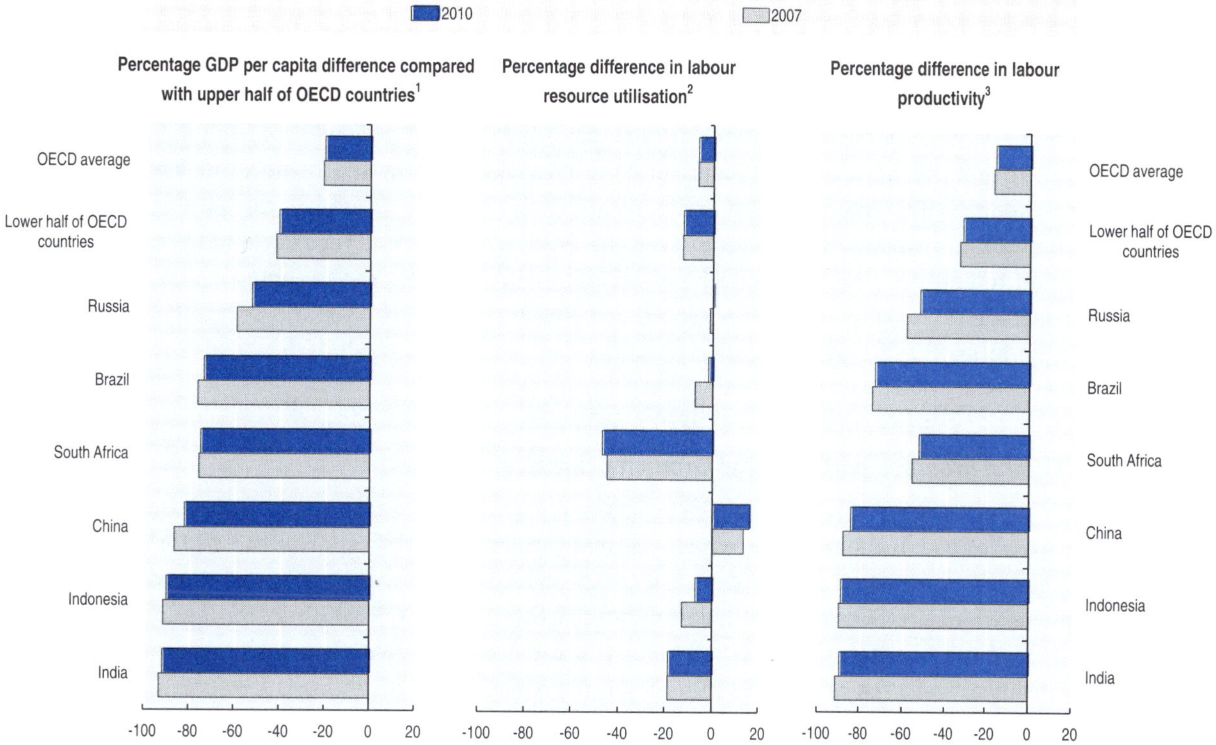

1. Compared to the average of the highest 17 OECD countries in terms of GDP per capita, based on 2007 and 2010 purchasing power parities (PPPs) from the World Bank. The OECD average is based on a simple average of the 34 member countries. The sum of the percentage gap in labour resource utilisation and labour productivity does not add up exactly to the GDP per capita gap since the decomposition is multiplicative.
2. Labour resource utilisation is measured as employment as a share of working-age individuals in the population.
3. Labour productivity is measured as GDP per employee.

Source: World Bank (2011), *World Development Indicators (WDI) (Database)*; ILO (International Labour Organisation) (2011), *Key Indicators of the Labour Market (KILM) (Database)* for employment data on Brazil and Indonesia; Statistics South Africa for employment data on South Africa; India National Sample Survey (various years), annual population estimates from the Registrar General and OECD estimates for employment data on India; China Ministry of Human Resources and Social Security for employment data on China.

StatLink http://dx.doi.org/10.1787/888932564863

Policy priorities in OECD countries and the BRIICS

Overall, the balance of policy recommendations in *Going for Growth* by subject area has remained quite stable for OECD countries since 2007, with the share of productivity-enhancing recommendations remaining at approximately 60% (Table 1.1). This ratio slightly increased in the most recent rounds, reflecting new priorities in public sector efficiency, taxation structure, infrastructure, housing and social mobility. This was partly following new empirical research in these domains, as well as reflecting policy lessons emerging from the recent crisis. The predominance of labour productivity-enhancing challenges is more pronounced among the lower-income OECD economies. While detailed priorities vary widely across OECD countries depending on their particular performance and policy weaknesses, relaxing anti-competitive product market regulations and reforming social benefit systems are fairly common recommendations for raising productivity and labour utilisation, respectively.

For the BRIICS, four-fifths of the policy recommendations are aimed at improving productivity, reflecting these countries' relative weakness in this area (Figure 1.1, Panel B). There is a strong focus on product market regulation, which is often much more stringent than in upper-income OECD countries; and education systems, where quality and achievement levels are relatively low. Government/governance reform, strengthening intellectual property rights protection and basic financial liberalisation are also common recommendations for boosting productivity in the BRIICS. There are fewer recommendations aimed at enhancing labour utilisation than for OECD countries in general and the lower-income OECD countries in particular, partly because most of the BRIICS have relatively high overall employment rates. Instead, a number of recommendations are intended to address the major challenge of labour informality. These include increasing the coverage of social protection systems or containing labour costs and relaxing overly strict job protection for formal workers.

The role of the crisis in shaping reform patterns

Measuring progress on Going for Growth priorities

In order to assess progress on *Going for Growth* priorities over the past five years, this report makes use of the "reform responsiveness rate indicator", first constructed for *Going for Growth 2010* (see Box 1.1). The reform responsiveness indicator is a measure of the extent to which OECD countries have followed up on *Going for Growth* recommendations, but it does not aim to assess overall reform intensity *per se*, which would require both accounting for reforms carried out in non-priority areas and quantifying the importance of each individual measure.[5] It is defined annually for each individual *Going for Growth* policy priority area, each broad reform field (labour productivity or labour utilisation) and each

Box 1.1. **An indicator of reform action**

The reform responsiveness rate indicator is based on a scoring system in which each priority set in the previous edition of *Going for Growth* takes a value of one if "significant" action is taken the following year, and zero if not. The indicator is therefore the ratio of the total number of years in which some action is taken to address the policy priority to the total number of years in which the policy priority has been identified. By definition, it excludes the years before and includes the year in which the policy priority was first set.

Some policy areas appear to be more difficult to reform than others. Thus, the extent to which countries have followed up on *Going for Growth* priorities may be shaped by the nature of the recommendations. For instance, a country with recommendations in the areas of innovation and public sector efficiency might be expected to be more responsive than another country with similar appetite for reform but with priorities in the areas of job protection and wage formation, where political economy obstacles to reform are stronger. In order to account for this possibility a "corrected" responsiveness rate has also been computed. This weighs responsiveness on each individual priority according to the difficulty of undertaking the relevant reform. The difficulty is measured by the average responsiveness to priorities in this area across the OECD.

For more details see Box 2.2 and Annex 2.A1 in OECD, (2010), *Economic Policy Reforms 2010: Going for Growth*, OECD Publishing.

individual country. While this indicator is an imperfect substitute for proper reform assessments, it is used here because of its comprehensiveness and timeliness. The reform responsiveness indicator does not cover the countries that joined the OECD in 2010 (Chile, Estonia, Israel[6] and Slovenia) and the BRIICS, for which priorities were set for the first time in 2011. Actions these countries have taken over the past year – a much shorter time period than the other countries – are discussed in this report and detailed in the accompanying country notes (Chapter 2).

Reform patterns during the crisis

Overall, the crisis seems to have acted as a catalyst for structural reforms.[7] Compared with the pre-crisis period, responsiveness rates have increased on average to *Going for Growth* recommendations for enhancing both labour productivity and labour utilisation. For the latter, this partly reflects recent extensive labour market reforms undertaken in the context of the euro area debt crisis. Reform activity has gone through distinct phases since the start of the crisis (Figure 1.2). At first the recession markedly slowed action on *Going for Growth* priorities, probably reflecting much greater policy focus on macroeconomic stabilisation. The pace of reform slowed down most in the labour productivity area and less so for labour utilisation. The subsequent period saw reform action accelerate strongly, with the bounce-back strongest in reforms to boost labour productivity, such as product market or public sector reforms aimed at increasing efficiency.

Figure 1.2. **The crisis has acted as a catalyst for reforms**

Responsiveness to *Going for Growth* recommendations across the OECD, 2005-11[1]

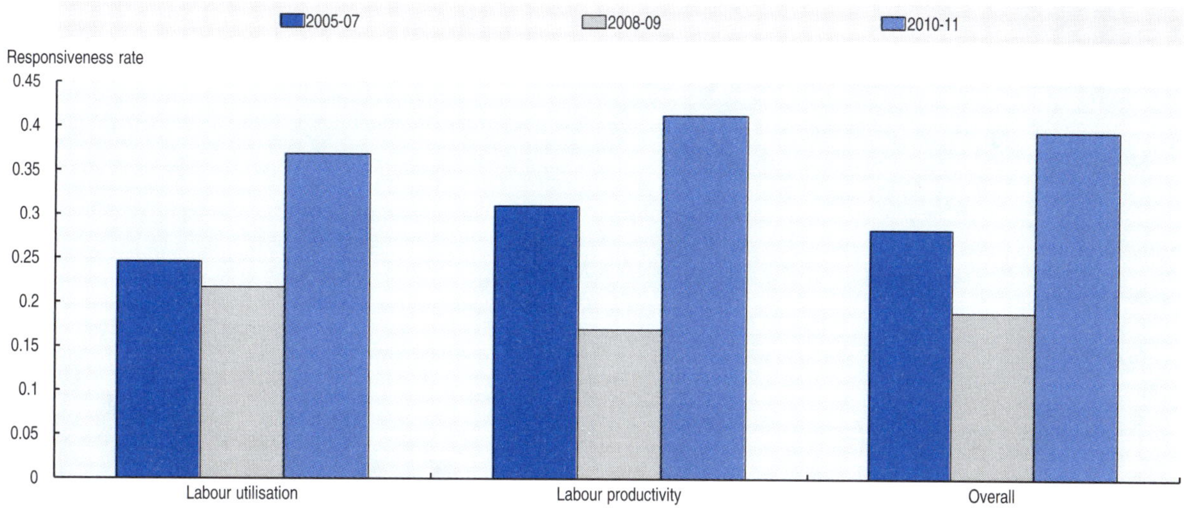

Note: See Box 1.1 for the definition of the responsiveness rate.

1. Average across OECD countries excluding Chile, Estonia, Israel and Slovenia.

StatLink http://dx.doi.org/10.1787/888932564882

During the 2010-11 recovery phase responsiveness to *Going for Growth* priorities increased in more than half of OECD countries compared with the 2005-07 pre-crisis period (Figure 1.3, Panel A). In the vast majority of these countries the picture is reinforced when comparing this phase and the crisis phase (Panel B). However, there are exceptions. For example, in Germany responsiveness has been declining, possibly reflecting reform "fatigue" after past efforts and the country's relatively good overall economic performance. Since 2010, there has been a major acceleration in reform action in countries either *i)* directly affected by the euro area debt crisis and therefore forced into reform as part of the European Union-International Monetary Fund (EU-IMF) financial aid package; or *ii)* experiencing tensions with sovereign bond spreads. Indeed Greece, Ireland and Portugal all appear among the countries whose responsiveness to *Going for Growth* recommendations increased the most between 2008-09 and 2010-11, especially for labour utilisation, and so does Spain. The acute crisis forced these countries to enact unpopular reforms in "difficult" areas, such as labour market regulation and social welfare systems (*e.g.* job protection, pension and welfare reforms). This can be seen in Figure 1.4, which compares responsiveness rates with corrected responsiveness rates (see Box 1.1 for methodological details on these indicators and Box 1.2 for a discussion of reforms in Greece, Ireland and Portugal).[8]

Figure 1.3. **Evolution of responsiveness to *Going for Growth* recommendations: OECD countries**

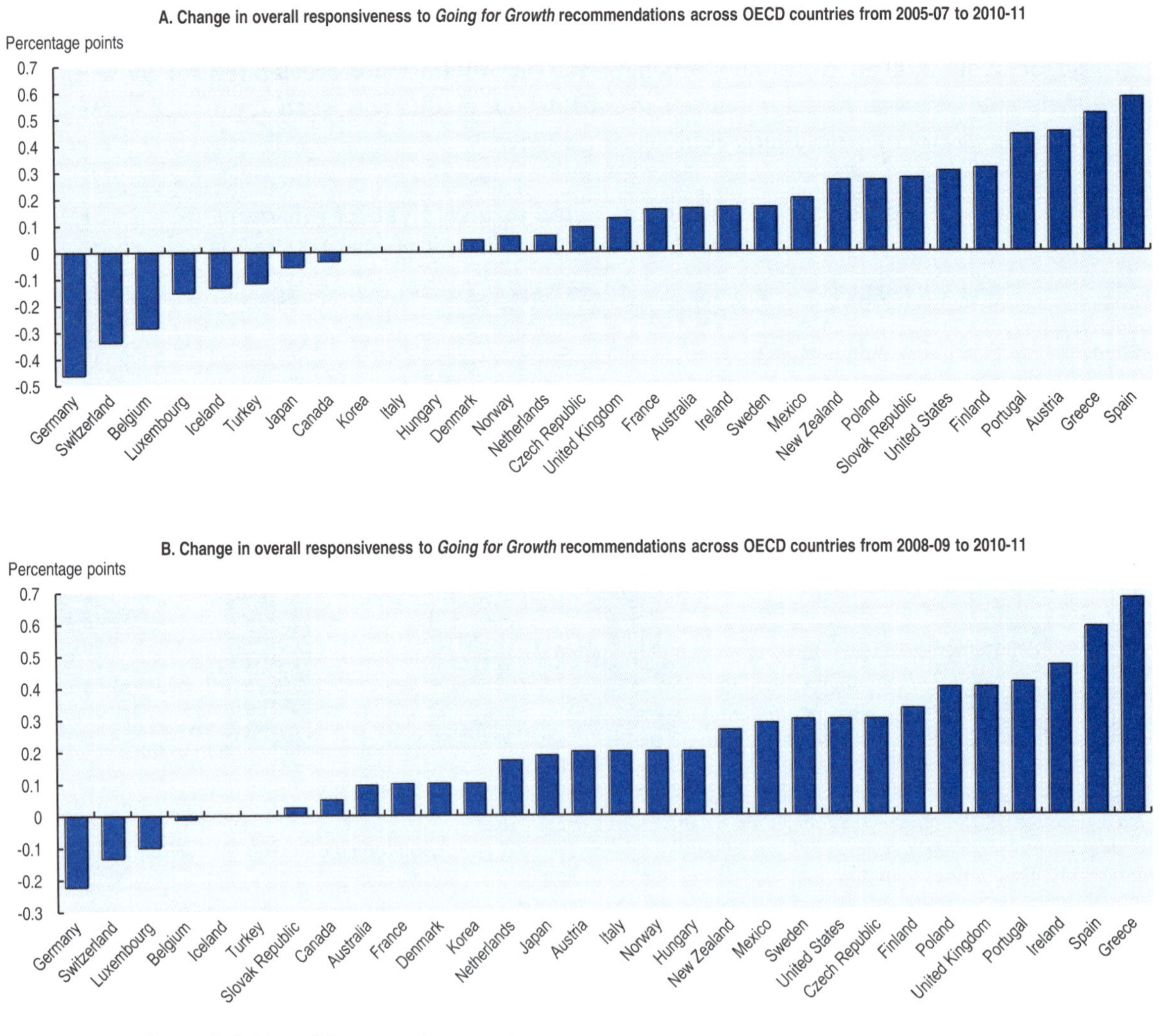

Note: See Box 1.1 for the definition of the responsiveness rate.

StatLink http://dx.doi.org/10.1787/888932564901

Figure 1.4. **Responsiveness to *Going for Growth* recommendations: OECD countries, 2007-11**

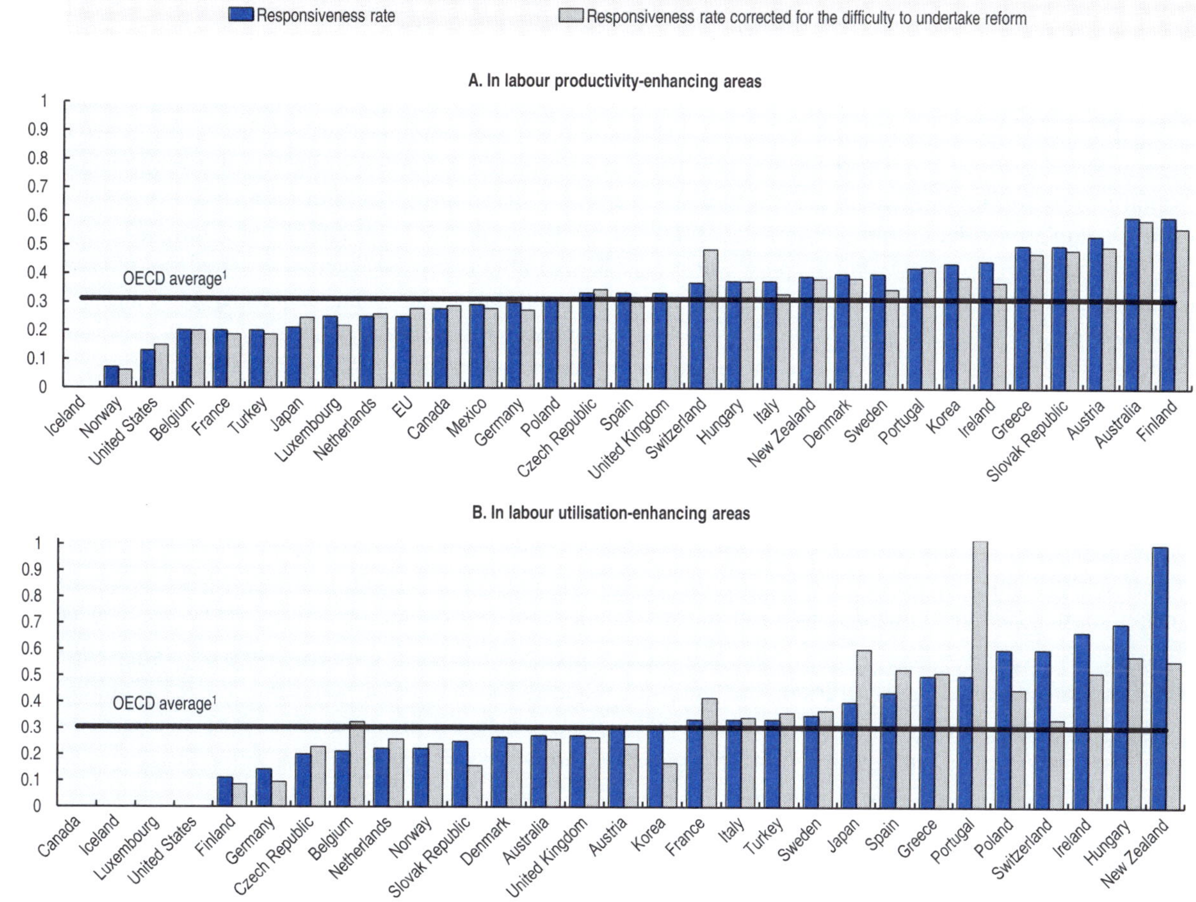

Note: See Box 1.1 for the definition of the responsiveness rate.

1. OECD average excludes Chile, Estonia, Israel and Slovenia.

StatLink http://dx.doi.org/10.1787/888932564920

Box 1.2. **Structural reforms catalysed by the euro area debt crisis: Greece, Ireland and Portugal**

As has often been the case in the past, the current crisis has acted as a catalyst for structural reforms. Reform impetus has been particularly strong in the euro area in countries that asked for assistance from the European Union and the IMF. For Greece, Ireland and Portugal, some of the measures announced in 2010 and 2011 were part of their conditions linked to financial assistance.

Most reforms implemented by these countries are aimed at delivering credible fiscal consolidation *e.g.* pension and welfare reforms, public sector reforms and privatisation programmes. In addition, labour market institutions, active labour market policies, and product and financial market regulations have been or are being reformed, partly as a way to boost growth and indirectly strengthen public budgets. This box summarises the most important structural reforms introduced by Greece, Ireland and Portugal in these policy areas, covering both measures that have already been undertaken as well as commitments to present future reform plans or studies. Some other European countries experiencing severe financial market stress, such as Italy and Spain, have taken similar measures on a voluntary basis. As will be seen below, a large number of these reform initiatives are among the *Going for Growth* policy recommendations. The accompanying country notes (Chapter 2) detail actions taken on those.

Box 1.2. Structural reforms catalysed by the euro area debt crisis: Greece, Ireland and Portugal *(cont.)*

Tax reforms

Tax reforms include: *i)* base broadening by rationalising personal income tax and eliminating a number of deductions (Greece, Ireland and Portugal) and broadening the value added tax (VAT) tax base (Greece and Portugal); *ii)* budget-neutral tax shifting aiming to lower labour costs (Ireland); *iii)* reforming property taxation, including increasing (Portugal and Greece) or introducing (Ireland) property taxation and introducing a new flat stamp duty on all residential property taxation, along with abolishing all existing exemptions (Ireland); *iv)* stepping-up environmentally-friendly taxation by increasing the level of carbon taxes and introducing water charges (Ireland) or increasing the car registration tax (Portugal); *v)* combating tax evasion and enhancing tax compliance, tax administration discipline and transparency by developing a risk-based analysis audit system, increasing fraud penalties, revising tax auditors' hiring rules and reinforcing their supervision and the legal measures to curb corruption by tax personnel (Greece).

Pension, welfare and active labour market policies reforms

Pension reforms include: *i)* increasing the legal and/or minimum retirement ages and lengthening the contribution periods required for a full pension (Greece and Ireland for the state contributory pension); *ii)* reducing the generosity of pension benefits (Greece), focusing on civil servants above a wage level threshold (Ireland); *iii)* reducing early retirement *via* reducing benefits and revising the list of arduous occupations (Greece); *v)* introducing a mechanism to index the retirement age to life expectancy (Greece).

Welfare and active labour market policy reforms include: *i)* reducing unemployment benefit rates (Ireland and Portugal) and duration (Portugal), introducing means-tested benefits (Greece), along with extending the population covered by these benefits (Portugal); *ii)* cutting other welfare payments such as child benefits (Ireland); and *iii)* strengthening active labour market policies (Ireland) through:

- Increasing the provision of training and internship.
- Enhancing efficiency in the Public Employment Services (PES), including enhanced profiling to better identify claimants at high risk of becoming unemployed.
- Strengthening the mutual obligations approach *e.g.* greater sanctions for refusal to engage in training.

Product market reforms

Product market reforms include: *i)* privatisation programmes – primarily aimed at raising public revenues – in various energy and transport sectors (Greece, Ireland and Portugal) and launch of public-private partnerships and concessions to develop some state-owned immovable assets (Greece); *ii)* strengthening the power, independence or effectiveness of the competition authority (Greece and Portugal) and the enforcement of competition law (Ireland); *iii)* easing the formalities to start a new business (Greece) and the complexity of licensing procedures (Greece and Portugal); *iv)* increasing competition in transport and network industries by reducing barriers to entry in road and maritime cruises (Greece) and phasing out regulated tariffs in electricity and gas (Greece and Portugal); *v)* increasing competition in retail trade (Portugal) and reducing barriers to entry in professional services (Greece, Ireland and Portugal).

Public sector reforms

Public sector reforms include efficiency-enhancing measures: *i)* reorganising local and central government (Greece, Ireland and Portugal), rationalising the public remuneration system (Greece and Ireland), rationalising management and improving efficiency and governance of state-owned enterprises (Greece and Portugal); *ii)* introducing cross public sector measures, including greater use of shared services and information technology solutions, reform of public procurement processes (Ireland and Portugal), regular comprehensive expenditure reviews and using new business models for service delivery (Ireland); *iii)* public healthcare sector measures, including strengthening and better monitoring of prescription rules and rationalising procurement procedures (Greece and Portugal), increasing co-payments (Portugal) and enhancing cost-accountability in the hospital sector (Greece and Portugal).

Box 1.2. **Structural reforms catalysed by the euro area debt crisis: Greece, Ireland and Portugal** *(cont.)*

Labour market reforms

Labour market reforms include: *i)* reductions in severance pay for regular contracts and some simplification of individual or collective dismissal procedures (Greece and Portugal), along with measures to boost temporary employment by increasing the maximum work time under temporary work agencies (Greece); *ii)* measures to boost flexibility in working-time arrangements by reducing overtime pay and earnings of part-time employees and making averaging of working time possible (Greece); *iii)* measures to enhance flexibility in wage determination such as easing the conditions for firms to opt out from higher-level collective bargaining agreements (Greece and Ireland) and reforming sectoral wage agreements (Ireland); *iv)* introducing a sub-minimum wage for young people (Greece).

Financial sector reforms

Financial sector reforms include: *i)* measures to help deleverage the banking system by progressively setting higher capital requirements than under the Basel III rules and requiring them be met earlier (Ireland and Portugal); *ii)* enhancing prudential regulation by reinforcing banking supervision (Ireland and Portugal) and restructuring the banking system (Ireland).

Impact of the crisis on reform action

While countries that have been most active in their priority areas since 2007 (Figure 1.4) are relatively diverse in terms of geography and size, those that were in greater need for reform – i.e. with lower GDP per capita levels in 2007 – have been most responsive to *Going for Growth* priorities on average, as can for example be seen in the cases of Greece, Hungary, New Zealand, Poland and Portugal (Figure 1.5).

Reforms have been more frequent in countries that have been more severely affected by the crisis. There is a particularly clear positive correlation between the severity of the labour market impact of the crisis (measured as the change in unemployment from trough

Figure 1.5. **Reform progress has been greater in lower-income countries**

Responsiveness to *Going for Growth* priorities and 2007 GDP per capita levels

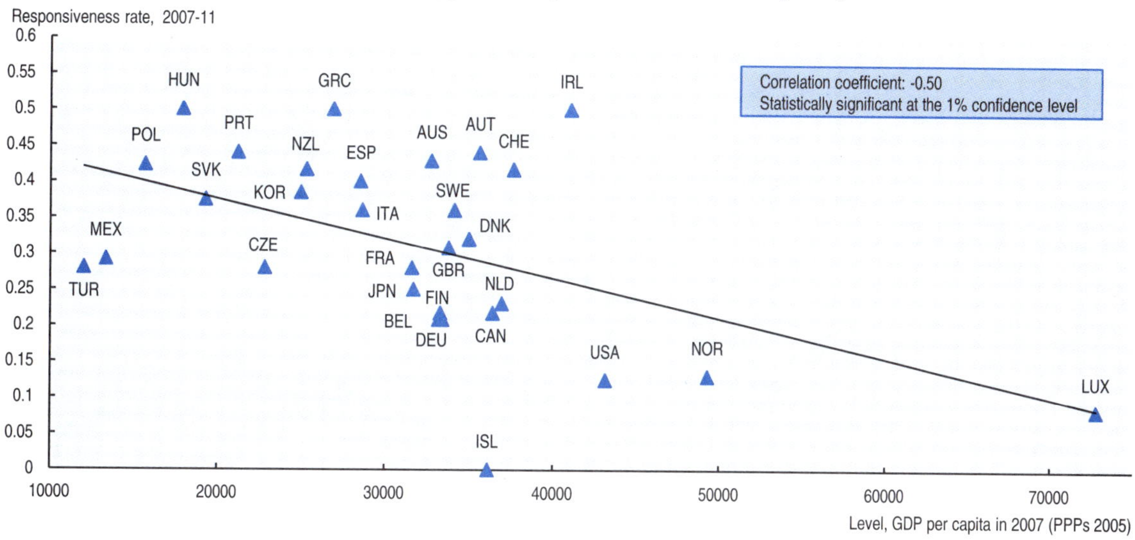

Note: See Box 1.1 for the definition of the responsiveness rate.

StatLink http://dx.doi.org/10.1787/888932564939

to peak) and responsiveness to *Going for Growth* recommendations for enhancing labour use (Figure 1.6, Panel A).[9] Major financial market pressure seems to have forced both fiscal consolidation and reforms. There is a significant positive correlation between recent reform intensity – measured by the responsiveness rate to *Going for Growth* priorities between 2010 and 2011 – and fiscal consolidation intensity – measured as the projected change in the underlying primary balance between 2010 and 2012 (Figure 1.6, Panel B).[10, 11] This suggests that countries facing major economic and fiscal crises simultaneously may have had little choice but to address both growth and fiscal consolidation objectives, as the examples of Greece, Ireland and Portugal show (Box 1.2). In the current situation, it is therefore difficult to disentangle structural reforms genuinely aimed at raising long-term living standards from fiscal consolidation actions. Reforms that are associated with rapid and unprecedented fiscal retrenchment are likely to have weaker positive effects on growth than fiscally-neutral reforms (see discussion in Chapter 4).

Figure 1.6. **The need to address job and fiscal sustainability concerns has given impetus to reform**

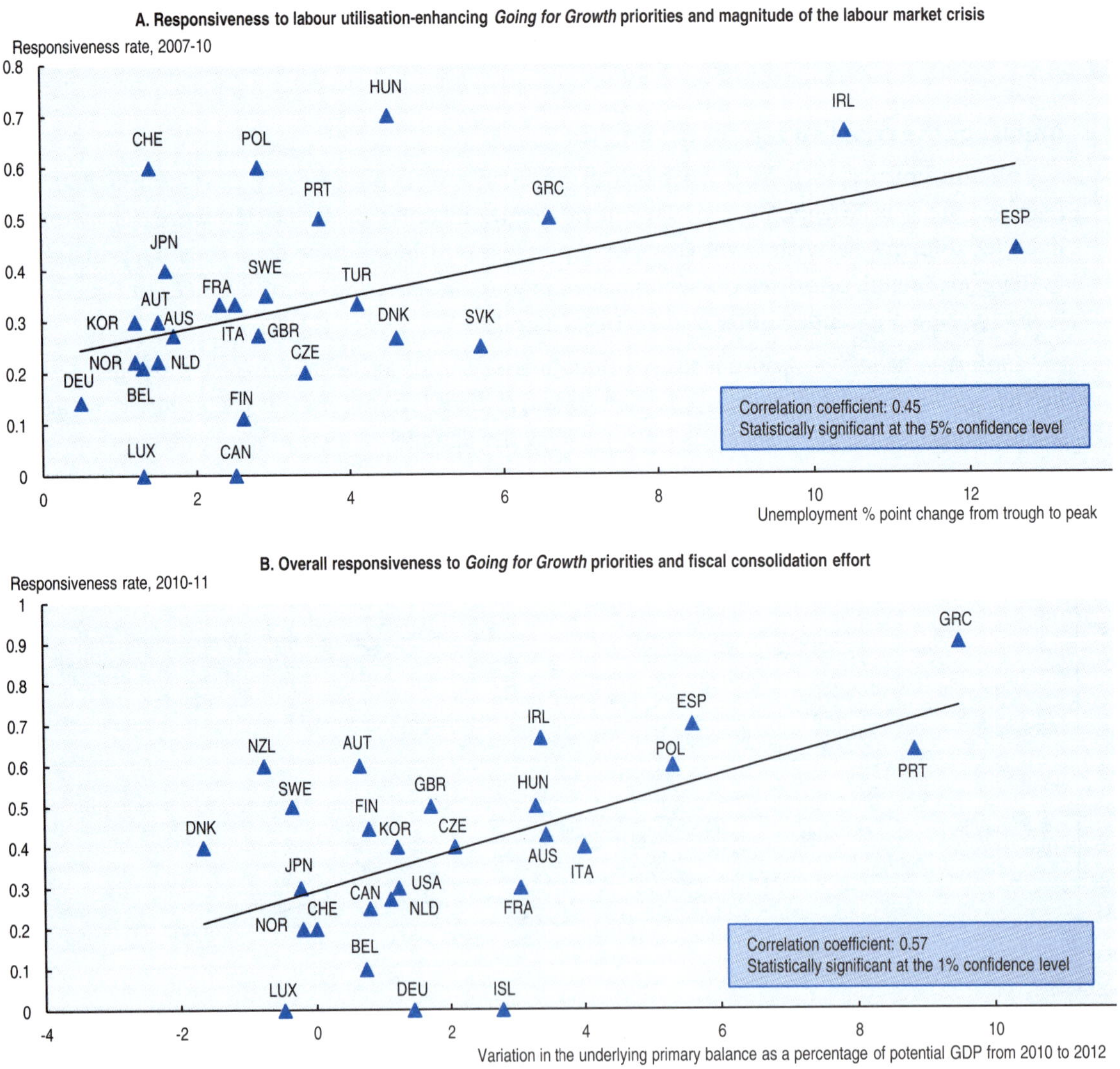

Note: See Box 1.1 for the definition of the responsiveness rate.

Source: *OECD Quarterly National Accounts (Database)*; *OECD Main Economic Indicators (Database)* and *OECD Economic Outlook No. 90: Statistics and Projections (Database)*.

StatLink http://dx.doi.org/10.1787/888932564958

The crisis and structural reforms: a detailed review of progress since 2007

This section reports on progress in implementing *Going for Growth* priorities since 2007, distinguishing labour-utilisation and labour productivity-enhancing priorities. The associated actions are detailed in separate country notes (Chapter 2). Furthermore, as already noted above and against the background of the crisis, key labour market reforms and interventions in non-priority areas are also covered (in the labour utilisation section), based on the accompanying country notes as well as on other recent OECD work (see OECD, 2009; 2010b; 2011d; 2011e).

Progress in reforming policies to improve labour utilisation in the context of the crisis

Since 2007, recommendations to remove impediments to labour utilisation have been made primarily to continental European countries, where trend labour utilisation rates remain comparatively low despite some heterogeneity and some progress prior to the crisis (Figure 1.1). Identified policy priorities have included reducing disincentives to work at older ages, obstacles to female participation, and labour taxation, as well as improving the design of disability and sickness benefit schemes and other labour market policies such as job protection, unemployment benefits and activation policies. Priorities have also been identified in these areas outside Europe, often as a way to address more specific labour market performance weaknesses, *e.g.* widespread informality in the BRIICS. Among the various types of *Going for Growth* labour utilisation-enhancing priorities, countries have been most active in the areas of labour taxation, retirement systems, disability schemes and active labour market policies (Figure 1.7).

Figure 1.7. **Responsiveness to *Going for Growth* recommendations across labour utilisation-enhancing areas**

2007-11 average

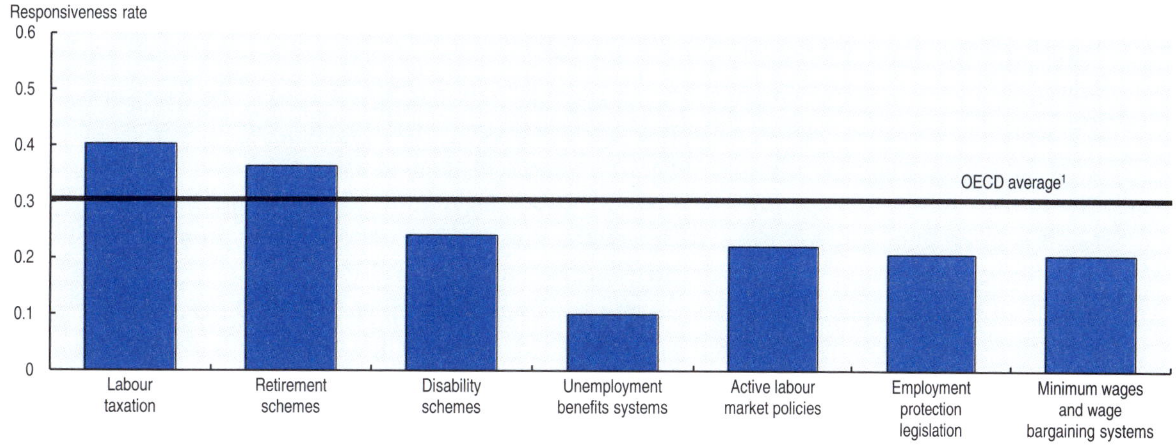

Note: See Box 1.1 for the definition of the responsiveness rate.

1. OECD average excludes Chile, Estonia, Israel and Slovenia.

StatLink http://dx.doi.org/10.1787/888932564977

Average and marginal taxation of labour income

Most countries for which labour taxation was identified as a priority in previous editions of *Going for Growth* implemented measures to sustain employment by lowering labour taxation, either on a permanent or a temporary basis. Despite high responsiveness, policy action has never been judged sufficient to justify the removal of the policy priority.

This does not point to some lack of major reform, but reflects the fact that labour taxation is an area where sustained reform efforts are often required to achieve major policy changes. Countries with a *Going for Growth* priority in this area have reduced income tax rates or increased tax relief (Austria, Belgium, the Czech Republic, Denmark, Finland, Hungary, Netherlands, Poland and Sweden), introduced or raised in-work tax credits (Denmark, Netherlands, Sweden and the Slovak Republic), and lowered social security contributions (Austria, Germany, Hungary, Poland, Sweden and Turkey).[12] Italy reduced the labour tax wedge for young people and women by making the payroll tax deductible against income tax. In some of these countries, reductions in labour taxation were accompanied or, more recently in the context of fiscal consolidation packages, followed by compensatory increases in consumption (Germany, Finland and Italy), environmental or energy (Austria, Finland and Germany) and financial sector taxes (Austria).

Many OECD countries – including some for which labour taxation was not identified as a priority in previous editions of *Going for Growth* – further implemented new job or hiring subsidy schemes in response to the crisis, often targeting vulnerable job seekers such as youth, older workers, or the long-term unemployed (Finland, France, Greece, Hungary, Portugal and Turkey, for which reducing the cost of labour was identified as a *Going for Growth* priority, as well as Ireland and Spain who did not have a priority in this area). Going forward, to minimise potential productivity losses resulting from labour misallocation, hiring subsidies should eventually be withdrawn. Conditional on the pace of fiscal consolidation, reductions in social security contributions are to be envisaged on a longer time frame in countries where non-wage labour costs remain high, and could be coupled with a shift in the tax burden towards tax bases that are more friendly for employment and growth, *e.g.* immovable property, consumption, or environmental taxation. Tax structure reforms along these lines were recommended for ten countries in the 2011 edition of *Going for Growth* (OECD, 2011b).

Social benefits and active labour market policies

Retirement schemes. There has been progress since 2007 in reducing financial disincentives to work at older ages embedded in old-age pension systems and/or available social transfer programmes in countries where this was deemed a *Going for Growth* priority. The crisis and the ensuing fiscal sustainability problems in many OECD countries have led to an acceleration of pension reforms over the most recent period. Major reforms have been implemented in European countries, especially – but not exclusively – in EU-IMF programme countries (see Box 1.2). Some of the reforming countries phased out or restricted access to early retirement schemes by tightening eligibility conditions (Austria, Belgium, Greece, Poland, the Slovak Republic and Spain) or progressively closing *de facto* early retirement routes by abolishing job-search exemptions for older unemployed (France). Others raised minimum and statutory retirement ages (Belgium for females, France, Greece, Hungary and Spain), or sought to increase the effective retirement age by lengthening contribution requirements to claim full pensions (France, Greece and Spain), reducing the level of pension benefits (Greece and Hungary), or adjusting benefits or the retirement age in line with life expectancy (Greece, Norway and Spain). Reforms aimed at enhancing the long-term sustainability of public pensions systems have in some cases been accompanied by concomitant backtracking with the downsizing of the fully-funded, defined-contribution "second pillar", especially in some Central and Eastern European countries. Among the OECD countries that had a *Going for Growth* priority in this area,

Hungary dismantled the "second pillar" altogether while Poland partially diverted contributions from the private to the public pillar. In Turkey, where reform of retirement schemes was identified as a policy priority, the phasing-in of the pension reform remains excessively slow.

One notable feature of this crisis has been that older workers have remained in the labour market, contrary to the experiences of previous recessions, where early retirement incentives sometimes encouraged labour market withdrawal (OECD, 2011b, 2011d and 2011e). This may reflect not just the comparatively mild deterioration in labour market conditions (given the magnitude of the recession) in a number of OECD countries, but also the benefits of recent reforms. Still, given that severe recessions have in the past led to significant labour market withdrawal with a notable lag (Duval *et al.*, 2011), further reductions of financial disincentives to continued work – not least faster phasing out of special or *de facto* early retirement routes – would help ensure that laid-off older workers remain attached to the labour market. Furthermore, such reforms would improve the long-run sustainability of pension systems, which recent OECD analysis (OECD, 2011e, *OECD Pensions at a Glance 2011*) shows is not currently ensured. Such reforms can be designed in ways that protect the most vulnerable (low income earners and people with interrupted careers), as has been done in some OECD countries.[13]

Disability schemes. Long-term sickness and disability benefit schemes have in the past provided an exit pathway from the labour force to both older and prime-aged workers. A look at the past cyclical profiles of unemployment and disability rates shows that in a number of countries, unemployment peaks associated with recessions have tended to be followed by spikes in disability rates a number of years later.[14]. This partly explains why disability benefit reform ended up being identified as a priority in countries such as Australia, Denmark, Norway, the Netherlands, the United Kingdom and the United States.[15] While it is too early to draw definitive conclusions regarding the impact of this crisis, preliminary evidence (OECD, 2011d) suggests that recipiency rates have started trending upward or have continued to rise in a number of OECD countries since the onset of the crisis (Australia, Denmark, Estonia, Iceland, Israel, Korea, Norway and the United States).[16] Cross-country heterogeneity in post-crisis developments has been wide, partly reflecting differences in the design of disability benefit schemes and the extent of past reforms.[17] Some of the countries with a *Going for Growth* priority in this area (the Netherlands, Sweden and the United Kingdom) reformed their schemes just prior to the onset of the crisis, with the view to stemming the "excess" inflow of recipients and, in some cases, to helping existing recipients with work capacity to (re-) join the labor market. Preliminary recipiency rates data suggest that past reforms in these countries helped cushion the impact of the crisis in this area. While similar reforms are being implemented in Australia starting in 2011, action was rather limited in other countries for which disability schemes reforms were identified as a *Going for Growth* priority, in particular in the United States which have experienced what seems to be a structural rise in the beneficiary rate.

Unemployment benefit systems. The crisis led a number of countries to better protect the incomes of the unemployed, which was needed in a context where job opportunities fell dramatically. Many of the changes made to unemployment benefit schemes during the crisis were therefore temporary measures, rather than structural reforms *per se*. These short-run imperatives legitimately constrained policy action, which explains low responsiveness in this area (Figure 1.7). Indeed, none of the countries with a recommendation took significant action in line with the priority, except for Portugal, whose authorities committed to reduce the generosity of unemployment benefits in 2012 under the EU-IMF financial aid package.

Crisis-response measures (including in countries where unemployment benefit reform was not identified as *Going for Growth* priority) included:[18]

- Moderate increases in benefit replacement rates (Belgium and Finland where unemployment benefit reform was a *Going for Growth* priority, but also the Czech Republic, Greece and Poland);
- Increases in benefit duration (Canada, Iceland, Portugal and the United States);
- Looser eligibility criteria, a long-standing *Going for Growth* recommendation for certain countries (*e.g.* Japan) in order to increase the social insurance coverage of non-regular workers. For instance, changes in eligibility in Finland, France, Israel, Japan, Portugal and Spain are likely to have made it easier for temporary or irregular workers to access unemployment benefits.

Once the labour market recovers, phasing out crisis-related increases in benefit levels and duration (where these were already high) would amplify the pick-up in labour utilisation, with direct co-benefits for public budgets. In a number of countries, crisis-related increases in unemployment income support have already been phased out – increases in benefit duration have been phased out in Canada for instance[19] – and some countries have recently taken some steps to reduce the generosity of unemployment benefits – especially those under fiscal pressure such as Ireland and Portugal. By contrast, some of the extensions in the coverage of unemployment benefits from previously low rates could be made permanent provided they are coupled with conditionality and activation measures.

Active labour market policies. OECD countries have been endorsing the need to develop sound ALMPs as a key tool to activate the long-term unemployed. In the crisis context, reforms to increase spending on or enhance the efficiency of ALMPs have been implemented in all the countries for which this was identified as a priority. Efficiency has been improved through more regular assessments of job search activity (Estonia), greater sanctions for refusing job or training offers (Ireland since 2011) or not participating in active labour market programmes (Finland) and the reorganisation of Public Employment Services (PES) (merger of benefit administration and public employment services into a single department in Ireland, enhanced coordination between regional placement agencies in Belgium). South Africa committed to increase funding devoted to employment services and to improve information about training and employment opportunities. More broadly and including outside *Going for Growth* priorities, more than two-thirds of OECD countries raised resources for job-search assistance and training programmes in order to facilitate re-employment and re-deployment during the crisis. Despite the additional resources devoted to PES, the average staff caseload increased in most countries during the crisis due to the surge in the number of registered jobseekers. Additional PES resources have therefore been typically targeted to provide job-search assistance to particular groups such as young people, immigrants, and people with short-term contracts or not receiving benefits (OECD, 2010b).

In countries where the average caseload per staff providing PES has risen substantially during the crisis as a result of a sharp increase in the number of job seekers, there is a case for ensuring that resources devoted to job-search assistance are commensurate to the task of returning to pre-crisis employment levels. Still, the relevance of different ALMP spending programmes differs depending on the state of the labour market, suggesting a case-by-case approach:

- In countries that have experienced large increases in long-term unemployment, and in particular where its level is now also high (see Figure 1.8), unemployment persistence is the most pressing concern. The longer individuals remain unemployed, the more difficult it becomes for them to find a job and the more unqualified and discouraged they may be, a phenomenon referred to as *hysteresis*. One particular concern is that some of the most affected countries invested relatively little in ALMPs prior to the crisis (OECD, 2011d). In this context, training programmes implemented in response to the crisis could be maintained where unemployment outflows remain depressed and the public budget situation allows. Some of the hardest-hit countries were also most affected by a strong boom-bust pattern in the construction sector (*e.g.* Ireland, Spain and the United States), implying a likely need for substantial labour reallocation, which further strengthens the case for maintaining adequate training to facilitate reallocation of workers.
- In countries where the risk of persistently high unemployment is low, especially where labour hoarding or some form of work sharing dampened the labour market impact of the recession, efforts should concentrate on ensuring that PES provide effective job-search support and incentives. More generally, as the labour market situation normalises, the value of job search relative to training programmes increases, calling for putting greater weight on activation.

Figure 1.8. **Long-term unemployment has increased dramatically in some OECD countries**

Share of people unemployed for more than 12 months in total unemployment[1]

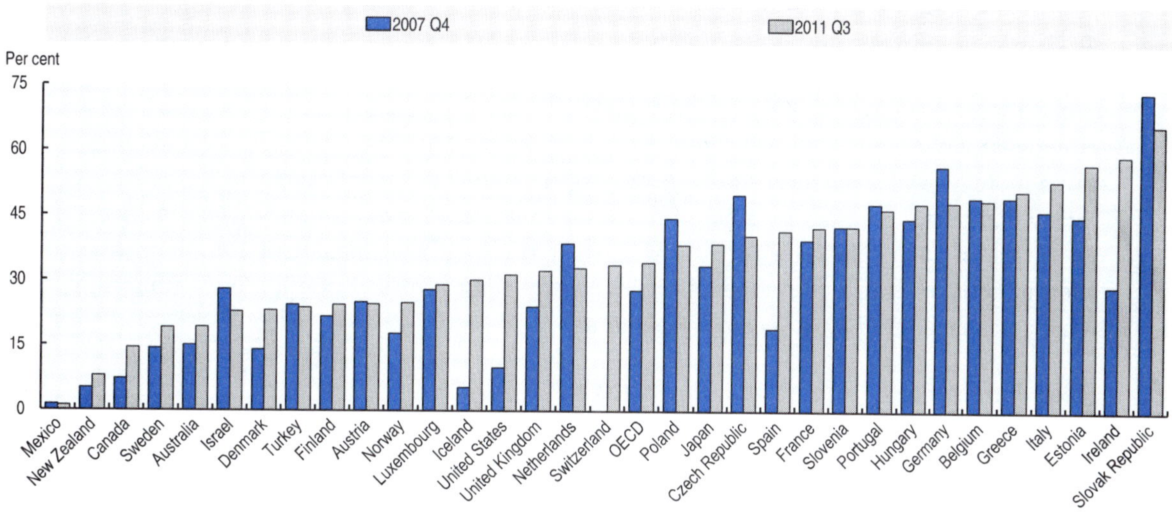

1. Series are smoothed using a three-quarter centred moving averages. 2011Q4 for Canada and the United States.

Source: OECD (2012), *Quarterly Labour Market Indicators (Database)*, Directorate for Employment, Labour and Social Affairs unpublished data (January).

StatLink http://dx.doi.org/10.1787/888932564996

Short-time working schemes. Among crisis-related labour market interventions, work-sharing arrangements and in particular short-time working schemes (STW) have played a prominent role, with measures in place in two-thirds of OECD countries.[20] Such measures typically aim at cushioning the labour market impact of downturns, and for this reason they have not been covered in *Going for Growth*, whose focus is on longer-term growth. Nevertheless, given the highly persistent employment impact of the crisis in some countries, STW schemes may have protected permanent jobs and prevented large income losses where they were in place. New STW schemes were introduced in Poland, the Netherlands, Hungary, the Czech Republic, the Slovak Republic, Mexico and New Zealand. In addition, many countries extended the coverage or generosity of existing schemes, or relaxed eligibility or administrative requirements in order to encourage take-up. The share of employees participating in pre-existing STW schemes expanded substantially in Belgium, Germany, Finland, Italy, Japan and Luxembourg, contributing to relatively benign labour market effects of the crisis (OECD, 2010b; Hijzen and Venn, 2011). Although an empirical assessment of the long-term effects of STW schemes is not yet available, the crisis experience suggests that having such options in place and being able to activate them in severe downturns can be useful, insofar as they may avoid losses of specific human capital in the wake of shocks that are temporary and do not imply a need for reallocation.

At the same time, as with any form of public wage subsidy, STW schemes entail some risks: *i)* deadweight losses may be incurred if subsidies are paid for jobs that employers would have maintained even without public support; *ii)* displacement effects may occur if STW schemes help preserve jobs that are not viable in the long run, hampering the reallocation of resources across firms and industries and resulting in persistent declines in hours worked and productivity; *iii)* wage pressures may arise, mitigating the success of STW schemes in containing the rise in unemployment. In order to minimize these risks, certain features in the design of STW schemes are desirable (OECD, 2011d; 2011e): *i)* tight eligibility conditions (*e.g.* proof of minimum and abrupt reduction in production or sales), co-financing by firms and (as is the case in Germany and the Netherlands) built-in incentives for workers and firms to withdraw from STW schemes once they have outlived their conjunctural purpose can help reduce deadweight losses; *ii)* quick phasing out as the economy recovers can mitigate displacement effects. Also, such schemes may work more effectively when implemented in the context of wage bargaining that provide individual firms more leeway (such as opt-out clauses) in the application of collective agreements, as this will allow for greater flexibility in the determination of working conditions during the operation of such schemes. For example, in Germany, those measures complemented spontaneous private-sector adjustment in average hours worked, the implementation of which was facilitated by collective agreements.

Policy barriers to full-time female participation

Some of the impediments to full-time female participation have been reduced since 2007 in all nine countries where this had been put forward as a policy priority. This has been achieved by expanding childcare facilities (Germany, Ireland and Switzerland), increasing childcare subsidies (Korea, New Zealand and the Slovak Republic), stepping up the childcare components of tax credits (Switzerland and the United Kingdom), lowering the compulsory schooling age or promoting full-day schools (Germany and Switzerland), reducing differences in taxation between main and second earners (Australia and Switzerland) and restructuring income support for single parents or second earners to promote participation (Australia and the United Kingdom). Chile increased the length of paid maternity leave and created a paternity leave, though empirical evidence suggests that childcare support may be more conducive to high female labour force participation (see *e.g.* Jaumotte 2003; Bassanini and Duval, 2006).

Labour market regulations and collective wage agreements

Job protection and other policies to reduce labour market dualism. Firing restrictions may have cushioned unemployment to some extent during the crisis, but excessive gaps in protection between permanent and temporary contracts contribute to duality in the labour market, which in turn hampers employment and productivity (Bassanini *et al.*, 2009). Actions taken in countries that had a *Going for Growth* recommendation in this area were more frequent and radical in nature during the crisis than before, especially in European countries where the surge in unemployment highlighted the weaknesses of partial employment protection reform strategies – *i.e.* reforms reducing job protection on temporary contracts while maintaining high protection on regular contracts.[21] Greece and Spain introduced major EPL reforms in 2010 aimed at reducing severance payments on permanent contracts. In Portugal, the 2009 job protection reform, which implied a substantial easing of job protection on regular contracts through a simplification of dismissal procedures, is being followed up – as part of the EU-IMF financial assistance package – by reductions in severance payments for regular contracts and a narrower definition of unfair dismissal. The Netherlands have been gradually reducing *de facto* severance payments, first by reforming judicial procedures for local courts and then by introducing a cap (although limited to public and care sector workers). The Czech Republic also reformed severance payments by linking their level to job tenure. The provision for termination of a work contract by mutual consent was instituted in France in 2008 with the goal of reducing uncertainty about dismissal costs but it had a limited impact on reducing dualism so far. Finally, some countries have sought to reduce labour market duality by strengthening training (Korea) or work-study schemes (France). Such measures are likely to work best if targeted to marginal groups in the labour market in order to enhance their regular employability. No actions were taken in respect of the priority to reduce job protection on regular workers in Germany, Italy, Korea, Luxembourg, Slovenia and Sweden.

EPL or targeted training reforms have also been recommended to lower-income countries as a way to tackle labour informality, which is an extreme form of labour market duality. Brazil recently introduced a programme for vocational training of low-skilled workers. Turkey progressively eased the conditions for establishing temporary work contracts. Little progress has been achieved in India over the past year to reduce employment protection legislation that discriminates against larger firms. No action was taken over the past year in Chile and Indonesia, where reducing job protection had been recommended along with introducing (Indonesia) or stepping up (Chile) unemployment benefits.

Minimum wages and wage bargaining systems. Reductions in the relative level or growth rate of minimum wages *vis-à-vis* average wages have been recommended as a means to encourage low-skilled and formal employment in both some OECD and large emerging countries (Australia, Greece, Indonesia, Israel, South Africa and Turkey). Greater flexibility in wage determination has also been recommended for Australia, Belgium, Finland, Italy, Slovenia, Spain and South Africa in order to better align wages with firm-and regional-level productivity conditions and thereby encourage demand for low-skilled workers. Similarly to the trend observed in the area of job protection, responsiveness to such recommendations has been stronger during the crisis than before. Greece introduced sub-minimum wages for young workers and apprentices. While no change in this area has been achieved in Belgium, Finland decentralised wage bargaining, as did Australia by strengthening wage bargaining at the firm level, Italy by agreeing on a new labour contract promoting greater wage differentiation in the private sector and Spain by easing the conditions for firms to opt out from higher-level collective bargaining agreements. Reforms in this area have been accelerating over the past year, especially in southern European countries in need to regain competitiveness. Spain recently introduced a reform facilitating company-level agreements over any other negotiation level on issues such as wages and distribution of working time and accelerating arbitration procedures. Similarly, in Italy, the 2011 emergency budget allows local enterprise bargaining to undercut national wage agreements, provided a representative union in the firm accepts to opt out of the collective agreement and signs the new agreement with the employer. Responsiveness to priorities was more limited in the new OECD members and in Indonesia and South Africa since 2011, when associated *Going for Growth* priorities were set. In South Africa, the *New Growth Pact* strategy includes broad proposals to reform wage bargaining, which could help raise the very low employment rate in the formal sector. In Israel and Slovenia, increases in relative minimum wage levels were agreed for 2011 and 2012, in contrast with *Going for Growth* recommendations in this area.

Housing policies

Housing policies can affect living standards through both labour productivity and labour utilisation (see Special Chapter 4 in *Going for Growth 2011*, OECD, 2011b). However, *Going for Growth* priorities in this area have focused somewhat more on boosting labour utilisation. Responsiveness to these recommendations has clearly increased over the past few years, possibly reflecting growing recognition that badly designed policies contributed to the build-up of housing bubbles. Some countries have been revising housing subsidies (Iceland and the Slovak Republic), in some cases replacing them with less distortive targeted cash benefits (Spain). The United Kingdom simplified the planning process in order to increase the responsiveness of housing supply to demand, while Sweden took some actions to introduce market principles for municipal housing companies. Some countries reduced tax distortions that favour home ownership by reducing mortgage interest deductions from income taxation (Denmark) or by equalising the tax treatment of rented and owner-occupied housing (Spain). Rent regulations that prevent the development of the rental market have been eased in the Netherlands, Poland and Spain. No actions were taken in Luxembourg to address housing rigidities.

Progress in reforming policies to improve labour productivity

Policy priorities aimed at improving productivity performance have been more prevalent for countries with a large gap in output per hour worked *vis-à-vis* the most productive OECD economies or with weak productivity growth over the past decade. Such countries have included some North American and Asia-Pacific member countries, some smaller European countries, the European Union as a whole, and starting in 2011, all of the BRIICS. Suggested policy reforms to boost productivity have included the easing of entry restrictions and controls over business operations in specific product markets, policies to boost educational outcomes, cuts in agricultural support to improve resource allocation throughout economies, and various other measures such as tax system reforms and innovation policies. Progress has been mixed since 2007 in the area of agriculture, but more actions in line with prior *Going for Growth* recommendations have been taken in other areas, notably innovation,[22] but also human capital and product market regulation (Figure 1.9).

Figure 1.9. **Responsiveness to *Going for Growth* recommendations across labour productivity-enhancing areas**

2007-11 average

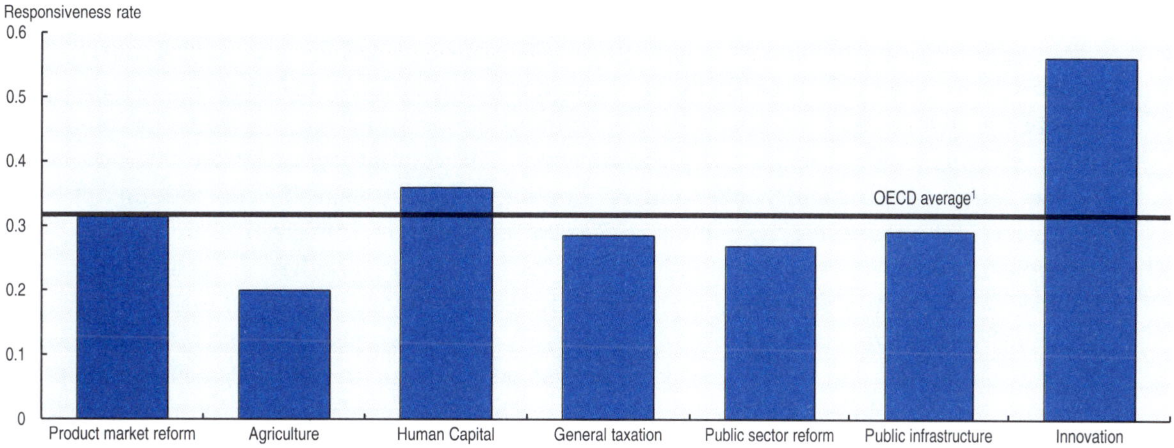

Note: See Box 1.1 for the definition of the responsiveness rate.
1. OECD average excludes Chile, Estonia, Israel and Slovenia.

StatLink http://dx.doi.org/10.1787/888932565015

Product market reforms

The easing of unduly restrictive regulations in product markets has been identified as a priority for most OECD countries – especially those with sub-par productivity performance – and would in many cases also help them kick-start the recovery. While action on these priorities has been relatively frequent, it has rarely been followed by a removal of the corresponding *Going for Growth* priority, hinting at some lack of major reforms. Specifically, around two-thirds of the countries concerned have followed up on recommendations to ease product market regulations since 2007, but the actions taken have been deemed sufficient to result in a removal of the corresponding priorities in only around one-fifth of them. The main product market reforms have been the following:

- All countries that had been recommended to reduce economy-wide regulatory burdens have taken some measures to address this priority by: *i)* streamlining registration and licensing procedures (Belgium, Chile, the Czech Republic, Greece, Korea and Turkey) including in some specific sectors (construction in Israel, services in Portugal and food in Turkey); *ii)* creating a one-stop shop for start-ups (the Czech Republic, Greece, Israel and Poland); *iii)* simplifying bankruptcy procedures (the Czech Republic and Estonia); and *iv)* promoting competition for public contracts and cutting business red tape (Denmark and Poland). Policy responsiveness has been limited in Iceland, India and Indonesia, where sustained efforts will be needed to reduce economy-wide regulatory burdens.

- In line with *Going for Growth* recommendations, efforts have been made to strengthen the competition framework in Denmark, France and Greece, Italy, as well as in New Zealand through the establishment of an independent Productivity Commission in 2010, and in South Africa through the introduction of regulatory impact assessment for new regulation. In the European Union, the transposition of the Services Directive, albeit incomplete, is well advanced and the creation of a Single European Payments Area has reduced cross-border financial transactions costs. Norway took action that goes against *Going for Growth* recommendations in 2008 with the simplification of government procedures to overrule competition authorities.
- Most countries that had been recommended to strengthen competition in network industries have taken some measures to address this priority by: *i)* unbundling energy networks (Hungary, Portugal); *ii)* improving third-party access and easing entry restrictions (Austria and Mexico in telecommunications, Greece and Portugal in various network sectors and Switzerland in telecommunications and electricity transmission); *iii)* introducing or consolidating the power of the regulatory authority (Mexico, New Zealand, Poland and Switzerland) or adopting an industry-specific competition Act (Austria in the gas sector); *iv)* reducing price controls (Belgium, Hungary, Ireland where a wholesale electricity market was set up in 2007 and Portugal where a roadmap for phasing out regulated energy prices was drafted in July 2011) and; *v)* introducing incentive-based regulation (Germany and Israel). In the European Union, competition has been enhanced in air services by the first-stage EU-US Air Transport Agreement and postal services will be fully liberalised in 2012. The Netherlands took action that goes against *Going for Growth* recommendations in 2010, when the court of appeal overruled the 2006 law stipulating ownership separation of the energy distribution networks. No significant action was taken in Canada and South Africa to address priorities to enhance competition in network industries, nor in Japan where the privatisation of Japan Post and Japan Post Insurance – planned to be completed by 2017 – was suspended.
- In countries that had been recommended to reduce barriers to competition in retail trade, measures have been taken to: *i)* ease entry barriers, including for large retailers (Italy, Belgium, Portugal and Spain), *ii)* retail pricing regulation (France) and *iii)* sales regulations (Belgium) and; *iv)* reduce restrictions on shop opening hours (Austria, Denmark, Finland, Italy and Portugal). In line with *Going for Growth* recommendations, barriers to entry in professional services have been reduced in Austria, Canada (where the focus has been barriers to inter-provincial mobility), Germany, Greece, Ireland, Korea and Portugal (a commitment associated with the EU-IMF aid package). No progress has been achieved to increase competition in retail trade and professional services in Luxembourg, where even the transposition of the EU Services Directive remains to be legislated, or in the Netherlands to promote competition in retail trade.
- Reducing the scope of public ownership has often been recommended as part of a broader policy package aimed at strengthening competition. Privatising SOEs could bring efficiency gains while helping restore the sustainability of public finances in cases where public administration and management had clearly proven to hurt efficiency. Well-designed privatisation processes, however, need to consider competition principles and apply competition law. Reducing the scope of public ownership has also been specifically advised to some OECD countries as well as in 2011 to China and Russia, where public ownership is particularly high. In China, private equity firms are progressively being

allowed to restructure state-owned companies and the share of state capital in state-owned enterprises is being decreased. Italy privatised its public airline Alitalia in 2009. Mexico has been gradually increasing the independence and accountability of PEMEX, the national oil company. Privatisations took place in Poland and Turkey. More broadly, against the background of fiscal sustainability concerns, the crisis has accelerated the pace of privatisation, and especially so in European countries in the context of the sovereign debt crisis (see Box 1.2). In Russia, where State intervention remains pervasive, no significant progress has been recorded over the past year.

- Among the 11 countries (8 OECD countries and in 2011 India, Indonesia and Russia) where reducing barriers to foreign direct investment had been recommended, policy responsiveness has been rather limited, with countries often combining small steps forward with policy relapses. As a result, all priorities in this area have yet to be fully addressed. Approval processes for foreign direct investment (FDI) were removed in the non-state-owned banking sector in Russia over the last year and were simplified across the board in Korea. Efforts to improve transparency and simplify procedures for prospective foreign investors have also been undertaken in India since 2011 as well as in Japan through the "Inward Investment Promotion Programme" (2010) which features some deregulation of investment procedures. Reductions of ownership restrictions have taken place for satellites broadcasting in Canada and Korea and for retail trade in India. Little has been achieved in Australia, Iceland, Indonesia and New Zealand to reduce FDI restrictions.
- Openness to trade was improved in Switzerland – for which the removal of non-tariff trade barriers was identified as a priority in 2007 – in 2010, when remaining technical barriers to trade for over 80% of the imports from the European Union were eliminated. In Russia, action to remove distortions in trade policy has been limited since 2011, apart from some reduction in tariffs for selected agricultural products that were put in place in response to the food price shock resulting from the summer 2010 drought.

Agriculture

Limited action has also been taken on *Going for Growth* agricultural policy reform priorities as reflected in relatively low responsiveness rates and in the persistence of the recommendations over time. This partly stems from the political difficulty of reform in this area, as also testify increases in restrictions of agricultural exports in the past few years. Agricultural subsidies have been mechanically reduced as a consequence of higher world market prices. However, some progress has also been made towards reducing the economic distortions associated with policy interventions, *i.e.* the composition of producer support to agriculture has shifted from price support towards more direct income support (European Union and Switzerland), and in some countries new direct payments supplement existing market price support measures (Japan and Korea). The European Union is progressively decoupling producer support from production and will abolish milk quotas by 2015. However, the renewed use of export subsidies for dairy products in 2009 was a step back. Korea, Iceland and Switzerland are reducing export subsidies and tariff and non-tariff barriers. The United States went a step back in 2008 by providing new incentives for the local production of cellulosic bio-fuels and little progress has been achieved in Norway in this area.

Human capital

Raising human capital has been recommended to lift productivity levels in the vast majority of OECD countries since 2007 and in 2011 in all BIICS. Concrete priorities have aimed at improving the quality and efficiency of education systems, their responsiveness to labour market needs, as well as at reducing educational inequalities. While action has been very frequent and increasingly so over time, many of the priorities remain as education reform typically requires sustained efforts. The crisis context did not halt longstanding policy efforts in this area but, as discussed in the 2011 edition of *Going for Growth*, there remains significant room for improving the efficiency of public education spending.

About half of the countries have taken actions on *Going for Growth* recommendations to reform primary and secondary education. General education reforms have included: *i)* curricula reforms (Greece, Iceland, Luxembourg, Mexico and Turkey); *ii)* increased supply of vocational education at the upper secondary level and greater responsiveness to the needs of the labour market (Australia, Portugal, Spain and Turkey and the United Kingdom) – including by developing second-chance programmes for low-educated adults (Brazil and Portugal); and *iii)* stronger qualification requirements, training or certification for teachers (Chile, Greece, Indonesia, Mexico, Norway, South Africa, Spain and Sweden). Accountability has been reinforced through: *i)* teacher or school performance evaluations (Greece, Mexico, Portugal and the United States); *ii)* reforms or wider use of standardised exams (the Czech Republic, Germany, Denmark, Israel, Sweden and Spain); *iii)* national standards or indicators (Norway, New Zealand, Turkey and the United States), annual reporting (New Zealand); and *iv)* evaluation by a quality assurance agency (Chile). Countries have taken measures to increase equality of educational opportunities, such as: *i)* financial incentives for under-performing schools or for teachers to raise student achievement (Chile and the United States); *ii)* increased support for students from disadvantaged backgrounds (Chile, New Zealand, the United States and the United Kingdom); *iii)* reduced grade repetition (Luxembourg); *iv)* the progressive postponing of tracking (Austria and Germany); and *v)* an increase in compulsory years of schooling (Portugal and Israel). Funding for basic education and school infrastructure has been increased in emerging economies, including in Brazil, China, Chile and South Africa, as well as in Israel where it has financed increased teacher pay and reductions in class size.

Reform of higher education systems has been flagged as a priority in *Going for Growth* for many continental European countries. Most of them have taken some measures, although further action is still needed to address long-standing deficiencies. The reforms undertaken since 2007 in countries with a recommendation in this area have included:

- Revising the functioning of students' financial aid (Denmark and Finland) and introducing or extending tuition fees (Germany, Ireland through increases in the contribution charge for tertiary students, and Sweden but in the latter case only for students from outside the European Economic area);
- Improving the governance of universities, including through greater autonomy (France, Germany, Italy and Portugal) and the reinforcement of financial incentives to improve performance *inter alia* by strengthening evaluation mechanisms (Italy), partly conditioning government funding on outcomes (New Zealand and the Slovak Republic), and *via* cost benchmarking across institutions (Switzerland);

- Reforming higher education assessment frameworks, including by establishing a new framework law for higher education (Greece) or by creating or reforming the accreditation agency to support internal quality assessments of universities (Portugal and Switzerland);
- Encouraging earlier completion by adjusting university funding and study programmes (Denmark), or earlier entry into tertiary education by reforming admission criteria (Sweden and Finland);
- Developing higher education technical and professionally-oriented courses (Portugal, Spain and Turkey) with facilitated transition to university (Portugal and Spain).

General taxation

Tax reform has gained increasing prominence in the *Going for Growth* exercise over the years. This reflects mounting evidence of the impact of the tax structure on economic growth (see *e.g.* Arnold *et al.*, 2011) and the pressing need to restore fiscal sustainability in many OECD countries, which calls for designing growth-friendly fiscal consolidation strategies – or for implementing revenue-neutral tax reforms where there is fiscal space. While Brazil took no action to reduce the fragmentation and complexity of its tax system since 2011 (when the corresponding priority was set) reforms have been widespread over the last five years in the 13 OECD countries where improving the efficiency of the tax system had been identified as a priority. Greece and Portugal have been implementing tax reforms largely consistent with their *Going for Growth* priorities. In particular, both countries have sought to broaden the tax base by combating tax evasion (Greece) and curbing tax expenditures (Portugal). Portugal also took action to simplify tax collection and reduce tax compliance costs. In 2011, Italy undertook a number of fiscal consolidation-driven tax changes which should improve the efficiency of the tax structure, *e.g.* cutting labour and corporate taxes along with raising value added tax (VAT) and local property tax rates. In Germany and Finland, cuts in labour taxation implemented as part of the crisis-related measures have been financed through permanent increases in less distortive consumption and environmental taxes. Canada and Israel have been reducing the corporate tax rate – as well as personal income tax rates in the case of Israel, as will Australia by 2013. Japan broadened the tax base by abolishing a number of tax exemptions in 2010. Tax reform was also implemented in Korea by broadening the consumption tax base and in Mexico, first by reducing corporate tax loopholes and then by increasing the VAT rate in 2010. Norway partly reformed its wealth tax system by bringing the housing valuation component of the tax closer to market values. No significant action was taken in the United States to address tax distortions and broaden the tax base.

Other policies

Policy priorities have also covered a broad range of other areas relevant to productivity performance, some of which – especially in the area of the financial sector and public sector efficiency – could also help address public and private sector financial imbalances:

- *Financial services.* Financial market reform has in general not featured among the *Going for Growth* priorities and has been treated separately (*e.g.* in Box 1.1 of *Going for Growth 2011* and in *Going for Growth 2010*), as it is a key challenge in many OECD countries and in need of broad international coordination. Reforms in this area had also been specifically identified as policy priorities for the European Union since 2007, and for Iceland and the United States against the background of the financial crisis. Most OECD countries – including those with a previous priority in this area – have taken steps towards overhauling financial supervision, in an attempt to correct some of the institutional failures that led to the financial crisis. Together with actions by individual countries and the European Union, a regulatory reform has been taking place at the international level in recognition of the need for co-ordinated rules to strengthen financial stability and reduce opportunities for regulatory arbitrage. One vital component of such a regulatory regime has been the Basel III agreement, which effectively triples the size of capital reserves that banks must hold against losses over the period 2011-18.[23] Despite this progress, areas where international coordination still needs to advance include the regulation of the over the counter derivatives market and accounting standards. International coordination of prudential supervision is particularly important for the euro area, where further efforts to develop an effective system of cross-border supervision and an integrated crisis management framework should feature on top of the policy agenda. *Going for Growth* 2011 recommended more basic financial liberalisation in most non-member economies, including Brazil and India, where bank credit is not fully allocated by the market. Since 2011, no action was taken in Brazil to reduce its very high level of reserve requirements, but the authorisation of credit registries should improve banks' access to information on borrowers. Over the last year, India eased restrictions on access to local capital markets with foreign individuals allowed to invest directly (from 2012).

- *Public sector reform*. Responsiveness has been relatively high among the OECD countries where improving the efficiency of government expenditure had been recommended, likely reflecting the need to consolidate public budgets. General public sector reforms have included a rationalisation of public services (Hungary and Portugal) and introducing performance assessment (Portugal). Efficiency-enhancing public sector reforms have taken place in the healthcare sector through the re-organisation of public providers and the introduction of benchmarking (Hungary and New Zealand), patient co-payments (the Czech Republic) or the decentralisation of expenditures to enhance cost-awareness (New Zealand and the United Kingdom). Broader healthcare sector reforms have been recommended for Switzerland, the United States and Russia. The 2010 reform in the United States made health insurance compulsory and provided means-tested subsidies for its purchase. Switzerland has been enhancing cost-effectiveness in the pharmaceutical sector by increasing co-payments on branded drugs and by progressively introducing diagnosis-related funding in the hospital sector. Since 2011, the Russian Federation has allowed citizens to choose a primary care doctor and an insurance company within the mandatory insurance system. No significant progress has been registered in Iceland with respect to public sector reform.
- *Public infrastructure*. Addressing public infrastructure deficiencies has been a priority for several OECD and large emerging countries. Against the background of fiscal adjustment needs, raising expenditure on infrastructure has proven more challenging in the aftermath of crisis-related fiscal stimulus packages implemented in most OECD countries in 2008 and 2009 (see Chapter 1 in OECD, 2010a). Policies to make cost-effective use of existing infrastructure have included the introduction of a combined property and water charge in 2012 (and meter-based water charges scheduled for 2013) in Ireland and the introduction of toll roads to restrain demand in Australia and New Zealand. Australia also focused on enhancing transparency in the selection of projects through the publication of cost-benefit analyses and *ex post* evaluation mechanisms. While the UK

government halted the trend increase in public investment amid austerity measures, Poland could rely on EU structural funds to continue upgrading its transport and communication infrastructure. In emerging economies, where enhancing infrastructure provision is key to boosting living standards and where public finances are generally in better shape, public spending on infrastructure continued to rise. At the same time, though, backtracking took place with respect to the opening of infrastructure industries to foreign investors, with India raising limits for foreign institutional investment in debt issued by Indian infrastructure companies and Brazil restricting private equity participation in the oil and gas sectors.

- *Innovation-promoting policies.* As a key driver of long-term growth, innovation-related reforms have been recommended in seven OECD countries and in the Russian Federation as well as in China, where the focus was to speed up absorption of existing technology. As in the past, policy responsiveness has been rather high in this area, although it has declined more recently. All countries concerned followed up on *Going for Growth* recommendations since 2007 by raising public support for R&D activities through tax credits (Ireland and Italy), public grants (New Zealand) or subsidies targeted at innovative SMEs (Slovak Republic), as well as by strengthening university-industry linkages (Canada, Ireland, Japan and New Zealand) and better protecting intellectual property rights (Korea). In Russia, the recent creation of the Skolkovo "innovation city" may help improve innovation policy in the future, but with the risk of increasingly "picking the winners" through public support.

In some lower-income OECD countries (*e.g.* Mexico) and the BRIICS, a number of more specific productivity-enhancing policy initiatives have been recommended, such as land regulation, governance and legal reforms that would help strengthen the rule of law, clarify property rights and fight corruption, or phasing out of distortive energy subsidies. Action has been rather limited since 2011, when corresponding priorities were set. India and Indonesia have introduced reforms aimed at streamlining land acquisition processes. Since 2011 in Russia, all draft legislation is required to be subject to regulatory impact analysis, in order to identify unjustified bureaucratic interference in private sector activities and thereby reduce corruption risk. The new Mediation law introduced in China in 2011 should strengthen the judicial system by providing a firm basis to the first level dispute resolution mechanism commonly used at the local level for the resolution of private disputes. Little progress has taken place since 2011 in Indonesia and Mexico to improve governance systems. Energy subsidies were increased in Indonesia in 2011 compared to what was planned in the initial Budget, at odds with the corresponding *Going for Growth* priority.

Green Growth

Going for Growth priorities are aimed at promoting long-run growth, and a number of them would also boost *Green Growth* and contribute to environmental sustainability including *inter alia* in the areas of innovation, taxes and infrastructure. Responsiveness to *Going for Growth* priorities has been pro-*Green Growth* in a number of policy areas, among which:

- *Tax reforms*, where the focus was on reducing direct taxes by partly shifting the tax burden on environmental taxation. Germany lowered unemployment insurance contributions over the 2007-09 period while introducing a CO_2 element in the vehicle tax in 2009, and Finland cut income tax and social security contributions during the recession while increasing energy taxes. Other countries have been introducing carbon emission trading schemes, such as New Zealand. To the extent that the underlying trading permits are auctioned, such schemes could also be part of a growth-friendly tax reform package.

- *Public infrastructure reforms*, where the focus was on reducing CO_2 emissions and road congestion and curbing demand through price incentives more broadly. Water charges are being introduced in Ireland (in 2012 as a lump sum per household and in 2013 meter-based). Australia is developing a system of smart managed motorways embedding technologies aimed at improving traffic demand management in major cities, and New Zealand opened a toll road in 2009.

Notes

1. Several broader measures of well-being are being developed in the context of the OECD-wide work on measuring well-being and progress. Highlights of this work are provided by the OECD Better Life Initiative, which so far includes the 2011 report "How's life?" and the interactive wellbeing assessment tool "Your Better Life Index". Some measures that extend GDP numbers to non-market production, and thereby may come closer to indicators of well-being, have been explored in last year's edition of Going for Growth. While many alternative well-being measures are correlated with GDP per capita (see OECD, 2006, *Going for Growth* 2006), broader measures are important complements to evaluate issues such as, for example, income distribution, poverty, or environmental sustainability. On the latter issue, the OECD is providing analytical tools and policy recommendations to foster green growth, which will progressively be integrated in the Going for Growth exercise (see OECD, 2011a) starting with next year's edition.
2. See special chapter on the crisis-related policy interventions in *Going for Growth* 2010 (Chapter 1 in OECD, 2010a).
3. See Chapter 2 of *OECD Employment Outlook 2010* (OECD, 2010b) for a discussion on the impact of the crisis on emerging economies and the role of labour market and social policies to support affected workers and their families.
4. See Annex 1.A1 for a detailed presentation of the methodology used to select the priorities.
5. Box 2.2 in *Going for Growth 2010* (OECD, 2010a) discusses the caveats associated with reform intensity indicators.
6. The statistical data for Israel are supplied by and under the responsibility of the relevant Israeli authorities. The use of such data by the OECD is without prejudice to the status of the Golan Heights, East Jerusalem and Israeli settlements in the West Bank under the terms of international law.
7. Roughly comparable reform patterns emerge from a concomitant survey carried over the same period by the Business and Industry Advisory Committee to the OECD (BIAC) in its Member and Observer organisations – *i.e.* the major national business and employer organisations in OECD countries and certain emerging economies. The latter survey suggests that BIAC Member/Observer organisations perceive that most *Going for Growth* priorities have been addressed. Indeed, 69% of the reform priorities are considered to have been partly implemented since 2007, which is consistent with significant reform activity over the period considered. BIAC Member/Observer organisations rarely consider that *Going for Growth* recommendations have been *fully* implemented, in line with the current finding that policy action has been often piecemeal and that it rarely would imply the removal of the corresponding priority.
8. See also the latest Economic Survey on Greece (OECD 2011c).
9. The scatter excludes the four countries that had either no or only one labour-utilisation enhancing priority.
10. Based on *OECD Economic Outlook* 90 projections.
11. This finding is in contrast with past experience and empirical evidence, *e.g.* with Duval (2008) who found significant evidence of a general trade-off between undertaking reforms and consolidating public budgets.

12. Hungary achieved considerable progress in reducing labour taxation over the last two years, and, more recently, it even introduced a flat-rate personal income tax. While boosting labour utilisation in principle, such reform as implemented has been highly regressive and raises fiscal sustainability concerns.
13. See (OECD, 2011e).
14. See de Serres *et al.* (2012) and OECD (2010c), *Sickness, Disability and Work: Breaking the Barriers – A Synthesis of Findings across OECD Countries*
15. The Netherlands and the United Kingdom have had some success in reversing the trend rise in disability rates during 2000s.
16. See Box 1.3 and Panels A and B of Chapter 1 of *OECD Employment Outlook 2011* (OECD, 2011d).
17. Other influential factors factors include population ageing, since disability prevalence increases with age.
18. See Chapter 1 of *OECD Employment Outlook 2011* on income support to job losers (OECD, 2011d).
19. See web annex of Chapter 1 of *Employment Outlook 2011* (OECD, 2011d), Table 1.A1.6.
20. See *OECD Employment Outlook 2010* (OECD, 2010b) for a detailed assessment of STW schemes in OECD countries.
21. The Spanish labour market crisis is a topical case. See Blanchard and Landier (2002), Bentolila *et al.* (2010) and de Serres *et al.* (2012).
22. Actions in this area do not need to imply comprehensive reforms. Moreover, the bulk of measures were actually taken over the period 2007-09, with some slowdown more recently.
23. See *e.g.* Box 1.1 in Chapter 1 of OECD (2011b) on financial market reform.

Bibliography

Arnold, J., *et al.* (2011), "Tax Policy for Economic Recovery and Growth", *The Economic Journal*, 121, pp. F59-F80.

Bassanini, A. and R. Duval (2006), "Employment Patterns in OECD Countries: Reassessing the Role of Policies and Institutions", *OECD Economics Department Working Papers*, No. 486, OECD Publishing.

Bassanini, A., L. Nunziata, and D. Venn (2009), "Job Protection Legislation and Productivity Growth in OECD Countries", *Economic Policy*, Vol. 24, No. 58, pp. 349-402, April.

Bentolila, S., *et al.* (2010), "Two-tier Labor Markets in the Great Recession: France vs. Spain,"*IZA Discussion Paper series*, No. 5340.

Blanchard, O. and A. Landier (2002), "The Perverse Effects of Partial Labour Market Reform: Fixed-Term Contracts in France", *Economic Journal*, Vol. 112, No. 480, pp. F214-F244.

Duval, R. (2008), "Is There a Role for Macroeconomic Policy in Fostering Structural Reforms? Panel Evidence from OECD Countries over the Past Two Decades", *European Journal of Political Economy*, Vol. 24, No. 2, pp. 491-502.

Duval, R., M. Ehris and D. Furceri (2011), "The Effects of Downturns on Labour Force Participation: Evidence and Causes", *OECD Economics Department Working Papers*, No. 875, OECD Publishing.

Hijzen, A. and D. Venn (2011), "The Role of Short-Time Work Schemes during the 2008-09 Recession", *OECD Social, Employment and Migration Working Papers*, No. 115, OECD Publishing.

Jaumotte, F. (2003), "Female Labour Force Participation: Past Trends and Main Determinants in OECD Countries", *OECD Economics Department Working Papers*, No. 376, OECD Publishing.

OECD (2006), *Economic Policy Reforms 2006: Going for Growth*, OECD Publishing.

OECD (2009), *OECD Employment Outlook 2009: Tackling the Jobs Crisis*, OECD Publishing.

OECD (2010a), *Economic Policy Reforms 2010: Going for Growth*, OECD Publishing.

OECD (2010b), *OECD Employment Outlook 2010: Moving Beyond the Jobs Crisis*, OECD Publishing.

OECD (2010c), *Sickness, Disability and Work: Breaking the Barriers: A Synthesis of Findings across OECD Countries*, OECD Publishing.

OECD (2011a), "Strengthening *Going for Growth* and Other WP1 Work", Document prepared by the Economics Department for the Economic Policy Committee's Working Party No. 1, ECO/CPE/WP1(2011)16.

OECD (2011b), *Economic Policy Reforms 2011: Going for Growth*, OECD Publishing.

OECD (2011c), *OECD Economic Surveys: Greece 2011*, OECD Publishing.

OECD (2011d), *OECD Employment Outlook 2011*, OECD Publishing.

OECD (2011e), *Pensions at a Glance 2011: Retirement-income Systems in OECD and G20 Countries*, OECD Publishing.

de Serres, A. F. Murtin, and C. De la Maisonneuve, (2012), "Policies to Facilitate the Return to Work", *OECD Economics Department Working Papers*, OECD Publishing, forthcoming.

ANNEX 1.A1

How policy priorities are chosen for Going for Growth

The *Going for Growth* structural surveillance exercise seeks to identify five policy priorities for each OECD member country, the BRIICS and the EU. Three of these policy priorities are identified based on internationally comparable OECD indicators of policy settings and performance. The additional two priorities are often supported by indicator-based evidence, but may draw principally on country-specific expertise. These priorities are meant to capture any potential policy imperatives in fields not covered by indicators.

For the selection of the three indicator-based policy priorities, the starting point is a detailed examination of labour utilisation and productivity performance so as to uncover specific areas of relative strength and weakness. Each performance indicator is juxtaposed with corresponding policy indicators, where OECD empirical research has shown a robust link to performance, to determine where performance and policy weaknesses appear to be linked. This evaluation process is carried out for each of the approximately 50 areas where OECD policy indicators provide coverage.

As an example, Figure 1.A1.1 below shows, for a sample country, a scatter plot of pairings of policy indicators (on the horizontal axis) with corresponding performance indicators (on the vertical axis). Since many of the approximately 50 indicators are associated with more than one performance area, there are potentially more than 100 potential pairings to be examined. The indicators of policy and performance are standardised by re-scaling them so that each has a mean of zero and a cross-county standard deviation of one, with positive numbers representing positions more growth-friendly than the OECD average. The scatter plot is thus divided into four quadrants, depending on whether a country's policy-performance pairing is below or above the average policy or performance score.

Candidates for recommendations thus fall into the lower left quadrant, where policy indicators and corresponding performance are *both* below average. In most countries there are more than three unique policy areas that qualify as potential priorities (for instance, Germany had 16 candidates in the 2009 exercise). When there are more than three candidate policy priorities, the list has been narrowed using a combination of country expertise with the following criteria: *i*) the estimated quantitative impact of reforms in the policy area on GDP per capita as determined in previous OECD analysis, *ii*) the normalised distance of the policy stance from the benchmark (the OECD average), and *iii*) recent trends in policy and performance. The limit on the number of priorities means that for some countries, obvious policy imperatives may not be identified as priorities because other priorities are deemed as more important.

Figure 1.A1.1. **Example of selection of candidates for *Going for Growth* priorities**

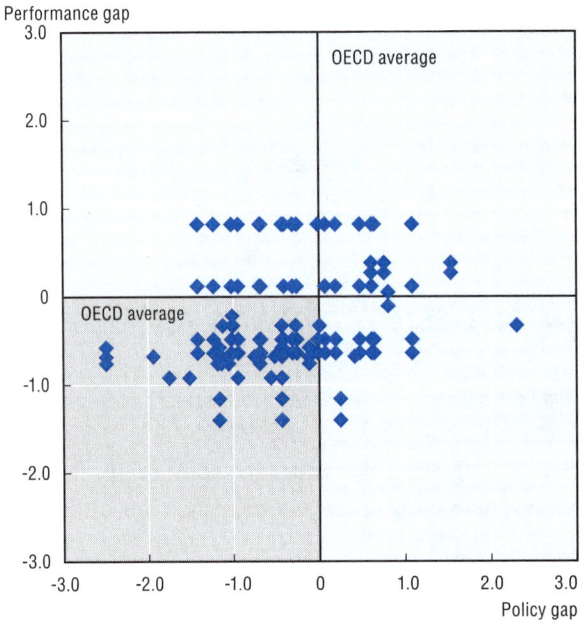

StatLink http://dx.doi.org/10.1787/888932372982

The empirical research linking policy with performance includes a long series of studies carried out by the Secretariat as well as the academic literature. OECD studies include for instance the OECD (2003), OECD (1994) and its reappraisal (OECD, 2006). Carrying out empirical analysis to strengthen the underpinnings of *Going for Growth* recommendations is an ongoing process. Some new empirical evidence on the policy and institutional drivers of long-term economic growth for both OECD countries and the BRIICS is featured in Bouis *et. al.* (2011).

Bibliography

Bouis, R., R. Duval and F. Murtin (2011), "The Policy and Institutional Drivers of Economic Growth: New Evidence from Growth Regressions", *OECD Economics Department Working Papers*, No. 843.

OECD (1994), *OECD Jobs Study; Facts, Analysis, Strategies*, OECD Publishing.

OECD (2003), *The Sources of Economic Growth in OECD Countries*, OECD Publishing.

OECD (2006), *OECD Employment Outlook 2006: Boosting Jobs and Incomes*, OECD Publishing.

Economic Policy Reforms 2012
Going for Growth
© OECD 2012

PART I

Chapter 2

Country notes

Note: Users of the data must be aware that they may not longer fully reflect the current situation in fast reforming countries.

AUSTRALIA

Priorities supported by indicators

Enhance capacity and regulation in infrastructure (2007, 2009, 2011)

Recommendations: Address the shortfall in infrastructure by rigorously selecting public projects and ensuring that existing capacity is efficiently used, for instance in road transport and water management.

Actions taken: Selection and funding of projects will rely more heavily on publication of cost-benefit analyses and *ex post* evaluation from 2012. The government will also invest in a smart managed motorway system to curb road congestion in agglomerations.

Relax barriers to foreign direct investment (2011)

Recommendations: Apply to other countries the lighter screening procedures granted to the United States. Involve specialist agencies (*e.g.* national security) in the screening procedure to enhance transparency.

Actions taken: No action taken.

Improve efficiency of the tax system (2011)

Recommendations: Lower further corporate and personal income taxes and raise the goods and services tax. Simplify and rationalise the states' tax system, especially on housing.

Actions taken: Parliament is discussing a reform increasing taxation of non-renewable resources. By 2013, the statutory corporate tax rate will be cut from 30% to 29%.

Reform disability benefit schemes (2007, 2009)

Recommendations: Tighten eligibility criteria for the Disability Support Pension (DSP) and encourage DSP recipients with substantial work capacity to look for a job.

Actions taken: A more rigorous DSP assessment process is being introduced in 2011 and higher wage subsidies will be granted to employers hiring people with disability. From July 2012, DSP recipients under 35 years with an assessed work capacity of at least 8 hours per week will be asked to look for a job.

Other key priorities

Improve education outcomes (2007, 2009, 2011)

Recommendations: Improve and promote apprenticeships and vocational education and training (VET).

Actions taken: Additional training places will be funded through the 2011-12 budget, co-financed by employers and tailored to industry skill needs. States will be given financial incentives from 2012-13 to reform the VET system so as to upgrade skill levels and increase completion rates.

Increase incentives for workforce participation (2007, 2009, 2011)

Recommendations: Reduce effective marginal tax rates on returning to work, especially for low-income families. Make childcare benefits for children under school age conditional on employment or job search of parents.

Actions taken: Payment of the low-income tax offset will be brought forward during the year from 2011-12. Dependent spouse tax offset will be phased out for spouse turning 40 after July 2011. As from 2013, income support for single parents will be restructured to promote participation.

Maintain a flexible wage bargaining system and cut minimum labour costs (2007, 2009)

Recommendations: Rationalise the award system and maintain wage negotiation at firm level.

Actions taken: In 2009, a nationwide system of industrial relations in the private sector reduced the number of awards, created a single regulator and enhanced worker protection. No action taken on minimum labour costs.

AUSTRALIA

- Per capita GDP has risen to the upper half of OECD countries but productivity has been lagging.
- Among key priority areas, progress has been made to improve the tax system, better use infrastructure capacity and promote workforce participation, but more needs to be done, in particular to further enhance the tax structure and to relax barriers to foreign direct investment.
- In non-priority areas, reform has been launched to promote a more sustainable low-pollution growth path by putting a price on carbon.

Performance and policy indicators

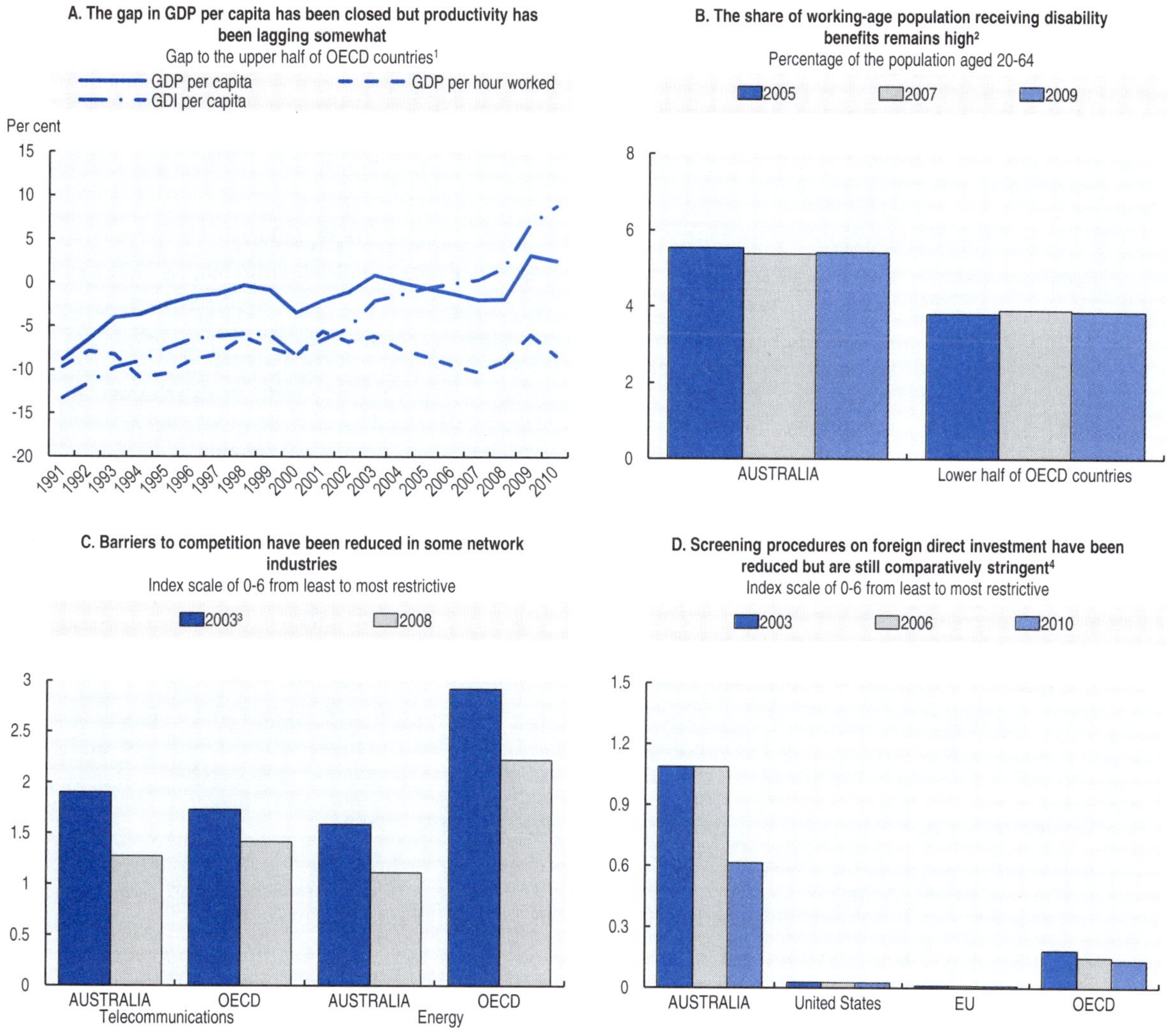

1. Percentage gap with respect to the simple average of the highest 17 OECD countries in terms of GDP per capita, GDP per hour worked and GDI per capita (in constant 2005 PPPs).
2. For Australia, the last available year is 2008. Lower half of OECD countries in terms of the share of working age population receiving disability benefits. This group excludes Chile, Iceland and Turkey.
3. The OECD average excludes Chile, Estonia, Israel and Slovenia.
4. The OECD FDI regulatory restrictiveness index looks only at statutory restrictions and does not assess the manner in which they are implemented.

Source: Chart A: OECD, *National Accounts and Economic Outlook 90 Databases*; Chart B: OECD (2010), *Sickness, Disability and Work: Breaking the Barriers: A Synthesis of Findings across OECD Countries*; Chart C: OECD, *Product Market Regulation Database*; Chart D: *http://www.oecd.org/investment/index*.

StatLink http://dx.doi.org/10.1787/888932565034

AUSTRIA

Priorities supported by indicators

Improve graduation rates from tertiary education (2007, 2009, 2011)

Recommendations: Postpone early tracking and strengthen language support to immigrant students. Extend performance-based funding in tertiary education and allow universities to reintroduce tuition fees, accompanied by a comprehensive income-contingent student loan system.

Actions taken: The "New Secondary School" (*Neue Mittelschule*), which unifies formerly separated pupils aged 10-14, was launched as a pilot project in 2008-09. The government announced in May 2011 that it will be extended to the entire secondary education system by 2015-16.

Reduce barriers to entry in network industries (2007, 2009, 2011)

Recommendations: Ensure that access prices are not kept artificially high. Relax ownership restrictions in and fully privatise the electricity sector. Stimulate competition in rail transportation. Reduce or eliminate remaining cross-subsidies in all network industries.

Actions taken: Further progress has been made in implementing EU directives in the gas and electricity sectors. A Natural Gas Act strengthening competition was adopted in 2011. New access obligations were set for telecommunication network operators identified as possessing significant market power in 2010.

Reduce incentives to exit early from the labour force (2007, 2009, 2011)

Recommendations: Phase in all provisions of past pension reforms without relaxing their conditions. Tighten eligibility criteria to ensure that disability pensions are only used in well-justified cases.

Actions taken: Some backtracking with respect to the 2003-04 reform resulted from halving the discount rate and the extension of special early retirement programmes in 2007-08. Eligibility to disability pension was tightened in 2011, and a tightening of access to early retirement schemes is planned for 2014. The initiative "fit2work" started in 2011, an information and consulting service on health at the workplace, aims to reduce invalidity and early exit from the labour market.

Other key priorities

Reduce barriers to competition in professional services and retail trade (2007, 2009, 2011)

Recommendations: Reduce the statutory regulations of trades and professions and curb sectoral self-regulations hindering competition in "professional" services. Abolish compulsory membership to professional associations in liberal professions. Further promote competition in retail trade.

Actions taken: The Crafts, Trade, Service and Industry Act was amended in 2008 and 2010 to facilitate entry in several professions. Shop opening hours were extended in January 2008. The Horizontal Services Act implementing the EU Services Directive at federal level was adopted in October 2011.

Lower marginal tax rates on labour income (2007, 2009, 2011)

Recommendations: Reduce marginal income tax rates especially for low-skilled workers, financed by further broadening the tax base through reducing the numerous tax allowances and possibly increasing taxes on property and consumption (including environmental taxes).

Actions taken: Personal income taxes were lowered somewhat in 2009, including through tax relief for families with children, entrepreneurs and freelancers. Unemployment insurance contribution rates were reduced for low-wage workers in 2008. Environmental and financial sector taxes were increased as part of the fiscal consolidation package at the beginning of 2011.

AUSTRIA

- The small GDP per capita gap relative to the upper half of OECD countries has declined since 2005, reversing the widening since the early nineties. This improvement is due both to gains in labour productivity and to an increase in labour force participation, notably of older workers.
- Among the key priority areas, some progress has been made in reducing incentives for early retirement and planned measures should be fully implemented. More needs to be done to raise graduation rates from tertiary education, increase competition in the services sector and network industries, and shift the tax burden away from labour.
- In other areas, labour market policy responses to the crisis such as reforms to the short-term working scheme and subsidised study leave, which are still in place, have prevented excessive layoffs.

Performance and policy indicators

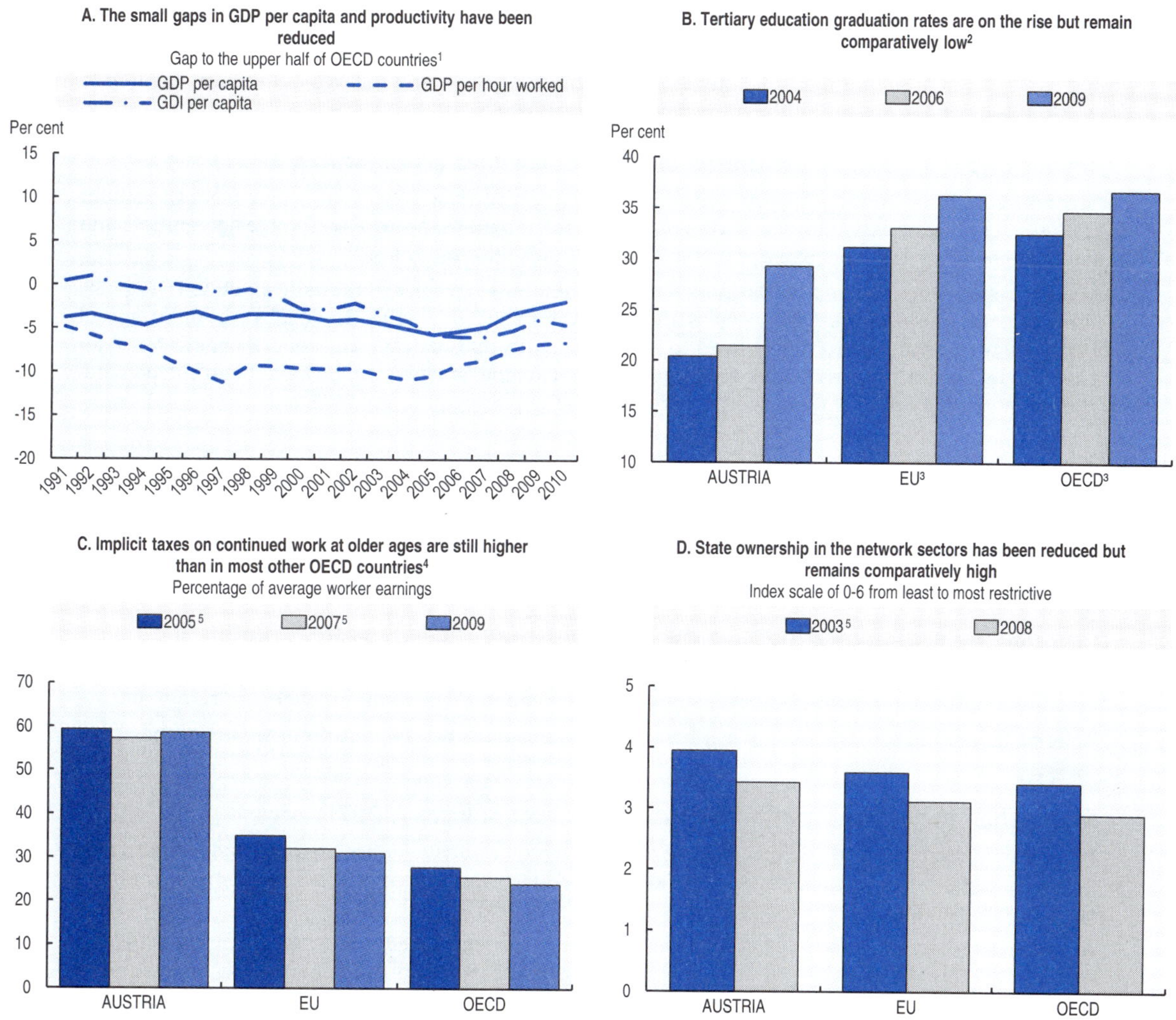

1. Percentage gap with respect to the simple average of the highest 17 OECD countries in terms of GDP per capita, GDP per hour worked and GDI per capita (in constant 2005 PPPs).
2. First-time graduation rates for single year of age at type A level.
3. Average of European countries in the OECD. EU and OECD averages exclude Belgium, Chile, Estonia, France and Korea.
4. Average implicit tax on continued work for five more years in "early retirement route" (as defined in Duval, 2003) for 55 and 60 year-olds.
5. Average of European countries in the OECD. EU and OECD averages exclude Chile, Estonia, Israel and Slovenia.

Source: Chart A: OECD, *National Accounts and Economic Outlook 90 Databases*; Chart B: OECD (2011), *Education at a Glance*; Chart C: Duval, R. (2003), "The Retirement Effects of Old-Age Pension and Early Retirement Schemes in OECD Countries", *OECD Economics Department Working Papers*, No. 370, OECD Publishing and OECD calculations; Chart D: OECD, *Product Market Regulation Database*.

StatLink http://dx.doi.org/10.1787/888932565053

BELGIUM

Priorities supported by indicators

Reduce the labour tax burden and enhance work incentives in the tax system (2007, 2009, 2011)

Recommendations: Target wages subsidies and reductions of social security contributions on low-wage workers. Address other labour market traps by removing spikes in effective marginal tax rates.

Actions taken: Since 2005, social security contributions have been lowered on several occasions for low-skilled, younger, older, R&D and shift-and-night workers as well as for the long-term unemployed.

Ease regulation in the retail sector and network industries (2007, 2009, 2011)

Recommendations: Scrap competition-inhibiting retail-sector regulation and liberalise zoning and shop opening hours regulation. Establish single independent regulators in all network industries and simplify universal service obligations while combining them with competitive tendering and government financing.

Actions taken: In 2010, Belgian-specific restrictions in the retail sector were relaxed, including through the authorisation of tied sales, fewer restrictions on sales with a loss, reducing the pre-sales black-out period and limiting it to clothing. Furthermore, the opening of large outlets was facilitated by removing the assessment of the impact on existing businesses.

Reduce implicit taxes on continued work at older ages (2007, 2009, 2011)

Recommendations: Phase out early retirement schemes and close other exit routes from the labour market, including by extending the surtax on employment benefit top-ups to all wage agreements and by phasing out occupational exemptions to the minimum retirement age.

Actions taken: Since the mid-2000s, job-search requirements have been gradually extended to age 58. Similarly, the minimum age for early retirement was raised to 60 and the legal retirement age of women was in several steps raised to 65 to be aligned with that of men. An in-work benefit for older unemployed and a pension bonus for staying longer in the labour market have been introduced. Thorough assessment of the early retirement schemes is planned for late 2011.

Other key priorities

Make wage setting more flexible (2007, 2009, 2011)

Recommendations: Decentralise wage negotiations and phase out the automatic wage indexation.

Actions taken: No action taken.

Improve job-search incentives in the unemployment benefit system (2009, 2011)

Recommendations: Reduce unemployment benefit over the unemployment spell to raise job-search incentives. Initial net replacement rates may have to go up to make room for such a phasing-out.

Actions taken: In 2009, the first year replacement rate was increased, but no other action has been taken.

Strengthen the efficiency of active labour market policies (2007)

Recommendations: Improve enforcement of job-search requirements for unemployed and co-ordination between regional placement agencies. Redirect ALMP funds from subsidised employment to compulsory training.

Actions taken: In 2008 and 2009, activation of younger unemployed was stepped up. In 2007, the regional placement agencies created an inter-regional association to exchange job offers and to co-operate on training. In 2009, Wallonia introduced commuting and childcare subsidies for newly hired low-wage workers. By contrast, Flanders stopped activation of older unemployed (above 52 years).

BELGIUM

- The GDP per capita gap relative to the upper half of OECD countries has stabilised. It is mostly explained by low labour utilisation, although there has been some progress in raising the low employment rate of older female workers. The erosion of the relatively high labour productivity level has come to a halt.
- Among the key priority areas, progress has been made to strengthen product market competition, particularly in the retail sector. Little progress has been achieved in labour market policies, notably regarding the wage determination process.
- In other areas, a massive expansion of the short-time work schemes was instrumental in preserving jobs during the crisis.

Performance and policy indicators

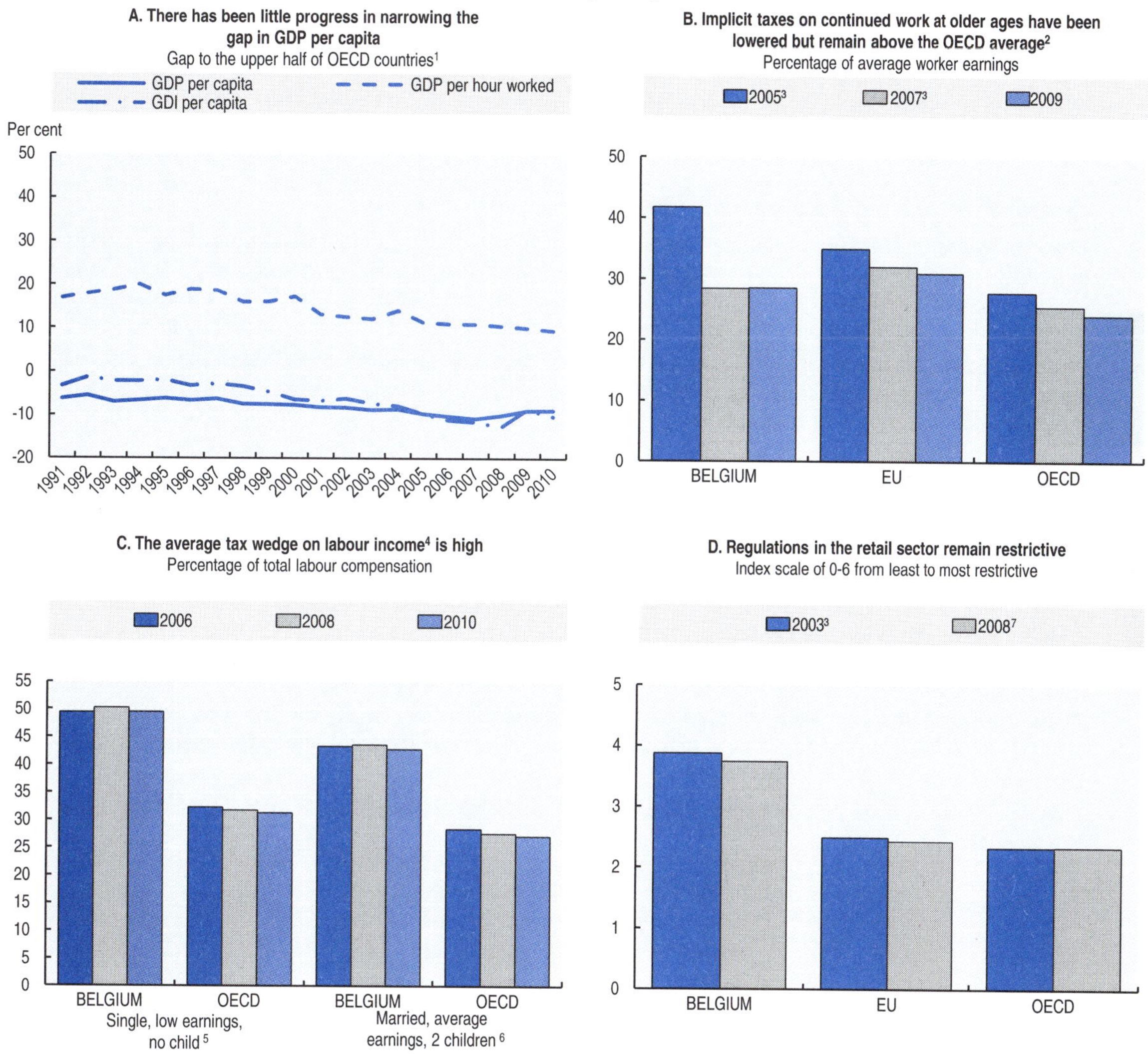

1. Percentage gap with respect to the simple average of the highest 17 OECD countries in terms of GDP per capita, GDP per hour worked and GDI per capita (in constant 2005 PPPs).
2. Average implicit tax on continued work for five more years in "early retirement route" (as defined in Duval, 2003) for 55 and 60 year-olds.
3. Average of European countries in the OECD. EU and OECD averages exclude Chile, Estonia, Israel and Slovenia and also Luxembourg in Panel D.
4. Labour taxes include personal income tax and employee plus employer social security contributions and any payroll tax less cash transfers.
5. Low earnings refer to two-thirds of average earnings.
6. At 100% of the average worker earnings for the first earner. Average of three situations regarding the wage of the second earner (0%, 33% and 67% of average earnings).
7. The 2008 figure does not include the most recent reforms which, however, only have a limited impact on the indicators.

Source: Chart A: OECD, *National Accounts and Economic Outlook 90 Databases*; Chart B: Duval, R. (2003), "The Retirement Effects of Old-Age Pension and Early Retirement Schemes in OECD Countries", OECD *Economics Department Working Papers*, No. 370 and OECD calculations; Chart C: OECD, *Taxing Wages Database*; Chart D: OECD, *Product Market Regulation Database*.

StatLink http://dx.doi.org/10.1787/888932565072

BRAZIL

Priorities supported by indicators

Increase the quality of education at all levels (2011)

Recommendations: Increase the quality of education at primary and secondary levels. Expand tertiary vocational and professional training to overcome skills shortages and reduce drop-out rates.

Actions taken: The new edition of the National Education Plan provides for further increases in funding for basic and professional education.

Improve the efficiency of financial markets (2011)

Recommendations: Gradually phase out directed credit provisions, including to the agriculture and housing sectors, to improve resource allocation. Ease bank reserve requirements over the medium term in accordance with the objective of ensuring both the stability and development of financial markets.

Actions taken: Credit registries containing positive information have been authorised in May 2011 and will improve banks' access to information on borrowers. Reserve requirements were raised in December 2010. The public development bank has announced a decrease in directed lending volumes for 2011.

Improve infrastructure provision (2011)

Recommendations: Reduce financial costs, the capital tax on productive investment and current expenditures in the public sector to allow higher infrastructure investment. Encourage States and municipalities to swiftly and efficiently undertake infrastructure projects. Lower regulatory uncertainties in the oil and gas sector and remove legal barriers to competition to spur private investment.

Actions taken: New laws dating from late 2010 have reduced regulatory uncertainty in the oil and gas sector, but private-sector equity participation has been restricted and equity participation by the state-owned oil company is mandatory.

Other key priorities

Reduce distortions in the tax system (2011)

Recommendations: Reduce the fragmentation and complexity of the tax system. Unify state-level VAT rates and bases and alleviate the burden on labour income.

Actions taken: No action taken.

Improve incentives for formal labour force participation (2011)

Recommendations: Encourage human capital accumulation on and off the job and lower social contributions for low-paid workers to tackle informality. Remove disincentives to formal labour force participation embedded in social programmes.

Actions taken: A new programme enacted in 2011 will provide funding for vocational training of low-skilled workers.

BRAZIL

- The GDP per capita gap with OECD countries is now diminishing and terms-of-trade gains have resulted in greater convergence in terms of income. Nevertheless, the gap remains large mainly due to comparatively weak labour productivity performance, which in turn reflects subdued investment rates, poor infrastructure and low levels of education.
- Among key priority areas, progress has been made in improving access to and the quality of education, promoting infrastructure investment and reducing informality in labour markets. The areas of financial markets and tax reform have seen less progress.
- In other areas, recent efforts to combat poverty and inequality through more equal access to education and conditional cash transfers have been very successful.

Performance and policy indicators

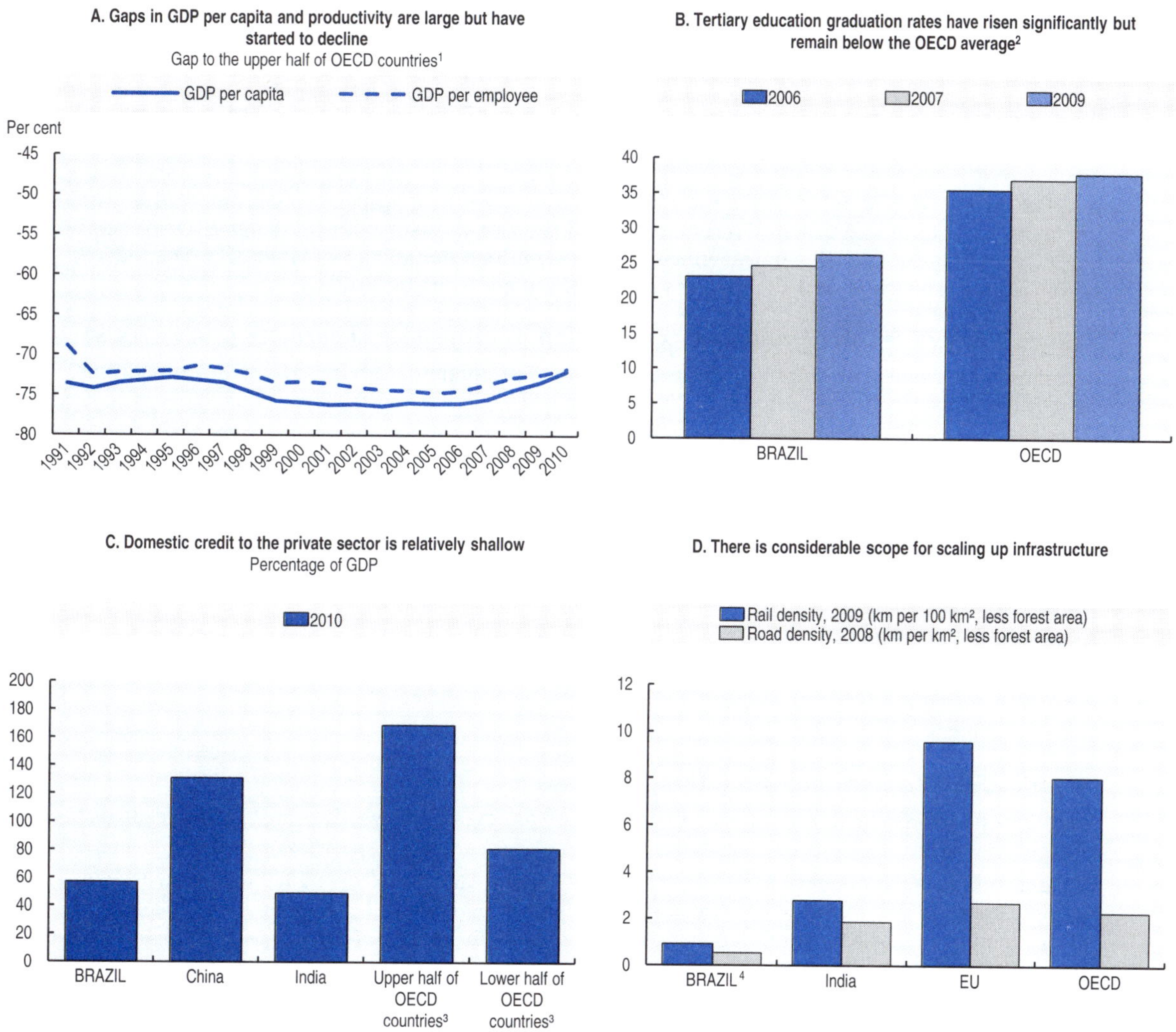

1. Percentage gap with respect to the simple average of the highest 17 OECD countries in terms of GDP per capita and GDP per employee (in constant 2005 PPPs).
2. First degree graduation rates for single year of age at tertiary-type A level.
3. Upper and lower half of OECD countries in terms of the level of domestic credit to the private sector. The last available year is 2009 for Australia, 2008 for Canada and the Slovak Republic and 2006 for Norway.
4. For road density, data refer to 2004.

Source: Chart A: World Bank (2011), *World Development Indicators (WDI)* and ILO (2011), *Key Indicators of the Labour Market (KILM) Databases*; Chart B: OECD (2011), *Education at a Glance*; Charts C and D: World Bank (2011), *World Development Indicators (WDI)*.

StatLink http://dx.doi.org/10.1787/888932565091

CANADA

Priorities supported by indicators

Reduce barriers to foreign direct investment (2007, 2009, 2011)

Recommendations: Reduce restrictions on foreign investment in the telecoms sector. Lift foreign ownership limits in air transport to complete the Canada-EU agreement and realise its potential benefits.

Actions taken: In 2010, foreign ownership restrictions were removed on satellites, and public consultations were held to lower them in telecoms. Legislation was approved in 2009 to raise the maximum foreign ownership limit on airlines from 25% to 49%, and regulations are being developed to complete the Canada-EU agreement for a transatlantic open aviation area.

Reduce barriers to competition in network industries (2007, 2009, 2011)

Recommendations: Reduce public ownership in the electricity sector and develop competitive retail and wholesale markets. Eliminate monopoly protections on Canada Post.

Actions taken: No action taken.

Reform the tax system (2007, 2009, 2011)

Recommendations: Make greater use of environmental, property or value-added taxes, and lower the corporate tax rate and personal income tax rates. Harmonise provincial sales taxes with the federal goods-and-services tax in remaining provinces.

Actions taken: The federal government will complete its series of corporate tax cuts in 2012. The provinces of Ontario and British Columbia replaced their sales taxes with the federal Harmonised Sales Tax in July 2010, but this move will be reversed in British Columbia by March 2013. The federal capital tax was abolished, and all provinces plan to eliminate theirs by 2012.

Reduce barriers to inter-provincial competition in professional services (2007, 2009)

Recommendations: Enhance inter-provincial mobility of professional services and trade occupations by fully implementing the Agreement on Internal Trade (AIT).

Actions taken: In 2009 the AIT was amended to mutually recognise occupational certifications across all regions. Additional agreements were introduced to further enhance mobility between certain provinces in 2009 and 2010.

Other key priorities

Reform the unemployment insurance system (2007, 2009, 2011)

Recommendations: Reduce unemployment persistence and foster labour mobility by introducing employer experience rating into Employment Insurance or scaling back access for seasonal or temporary workers in high-unemployment regions.

Actions taken: No action taken.

Improve R&D support policies (2007, 2011)

Recommendations: Evaluate current R&D support policies and use the findings to re-design programmes to improve business sector innovation.

Actions taken: An independent expert panel was established in October 2010 to review federal support for R&D and recommend ways to improve its effectiveness by October 2011. In 2011, the government introduced a programme to fund joint college-university commercialisation projects and provide greater support for small firms to adopt key technologies.

CANADA

- The small GDP per capita gap relative to the upper half of OECD countries has persisted due to comparatively weak labour productivity.
- In priority areas, progress has been made in enhancing labour mobility, reducing effective corporate tax rates and lowering foreign investment restrictions, but little action has been taken to liberalise post and electricity.
- In other areas, the extended duration of unemployment benefits and job-sharing agreements helped cushion the effects of the crisis, and are now being phased out. Targeted labour market initiatives have helped improve work incentives and skills of older workers, aboriginal Canadians, recent immigrants and young people.

Performance and policy indicators

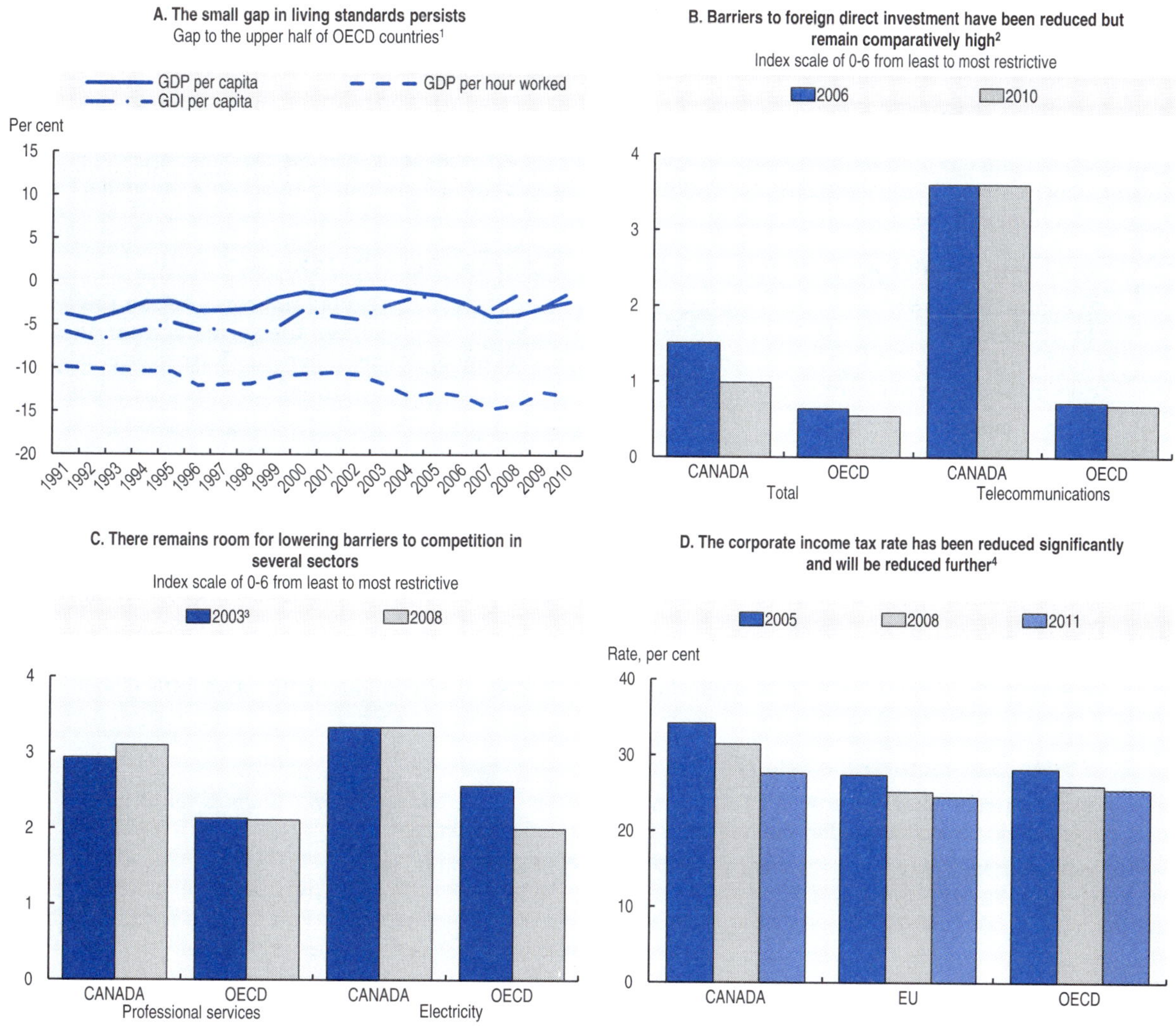

1. Percentage gap with respect to the simple average of the highest 17 OECD countries in terms of GDP per capita, GDP per hour worked and GDI per capita (in constant 2005 PPPs).
2. The OECD FDI regulatory restrictiveness index looks only at statutory restrictions and does not assess the manner in which they are implemented.
3. The OECD average excludes Chile, Estonia, Israel and Slovenia.
4. Combined central and sub-central (statutory) corporate income tax rate.

Source: Chart A: OECD, *National Accounts and Economic Outlook 90 Databases*; Chart B: *http://www.oecd.org/investment/index*; Chart C: OECD, *Product Market Regulation Database*; Chart D: OECD, *Tax Database*.

StatLink http://dx.doi.org/10.1787/888932565110

CHILE

Priorities supported by indicators

Ease product market regulation (2011)

Recommendations: Reduce administrative burdens for start-ups, shorten and reduce the costs of bankruptcy procedures and continue to ease access to credit for start-ups by further promoting the development of seed and venture capital markets.

Actions taken: In January 2011, a law was passed that lowered regulatory barriers for start-ups, and also reduced the time to start up a business from 22 to 7 days by easing the obtainment of permits and the payment of taxes as well as by streamlining notification requirements. The government is launching various programmes aimed at improving access to credit for small enterprises, such as the Fondo Capital Abeja, aimed at fostering women entrepreneurship by providing targeted subsidies.

Improve secondary and tertiary education outcomes (2011)

Recommendations: Upgrade teachers' qualifications through richer curricular and rigorous quality assurance in initial teacher education and on-the-job training. Enhance school accountability.

Actions taken: A new school quality assurance system was established in 2011 and the external exit exam for preschool and primary school teacher candidates was made mandatory. A Teacher Vocation Scholarship has been introduced aimed at encouraging good students to become teachers. Access to scholarships is being expanded and interests on the guaranteed student loan scheme for higher education reduced.

Ease employment protection legislation for regular workers (2011)

Recommendations: Lower the relatively high severance pay for regular workers to ease the adjustment of the regular labour workforce and thereby to encourage the formalisation of employment relationships. In return, consider increasing unemployment benefits further after a careful evaluation of recent reforms.

Actions taken: No action taken.

Other key priorities

Strengthen policies to foster female labour participation (2011)

Recommendations: Facilitate the reconciliation of work and family life, including by further extending publicly-financed childcare and early education together with strong quality control, and by reviewing relatively strict part-time work regulation.

Actions taken: In October 2011, a law was passed that lengthens paid maternity leave from 12 weeks to – at least – 24 weeks, extends the right to maternity leave to workers on temporary contracts and creates a paternity leave.

Strengthen competition law (2011)

Recommendations: Better enforce the competition law by increasing the maximum level of fines, which remain too low, and by making price fixing a criminal offence.

Actions taken: No action taken since the 2009 reform of competition law.

CHILE

- The GDP per capita gap with high-income OECD countries has decreased over the past decade, but it remains wide owing mainly to a weak labour productivity performance and, to a lesser extent, somewhat low utilisation of labour resources.
- Among key priority areas, progress has been made in easing product market regulations and improving secondary education; by contrast little action has been taken to ease employment protection legislation for regular workers along with increasing unemployment benefits.
- In other areas, the extension of unemployment benefits to workers with fixed-term contracts and the introduction of a wage subsidy for young low-wage workers during the crisis supported employment and attenuated the impact of layoffs on the economy. Also, income inequality has been slightly reduced, although further progress is needed.

Performance and policy indicators

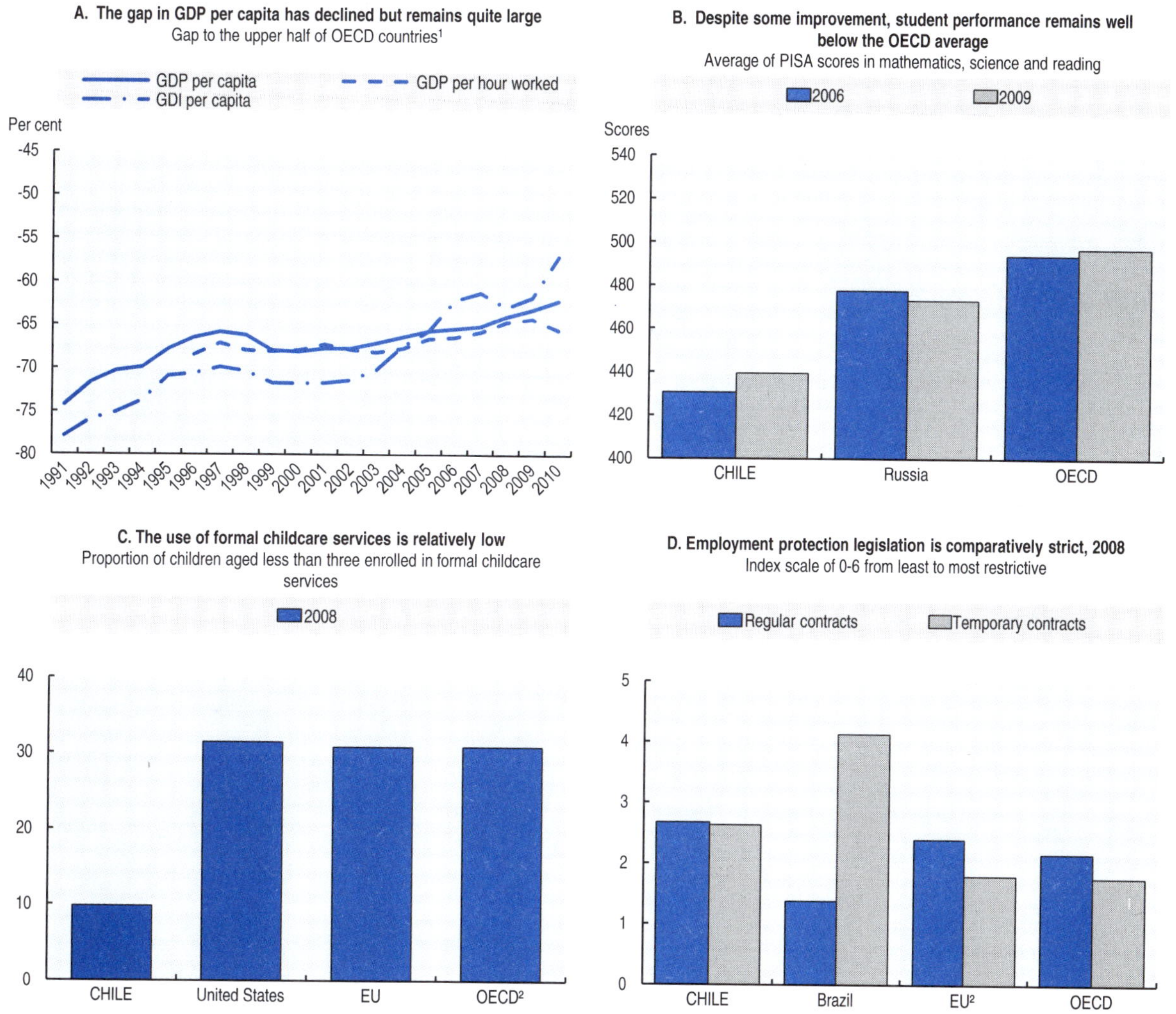

1. Percentage gap with respect to the simple average of the highest 17 OECD countries in terms of GDP per capita, GDP per hour worked and GDI per capita (in constant 2005 PPPs).
2. The OECD average excludes Israel, Switzerland and Turkey. Average of European countries in the OECD.

Source: Chart A: OECD, *National Accounts and Economic Outlook 90 Databases*, *Employment Outlook Database*; Chart B: OECD, *PISA 2009 Database*; Chart C: OECD (2011), *Doing Better for Families*; Chart D: OECD, *Employment Database*.

StatLink http://dx.doi.org/10.1787/888932565148

CHINA

Priorities supported by indicators

Reduce the importance of the state-owned sector in the economy (2011)

Recommendations: The formation of large "private equity" firms should no longer have to be approved by the government, in order to increase the funds available for restructuring poorly performing state-owned companies.

Actions taken: New regulations, introduced in January 2011, allowed foreign investors to purchase local currency for investment in private equity partnerships subject to an overall quota. Applications from foreign enterprises to create private equity firms have to be processed within 40 working days, thereby limiting possible delays.

Improve educational attainment (2011)

Recommendations: Inequalities in the provision of education need to be reduced both regionally and within urban areas. Quick implementation of the provisions for improving education of internal migrant is important.

Actions taken: In March 2011, the government announced it would promote a reform to allow children of internal migrants to take university entrance examinations where they lived.

Reduce administrative burdens on companies (2011)

Recommendations: Government institutions should be required to conduct a regulatory impact analysis before introducing new rules and should progressively review all regulations.

Actions taken: No action taken so far, although reducing government intervention in microeconomic activities will be one of the objectives of the 12th Five Year Plan (2011-15).

Other key priorities

Reduce barriers to urbanisation (2011)

Recommendations: Social expenditure should be further increased to provide broader coverage and a stronger social safety net. Provisions of the 2003 *Rural Land Contracting Law* need to be fully implemented to give all farmers full documentation for their rights, thus widening the rental market. The length of the use rights should be extended and household registration laws revised.

Actions taken: A new Social Insurance Law became effective in July 2011 stipulating that rural residents who migrate to urban areas shall be covered by social insurance.

Further enhance the rule of law (2011)

Recommendations: The effectiveness of enforcement should be enhanced further through the strengthening of the judicial institutions.

Actions taken: In January 2011, a new Mediation law became effective which gives a firm basis to the first-level dispute resolution mechanism commonly used at the local level for the resolution of private disputes.

CHINA

- GDP per capita has soared by close to 65% in the five years to 2010, thereby substantially narrowing the gap with OECD countries. As participation rates continue to be above average the difference in income per head essentially reflects lower productivity.
- Some progress has been made in key priority areas through widening the scope for foreign investment in Chinese companies, starting to lower the educational disadvantages of the children of internal migrants and enrolling migrants in social security programmes.
- In other areas, the government has announced the establishment of a system of general practitioners who will serve as the gatekeepers to the health system.

Performance and policy indicators

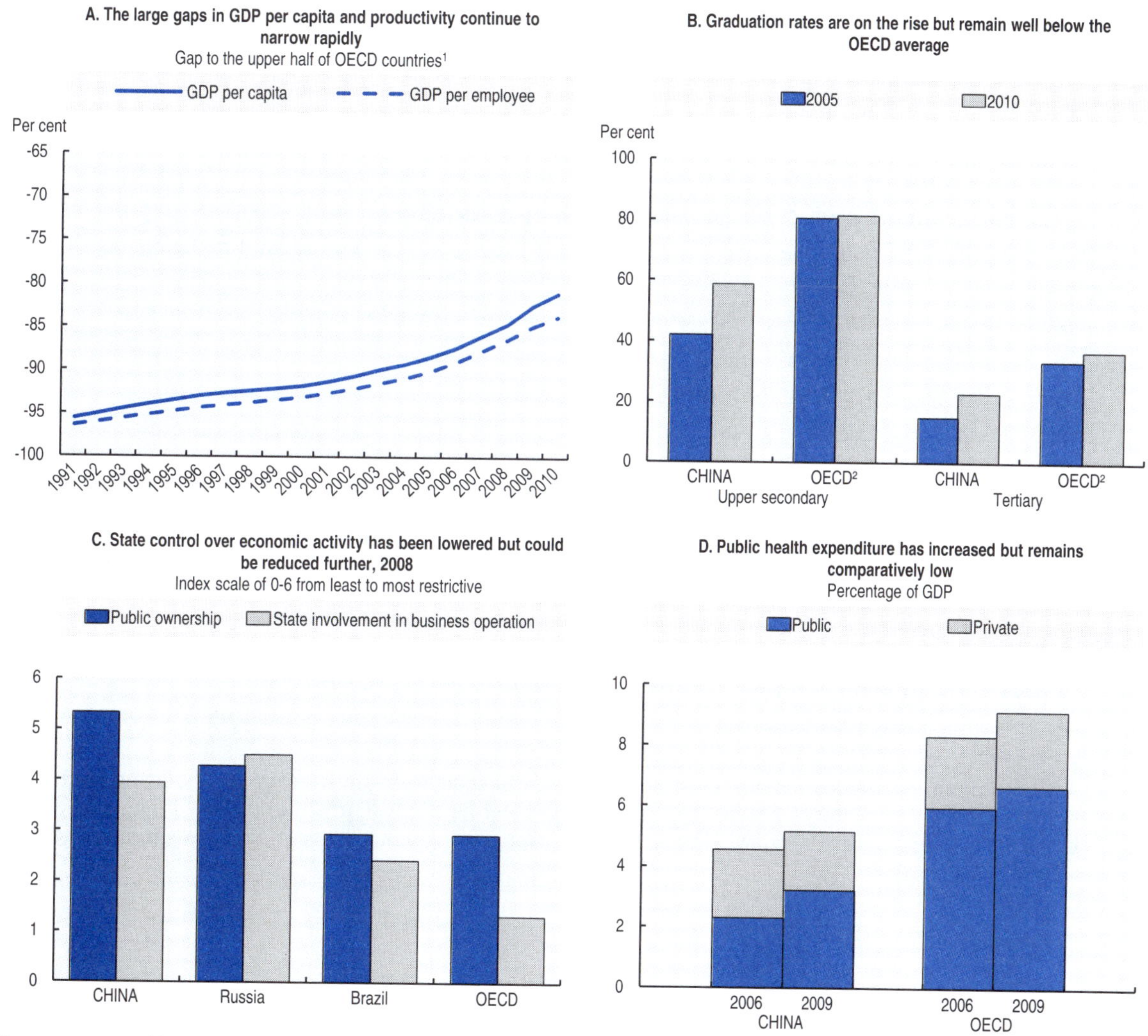

1. Percentage gap with respect to the simple average of the highest 17 OECD countries in terms of GDP per capita and GDP per employee (in constant 2005 PPPs).
2. Data refer to 2009. Graduation rate at upper secondary level (first-time graduate) and graduation rate for single year of age at tertiary-type A level (first-time graduate). For upper secondary education, average of OECD countries excluding Australia, Austria, Belgium, Estonia, France and the Netherlands; for tertiary education, average of OECD countries excluding Belgium, Chile, Estonia, France and Korea.

Source: Chart A: World Bank (2011), *World Development Indicators (WDI) Database* and China Ministry of Human Resources and Social Security; Chart B: OECD (2011), *Education at a Glance*; China Statistical Yearbook; Chart C: OECD, *Product Market Regulation Database*; Chart D: China Statistical Yearbook and World Bank (2011), *World Development Indicators (WDI)*.

StatLink http://dx.doi.org/10.1787/888932565167

CZECH REPUBLIC

Priorities supported by indicators

Reduce barriers to business entry (2007, 2009, 2011)

Recommendations: Reduce minimum capital requirements for business start-ups. Speed up and cut the costs of judicial proceedings for contract and bankruptcy enforcement. Strengthen competition in electricity and telecommunications.

Actions taken: A significant decrease in capital requirements for start-ups is being debated in Parliament. Business registration and notification of sole proprietors were streamlined in 2008 and 2009, supported by wider use of electronic communication channels. An improved bankruptcy law has been in force since 2008. The EU third Energy Package was implemented, enhancing competition in electricity market.

Enhance education outcomes (2007, 2009, 2011)

Recommendations: End too-early streaming in secondary schools and introduce a fee system for tertiary courses backed by income-contingent student loans. Enhance schools' accountability.

Actions taken: No action taken on early streaming. A first nation-wide school-leaving exam was carried out in 2011. The authorities have presented blueprints for tertiary education reform and a new system of financial assistance for students. Both should be legislated during 2012 and take effect the following year.

Relax employment protection legislation (2007, 2009, 2011)

Recommendations: Link severance pay and the notice period to job tenure, and make dismissal simpler more broadly, in particular for regular contracts.

Actions taken: An amendment to the labour code addressing the issue of severance pay came into effect in 2012.

Reform the tax-benefit system (2007, 2009, 2011)

Recommendations: Cut the high tax wedge on low earnings and reduce activity disincentives for second-income earners. Ensure better co-ordination of tax and benefit systems across the government.

Actions taken: A flat tax system was introduced in 2008 reducing the tax wedges, including for lower income earners. Benefits have been reformed, reducing average effective tax rates but spikes at benefit withdrawal points remain, and further system streamlining is scheduled for 2013-14.

Other key priorities

Improve the efficiency of public expenditure (2007, 2009, 2011)

Recommendations: Implement health care reform, focusing in efficiency savings within the existing system.

Actions taken: Patient co-payments were introduced in 2008. Reform in drugs price setting, and tightening of the regulatory framework is currently debated in the Parliament and should take effect in 2012. The authorities are reviewing the in-patient capacities with a view to streamlining them.

CZECH REPUBLIC

- The GDP per capita gap relative to the upper half of OECD countries remains sizeable due to a large labour productivity shortfall. Both gaps narrowed prior to the crisis, but convergence has essentially stalled since 2008. Labour utilisation remains high.
- A number of reforms have been implemented in most of the priority areas, with the strongest progress achieved in increasing tertiary education graduation rates and reducing administrative burdens on start-ups.
- In other areas, a flexible working-time arrangement introduced in the labour code in 2007 proved very popular during the downturn and helped mitigate lay-offs.

Performance and policy indicators

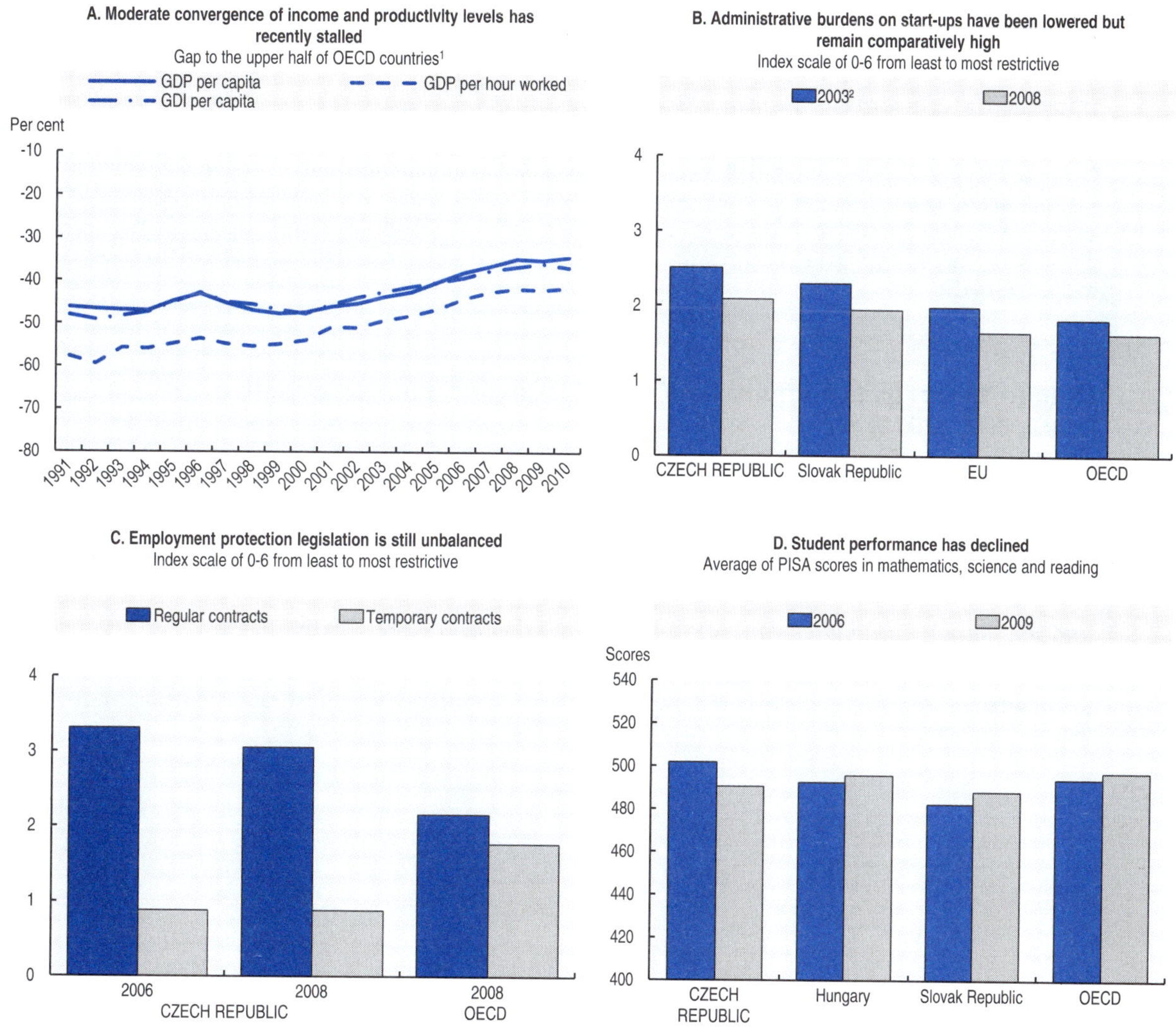

1. Percentage gap with respect to the simple average of the highest 17 OECD countries in terms of GDP per capita, GDP per hour worked and GDI per capita (in constant 2005 PPPs).
2. Average of European countries in the OECD. EU and OECD averages exclude Chile, Estonia, Israel and Slovenia.

Source: Chart A: OECD, *National Accounts and Economic Outlook 90 Databases*; Chart B: *Product Market Regulation Database*; Chart C: OECD, *Employment Database*; Chart D: OECD, *PISA 2009 Database*.

StatLink http://dx.doi.org/10.1787/888932565186

DENMARK

Priorities supported by indicators

Reduce marginal taxes on labour income (2007, 2009, 2011)

Recommendations: Reduce disincentives to work longer hours by continuing to cut income taxes, notably for wages above the average, while better controlling public expenditure growth.

Actions taken: The Parliament adopted a tax reform in 2009 lowering the top marginal income tax rate. The in work tax credit was expanded in 2008 and 2009.

Reform sickness leave and disability benefit schemes (2007, 2009, 2011)

Recommendations: Increase incentives to return to ordinary employment for the sick and disabled with some ability to work; lower subsidies to the disabled employment programme (*Fleksjob*) that has created some lock-in effects.

Actions taken: In 2009, the Parliament adopted new rules for sickness leave that increased control and put more emphasis on rehabilitation. However, access to the disability scheme was eased in 2011.

Improve the efficiency of the education system (2007, 2009, 2011)

Recommendations: Develop the culture of evaluation of compulsory education; strengthen its educational content; speed up tertiary education completion.

Actions taken: In 2010, mandatory national tests in compulsory education were introduced and the system of student grants and loans were changed. Also, various incentives to speed up completion at university, including extra funding to universities for timely completion, were introduced in 2008 in 2010.

Other key priorities

Enhance the competition framework and relax product market regulation (2007, 2009, 2011)

Recommendations: Enhance competition in specific sectors; streamline competition institutions.

Actions taken: Measures to cut business red tape in 2009, to loosen regulation of opening hours in the retail sector in 2010, and to promote competition for public contracts were introduced in 2011. The Parliament adopted legislation in 2010 that grants the competition authorities more powers to intervene in mergers.

Reduce housing subsidies and abolish rent regulation (2007, 2009, 2011)

Recommendations: Ease rent regulations, cut housing subsidies and raise housing taxation.

Actions taken: The 2009 tax reform reduced the value of the mortgage interest rate deduction from income taxation starting from 2012. No action has been taken on rent regulation.

DENMARK

- The income gap *vis-à-vis* the upper half of OECD countries has widened over the past decade, with rising labour utilisation more than offset by lower productivity growth. Employment rates are high but working hours remain low. The remaining income gap reflects mainly a labour productivity shortfall.
- Among key priorities, progress has been made in reducing marginal taxes on labour income, improving the performance of the education system and enhancing product market competition; by contrast, less progress has been achieved in getting recipients of sickness and disability benefits into work and reducing distortions in the housing market.
- In other areas, measures taken in 2008 and 2009 to support the financial sector, including capital injections, guarantees and extra liquidity support, have limited the impact of the crisis.

Performance and policy indicators

A. The widening of gaps in GDP per capita and productivity has stopped most recently

Gap to the upper half of OECD countries[1]

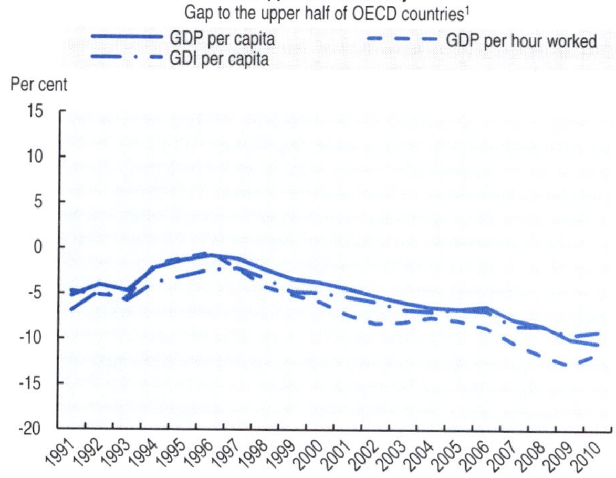

B. The marginal tax wedge on high incomes[2] has been reduced but is still substantial

Percentage of total labour compensation[3]

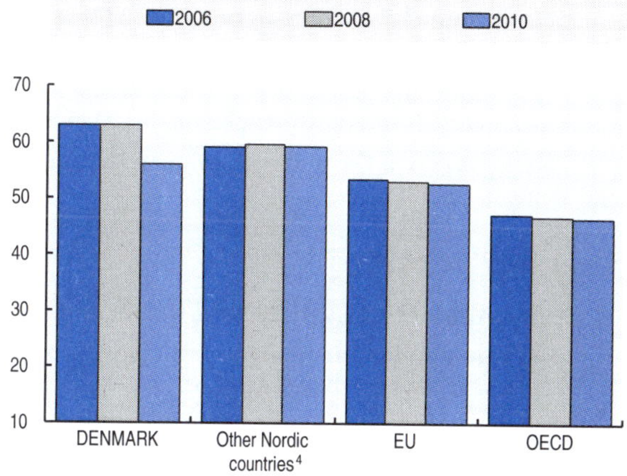

C. Student performance has not improved

Average of PISA scores in mathematics, science and reading

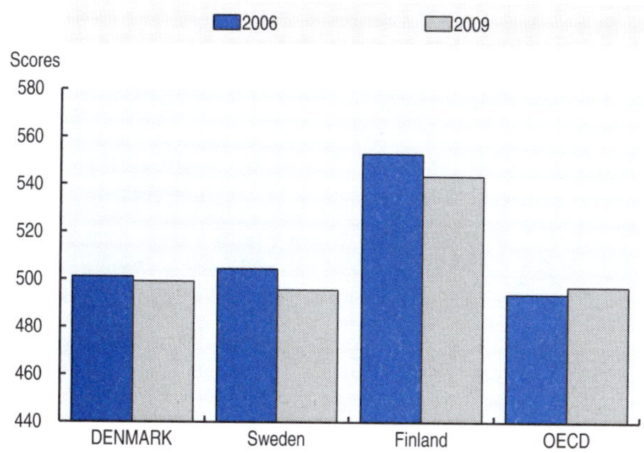

D. The share of working-age population receiving disability benefits is still above the OECD average and increasing

Percentage of the population aged 20-64

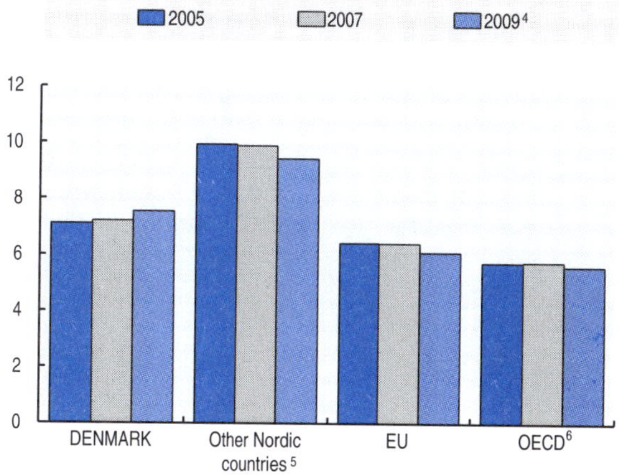

1. Percentage gap with respect to the simple average of the highest 17 OECD countries in terms of GDP per capita, GDP per hour worked and GDI per capita (in constant 2005 PPPs).
2. Labour taxes include personal income tax and employee plus employer social security contributions and any payroll tax less cash transfers.
3. Evaluated at 167% of average earnings for a single person with no child.
4. For Denmark, data refer to 2010.
5. Average of Finland, Norway and Sweden.
6. Excluding Chile, Iceland and Turkey.

Source: Chart A: OECD, *National Accounts and Economic Outlook 90 Databases*; Chart B: OECD, *Taxing Wages Database*; Chart C: OECD, *PISA 2009 Database*; Chart D: OECD (2010), *Sickness, Disability and Work: Breaking the Barriers: A Synthesis of Findings across OECD Countries*.

StatLink http://dx.doi.org/10.1787/888932565224

ESTONIA

Priorities supported by indicators

Reduce entry barriers in network industries (2011)

Recommendations: Open the electricity market for more suppliers. Use more market incentives to increase energy efficiency, including a better public/private mix in passenger transport.

Actions taken: The wholesale electricity market was opened in 2010. The integration with regional Nordic-Baltic electricity networks is being improved and the power market will be fully liberalised in 2013.

Reduce administrative burdens on business (2011)

Recommendations: Consider relaxing existing restrictions on land purchases by non-EU permanent residents.

Actions taken: The restrictions on land purchases have been abolished. Legislation changes reducing administrative burdens were adopted in several areas. Ongoing development of e-services included the launch of a Central Commercial Register portal.

Improve the attractiveness for FDI in manufacturing (2011)

Recommendations: Monitor the effectiveness of implemented entrepreneurship policies, and in particular the grants-based approach to supporting businesses, which requires the ability to pick winners. Make sure those policies are also effective at enhancing attractiveness for FDI.

Actions taken: The mid-term evaluation of support programmes for business and innovation is scheduled in 2011.

Other key priorities

Improve the quantity and quality of job placement services (2011)

Recommendations: Further improve the capacity of the unemployment fund to provide efficient job-search assistance, including for those unemployed whose benefits have expired.

Actions taken: A more flexible model of financing of labour market services was introduced in 2011 allowing a temporary employment programme. Individual action plans were made more flexible and are now regularly assessed. A full range of job-search activities is now available to the unemployed and employers through an online database. The existing voucher programme was extended to retraining. Three-day job tryouts were introduced.

Improve private bankruptcy procedures (2011)

Recommendations: Review private bankruptcy procedures, including debt restructuring by relocating owner-occupiers to smaller, more affordable housing. Make sure banks cannot develop excessively high interest rates or unfair fee structures.

Actions taken: The Debt Restructuring and Debt Protection Act that came into force in April 2011 enables debtors to restructure debt more flexibly and protects them from excessive interests or penalties for late payment. Simultaneously, an amendment to the Bankruptcy Act shortened the minimum period after which the court may, under specific conditions, partially relieve a person of remaining obligations.

ESTONIA

- There had been rapid catch-up in living standards in the wake of EU entry, but the large gap *vis-à-vis* the upper half of OECD countries widened again in the aftermath of the crisis. The GDP per capita gap reflects a productivity shortfall, while labour utilisation is relatively high.
- In priority areas, Estonia continued to reduce administrative burdens on business through legislative changes and development of e-services. Progress has been made in strengthening active labour market policies and improving bankruptcy procedures. Barriers to entry in energy markets have been reduced and restrictions on land purchases by non-EU residents removed.
- In other areas, the cross-border banking supervisory framework has been improved.

Performance and policy indicators

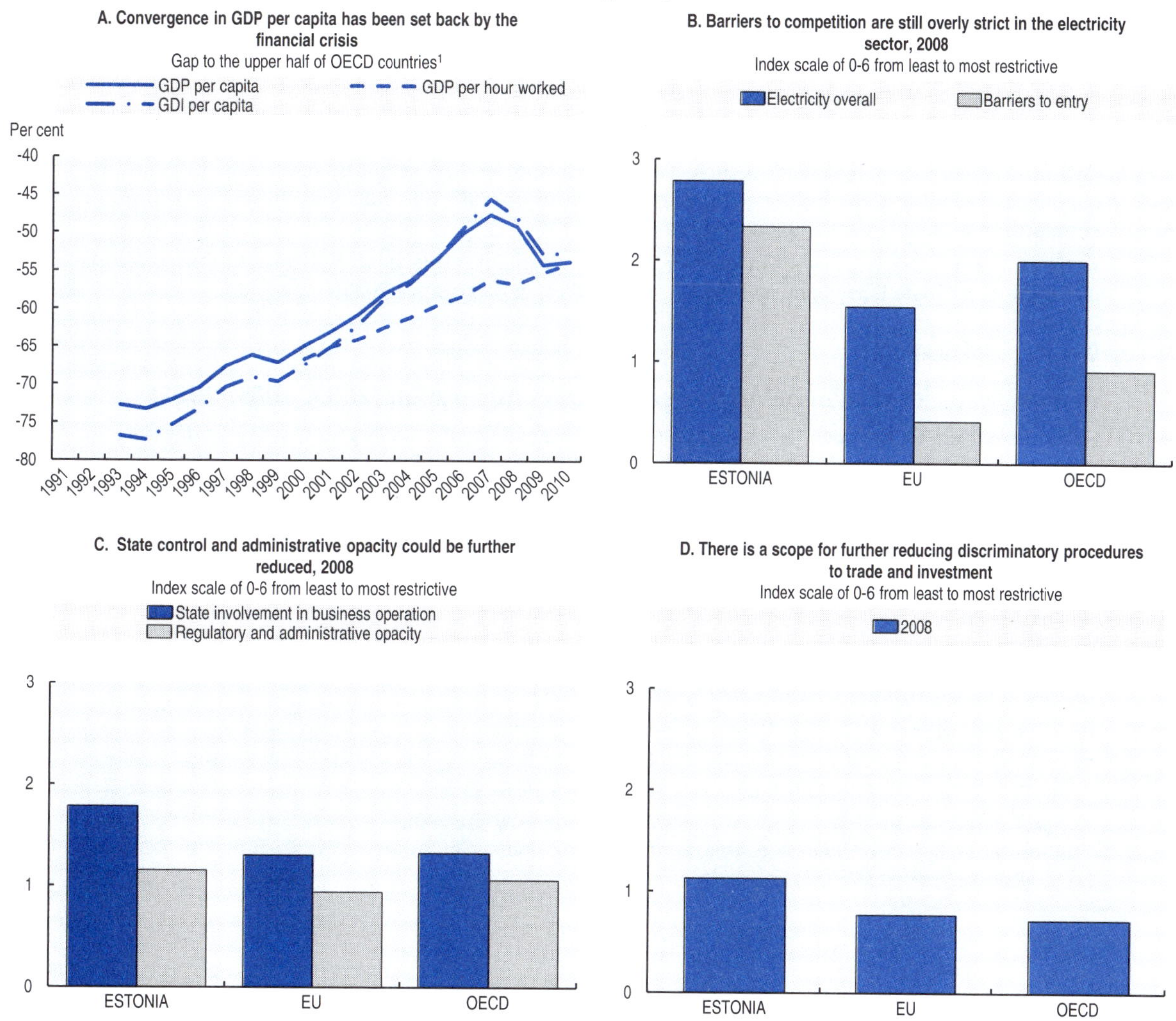

1. Percentage gap with respect to the simple average of the highest 17 OECD countries in terms of GDP per capita, GDP per hour worked and GDI per capita (in constant 2005 PPPs).

Source: Chart A: OECD, *National Accounts and Economic Outlook 90 Databases*; Charts B, C and D: OECD, *Product Market Regulation Database*.

StatLink http://dx.doi.org/10.1787/888932565262

EUROPEAN UNION

Priorities supported by indicators

Increase competition in network industries (2007, 2009, 2011)

Recommendations: Increase competition in transport, postal, telecommunications, port services and energy markets.

Actions taken: Electricity generation and transmission have been separated, although this falls short of full ownership unbundling. Competition has been enhanced in air services by the first-stage EU-US Air Transport Agreement. Postal services will be fully liberalised in 2012.

Reduce producer support to agriculture (2007, 2009, 2011)

Recommendations: Extend full decoupling of payments to livestock meat production and further decouple payments from production across other areas. Reduce barriers to market access for non-EU countries. Lower support prices. Reduce biofuel subsidies.

Actions taken: Since 2003, decoupling has been progressively introduced across numerous sectors. Milk quotas will be phased out by 2015. The re-introduction of export subsidies for dairy produce in 2009 was a step back.

Increase competition in the services sector (2007, 2009, 2011)

Recommendations: Increase competitive pressures in the services sector by reducing administrative barriers to entry and easing the regulatory burden of operating in national markets. Strengthen competition in the EU public procurement regime.

Actions taken: The transposition of the 2006 Services Directive is well advanced but remains incomplete. A Single European Payments Area has been in place since 2010.

Other key priorities

Reform financial regulation and deepen market integration (2007, 2009, 2011)

Recommendations: Improve the robustness of the financial system and put in a new framework for cross-border financial oversight and crisis management.

Actions taken: Wide-ranging reforms have raised and will continue to improve regulatory standards for banks and insurance companies in areas such as bank capital, liquidity management and deposit insurance arrangements. In 2011, European Supervisory Authorities (ESAs) and a European Systemic Risk Board were created. All countries have committed to putting in place bank resolution mechanisms.

Improve the functioning of the labour market and raise labour market mobility within the European Union (2007, 2009, 2011)

Recommendations: Although EU labour market objectives are primarily to be achieved through national instruments, EU policy should increase the portability of welfare and pension rights and can support national initiatives through surveillance and peer pressure.

Actions taken: Restrictions on worker mobility for the new EU member states are being phased out. The Job Mobility Action Plan contains a range of measures, including strengthening the European Employment Services (EURES) network.

EUROPEAN UNION

- There remains a substantial income gap relative to the upper half of OECD countries. While labour utilisation is lower than for the top performers, the labour productivity gap is the main factor behind lower living standards. Labour productivity has grown at a sluggish pace over the past decade.
- In priority areas, the on-going implementation of the Services Directive strengthens competition. Progress has been made to overhaul financial regulation. A wide range of growth-enhancing measures is proposed under the Single Market Programme.
- In other areas a new framework for economic governance is being established to improve economic, fiscal and financial stability. The Europe 2020 Agenda sets ambitious economic and social targets, including on climate, education and poverty.

Performance and policy indicators

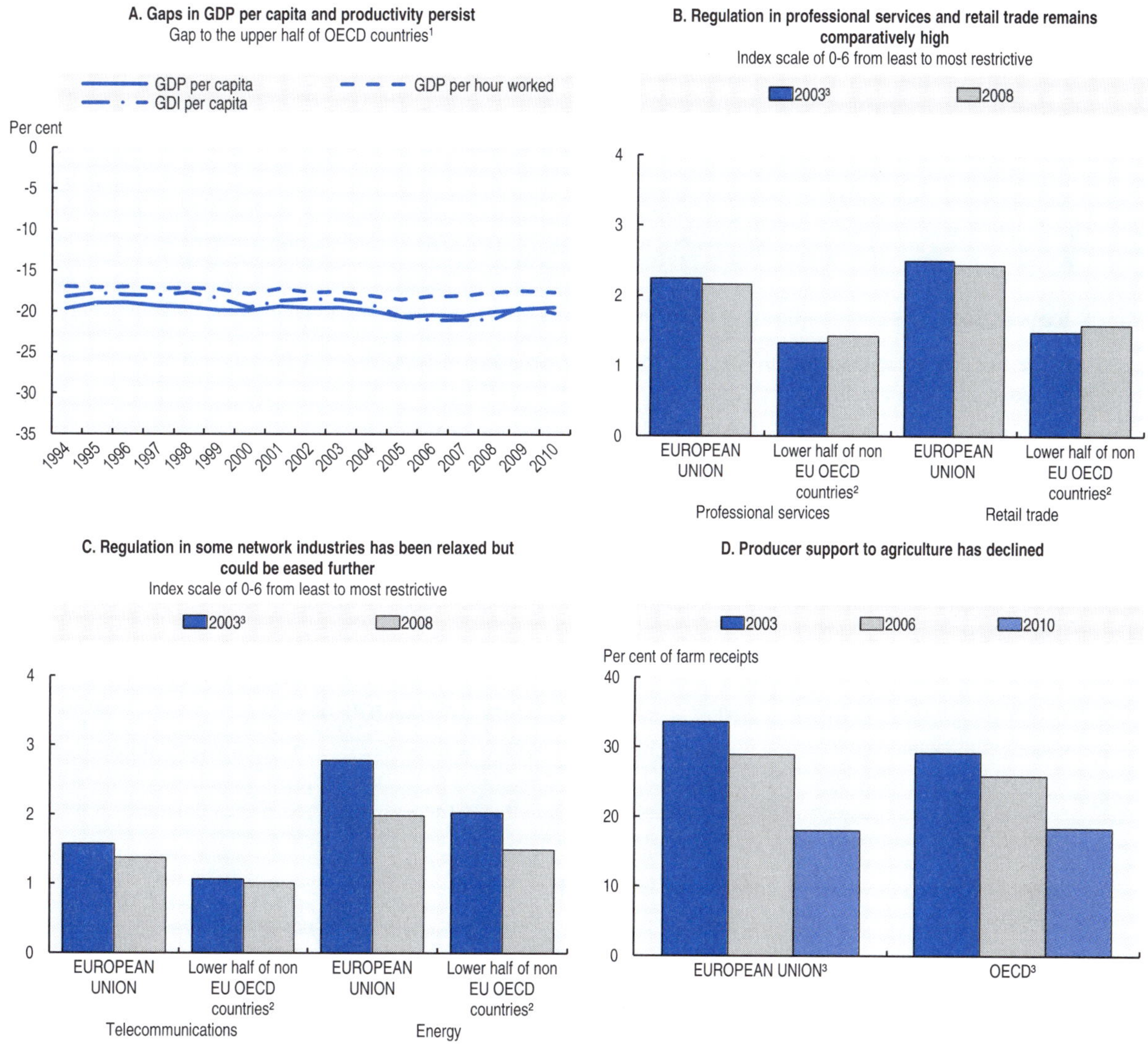

1. Percentage gap with respect to the simple average of the highest 17 OECD countries in terms of GDP per capita, GDP per hour worked and GDI per capita (in constant 2005 PPPs).
2. Lower half of non-EU OECD countries in terms of the stringency of regulation in professional services and retail trade (Panel B) or in telecommunications and energy (Panel C).
3. Average of European countries and non-European countries in the OECD, excluding Estonia and Slovenia in Panels B and C.

Source: Chart A: OECD, *National Accounts and Economic Outlook No. 90 Databases*; Charts B and C: *Product Market Regulation Database*; Chart D: OECD, *Producer and Consumer Support Estimates Database*.

StatLink http://dx.doi.org/10.1787/888932565281

FINLAND

Priorities supported by indicators

Reduce the labour tax wedge and improve efficiency of the tax structure (2007, 2009, 2011)

Recommendations: Continue to shift taxation from labour to indirect and property taxes. Align property tax assessment values with property market valuations and eliminate reduced VAT rates.

Actions taken: The government cut income tax and social security contribution rates during the recession as part of fiscal stimulus measures. More revenue is being raised through higher VAT rates – except on food – and energy taxes. However, social contribution rates will increase during 2011-14.

Reduce disincentives to work at older ages (2007, 2009, 2011)

Recommendations: Raise the minimum statutory retirement age, review the disability pension system and close the unemployment pathway into retirement. Increase pension accrual rates after 65 and extend the actuarial adjustment of pensions to the full working life.

Actions taken: The government and stakeholder organisations agreed in 2009 to gradually increase the average effective retirement age by three years but no concrete measures have been implemented so far.

Reform the unemployment benefit system (2007, 2009, 2011)

Recommendations: Reduce replacement rates and taper them off throughout the unemployment spell. Ensure earlier mandatory activation for the unemployed.

Actions taken: A relocation allowance was introduced in 2007 and receipt unemployment benefits after 500 days have been made conditional on participation in active labour market programmes. In response to the recession, replacement rates were raised.

Other key priorities

Improve the efficiency of the tertiary education system (2009, 2011)

Recommendations: Reform selection procedures slowing access to upper education and introduce tertiary tuition fees together with government student loans with income-contingent repayments.

Actions taken: To speed up graduation and secure income during full-time studies, student selection procedures in higher education are being reviewed and financial aid is being rationalised.

Increase productivity in municipalities (2011)

Recommendations: Open up further the municipal purchasing of non-core services to competitive bidding, promote municipal mergers and municipal-level productivity programmes with increased reliance on benchmarking.

Actions taken: No significant action taken.

Align wage determination better with productivity (2007, 2009)

Recommendations: Reform the wage setting system so that wages are better aligned with individual productivity performance.

Actions taken: Wage negotiations have been decentralised to the industry level since 2007, but local flexibility remains low.

Increase product market competition (2007)

Recommendations: Increase competition in product markets, especially in the retail sector.

Actions taken: Since 2009 all shops have been allowed to open on Sundays all year round. Nevertheless, the rules on shop opening hours remain very prescriptive.

FINLAND

- The GDP per capita gap *vis-à-vis* the best performing countries narrowed from the mid-1990s until 2008, but widened again during the crisis. The gap mainly reflects a labour productivity shortfall.
- In priority areas, recent pension reforms have reduced disincentives to work, activation policies have been strengthened to encourage return to work, and the tertiary education system is being reviewed, *e.g.* in the area of students' selection.
- In other areas, to mitigate hardship on the non-employed during the crisis, various social benefits have been raised permanently.

Performance and policy indicators

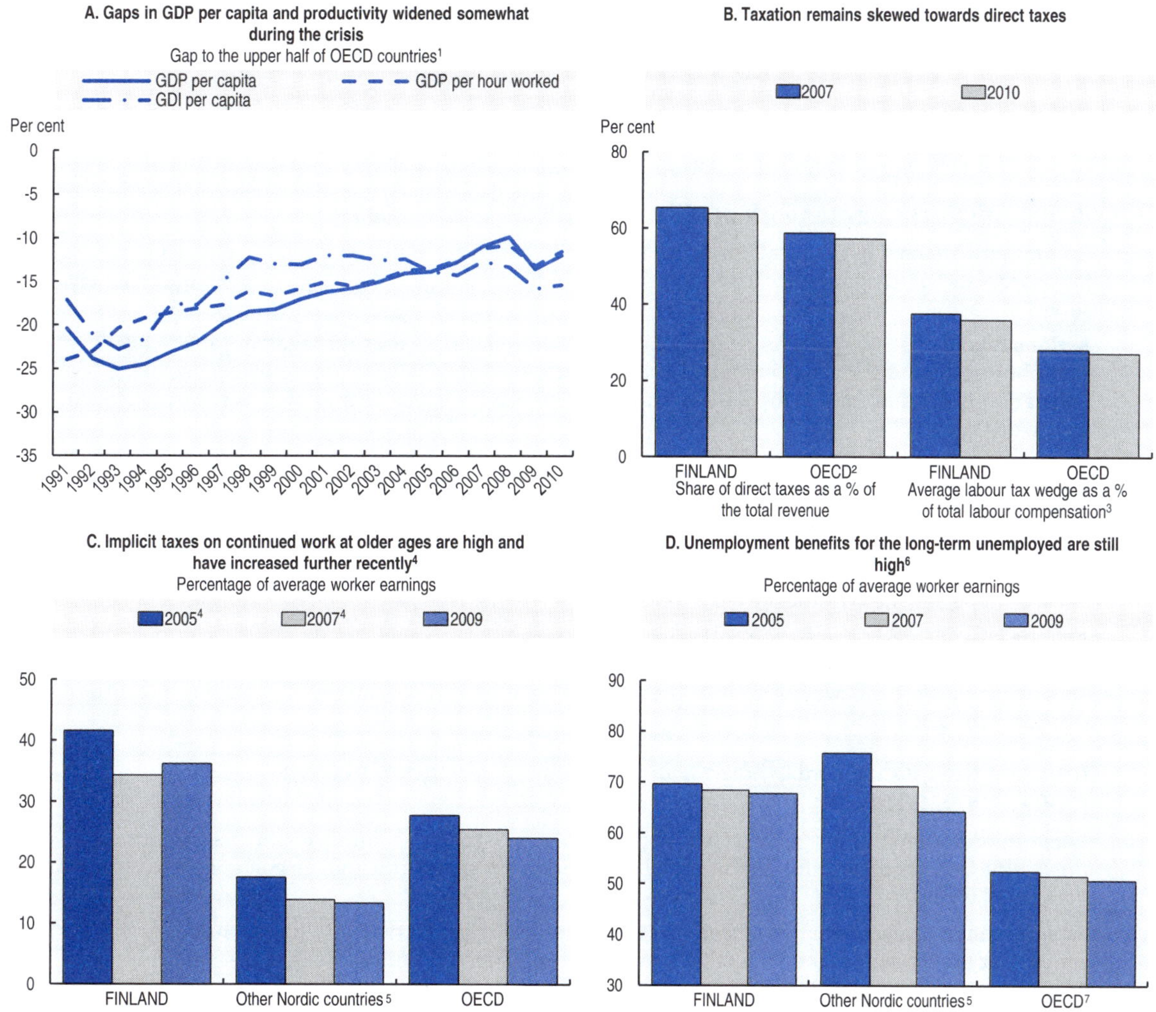

1. Percentage gap with respect to the simple average of the highest 17 OECD countries in terms of GDP per capita, GDP per hour worked and GDI per capita (in constant 2005 PPPs).
2. Data refer to 2009 for Australia, the Netherlands and Poland.
3. Labour taxes include personal income tax and employee plus employer social security contributions and any payroll tax less cash transfers. Couple with two children, at 100% of the average worker earnings for the first earner. Average of three situations regarding the wage of the second earner (0%, 33% and 67% of average earnings).
4. Average implicit tax on continued work for five more years in "early retirement route" (as defined in Duval, 2003) for 55 and 60 year-olds. For 2005 and 2007, average of OECD countries excluding Chile, Estonia, Israel and Slovenia.
5. Average of Denmark, Norway and Sweden.
6. Average of net replacement rates after five years of unemployment for unemployed persons who earned 67% and 100% of average worker earnings.
7. Average of OECD countries excluding Chile and Mexico.

Source: Chart A: OECD, *National Accounts and Economic Outlook 90 Databases*; Chart B: OECD, *Taxing Wages Database*; Chart C: Duval, R. (2003), "The Retirement Effects of Old-Age Pension and Early Retirement Schemes in OECD Countries", OECD *Economics Department Working Papers*, No. 370, OECD Publishing and OECD calculations; Chart D: OECD, *Benefits and Wages Database*. *StatLink* http://dx.doi.org/10.1787/888932565300

FRANCE

Priorities supported by indicators

Reduce labour market dualism (2007, 2009, 2011)

Recommendations: Reduce the level and unpredictability of dismissal costs. In order to enhance inclusion of the young people with low qualifications, target the work-study schemes more on the less skilled, and evaluate their efficiency regularly.

Actions taken: The provision for amicable termination of a work contract instituted in 2008 is a first step towards limiting dismissal costs uncertainty but has had only a limited impact in reducing dualism. The government passed a law in July 2011 which facilitates the use of work-study arrangements.

Reduce the labour tax wedge and the minimum cost of labour (2007, 2009, 2011)

Recommendations: Continue to allow the minimum cost of labour to fall relative to the average. Increase work incentives facing low-wage earners. Shift the tax burden away from labour.

Actions taken: Consistent with the recommendations of a commission of independent experts created in 2009, the rise in the minimum wage has been limited to the minimum legal requirement. In 2009 the government introduced a social scheme improving incentives to find employment.

Reduce disincentives to work at older ages (2007, 2009, 2011)

Recommendations: Phase out all forms of early retirement and reinforce the link between benefits, job search and participation in active measures relying on efficient delivery of public employment services.

Actions taken: The 2010 pension reform included a two-year increase in the legal retirement age. The contribution period for a full pension has been extended in line with rising life expectancy, but indexation is not automatic. The job-search exemption for the older unemployed is set to disappear in 2012.

Other key priorities

Reduce regulatory barriers to competition (2007, 2009, 2011)

Recommendations: Remove regulatory entry barriers in potentially competitive sectors or segments of network industries. Ease restrictions to price competition in the retail sector and to setting up new stores.

Actions taken: A new competition authority was created in 2009. Retail distributors have been granted more flexibility to negotiate prices with suppliers. While zoning restrictions have been eased somewhat, a draft bill would tighten them again by integrating commercial zoning into urban development law.

Improve the quality and efficiency of the tertiary education system (2007, 2009, 2011)

Recommendations: Boost private funding for tertiary education, and extend the autonomy of universities. Incorporate information on labour market prospects into career guidance and expand vocational education.

Actions taken: Universities have been given more autonomy, but they still have limited leeway on remuneration. No action has been taken on student selection and tuition fees. The establishment of "centres of excellence" will continue to increase co-operation between the *grandes écoles* and the universities.

FRANCE

- After a steady deterioration since the early 1990s, the GDP per capita gap *vis-à-vis* the upper half of OECD countries has stabilised over the past five years. The gap mainly reflects low employment rates at both ends of the age spectrum.
- Among key priority areas, universities have been granted greater autonomy and the pension system has been reformed to boost the effective retirement age. By contrast, limited progress has been made in reducing labour market dualism, developing active labour market policies, and shifting the tax burden away from labour.
- In other areas, part-time unemployment measures and unemployment benefit duration were extended, and subsidised work contracts revived, to cushion the impact of the recession. The "taxe professionnelle", which penalised investment, was eliminated in 2010, and a new "independent entrepreneur" status simplified administrative procedures and tax rules.

Performance and policy indicators

A. The gap in GDP per capita widened before the recession

Gap to the upper half of OECD countries[1]

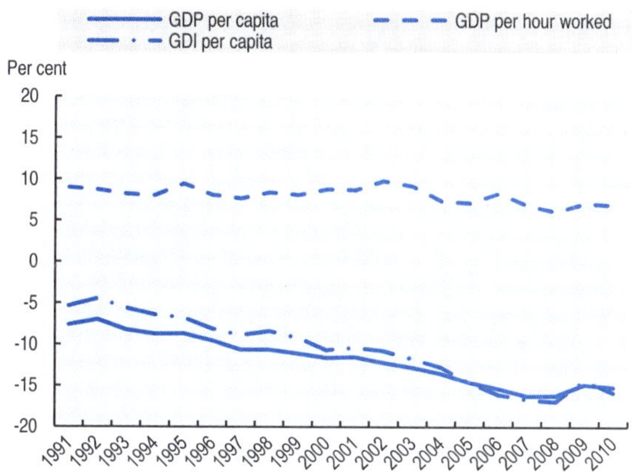

B. The high average tax wedge on labour income[2] has not been reduced

Percentage of total labour compensation[3]

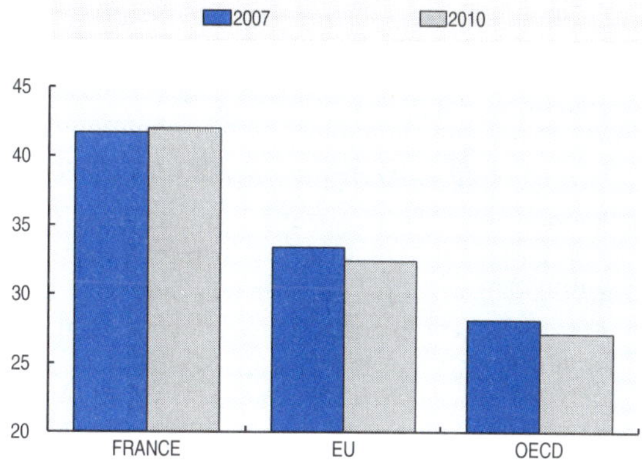

C. The minimum cost of labour is still comparatively high

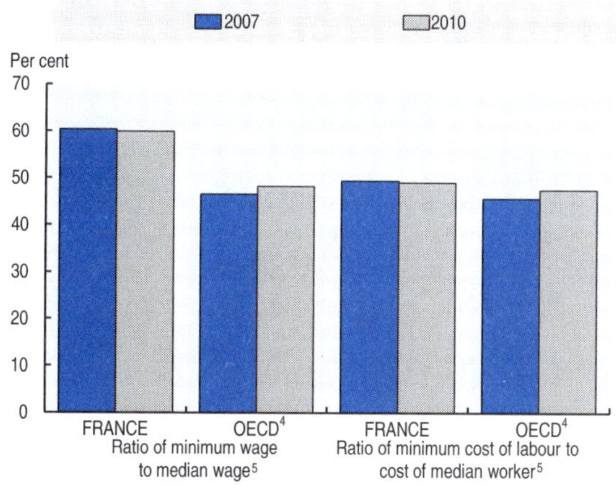

D. Labour market policies are still some way from a flexicurity model

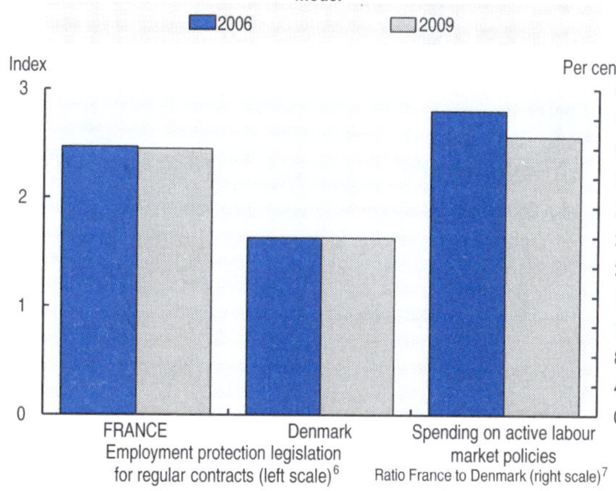

1. Percentage gap with respect to the simple average of the highest 17 OECD countries in terms of GDP per capita, GDP per hour worked and GDI per capita (in constant 2005 PPPs).
2. Labour taxes include personal income tax and employee plus employer social security contributions and any payroll tax less cash transfers.
3. Couple with two children, at 100% of the average worker earnings for the first earner. Average of three situations regarding the wage of the second earner (0%, 33% and 67% of average earnings).
4. The OECD average excludes some OECD countries which do not have a national statutory minimum wage, as well as Mexico for which data are not available.
5. Exactly half of all workers earn less than the median wage for the OECD countries. The cost of labour is the sum of the wage level and the social security contributions paid by employers.
6. Index scale of 0-6 from least to most restrictive.
7. Ratio of spending on total active labour market policies per unemployed between France and Denmark, using 2005 PPPs. For active labour market policies, average of ratios over the period 2002-05 for 2006 and average of ratios over the period 2005-08 for 2009.

Source: Chart A: OECD, *National Accounts and Economic Outlook 90 Databases*; Chart B: OECD, *Taxing Wages Database*; Chart C: OECD (2011), *Employment Outlook Database and Taxing Wages Databases*; Chart D: OECD, *Labour Market Programmes and Economic Outlook 90 Databases*.

StatLink http://dx.doi.org/10.1787/888932565319

GERMANY

Priorities supported by indicators

Reduce tax wedges on labour income and shift taxation to property and consumption taxes (2007, 2009, 2011)

Recommendations: Raise work incentives by reducing the labour tax wedge, notably social security contributions, and shift taxation towards less distortive taxes.

Actions taken: Unemployment insurance contributions have been lowered over 2007-09 (with the last decrease partly reversed in 2011), partly financed through higher consumption taxes. The standard VAT rate was raised in 2007, but reduced VAT rates remain widespread. Environmental taxation was increased in 2009 by introducing a CO_2 element in the vehicle tax.

Reduce regulatory barriers to competition (2007, 2009, 2011)

Recommendations: Lower barriers to entrepreneurship, notably in professional services, and facilitate non-discriminatory entry into network industries.

Actions taken: Architects' fees regulation has been adjusted and simplified in 2009. Competition in network industries has been fostered *inter alia* through the introduction of incentive-based regulation in the electricity and gas market in 2009, and the government envisages liberalising inter-city bus services in 2011.

Improve education outcomes (2007, 2009, 2011)

Recommendations: Strengthen early childhood education, make schools and teachers more accountable for outcomes, reduce tracking in the school system, and allow all universities greater autonomy.

Actions taken: External exit exams were introduced in 2007 and 2008 in some *Länder*. Some *Länder* have lowered the number of school tracks in 2009 and 2010. Autonomy was raised with more universities selecting students and further *Länder* introducing tuition fees in 2007.

Other key priorities

Reduce impediments to full-time female labour force participation (2007, 2009, 2011)

Recommendations: Improve incentives for women to work full time by lowering the marginal tax burden for second earners and by increasing the supply of childcare places and full-day schooling.

Actions taken: It was decided in 2007 to increase the supply of public childcare places with the aim to provide access for around 35% of all children by 2013. Full-day schooling is also being expanded.

Ease job protection for regular workers (2009, 2011)

Recommendations: Relax employment protection legislation for regular workers for instance by shortening the period before dismissal notice can be given and by reducing the notice period for workers with a long tenure and by reforming the procedures for dismissal for economic reasons.

Actions taken: No action taken.

Improve the placement of long-term unemployed into jobs (2007)

Recommendations: Clarify administrative responsibilities related to job placement between municipalities and the Federal Employment Agency, revisit the level and strengthen the conditionality of benefits.

Actions taken: The supplementary benefit layer between unemployment insurance and the basic benefit for jobseekers is being phased out in 2011 in the context of fiscal consolidation. Administrative responsibilities for placing recipients of the basic jobseeker benefit have been clarified in 2011.

GERMANY

- The GDP per capita gap relative to the upper half of OECD countries has narrowed since 2005, partly reversing the widening since the mid-1990s. The remaining gap reflects exclusively weaker labour utilisation while Germany is ranking among the best performing OECD countries in terms of GDP per hour worked, notwithstanding some recent decline.
- Among key priority areas, progress has been made in improving education outcomes, bringing the long-term unemployed back into work and strengthening work incentives; less has been achieved in the areas of product market competition and employment protection legislation.
- In other areas, reforms of the short-time work scheme during the crisis have prevented excessive layoffs.

Performance and policy indicators

A. The GDP per capita gap has continued to narrow
Gap to the upper half of OECD countries[1]

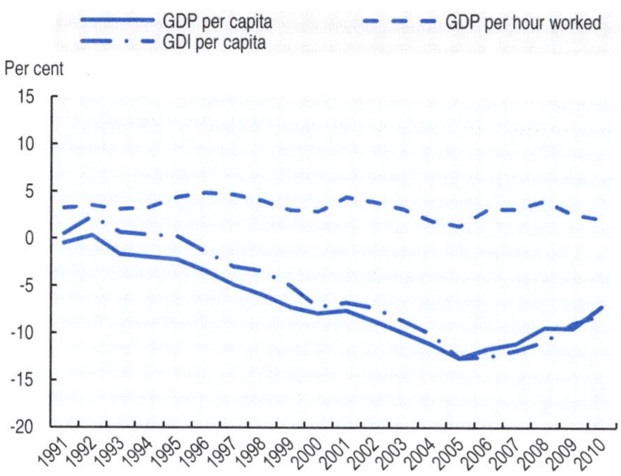

B. Taxation remains skewed towards direct taxes

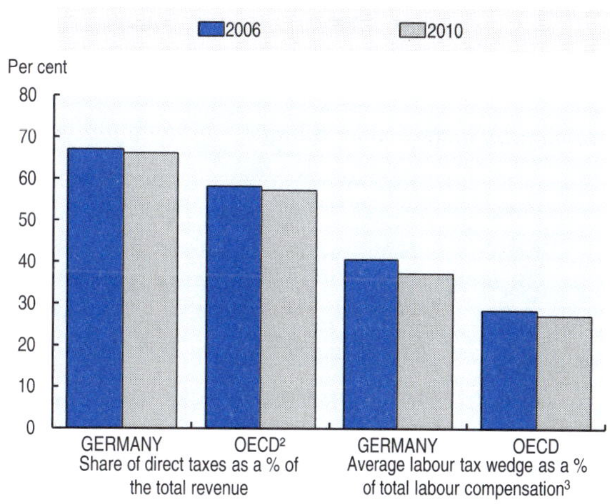

C. Barriers to entrepreneurship remain high
Index scale of 0-6 from least to most restrictive

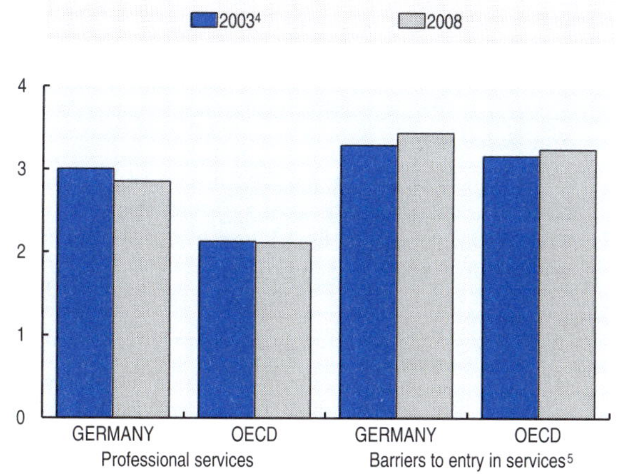

D. Tertiary graduation rates are still relatively low despite significant progress[6]

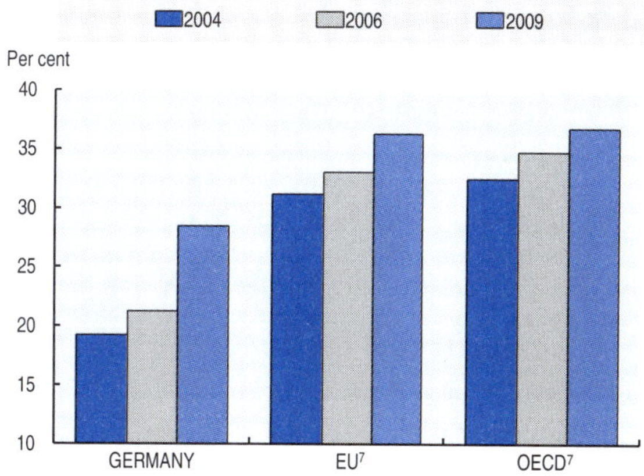

1. Percentage gap with respect to the simple average of the highest 17 OECD countries in terms of GDP per capita, GDP per hour worked and GDI per capita (in constant 2005 PPPs).
2. Data refer to 2009 for Australia, the Netherlands and Poland.
3. Labour taxes include personal income tax and employee plus employer social security contributions and any payroll tax less cash transfers. Couple with two children, at 100% of the average worker earnings for the first earner. Average of three situations regarding the wage of the second earner (0%, 33% and 67% of average earnings).
4. OECD average excludes Chile, Estonia, Israel and Slovenia.
5. Barriers to entry in services cover barriers to entry in professional services and retail trade.
6. First-time graduation rates for single year of age at type A level.
7. Average of European countries in the OECD. EU and OECD averages exclude Belgium, Chile, Estonia, France and Korea.

Source: Chart A: OECD, *National Accounts and Economic Outlook No. 90 Databases*; Chart B: OECD, *Taxing Wages and Tax Databases*; Chart C: OECD, *Product Market Regulation Database*; Chart D: OECD (2011), *Education at a Glance*.

StatLink http://dx.doi.org/10.1787/888932565205

GREECE

Priorities supported by indicators

Reduce implicit taxes on continued work at older ages (2007, 2009, 2011)

Recommendations: Boost labour force participation of older workers through pension reform, aiming *inter alia* to restrict early retirement.

Actions taken: The 2010 pension reform tightened conditions for early retirement, including for workers in heavy and arduous professions, and reduced benefits for those retiring before 65. It also included an indexation of the retirement age on life expectancy.

Reduce regulatory barriers to competition (2007, 2009, 2011)

Recommendations: Remove administrative burdens on business and reduce barriers to competition in professional services and network industries.

Actions taken: A new competition law was enacted, a General Commercial Registry (GEMI) was created and one-stop-shops for business start-ups became operational in 2011, while other reforms including simplified licensing procedures, opening of over 150 closed professions, and liberalisation of the energy sector were approved by Parliament. A 2010 law liberalised the road freight sector. An ambitious privatisation plan for 2011-15 was adopted in mid-2011 but implementation is lagging behind.

Reduce the tax wedge on labour income and broaden the tax base (2007, 2009, 2011)

Recommendations: Reduce incentives for tax evasion and informality by broadening the tax base and lowering the high tax wedge on labour over the medium term, once fiscal targets are achieved.

Actions taken: Reforms adopted since April 2010 have broadened the tax base and improved tax collection by simplifying the tax system. Measures have also aimed to tackle widespread tax evasion through risk-based audits, increased fraud penalties and a more accountable tax administration. The pace of implementation has however been slow so far.

Reform employment protection legislation (2007)

Recommendations: Reduce differences in the strictness of employment protection legislation across different groups of workers to improve labour turnover and facilitate labour market adjustment.

Actions taken: In late 2010 job protection of white-collar workers was relaxed by lowering total severance costs. More flexible rules on settlements of severance payments have been enacted.

Other key priorities

Improve the efficiency and quality of the education system (2007, 2009, 2011)

Recommendations: Improve formal education through better teaching quality and school curricula and by raising the standards of higher education to international levels.

Actions taken: In 2010, the "New School" policy for primary and secondary education introduced flexible curricula, streamlined teaching modules, established a certificate of pedagogic competence for teachers and evaluations for teachers and schools. A new framework law for higher education was adopted in 2011, introducing *inter alia* an independent evaluation system of academics.

Ease entry into the labour market (2007, 2009, 2011)

Recommendations: Reduce barriers to entry for young workers by lowering the high cost of labour.

Actions taken: 2010 and 2011 laws provide for sub-minimum wages for workers between 18 and 25 and for apprentices between 15 and 18 years.

GREECE

- The economic crisis has widened the income gap relative to the upper half of OECD countries, largely reversing its pre-crisis decline.
- Against the background of the recession and the euro area sovereign debt crisis, Greece negotiated an EU/IMF financial assistance programme, under which a range of structural reforms are being implemented. Progress has been made on all key priorities including reducing regulatory barriers to competition, improving the functioning of labour markets, the quality of education and work incentives for older workers. The vigorous reform process needs to continue and the pace of implementation should be speeded up including in the area of tax reform.
- In non-priority areas, recent reforms in the health care sector have aimed at improving spending control and the quality of services. The public remuneration system is being rationalised.

Performance and policy indicators

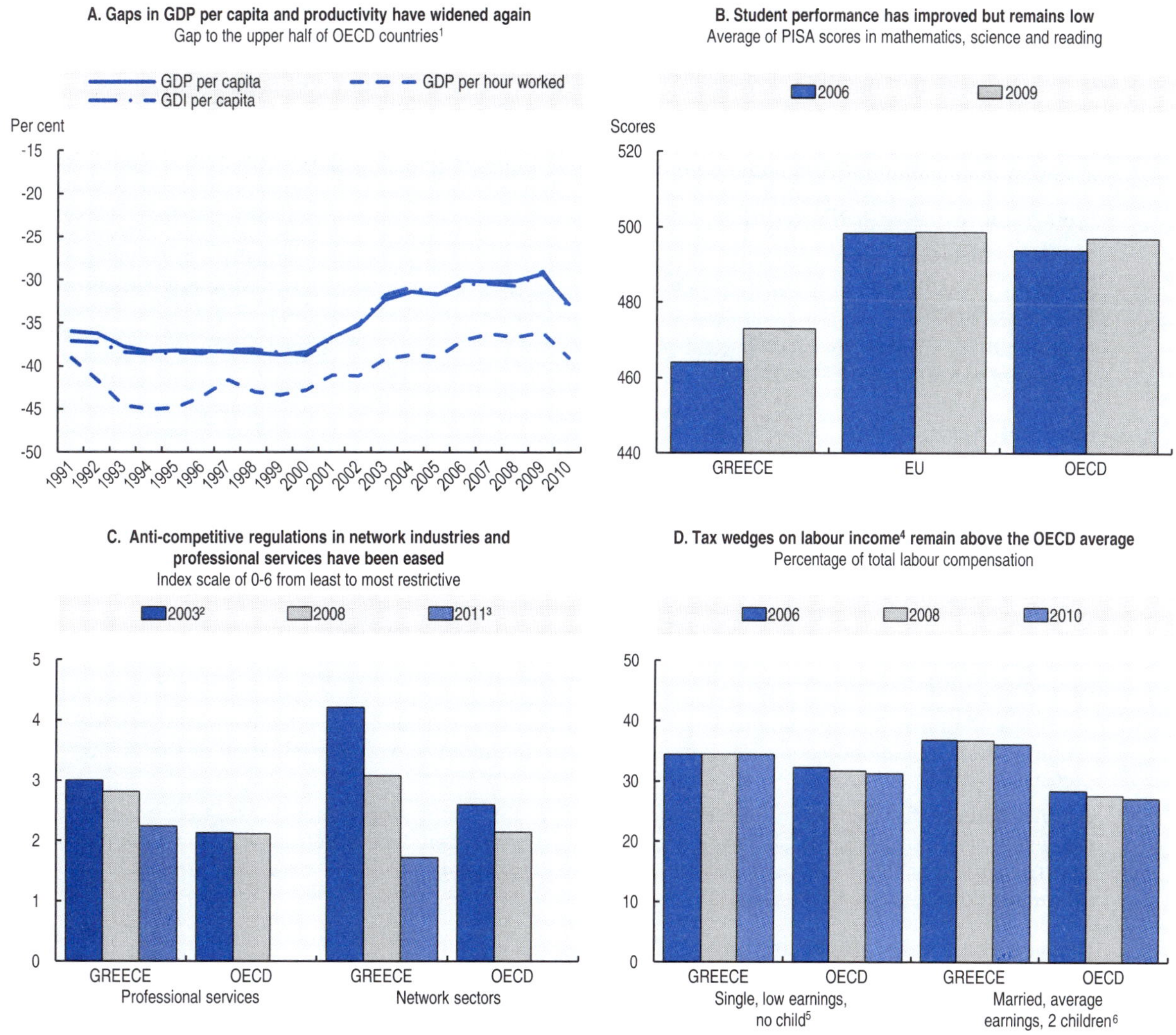

1. Percentage gap with respect to the simple average of the highest 17 OECD countries in terms of GDP per capita, GDP per hour worked and GDI per capita (in constant 2005 PPPs).
2. The OECD average excludes Chile, Estonia, Israel and Slovenia.
3. The PMR indicators for 2011 are based on an intermediate and partial update conducted in the context of the 2011 OECD Economic Survey of Greece, rather than on a full update for all countries.
4. Labour taxes include personal income tax and employee plus employer social security contributions and any payroll tax less cash transfers.
5. Low earnings refer to two-thirds of average earnings.
6. At 100% of the average worker earnings for the first earner. Average of three situations regarding the wage of the second earner (0%, 33% and 67% of average earnings).

Source: Chart A: OECD, *National Accounts and Economic Outlook No. 90 Databases*; Chart B: OECD, *PISA 2009 Database*; Chart C: OECD, *Product Market Regulation Database*; Chart D: OECD, *Taxing Wages Database*.

StatLink http://dx.doi.org/10.1787/888932565357

HUNGARY

Priorities supported by indicators

Reduce the tax wedge on labour income (2007, 2009, 2011)

Recommendations: Lower tax wedges by reducing social charges. Continue efforts to replace tax allowances and deductions with earned-income tax credits.

Actions taken: In 2009-10, personal income taxes and employer social contributions were cut by around 6.5 percentage points. In 2011, a shift to a flat-rate personal income tax and new tax reliefs for families with children further lowered the tax wedge. In 2012, despite the narrowing of the tax base below the average wage, the tax wedge on low-income workers will rise due to increased social security contributions and the removal of the employment tax credit.

Reduce disincentives to continued work at older ages (2007, 2009, 2011)

Recommendations: Tighten eligibility for disability benefits, increase the statutory retirement age and phase out access to early retirement programmes.

Actions taken: The unwelcome dissolution of the second pillar of the pension system in 2011 incidentally diminished expected replacement rates, and the statutory retirement age will increase from 62 to 65 years by 2022. From 2012, new and existing retirement benefits of special pension regimes will be reduced by the amount of the income tax (up to the statutory retirement age), but eligibility conditions for all early retirement options will be left unchanged.

Ease business regulations (2009, 2011)

Recommendations: Further limit state involvement in the operations of network industries by reducing price controls. Lift remaining constraints preventing freedom of choice between telecommunications service suppliers.

Actions taken: Stronger forms of vertical separation and price deregulation have been introduced in the energy sector in two steps in 2007 and 2009.

Other key priorities

Make the education system more efficient and equitable (2007, 2009, 2011)

Recommendations: Postpone early tracking of students and reform teachers' lifelong training to enhance the performance of secondary education. Make vocational training better attuned to labour market needs, and introduce university student fees backed by greater availability of income-contingent loans.

Actions taken: A 2008 referendum abolished tuition fees for tertiary education.

Increase public sector efficiency (2007, 2009, 2011)

Recommendations: Ensure cost-efficient delivery of services. Provide more effective incentives for municipalities to exploit economies of scale. Facilitate the monitoring and evaluation of the public sector.

Actions taken: Efficiency was enhanced with a reduction in public employment in 2004-08, but this has been partly offset by public works programmes since then. The creation of one-stop shop government agencies at a local level is under way and preparations for hospital and school rationalisation have also started in 2011.

Reduce shadow-economy activity (2007)

Recommendations: Access to health care services should be tied more to the payment of contributions, social benefits should be made more employment-friendly, and sanctions against abuse should be scaled up.

Actions taken: Tax inspections have been strengthened and should become more efficient with a merger of two main tax authorities into a single institution in 2011.

HUNGARY

- The gradual closing of the income and productivity gaps relative to the upper half of OECD countries had already ceased before the global recession hit. This gap mainly reflects weak productivity but there is also considerable room for raising employment rates.
- Among key priority areas, significant progress has been made in lowering tax wedges, extending the statutory retirement age and reducing incentives for early retirement, which should help raise labour utilisation.
- Policy measures were also taken in several other areas, such as a major cut in unemployment benefit generosity.

Performance and policy indicators

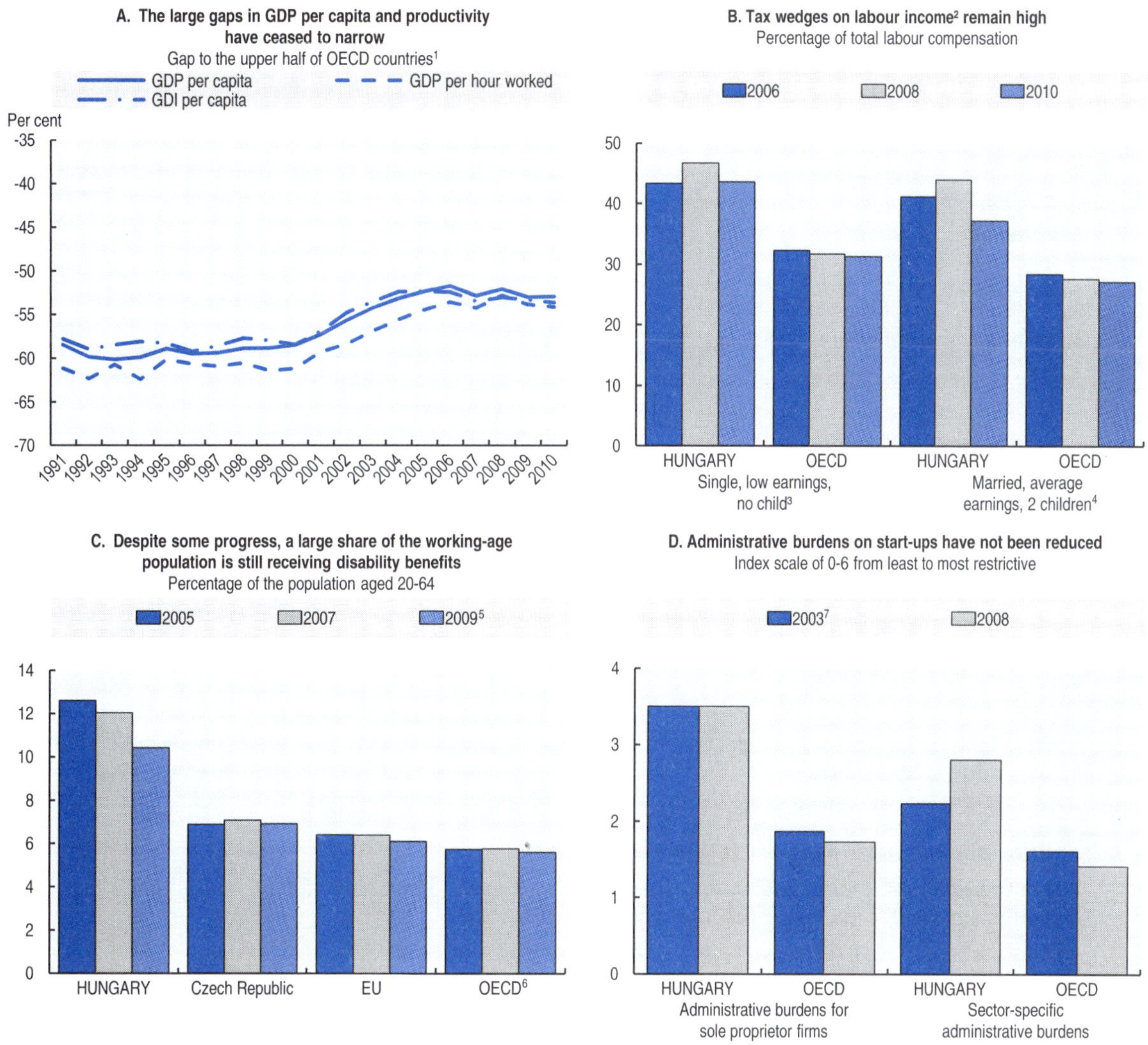

1. Percentage gap with respect to the simple average of the highest 17 OECD countries in terms of GDP per capita, GDP per hour worked and GDI per capita (in constant 2005 PPPs).
2. Labour taxes include personal income tax and employee plus employer social security contributions and any payroll tax less cash transfers.
3. Low earnings refer to two-thirds of average earnings.
4. At 100% of the average worker earnings for the first earner. Average of three situations regarding the wage of the second earner (0%, 33% and 67% of average earnings).
5. For Hungary, data refer to 2010.
6. Excluding Chile, Iceland and Turkey.
7. The OECD average excludes Chile, Estonia, Israel and Slovenia.

Source: Chart A: OECD, *National Accounts and Economic Outlook No. 90 Databases*; Chart B: OECD, *Taxing Wages Database*; Chart C: OECD (2010), *Sickness, Disability and Work: Breaking the Barriers: A Synthesis of Findings across OECD Countries*; Chart D: OECD, *Product Market Regulation Database*.

StatLink http://dx.doi.org/10.1787/888932565376

ICELAND

Priorities supported by indicators

Improve education outcomes (2007, 2009, 2011)

Recommendations: Make schools more accountable. Raise teacher quality, effective teaching time and student-teacher ratios, and reduce drop-out rates.

Actions taken: The 2009 secondary education reforms are expected to reduce drop-out rates by enabling students to complete programmes more quickly and by providing incentives to offer new and shorter programmes.

Reduce producer support to agriculture (2007, 2009, 2011)

Recommendations: Lower tariffs and excise duties, abolish quotas on agricultural production, reduce other forms of producer support and delink it from production.

Actions taken: Excise taxes on imported food (other than sugar and sweets) were abolished in 2007 and the general tariff on imported meat products was lowered significantly.

Lower barriers to entry for domestic and foreign firms (2007, 2009, 2011)

Recommendations: Reduce foreign ownership restrictions in the electricity and fisheries sectors and divest the National Power Company's generation activities.

Actions taken: No action taken.

Other key priorities

Accelerate public sector reform (2007, 2009, 2011)

Recommendations: Introduce outcome-based budgeting and strengthen conflict of interest disclosure.

Actions taken: No action taken.

Reduce barriers to product market competition (2011)

Recommendations: Reduce red tape, use plain language in regulations and reduce entry barriers in electricity, telecommunications and transport sectors.

Actions taken: No action taken.

Improve financial sector regulation and supervision (2009)

Recommendations: Tighten rules on large exposures, connected lending and quality of bank owners and give the macro-prudential regulator a legal basis to restrain bank behaviour.

Actions taken: The Act on Financial Undertakings 2010 tightens rules on large exposures, connected lending and quality of owners. The macro-prudential regulator signed a co-operation agreement with the micro-prudential regulator in 2011 but does not control the tools to restrain bank behaviour.

Reduce government support to housing (2007)

Recommendations: Charge the state-owned Housing Finance Fund (HFF) for the value of its loan repayment guarantee and lower the mortgage interest tax rebate.

Actions taken: The government is preparing a comprehensive restructuring plan for the HFF in response to a ruling of the European Surveillance Authority that requires that state aid for the HFF only benefit its public service activities. By contrast, mortgage interest tax rebates have been temporarily *increased* in 2009-11 and a temporary mortgage interest subsidy for households with net income below a certain limit was introduced in 2011.

ICELAND

- After some convergence in the decade to the mid-2000s, the GDP per capita gap relative to the upper half of OECD countries has widened since the financial crisis began. This income gap reflects relatively low labour productivity partially offset by one of the highest rates of labour utilisation in the OECD.
- Among key priority areas, some efforts have been made to improve financial sector regulation, strengthen the education system and reduce protection of the agricultural sector. By contrast, little has been achieved to enhance product market competition and public sector efficiency, and actions have gone in the wrong direction for government support to housing.
- In other areas, substantial increases in resources for the public employment service and for active labour market programmes have reduced the risk of the crisis-driven increase in unemployment becoming structural.

Performance and policy indicators

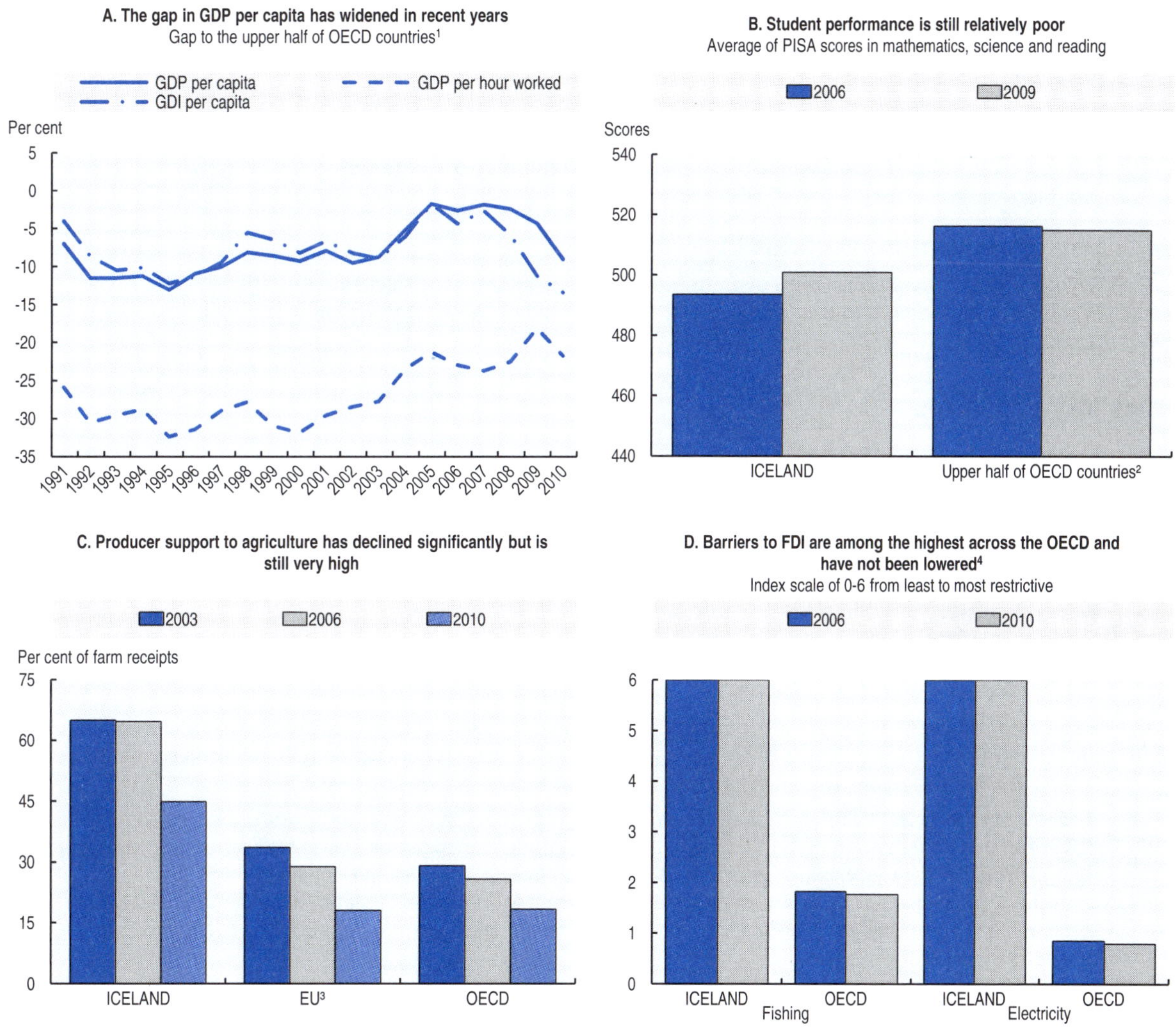

1. Percentage gap with respect to the simple average of the highest 17 OECD countries in terms of GDP per capita, GDP per hour worked and GDI per capita (in constant 2005 PPPs).
2. Upper half of OECD countries in terms of PISA scores in mathematics, science and reading.
3. Average of European countries in the OECD.
4. The OECD FDI regulatory restrictiveness index looks only at statutory restrictions and does not assess the manner in which they are implemented.

Source: Chart A: OECD, *National Accounts and Economic Outlook No. 90 Databases*; Chart B: OECD, *PISA 2009 Database*; Chart C: OECD, *Producer and Consumer Support Estimates Database*; Chart D: *http://www.oecd.org/investment/index.*

StatLink http://dx.doi.org/10.1787/888932565452

INDIA

Priorities supported by indicators

Reduce trade and FDI barriers as well as administrative burdens (2011)

Recommendations: Ease FDI restrictions in services sectors, especially in retail. Reduce trade barriers, especially in sectors where they are particularly high, including automotive manufacturing. Reduce red tape and legal and regulatory uncertainty.

Actions taken: In April 2011, the government issued revised regulations removing a requirement for foreign investors in some joint ventures to gain government approval before making a separate investment in the same sector. In January 2012, the government eased FDI restrictions in the retail sector, raising the foreign ownership limit for companies owning single-brand retail stores from 51% to 100%.

Improve the education system (2011)

Recommendations: Improve teacher effectiveness by strengthening accountability and improving quality of and access to training. Expand teaching resources in a cost-effective manner. Reform regulatory and quality-assessment arrangements in higher education. Provide institutions with greater autonomy.

Actions taken: The government has proposed legislation to establish a new higher education regulator. Parliament is also considering new legislation to broaden the quality assessment framework, reduce false advertising and clarify regulatory arrangements for foreign education providers.

Improve labour market flexibility (2011)

Recommendations: Reform employment protection legislation that discriminates against large firms, especially provisions requiring government approval to terminate employment contracts.

Actions taken: No action taken.

Other key priorities

Enhance infrastructure provision (2011)

Recommendations: Reduce regulatory uncertainty in the infrastructure sector in order to promote greater private sector involvement. Streamline land acquisition processes to reduce costs and delays. Eliminate cross-subsidies in the electricity and transport sectors.

Actions taken: The government raised limits for foreign institutional investment in debt issued by Indian infrastructure companies. The central government has prepared legislation to reform land titling and arrangements for public land acquisition.

Undertake wide-ranging financial sector reforms (2011)

Recommendations: Allow greater participation by foreign investors in the financial services sector and promote the entry of new private banks. Reform wide-ranging operational regulations for banks. Establish a new independent debt management authority.

Actions taken: In 2011 the government announced that it would issue additional licences for new private sector banks. A Financial Stability and Development Council has been established to monitor macro-prudential supervision and improve regulatory co-ordination. The government is proceeding with the establishment of a new independent Public Debt Management Agency. Restrictions on access to Indian capital markets have been eased with foreign individuals allowed from 2012 to invest directly in local stock markets.

INDIA

- The Indian economy has continued to expand rapidly, ensuring strong growth in per capita incomes and a decrease of the income gap with OECD countries. However, the latter remains very large, reflecting low labour productivity.
- Among key priority areas, the government has proposed legislative changes to higher education regulations aimed at enhancing quality and encouraging participation by foreign providers. There have also been significant achievements in key infrastructure sectors, although major bottlenecks persist.
- In other areas, further progress has been made in deregulating energy prices, enhancing energy efficiency.

Performance and policy indicators

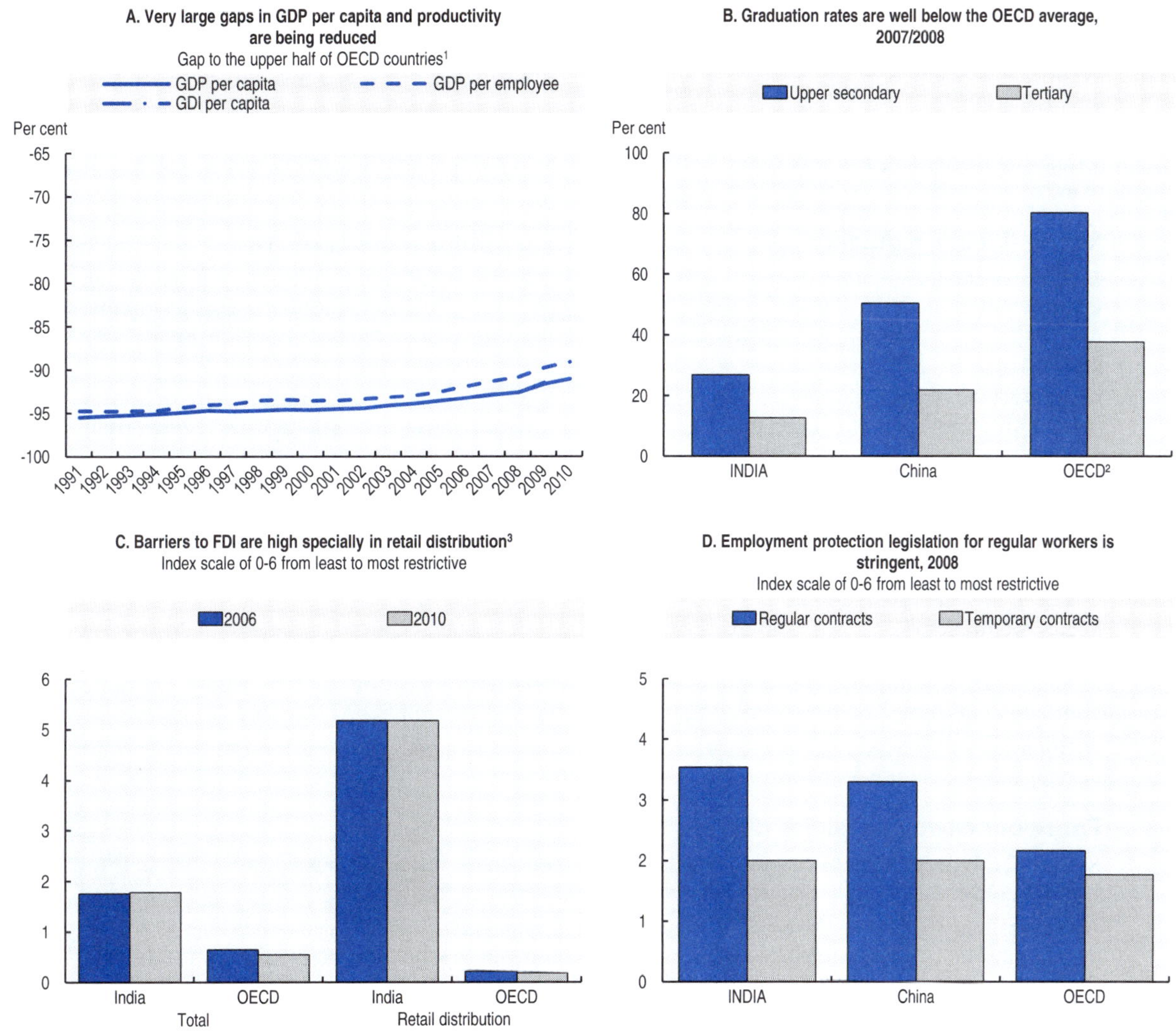

1. Percentage gap with respect to the simple average of the highest 17 OECD countries in terms of GDP per capita, GDP per employee and GDI per capita (in constant 2005 PPPs).
2. Graduation rate at upper secondary level (first-time graduate) and graduation rate for single year of age at tertiary-type A level (first-time graduate). For upper secondary education, average of OECD countries excluding Australia, Austria, Belgium, Estonia, France and the Netherlands; for tertiary education, average of OECD countries excluding Belgium, Chile, Estonia, France and Korea.
3. The OECD FDI regulatory restrictiveness index looks only at statutory restrictions and does not assess the manner in which they are implemented.

Source: Chart A: World Bank (2011), *World Development Indicators (WDI) Database*, National Sample Survey (various years), annual population estimates of the Registrar General and OECD estimates; Chart B: OECD (2011), *Education at a Glance*; India National Sample Survey (2007/8) and China Statistical Yearbook; Chart C: *http://www.oecd.org/investment/index*; Chart D: OECD, *Employment Database*.

StatLink http://dx.doi.org/10.1787/888932565414

INDONESIA

Priorities supported by indicators

Strengthen resources for secondary education and improve the overall efficiency of the education system (2011)

Recommendations: Make income transfer programmes conditional on children attending secondary school, and eliminate the secondary school enrolment fee for disadvantaged children in order to boost enrolment rates. To improve teaching quality, assess teachers' pedagogical skills regularly.

Actions taken: The National Education Strategy Plan is being implemented with the view to reducing disparities in access, enhancing the quality of teaching and improving management and accountability.

Improve the regulatory environment for infrastructure (2011)

Recommendations: Reduce regulatory barriers and uncertainties to entice private investment. Grant independence to regulatory bodies, strengthen their public accountability, and establish new ones in sectors lacking them. Reform land expropriation procedures to expedite reaching fair compensation decisions.

Actions taken: A draft Land Acquisition Law that seeks to secure land acquisition procedures for infrastructure projects has been submitted to Parliament. The President has announced a new master plan for improving connectivity between provinces.

Reform labour regulation to address the problem of informality (2011)

Recommendations: In order to improve the labour income insurance system, introduce some form of unemployment benefit while simplifying dismissal procedures and reducing severance payments. Also, cap real increases in the minimum wage to ensure they do not to exceed labour-productivity gains.

Actions taken: A regulation set the minimum wage increase at 15.4% in 2011 in the province of Jakarta (which amounts to about three times the economy-wide increase implemented in the first half of 2010).

Other key priorities

Ease barriers to entrepreneurship and investment and strengthen institutions to fight corruption (2011)

Recommendations: Simplify administrative procedures for establishing new firms by reducing the number of business licenses and setting up one-stop shops in districts where these are currently lacking. Further reduce FDI restrictions especially in telecommunications and transport. Continue efforts to fight corruption by reforming the tax office and further simplifying business licensing.

Actions taken: In May 2011, the government temporarily stopped allowing foreign investors to develop new oil palm plantations.

Phase out energy subsidies (2011)

Recommendations: Stick to the planned timetable to eliminate fossil-fuel subsidies and extend the commitment to electricity subsidies, while offering more effective targeted income support to the poor.

Actions taken: The planned rise in electricity tariffs for January 2011 was postponed. In April 2011, the overall amount of energy subsidies were increased compared to what was planned in the budget. In the State Budget, the government is scheduled to reduce electricity and fuel subsidies for 2012.

INDONESIA

- Per capita incomes are converging towards OECD levels but the gap remains very large, owing mainly to a labour productivity shortfall.
- Among priority areas, progress has been made to strengthen education and infrastructure. By contrast, no significant action has been taken to reform labour market regulation, and policy changes in the areas of business environment, the phasing out of energy subsidies and limitation of real minimum wage increases have gone in the wrong direction.
- In other areas, the government launched a National Plan of Action on Food and Nutrition in 2011 to fight against maternal and youth malnutrition.

Performance and policy indicators

A. Gaps in GDP per capita have diminished rather slowly
Gap to the upper half of OECD countries[1]

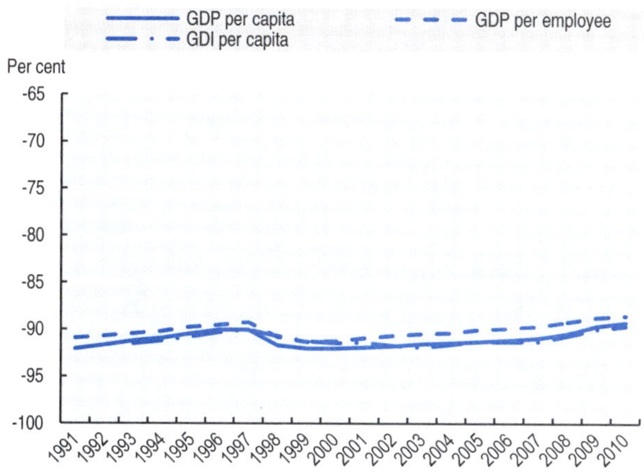

B. Secondary and tertiary education graduation rates remain low, 2009[2]

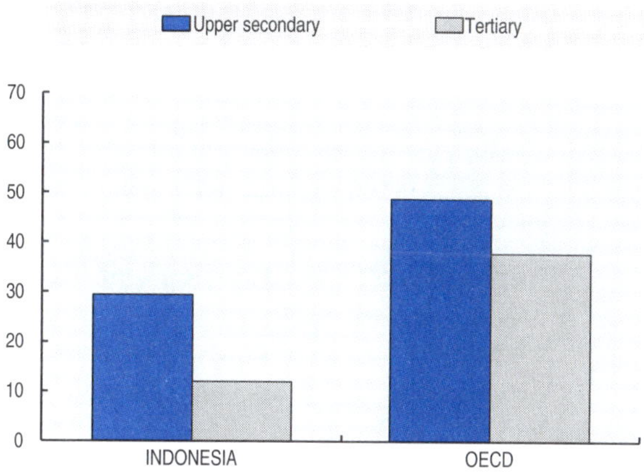

C. Product market regulation is stringent, 2008
Index scale of 0-6 from least to most restrictive

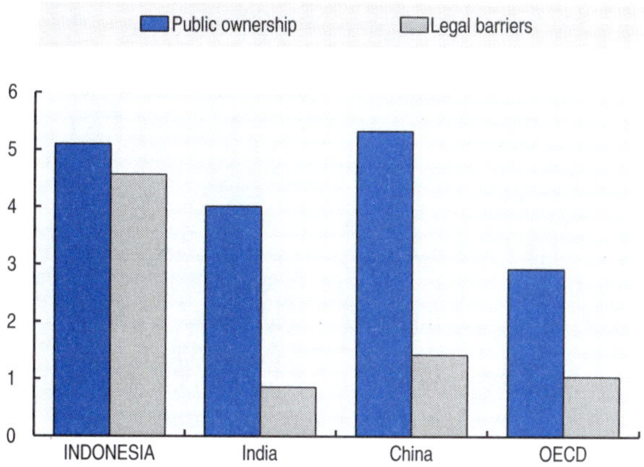

D. Employment protection legislation is strict especially for regular contracts, 2008
Index scale of 0-6 from least to most restrictive

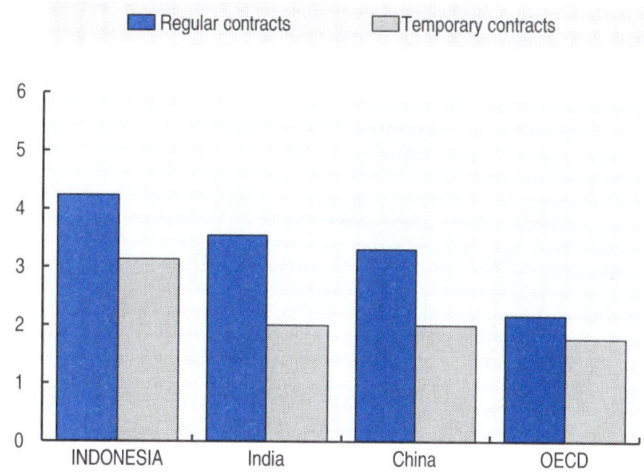

1. Percentage gap with respect to the simple average of the highest 17 OECD countries in terms of GDP per capita, GDP per employee and GDI per capita (in constant 2005 PPPs).
2. Graduation rate at upper secondary level for single year of age from the general programmes and graduation rate for single year of age at tertiary-type A level (first degree). For upper secondary education, average of OECD countries excluding Greece and the United Kingdom; for tertiary education, average of OECD countries excluding Greece and Luxembourg.

Source: Chart A: World Bank (2011), *World Development Indicators (WDI) and ILO (2011), Key Indicators of the Labour Market (KILM) Databases*; Chart B: OECD (2011), *Education at a Glance*; Chart C: OECD, *Product Market Regulation Database* and Woefl, A. *et al.* (2010), "Product Market Regulation: Extending the Analysis Beyond OECD Countries", OECD *Economics Department Working Papers*, No. 799, OECD Publishing; Chart D: OECD, *Employment Database*.

StatLink http://dx.doi.org/10.1787/888932565395

IRELAND

Priorities supported by indicators

Strengthen work incentives for women (2007, 2009, 2011)

Recommendations: Improve access to childcare and reconsider how second earners are taxed.

Actions taken: In 2010 the government replaced the Early Childcare Supplement by a free Pre-School year, open to 3 and 4 year-olds.

Strengthen competition in non-manufacturing sectors (2007, 2009, 2011)

Recommendations: Increase competition in utilities and services sectors.

Actions taken: A wholesale electricity market was set up in 2007 and interconnection with the United Kingdom was improved. In 2011, the government reduced margins paid to pharmacies and introduced legislation to parliament to reduce restrictions on the number of General Practitioners treating public patients, set up independent regulators for the legal profession and increase penalties for violating competition law.

Enhance R&D spending and innovation (2007, 2009, 2011)

Recommendations: Improve incentives for R&D and streamline funding for public institutions.

Actions taken: The government made the R&D tax credit more generous in 2009, and announced in the 2012 Budget that it would introduce greater flexibility and scope to the R&D tax credit, which should particularly benefit SMEs. The authorities have scaled up several initiatives to increase linkages between industry and researchers, including innovation vouchers, joint research centres and awards.

Improve access to education and increase tertiary education funding (2007, 2009)

Recommendations: Extend pre-primary education. In tertiary education, introduce tuition fees coupled with income-contingent repayments.

Actions taken: The contribution charge for tertiary students will increase from EUR 1 500 in 2010-11 to EUR 2 000 in 2011-12 and EUR 2 250 in 2012-13.

Other key priorities

Further improve infrastructure (2007, 2009, 2011)

Recommendations: Close infrastructure gaps in a cost-effective way. Speed up the planning process. Introduce water charges to ensure efficient use of infrastructure.

Actions taken: The government will introduce a combined property and water levy of EUR 100 per household in 2012. It will introduce meter-based water charges for domestic users in 2013, in the context of a broad reform of the water services sector. The motorway network between major cities was completed in 2010.

Enhance activation policies (2011)

Recommendations: Tighten activation requirements for the unemployed and expand activation measures.

Actions taken: In 2011 the government continued transferring the Public Employment Service's (FÁS) employment and community services to the Department of Social Protection (DSP) to combine benefit provision and activation. In 2011, DSP introduced profiling to better target those at high risk of becoming long-term unemployed. In April 2011, sanctions for refusing a job offer or training were increased. The number of training and internship places was further expanded in 2011.

IRELAND

- GDP per capita relative to the upper half of OECD countries has fallen from 2007 to 2011, turning the gap from positive to negative. This negative gap is entirely due to lower labour utilisation, as hourly labour productivity remains high.
- Against the background of a major economic and financial crisis, Ireland negotiated an EU/IMF financial assistance programme, under which certain structural reforms are being implemented. Among key priorities, progress has been made in improving early childhood education, encouraging innovation and enhancing infrastructure. Activation measures continue to be stepped up but potential for further improvement remains large.
- Beyond the strengthening of activation policies, the main labour market measure taken during the crisis was to expand training programmes for the unemployed. Further training places were added in 2011.

Performance and policy indicators

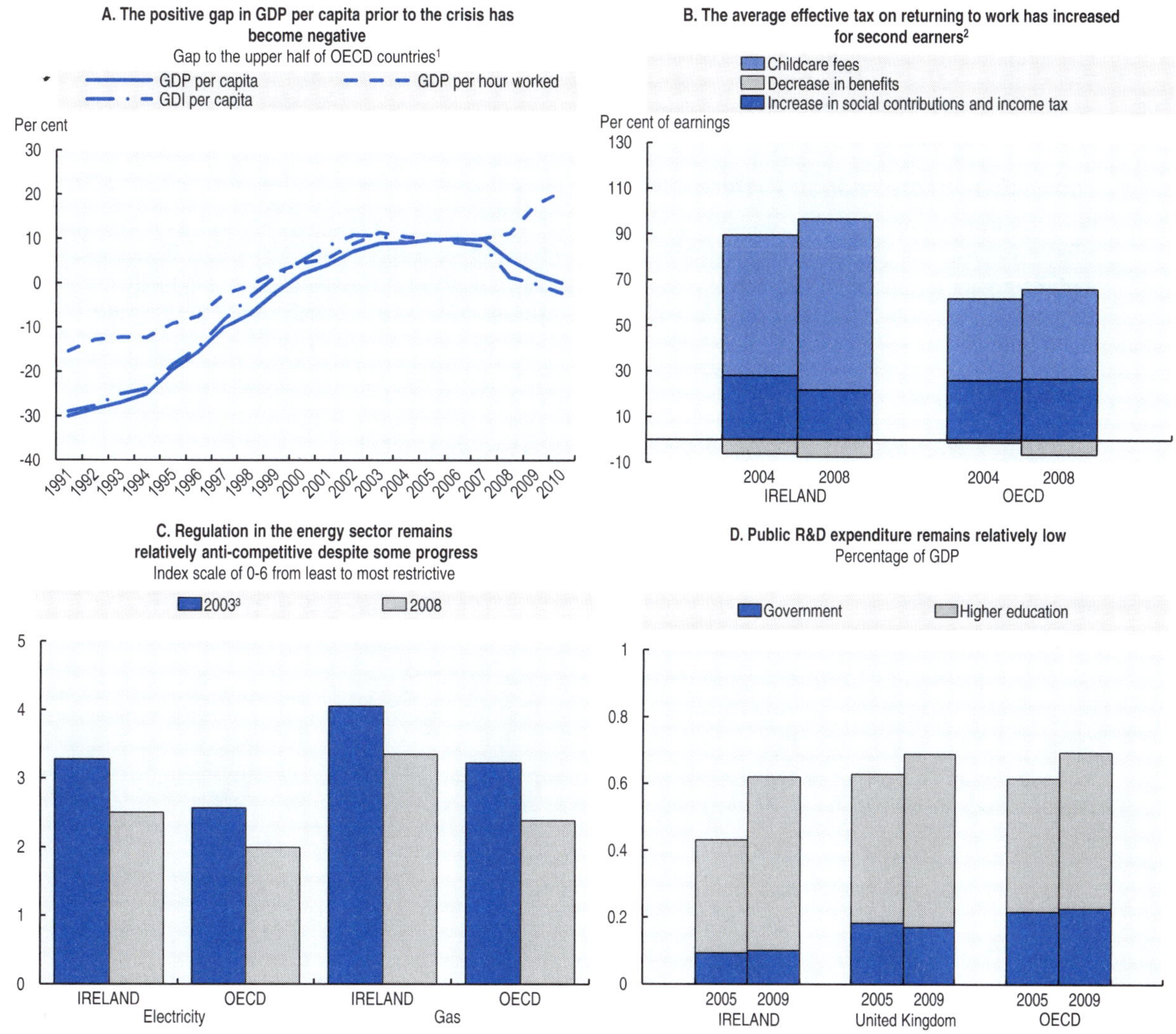

1. Percentage gap with respect to the simple average of the highest 17 OECD countries in terms of GDP per capita, GDP per hour worked and GDI per capita (in constant 2005 PPPs).
2. Based on implicit tax on returning to work, defined as the cost of childcare, reductions in income-related benefits and increases in social contributions and personal income taxes, all relative to earnings in the new job. Measured for second earner with income equal to two-thirds of average earnings. The OECD average excludes Chile, Estonia, Israel, Italy, Mexico, Turkey and Slovenia.
3. Average of OECD countries excluding Chile, Estonia, Israel and Slovenia.

Source: Chart A: OECD, *National Accounts and Economic Outlook No. 90 Databases*; Chart B: *Benefits and Wages Database*; Chart C: OECD, *Product Market Regulation Database*; Chart D: OECD, *Main Science and Technology Indicators Database*. StatLink http://dx.doi.org/10.1787/888932565433

ISRAEL

Priorities supported by indicators

Improve education outcomes (2011)

Recommendations: Raise the quality of state-run compulsory education, notably for Arab pupils. As regards the independent ultra-orthodox schools, expand and properly enforce curriculum requirements for state funding. Introduce tuition fees in tertiary education along with student loans with income-contingent repayment.

Actions taken: Upper secondary education reforms beginning in the 2011/12 school year will include higher teacher pay in exchange for increased working hours and a range of pedagogical and other reforms. Other ongoing reforms include raising the school-leaving age, reducing class sizes, as well as reforming final examinations and school-funding formulae.

Cut red tape for businesses (2011)

Recommendations: Follow through on plans to ease building regulations, and continue efforts to streamline the number of, and processing times for business licences.

Actions taken: Partial liberalisation of land ownership is under way, but attempts to streamline and decentralise planning and approval procedures have stalled. Yet, measures aiming to expedite housing construction have been taken to counter rapid house-price growth. A one-stop shop system for SMEs is being developed.

Complete network-industry reform (2011)

Recommendations: Resolve deadlock in the electricity sector, establish an independent telecommunications regulator, and increase competition in post, rail and water services.

Actions taken: In telecoms, the mobile phone connectivity fee was cut further in 2011. In electricity generation, progress towards private production continues with approval of a large plant given in 2011.

Other key priorities

Encourage employment among low-income households (2011)

Recommendations: Pursue welfare-to-work programmes more vigorously, increase the coverage and value of the earned-income tax credit (EITC), and combine stronger enforcement of labour regulation with reduction in the value of the minimum wage relative to average earnings.

Actions taken: A promising pilot private-sector job-placement scheme was abandoned. Also, exceptional increases in the minimum wage have been agreed for July 2011 and October 2012. The EITC is due to apply country-wide, but no increase in its value is planned.

Shift the burden of taxation away from direct taxes (2011)

Recommendations: Pursue feasible avenues for raising indirect taxes and continue cutting income taxes.

Actions taken: The corporate income tax rate was reduced in January 2011 along with cuts in some personal-income tax rates.

ISRAEL[1]

- GDP per capita has been gradually moving towards the upper half of OECD countries since the mid-2000s, but a large gap remains, reflecting a shortfall in productivity.
- Among key priority areas, some progress has been made in tax and education reforms, but there have been some backward steps in welfare-to-work measures.
- In other areas, the fiscal regime applying to offshore natural gas has been improved, and several steps have been taken to cool the housing market.

Performance and policy indicators

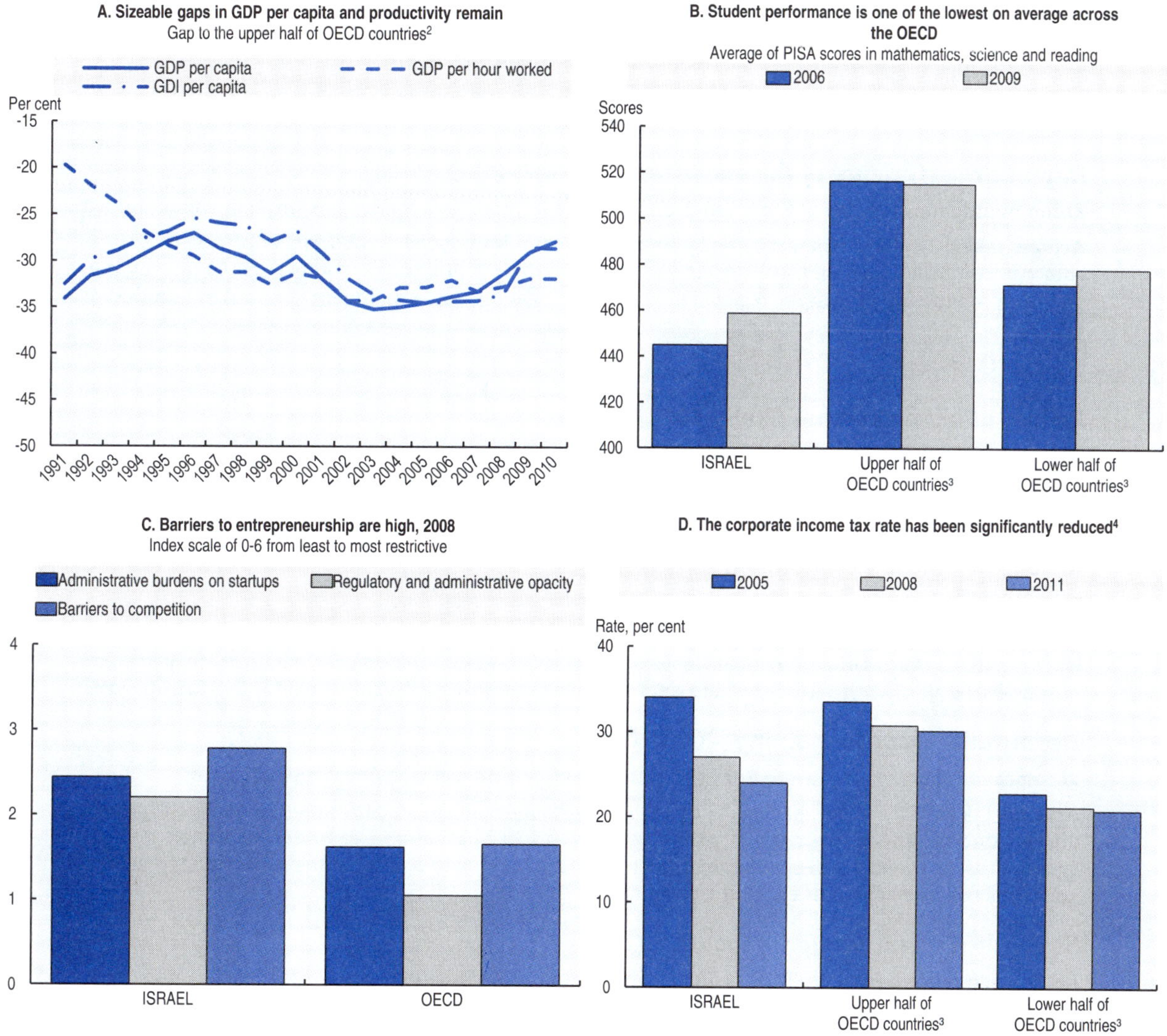

1. The statistical data for Israel are supplied by and under the responsibility of the relevant Israeli authorities. The use of such data by the OECD is without prejudice to the status of the Golan Heights, East Jerusalem and Israeli settlements in the West Bank under the terms of international law.
2. Percentage gap with respect to the simple average of the highest 17 OECD countries in terms of GDP per capita, GDP per hour worked and GDI per capita (in constant 2005 PPPs).
3. Upper and lower half of OECD countries in terms of PISA scores in mathematics, science and reading in Panel B and in terms of the level of the corporate income tax rate in Panel D.
4. Combined central and sub-central (statutory) corporate income tax rate.

Source: Chart A: OECD, *National Accounts and Economic Outlook No. 90 Databases*; Chart B: OECD, *PISA 2009 Database*; Chart C: OECD, *Product Market Regulation Database*; Chart D: OECD, *Tax Database*.

StatLink http://dx.doi.org/10.1787/888932565471

ITALY

Priorities supported by indicators

Reduce regulatory barriers to competition (2007, 2009, 2011)

Recommendations: Reduce barriers to competition in network industries and professional, retail trade and local services.

Actions taken: The December 2011 decree introduced measures to liberalise retail trade *e.g.* lifting restrictions on shop opening hours and easing various entry barriers, including for large retailers. Such measures could, however, be partly overruled by regional authorities' territorial policy. The decree also gave the competition authority the power to challenge regulations in the courts. The government introduced significant measures to liberalise the liberal professions and transport services in early 2012.

Improve access to and graduation from tertiary education (2007, 2009, 2011)

Recommendations: Link teachers' careers to performance, gradually introduce tuition fees and income-contingent repayment loans, decentralise the financing and management of universities.

Actions taken: A 2011 law separated university administrative management from teaching and research and reinforced evaluation mechanisms.

Improve the efficiency of the tax structure (2007, 2009, 2011)

Recommendations: Reduce the tax wedge on labour. Shift more taxation to consumption and property.

Actions taken: The 2011 emergency budget raised VAT and introduced an allowance for new corporate equity in company taxation. Labour taxation was reduced for young people and women by making the payroll tax deductible against the regional income tax. A new, higher, local property tax will be introduced in 2012.

Other key priorities

Reduce public ownership (2009, 2011)

Recommendations: Reduce state ownership, especially in TV media, transport, energy and local services.

Actions taken: Plans to privatise water services were overturned by referendum in 2011. The new government plans to pursue privatisation.

Reduce labour market dualism (2011)

Recommendations: Relax job protection on standard contracts.

Actions taken: No significant action taken but the new government is considering a comprehensive labour market reform aimed at relaxing job protection on standard contracts. Such reform is expected to be introduced along with a major welfare reform aimed at improving the safety net for the unemployed.

Decentralise wage bargaining (2007, 2009)

Recommendations: Promote greater wage differentiation by decentralising wage bargaining.

Actions taken: The social partners signed (2009) an agreement to promote private sector wage differentiation. The 2011 emergency budget allowed local bargaining to undercut national wage agreements, provided a representative union in the firm accepts to opt out of the collective agreement and signs the new agreement with the employer.

Strengthen incentives for innovation (2009)

Recommendations: Increase R&D tax incentives and improve business-academic research links.

Actions taken: The 2011-13 Budget introduced a tax credit for firms commissioning research activities to universities or public research centres.

Reform corporate governance (2007)

Recommendations: Reform bankruptcy legislation and enhance corporate governance and transparency of financial instruments.

Actions taken: In 2010, disincentives for creditors to lend and obstacles to the participation of shareholders in general meetings were reduced. The December 2011 decree prohibited cross-membership of directors and senior officers on the boards of competing financial institutions.

ITALY

- Italian GDP per capita stagnated over the past decade, significantly widening the gap relative to the upper half of OECD countries.
- Among the key priority areas, some progress has been made in reforming tertiary education, decentralising wage bargaining and strengthening corporate governance. But little has been achieved in reducing public ownership and regulatory barriers to competition, as well as on relaxing job protection on standard employment contracts. A decree in December 2011 tackles some of these issues and further action has been taken in early 2012.
- In other areas, the expanded short-time working compensation scheme (Cassa Integrazione Guadagni), which is still in place, contributed to social protection and moderated job losses during the crisis.

Performance and policy indicators

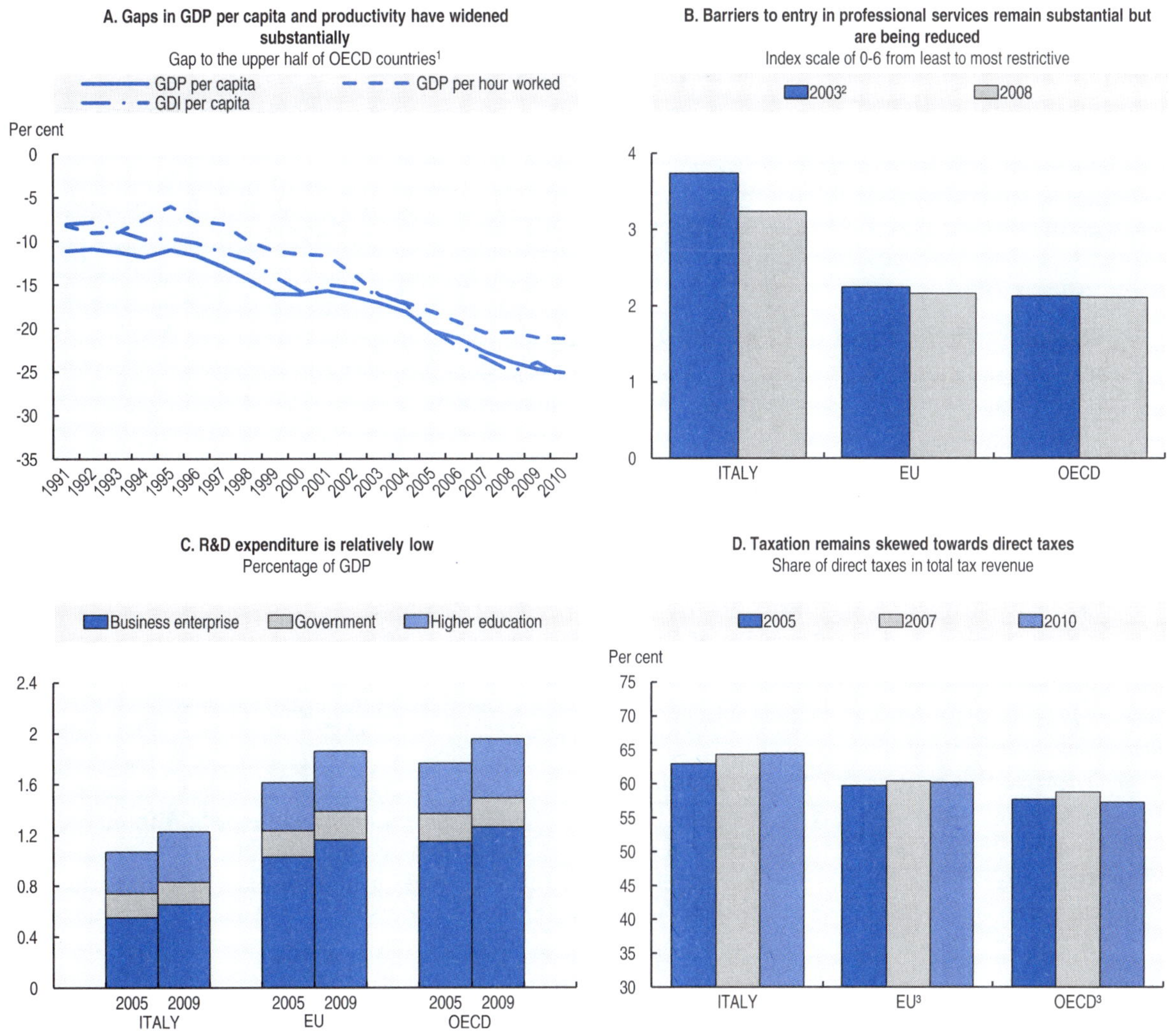

1. Percentage gap with respect to the simple average of the highest 17 OECD countries in terms of GDP per capita, GDP per hour worked and GDI per capita (in constant 2005 PPPs).
2. Average of European countries in the OECD. EU and OECD averages exclude Chile, Estonia, Israel and Slovenia.
3. Data refer to 2009 for Australia, the Netherlands and Poland.

Source: Chart A: OECD, *National Accounts and Economic Outlook No. 90 Databases*; Chart B: OECD, *Product Market Regulation Database*; Chart C: OECD, *Main Science and Technology Indicators Database*; Chart D: OECD, *Tax Database*.

StatLink http://dx.doi.org/10.1787/888932565490

JAPAN

Priorities supported by indicators

Strengthen competition in non-manufacturing sectors (2007, 2009, 2011)

Recommendations: Accelerate regulatory reform in network sectors, while strengthening competition policy. Follow through on the privatisation of Japan Post, as outlined in the 2005 law.

Actions taken: The privatisation of Japan Post Bank and Japan Post Insurance, which was to be completed by 2017, has been suspended. The 2010 revision of the Broadcast Act integrates broadcasting services and communications.

Break down labour market dualism (2007, 2009, 2011)

Recommendations: Reduce effective employment protection for regular workers, while increasing the social insurance coverage of non-regular workers and upgrading training programmes for them.

Actions taken: A 2008 law encouraged balanced treatment of part-time workers relative to regular workers, although this may discourage their hiring. The government relaxed the eligibility conditions for employment insurance in 2009 and 2010 from one year of work to 31 days.

Reduce producer support to agriculture (2007, 2009, 2011)

Recommendations: Scale back the high level of agricultural protection and shift its composition away from price support towards direct support to farmers, in order to reduce distortions to trade and production and facilitate regional economic integration.

Actions taken: The government implemented a direct income support programme for farmers in 2011 covering certain products, including rice, wheat and soy, with spending of 0.1% of GDP.

Other key priorities

Lower restrictions on FDI (2007, 2009, 2011)

Recommendations: Improve the FDI climate by further liberalising trade, lowering barriers to investment and ownership, accelerating reforms of administrative procedures and relaxing labour regulations.

Actions taken: The government decided to implement the "Inward Investment Promotion Programme" in 2010 to accelerate FDI through a cut in the corporate tax rate, deregulation of investment procedures, and incentives such as preferential tax treatment and subsidies.

Reform the tax system (2009, 2011)

Recommendations: Implement a comprehensive tax reform that broadens direct tax bases, while relying primarily on the consumption tax for additional revenue.

Actions taken: The government widened the tax base in 2010 by abolishing or reducing 41 special tax measures. The government is also considering doubling the consumption tax rate to 10% by the mid-2010s and cutting the corporate tax rate from 40% to 35%.

Improve the framework for innovation (2007)

Recommendations: Enhance co-operation between university, government and research institutes. Boost the share of public research funds for universities that is allocated competitively.

Actions taken: The third Science and Technology Basic Plan for 2006-10 increases the role of tertiary education in innovation, in part by policies to promote technology licensing by universities.

JAPAN

- The GDP per capita gap relative to the upper half of OECD countries has failed to narrow over the past decade, as relative productivity gains have been offset by a decline in labour input towards the OECD average. Average labour productivity remains 20% below the top half of OECD countries, while labour utilisation is slightly above.
- Key reforms in priority areas have included the introduction of (less harmful) direct income support to farmers and the expansion of social insurance coverage of non-regular workers. In addition, the corporate tax rate has been reduced, although it is still above the OECD average. However, less progress has been made in reforming regulations on FDI and network industries.
- In other areas, a subsistence allowance for workers not covered by employment insurance who participate in vocational training was introduced as part of the "*second safety net*" in 2009 and made permanent in 2011.

Performance and policy indicators

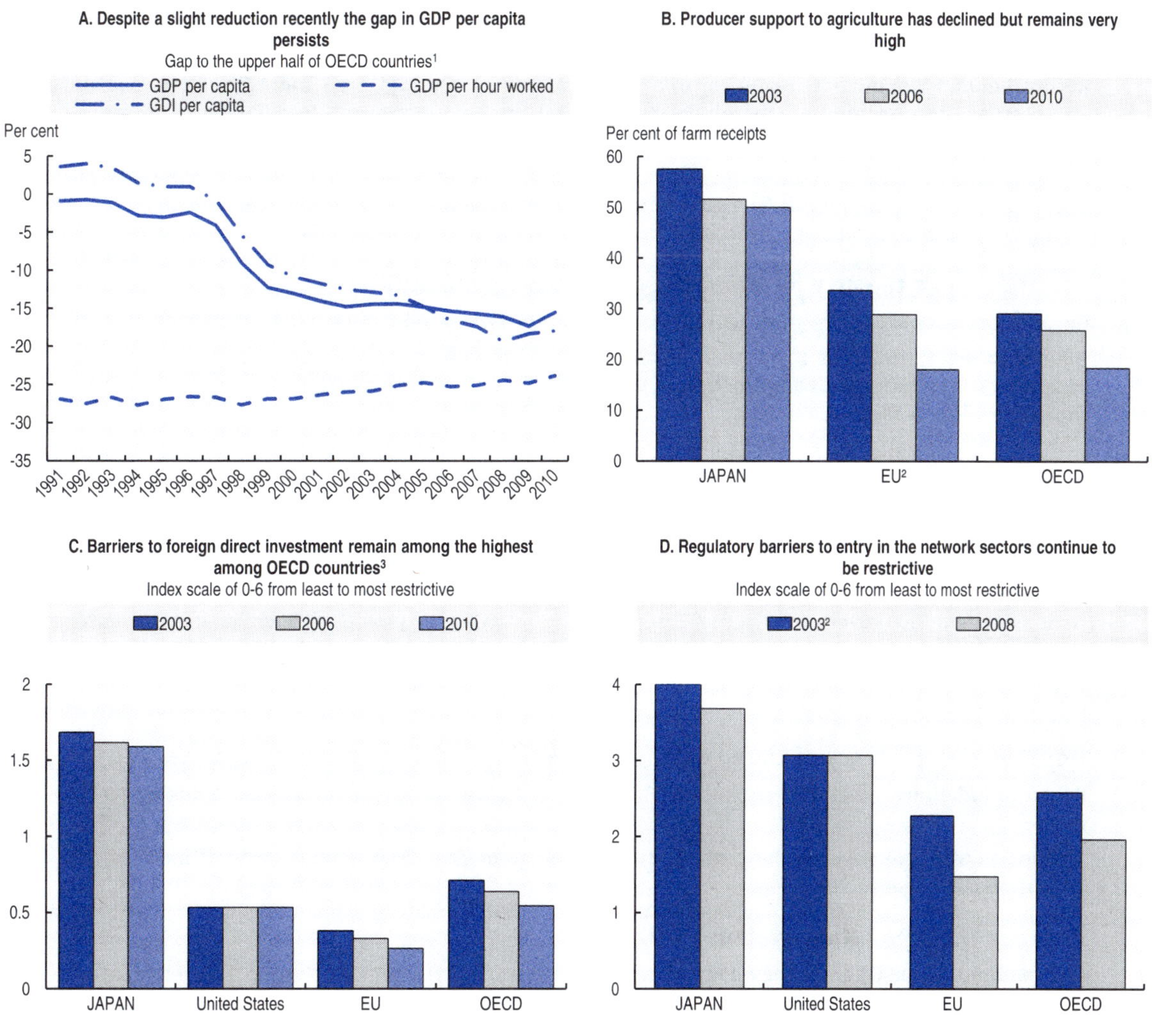

1. Percentage gap with respect to the simple average of the highest 17 OECD countries in terms of GDP per capita, GDP per hour worked and GDI per capita (in constant 2005 PPPs).
2. Average of European countries in the OECD. EU and OECD averages exclude Chile, Estonia, Israel and Slovenia in Panel D.
3. The OECD FDI regulatory restrictiveness index looks only at statutory restrictions and does not assess the manner in which they are implemented.

Source: Chart A: OECD, *National Accounts and Economic Outlook No. 90 Databases*; Chart B: OECD, *Producer and Consumer Support Estimates Database*; Chart C: *http://www.oecd.org/investment/index*; Chart D: OECD, *Product Market Regulation Database*.

StatLink http://dx.doi.org/10.1787/888932565509

KOREA

Priorities supported by indicators

Reduce labour market dualism (2009, 2011)

Recommendations: Expand the coverage of the social insurance system and ease employment protection legislation for regular workers. Increase training opportunities for non-regular workers.

Actions taken: The government introduced free training programmes for non-regular workers in 2009 and expanded them in 2010.

Ease regulation in network industries and services (2007, 2009, 2011)

Recommendations: Further reduce entry barriers, promote regulatory reform and create independent sectoral regulators. Relax FDI restrictions, including foreign ownership ceilings in key services.

Actions taken: The government relaxed 28 market entry regulations, primarily in services, in 2009-10. Foreign ownership ceilings were increased for satellite broadcasting and programme providers in 2009.

Reduce producer support to agriculture (2007, 2009, 2011)

Recommendations: Increase openness to agricultural imports through Free Trade Agreements (FTAs) and shift the composition of assistance from market price supports to direct payments to reduce distortions to trade and production.

Actions taken: Since 2007, Korea has implemented FTAs that include agriculture with the European Union, Peru, ASEAN and India. The government has expanded direct payment schemes, including a pilot project in 2010 aimed at promoting income stability for farm households.

Lower barriers to entry for domestic and foreign firms (2007)

Recommendations: Reduce entry barriers and encourage FDI by reducing regulatory obstacles.

Actions taken: In 2009, the government abolished the minimum capital requirement to create a firm and reduced the number of administrative procedures from ten to eight. The government simplified the approval process for FDI in 2009.

Other key priorities

Strengthen policies to support female labour force participation (2007, 2009, 2011)

Recommendations: Relax price controls on private childcare facilities and provide vouchers to parents.

Actions taken: The government introduced vouchers in 2009 that provide free childcare to children under the age of five in families with below-average incomes, expanding it to the lower 70% of income levels in 2011. It allowed private-sector childcare providers to set fees up to 50% above the ceiling on a trial basis in 2011.

Improve the efficiency of the tax system by relying more on indirect taxes (2011)

Recommendations: Rely more on indirect taxes for additional revenue, while broadening direct tax bases.

Actions taken: The government extended the coverage of the VAT to some areas of medical and educational services in 2011.

Improve the innovation system (2007, 2009)

Recommendations: Upgrade the quality of universities through greater competition and deregulation, and enhance intellectual property rights.

Actions taken: The government enacted a basic law on intellectual property rights in 2011. The disclosure of some key information by universities was mandated in 2008 to strengthen competition.

KOREA

- The gap in GDP per capita relative to the upper half of OECD countries continues to narrow. Korea's labour utilisation rate remains the highest in the OECD area, so the remaining income gap is entirely due to shortfalls in productivity, particularly in services.
- Key reforms have taken place in priority areas to relax market entry barriers for domestic and foreign firms, strengthen intellectual property rights and provide vouchers for childcare. However, much less progress has been made to overcome labour market dualism, reduce the level of support to agriculture and increase competition in network industries.
- In other areas, to cushion the labour market crisis, short-term public employment was temporarily doubled in 2009.

Performance and policy indicators

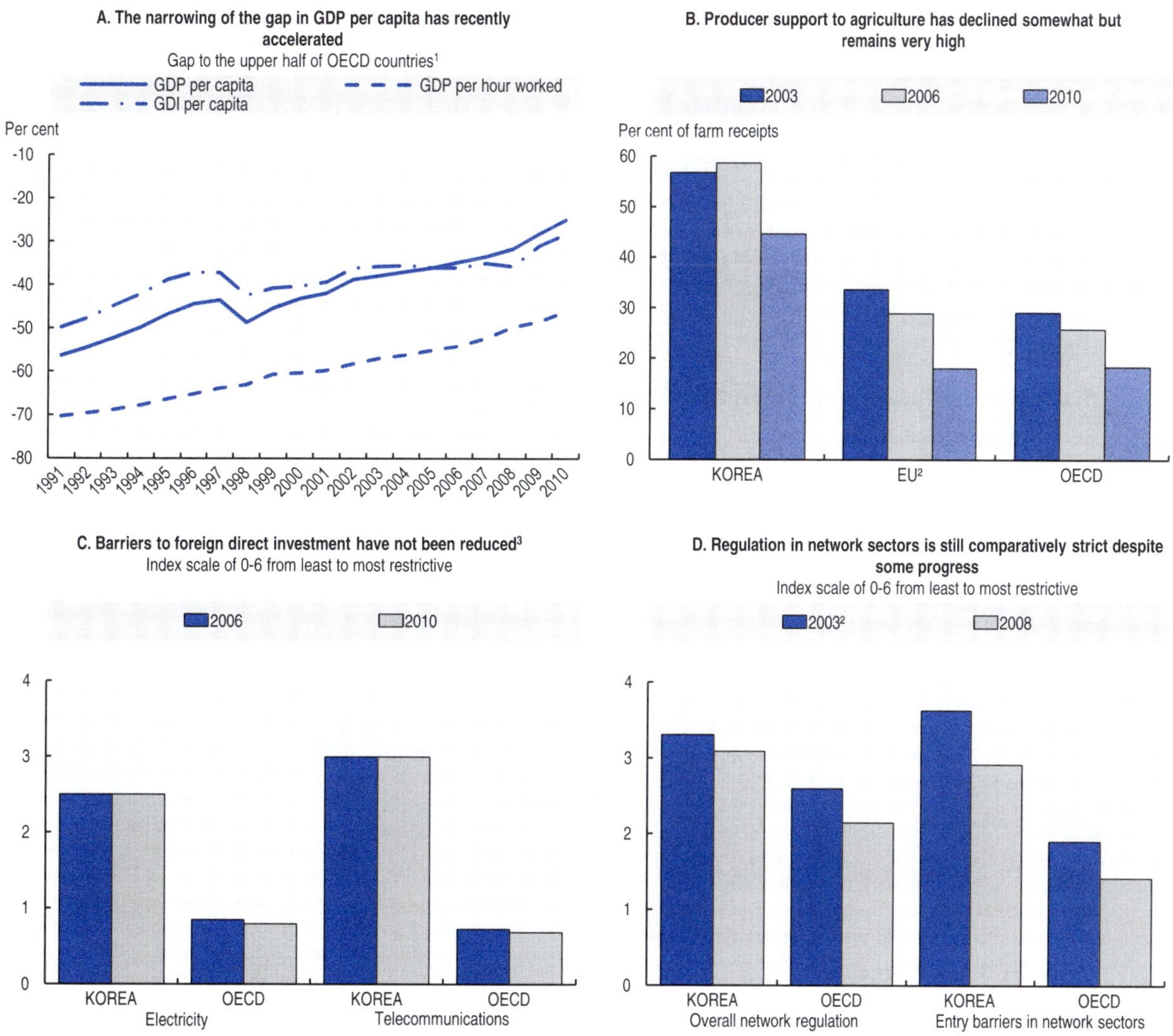

1. Percentage gap with respect to the simple average of the highest 17 OECD countries in terms of GDP per capita, GDP per hour worked and GDI per capita (in constant 2005 PPPs).
2. Average of European countries in the OECD. EU and OECD averages exclude Chile, Estonia, Israel and Slovenia in Panel D.
3. The OECD FDI regulatory restrictiveness index looks only at statutory restrictions and does not assess the manner in which they are implemented.

Source: Chart A: OECD, *National Accounts and Economic Outlook No. 90 Databases*; Chart B: OECD, *Producer and Consumer Support Estimates Database*; Chart C: *http://www.oecd.org/investment/index*; Chart D: OECD, *Product Market Regulation Database*.

StatLink http://dx.doi.org/10.1787/888932565528

LUXEMBOURG

Priorities supported by indicators

Improve work incentives (2007, 2009, 2011)

Recommendations: Lower replacement rates under ongoing social benefits and reduce unemployment benefits progressively throughout the period of entitlement. Tighten unemployment insurance eligibility conditions for young people without work histories. Strengthen activation requirements and improve the cost-effectiveness of labour market programmes.

Actions taken: No action taken to reform the unemployment benefit system. Activation is being improved by addressing organisational weaknesses in the public employment service (ADEM), such as high caseloads per case worker in some offices.

Reduce disincentives to continued work at older ages (2007, 2009, 2011)

Recommendations: Abolish early retirement schemes to raise the effective retirement age. A major reform of pensions should include a progressive reduction of the replacement rate, limiting credits for time spent outside work, introducing actuarial neutrality around the standard retirement age and indexing this age to longevity.

Actions taken: Proposals aimed at making the system more neutral around the retirement age and removing obstacles to continued work beyond that age have been made by the government.

Increase competition in the domestically-oriented services sector (2007, 2009, 2011)

Recommendations: For professional services, remove restrictions on advertising, facilitate co-operation between professions, and scrap minimum or reference prices. Shop opening hours should be made more flexible. The competition authority should be re-organised into a single body and be given sufficient resources.

Actions taken: No action taken, and transposition of the EU Services Directive remains to be legislated.

Strengthen primary and secondary education systems (2007, 2009)

Recommendations: Schools should be granted greater autonomy to allow headmasters and teachers to adjust their school programme in line with student needs. In addition, language education should be rebalanced to make school education better reflect labour market requirements.

Actions taken: Reforms aiming at improving language education and reducing class repetition were introduced starting with the 2009/10 school year.

Other key priorities

Improve the functioning of the labour market by easing employment protection legislation (2007, 2009, 2011)

Recommendations: Ease conditions on collective dismissal and social plans. Lengthen trial periods under regular contracts for the low-skilled. Extend the total duration of temporary contracts and facilitate their renewals.

Actions taken: No action taken.

Improve the functioning of the housing market (2011)

Recommendations: Overhaul the planning system to facilitate house building. Reduce implicit tax subsidies to home ownership and incentives to hoard building plots.

Actions taken: No action taken.

LUXEMBOURG

- GDP per capita is the highest in the OECD reflecting in part the importance of cross-border workers. However, labour productivity remains well below its pre-crisis peak.
- In priority areas, major reforms of the school system undertaken in recent years will improve education prospects for residents. The public employment service is being overhauled to improve matching and strengthen conditionality. Reforms have been limited in other priority areas.
- In other areas, action is being taken to curb greenhouse gas emissions and meet energy efficiency goals.

Performance and policy indicators

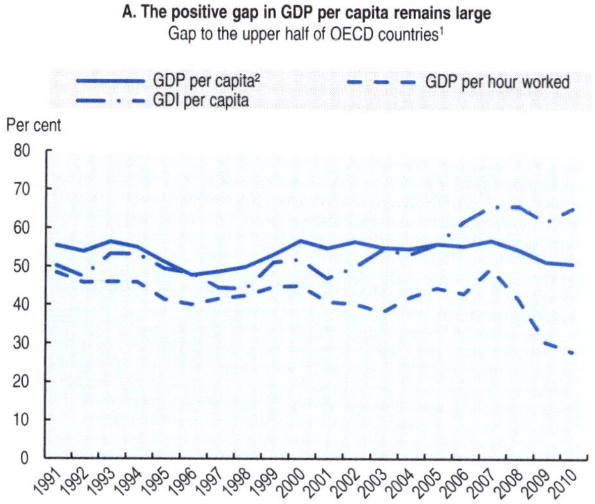

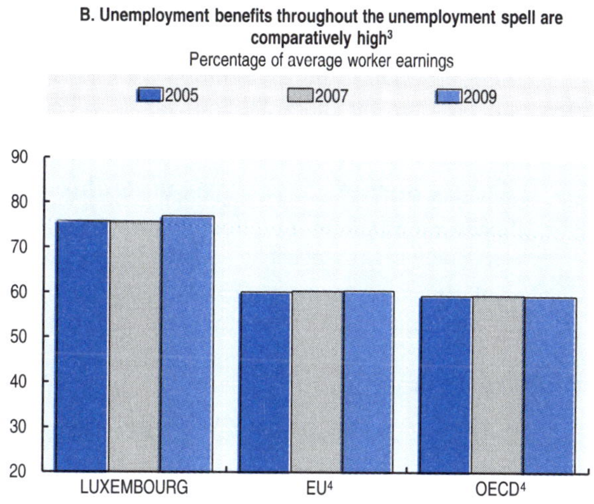

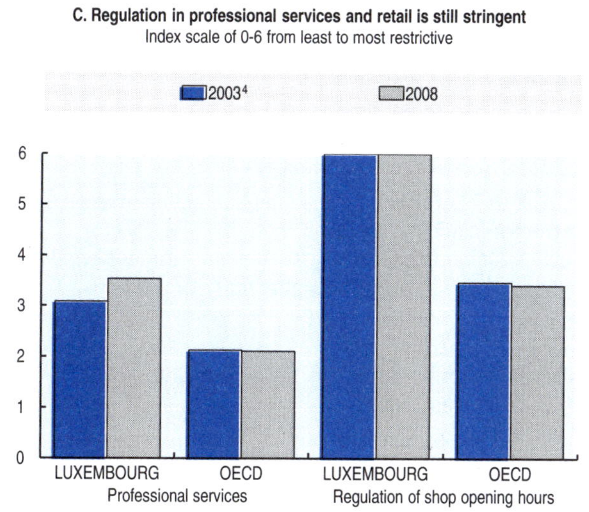

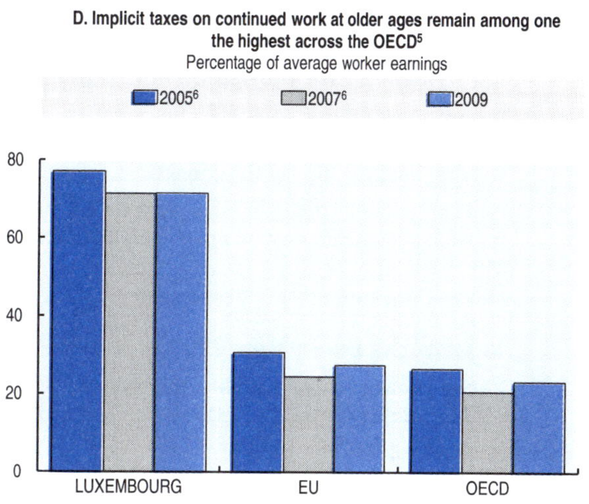

1. Percentage gap with respect to the simple average of the highest 17 OECD countries in terms of GDP per capita, GDP per hour worked and GDI per capita (in constant 2005 PPPs).
2. The population is augmented by the number of cross-border workers in order to take into account their contribution to GDP.
3. Average of replacement rates for short and long-term unemployed persons who earned 67% and 100% of average worker earnings at the time of losing job.
4. Average of European countries in the OECD. OECD average excludes Chile, Estonia, Israel and Slovenia.
5. Implicit tax on continued work for five more years embedded in the regular old-age pension scheme for 60 year olds.
6. Average of European countries in the OECD. EU and OECD averages exclude Chile, Estonia, Israel and Slovenia.

Source: Chart A: OECD, *National Accounts and Economic Outlook No. 90 Databases*; Chart B: OECD, *Benefits and Wages Database*; Chart C: OECD, *Product Market Regulation Database*; Chart D: Duval, R. (2003), "The Retirement Effects of Old-Age Pension and Early Retirement Schemes in OECD Countries", *OECD Economics Department Working Papers*, No. 370, OECD Publishing and OECD calculations.

StatLink http://dx.doi.org/10.1787/888932565547

MEXICO

Priorities supported by indicators

Raise achievement in primary and secondary education (2007, 2009, 2011)

Recommendations: Reallocate education funding to non-wage spending and improve the preparation and incentives for teachers to enhance students' learning outcomes.

Actions taken: The government has launched a programme in 2008 to progressively renovate and equip schools with computers. Since 2008 new teachers have been selected through a centralised exit exam and the government has started to implement a new incentive scheme focusing on teacher performance in 2010. Within education funding, non-wage expenditure increased by 24% in real terms between 2007 and 2010, whereas wage expenditure increased by 4%.

Reduce barriers to entry in network industries (2007, 2009, 2011)

Recommendations: Increase competition, in particular in the main network industries.

Actions taken: The 2011 competition policy reform increases fines and the scope for criminal prosecution for individuals engaged in collusion. The government auctioned part of the radio spectrum and a fibre-optic network in 2010.

Reduce barriers to foreign ownership (2007, 2009, 2011)

Recommendations: Ease restrictions on foreign direct investment in services and infrastructure, especially in the electricity sector and fixed line telephony.

Actions taken: The lower chamber of congress approved a law in 2008 reducing ownership restrictions in telecommunications. Approval in the upper chamber is pending.

Other key priorities

Improve the "rule of law" (2007, 2009, 2011)

Recommendations: Improve the rule of law by clarifying property rights and ensuring more predictable and effective law enforcement.

Actions taken: In 2011 the Supreme Court decided that telecommunication companies can no longer ignore rulings of the regulator on interconnection charges while challenging these in court.

Reform the state-owned oil company (2009, 2011)

Recommendations: Improve the governance and operating efficiency of PEMEX, the national oil company, by lifting investment constraints and strengthening accountability. Ease risk and profit sharing partnerships with other companies so as to facilitate access to technologies.

Actions taken: Since the Supreme Court approved in 2010 a reform launched by the government in 2008, PEMEX can now pay cash incentives to subcontractors, facilitating investment in the oil sector. The auction of the first incentive contracts between PEMEX and the private sector was concluded successfully in August 2011. However, PEMEX cannot share profits or property rights for hydrocarbons.

Reform the tax system (2007)

Recommendations: Simplify the system and broaden the tax base by limiting exemptions and preferential regimes to efficiently finance growth-enhancing investments.

Actions taken: The government introduced a minimum tax on businesses (Impuesto Empresarial a Tasa Unica, IETU) in 2007, which closes tax loopholes to some extent. The government increased the VAT rate along with other taxes in 2010, although without broadening the tax base.

MEXICO

- The wide income gap with the leading OECD economies is mainly due to low productivity, which has grown too slowly for catch-up in recent years.
- Among key priority areas, Mexico has made significant progress in aligning its competition policy framework with international best practice, but little action has been taken to ensure the efficiency of judicial procedures. Reforms have also been carried out to improve the quality of education and the tax structure. Progress in reducing barriers to foreign investment has been limited.
- Outside priority areas, Congress is debating a labour reform proposal that would reduce the cost of court procedures after dismissal and introduce probationary and training periods. The government also introduced a tax break for employers hiring workers who enter the formal economy for the first time. The well-targeted cash transfer programme, Oportunidades, is being expanded to further reduce high poverty and inequality.

Performance and policy indicators

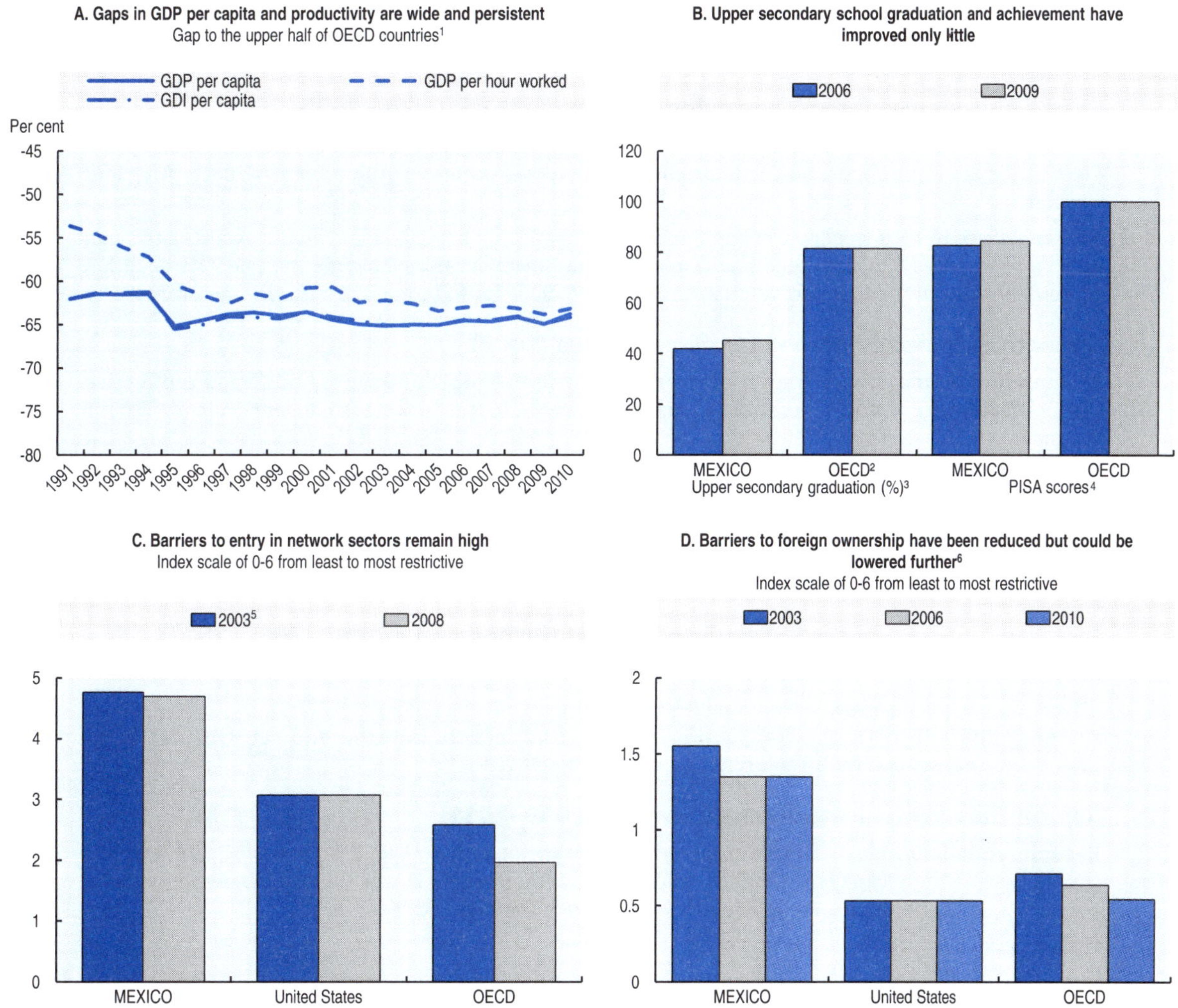

1. Percentage gap with respect to the simple average of the highest 17 OECD countries in terms of GDP per capita, GDP per hour worked and GDI per capita (in constant 2005 PPPs).
2. Average of OECD countries excluding Australia, Austria, Belgium, Estonia, France and the Netherlands.
3. First-time graduation rates for single year of age at upper secondary level.
4. Average score of student performance in mathematics, science and reading. Index OECD = 100.
5. The OECD average excludes Chile, Estonia, Israel and Slovenia.
6. The OECD FDI regulatory restrictiveness index looks only at statutory restrictions and does not assess the manner in which they are implemented.

Source: Chart A: OECD, *National Accounts and Economic Outlook No. 90 Databases*; Chart B: OECD (2011), *Education at a Glance* and OECD, *PISA 2009 Database*; Chart C: OECD, *Product Market Regulation Database*; Chart D: *http://www.oecd.org/investment/index*.

StatLink http://dx.doi.org/10.1787/888932565566

NETHERLANDS

Priorities supported by indicators

Lower marginal effective tax rates on labour income (2007, 2009, 2011)

Recommendations: Reduce subsidies for owner-occupied housing and broaden the VAT tax base to finance lower labour taxes. Reduce the effective marginal tax rate arising from benefits such as the family-income based tax credit, second-earner tax credit, housing and child benefits.

Actions taken: In 2009 the government introduced several income-based tax credits to reduce disincentives to higher participation and hours worked for low-income workers and second earners.

Reform disability benefit schemes (2007, 2009, 2011)

Recommendations: Tighten gate-keeping and medical controls for existing benefit recipients. De-couple benefits from past earnings over the disability spell and exclude them from wage agreements.

Actions taken: In 2010 some reforms to limit entry into the disability programme for young people (Wajong) came into force. The government's proposals to further restrict entry into disability schemes for those (partly) able to work and to make work pay by 2013 are still to be passed through parliament.

Ease employment protection legislation for regular contracts (2009, 2011)

Recommendations: Relax employment protection legislation for regular contracts by making the dismissal system simpler and more predictable. Cap severance payments, particularly for older workers.

Actions taken: In 2009 local courts adopted new guidelines on severance payments awarded through judicial procedures, which should result in somewhat lower severance payments. The 2010 coalition agreement stipulates capping severance pay at EUR 75 000, limited to public and care sector workers.

Strengthen competition in network industries (2007)

Recommendations: Privatise local-government-owned network industries and secure effective vertical separation. Introduce cost-based access pricing. Adopt a "silence is consent" rule for issuing licenses.

Actions taken: In 2006 a law was passed stipulating full ownership separation of the energy distribution networks from supply companies by 2011. This has been overruled by the court of appeal in 2010.

Other key priorities

Increase the scope of the unregulated part of the housing market (2007, 2011)

Recommendations: Deregulate the rental sector. Shift taxation of housing away from purchase to ownership and ease the strict land regulation.

Actions taken: In 2011, the transaction tax was temporarily lowered and rent regulation in high-scarcity areas and for high-income groups was loosened.

Reform the unemployment benefit system (2009, 2011)

Recommendations: Maximum unemployment benefit duration should be lowered and benefits should decline more rapidly throughout the unemployment spell. Lower the cap on unemployment benefits to further enhance the job-search incentives of the high-skilled.

Actions taken: No significant action taken.

Promote competition in retail distribution services (2007, 2009)

Recommendations: Phase-out existing restrictions on shop-opening hours. Facilitate the entry of large retail stores and ease zoning regulations.

Actions taken: No significant action taken.

NETHERLANDS

- Over the past two decades, GDP per capita has remained roughly in line with that of the upper half of OECD countries. The positive gap in hourly productivity has remained stable since the mid-2000s, and is being offset by relatively low hours worked.
- Among key priority areas, the government initiated reforms in the disability system to increase employment and improve gate-keeping, but most laws are yet to be approved. Current plans to reduce severance payments foresee limiting them for public and care sector workers. Some actions have been taken to improve the functioning of the housing market, but not in the area of unemployment benefits and retail trade regulation.
- Outside priority areas, temporary crisis-related measures that helped mitigate the employment impact of the downturn included a short-time work scheme and expanded opportunities for employers to offer temporary contracts.

Performance and policy indicators

A. There has been a relative decline in productivity levels
Gap to the upper half of OECD countries[1]

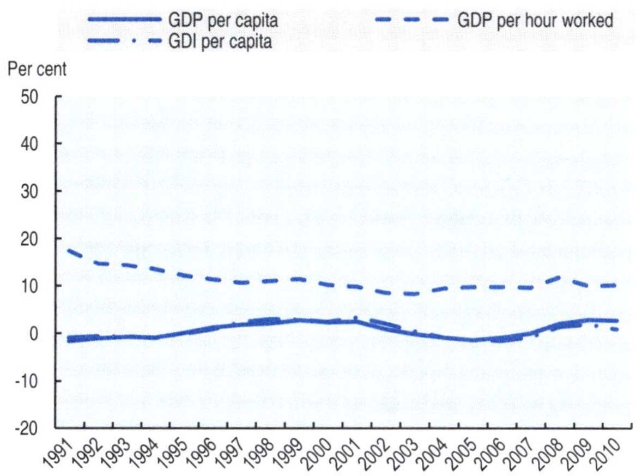

B. Marginal labour tax wedges remain relatively high for low-income workers[2]
Percentage of total labour compensation[3]

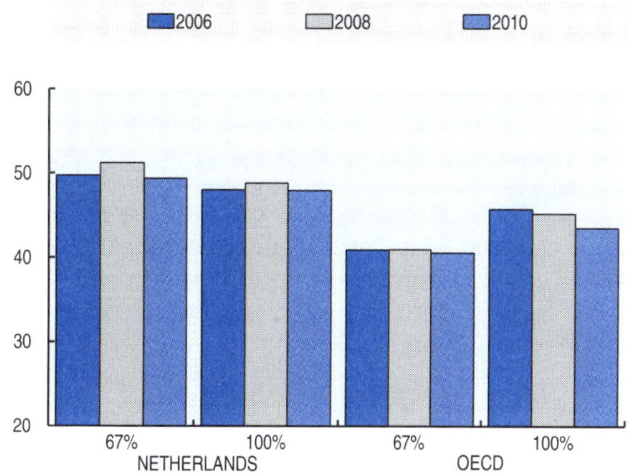

C. Despite some decline, the share of working-age population receiving disability benefits remains high
Percentage of the population aged 20-64

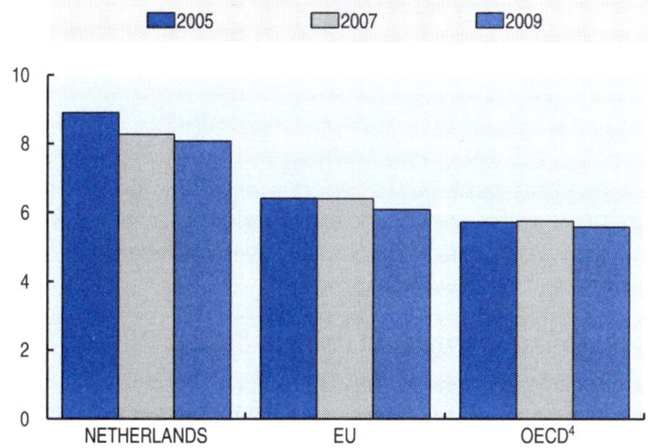

D. Employment protection legislation for permanent workers has been eased but is still comparatively strict
Index scale of 0-6 from least to most restrictive

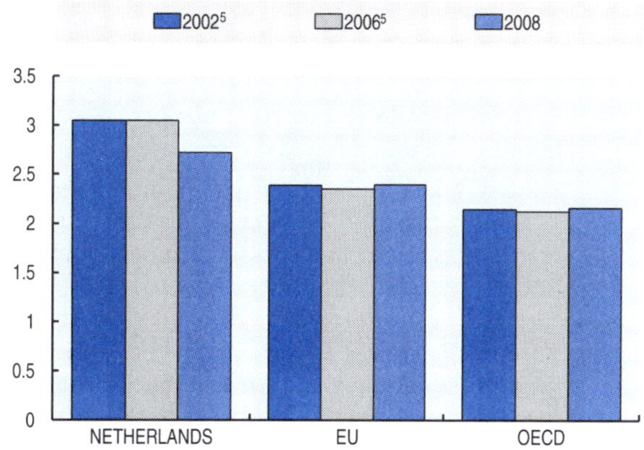

1. Percentage gap with respect to the simple average of the highest 17 OECD countries in terms of GDP per capita, GDP per hour worked and GDI per capita (in constant 2005 PPPs).
2. Labour taxes include personal income tax and employee plus employer social security contributions and any payroll tax less cash transfers.
3. Evaluated at 67% and 100% of average earnings for a single person with no child.
4. Excluding Chile, Iceland and Turkey.
5. Average of European countries in the OECD. EU and OECD averages exclude Chile, Estonia, Israel and Slovenia.

Source: Chart A: OECD, *National Accounts and Economic Outlook No. 90 Databases*; Chart B: OECD, *Taxing Wages Database*; Chart C: OECD (2010), *Sickness, Disability and Work: Breaking the Barriers: A Synthesis of Findings across OECD Countries*; Chart D: OECD, *Employment Database*.

StatLink http://dx.doi.org/10.1787/888932565585

NEW ZEALAND

Priorities supported by indicators

Reduce barriers to competition in network industries (2007, 2009, 2011)

Recommendations: Divest public ownership stakes and dismantle barriers to competition in energy, air transport, telecommunications and rail. Strengthen independence and accountability of network regulators.

Actions taken: An Electricity Authority and a Productivity Commission were established as independent agencies in 2010-11. The rail network was renationalised in 2008.

Reduce educational under-achievement among specific groups (2007, 2009, 2011)

Recommendations: Provide early intervention to raise numeracy and literacy of at-risk students. Support a high-quality teaching workforce by use of accountability incentives and ongoing teacher education.

Actions taken: The government funded strengthened teacher professional learning and development in 2009-10, with a particular focus on schools with high shares of disadvantaged students.

Relax barriers to foreign direct investment and reduce regulatory opacity (2011)

Recommendations: Pass a Regulatory Responsibility Act establishing transparent quality benchmarks and requiring clear net benefit tests for regulations. Ease FDI screening requirements, remove ministers' discretionary veto and clarify the criteria for protecting "sensitive land".

Actions taken: No significant action taken.

Facilitate access to childcare for working parents (2007)

Recommendations: Improve access to childcare for disadvantaged and 3 and 4 year-old children.

Actions taken: In 2007, the government introduced twenty universal, free hours of early childhood education and childcare per week for 3 and 4 year-olds.

Other key priorities

Improve efficiency in health and education (2007, 2009, 2011)

Recommendations: Increase incentives for efficiency and accountability by public health care and education providers. Continue to provide access and service quality for minority groups.

Actions taken: National standards have been developed and implemented in primary schools in 2011, with annual reporting as of 2012. From 2012, government funding in tertiary education will be partly conditioned on performance. Health reforms since 2009 have encompassed regional consolidation of hospitals and primary care organisations, increased use of benchmarking and greater decentralisation.

Raise the effectiveness of R&D support (2009, 2011)

Recommendations: Reinstate business R&D incentives, enhance the efficiency of direct public R&D funding and improve R&D policy co-ordination.

Actions taken: In 2010, the government introduced a new business R&D support scheme including targeted grants and vouchers, and it restructured key innovation agencies into a single Ministry for Science. A national network of commercialisation centres is being established and university research funding incentives have been adapted to facilitate applied and commercial research.

Deal with infrastructure bottlenecks, especially in transport and energy (2007, 2009)

Recommendations: Change regulations, notably by reducing discretion and inconsistency in local resource consenting, to unblock investments. Use tolls and congestion pricing to restrain demand.

Actions taken: The government reformed the Resource Management Act in 2009 to streamline procedures for obtaining resource exploitation consents. The first toll road opened in 2009.

NEW ZEALAND

- The GDP per capita gap relative to the upper half of OECD countries narrowed in the global recession but remains high. It is more than explained by a significant lag in hourly labour productivity, whereas labour utilisation remains among the highest in the OECD.
- Among key priority areas, reforms in health care, education and R&D support are going in the direction of more efficient public spending. By contrast, little has been done to eliminate barriers to FDI.
- In other areas, an emission trading scheme has been introduced and personal and corporate income tax rates are being reduced.

Performance and policy indicators

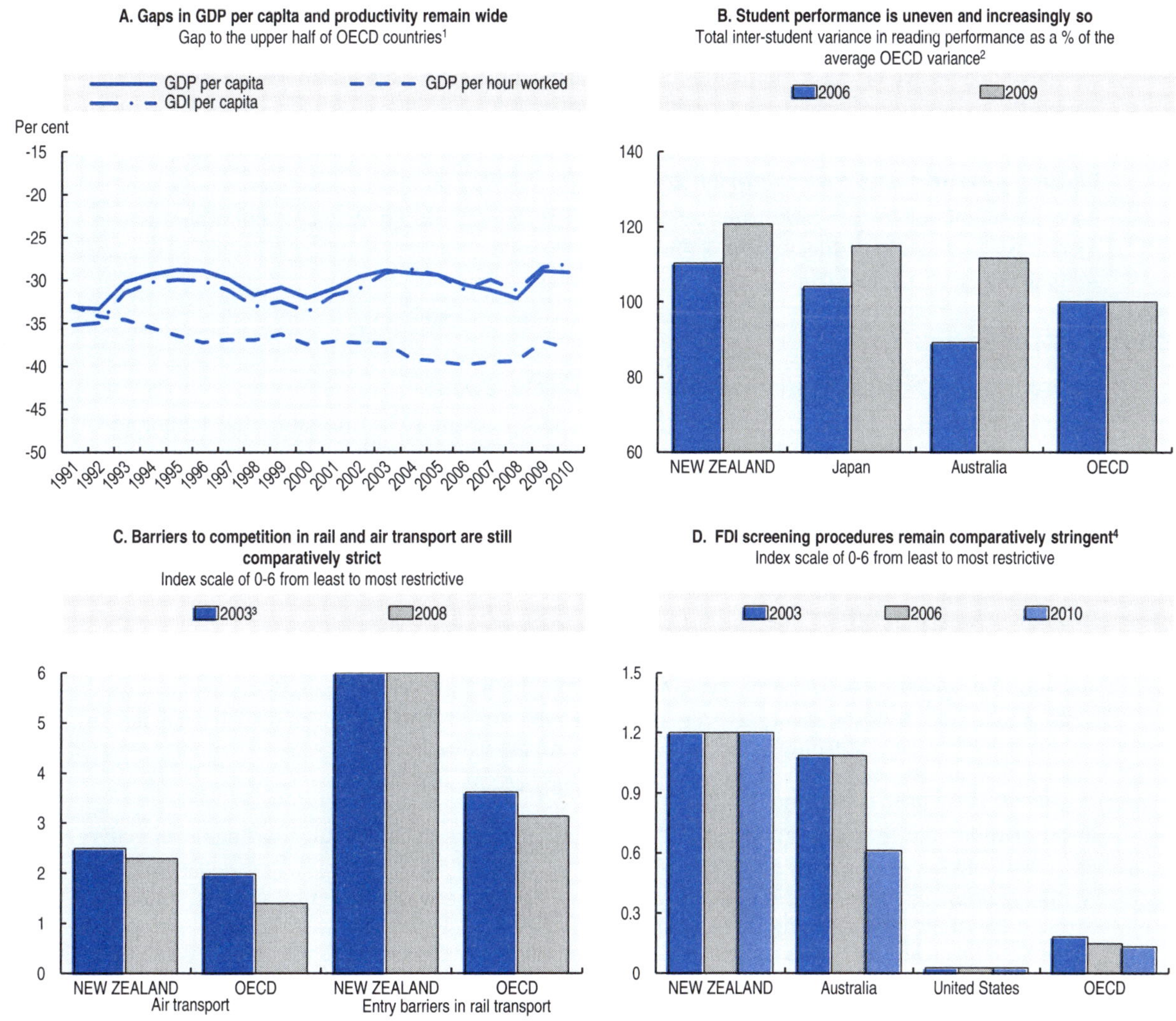

1. Percentage gap with respect to the simple average of the highest 17 OECD countries in terms of GDP per capita, GDP per hour worked and GDI per capita (in constant 2005 PPPs).
2. The variance components, in reading performance only, were estimated for all students in participating countries with data on socio-economic background and study programmes.
3. The OECD average excludes Chile, Estonia, Israel and Slovenia.
4. The OECD FDI regulatory restrictiveness index looks only at statutory restrictions and does not assess the manner in which they are implemented.

Source: Chart A: OECD, *National Accounts and Economic Outlook No. 90 Databases*; Chart B: OECD, *PISA 2006 and 2009 Databases*; Chart C: OECD, *Product Market Regulation Database*; Chart D: *http://www.oecd.org/investment/index.*

StatLink http://dx.doi.org/10.1787/888932565623

NORWAY

Priorities supported by indicators

Reform disability and sickness benefit schemes (2007, 2009, 2011)

Recommendations: Make increased use of independent doctors to certify sickness and disability and/or improve incentives by lowering replacement rates. Expand use of partial disability payments for the disabled who take up part-time work.

Actions taken: The 2008 requirement for a joint employer-employee back-to-work plan for each sickness benefit recipient failed to halt the trend. New measures were introduced in 2011, *e.g.* to sanction employers and employees and require mandatory training for certifying doctors.

Increase product market competition (2007, 2009, 2011)

Recommendations: Strengthen competition in network industries, especially in transport and postal services, as well as in the retail sector. Reduce public ownership.

Actions taken: The government sold a fibre-optic company, but some minor backward actions have also been taken such as the simplification of procedures for the government to overrule competition authority decisions in 2008 and the tightening of restrictions on establishing out-of-town shopping centres.

Reduce producer support to agriculture (2007, 2009, 2011)

Recommendations: Reduce tariffs, quotas and seasonal import restrictions on agricultural products. Reduce restrictions on trading in fishing quotas.

Actions taken: No action taken.

Other key priorities

Improve education efficiency and outcomes (2009, 2011)

Recommendations: Reduce the number of schools and focus more on migrants' needs. Enhance school and teacher accountability by making wider use of performance indicators. Improve teacher training and career paths.

Actions taken: From 2009, candidates for teacher training must meet more stringent entry requirements. The government requirement for municipalities to prepare performance reports was strengthened in 2010, but there is no obligation to publish performance at the school level.

Improve the efficiency of the tax structure (2009, 2011)

Recommendations: Reduce personal income taxation and shift the composition of taxes toward consumption and property. Remove the undervaluation of housing in the wealth tax.

Actions taken: In 2010, steps were taken to move the valuation of housing for the wealth tax closer to market values, but it is still only a fraction of the full market valuation.

Implement a comprehensive pension reform (2007)

Recommendations: Introduce an actuarially neutral pension system aimed at increasing the effective retirement age.

Actions taken: The reform of the National Insurance scheme was completed in 2011, ensuring actuarial neutrality and allowing for flexible retirement after 62. However, while the early retirement scheme in the private sector was adjusted in a similar way, the public sector retains high incentives to early retirement.

NORWAY

- Norway's non-oil economy has maintained a high level of GDP per capita relative to the upper half of OECD countries, owing mainly to high productivity.
- In key priority areas, measures have been taken to improve education efficiency, and the private sector pension system has been reformed. Little has been done to contain sickness and disability benefit take-up and to increase product market competition.
- In other areas, the merger of the Public Employment Services and National Insurance Services was completed in early 2011.

Performance and policy indicators

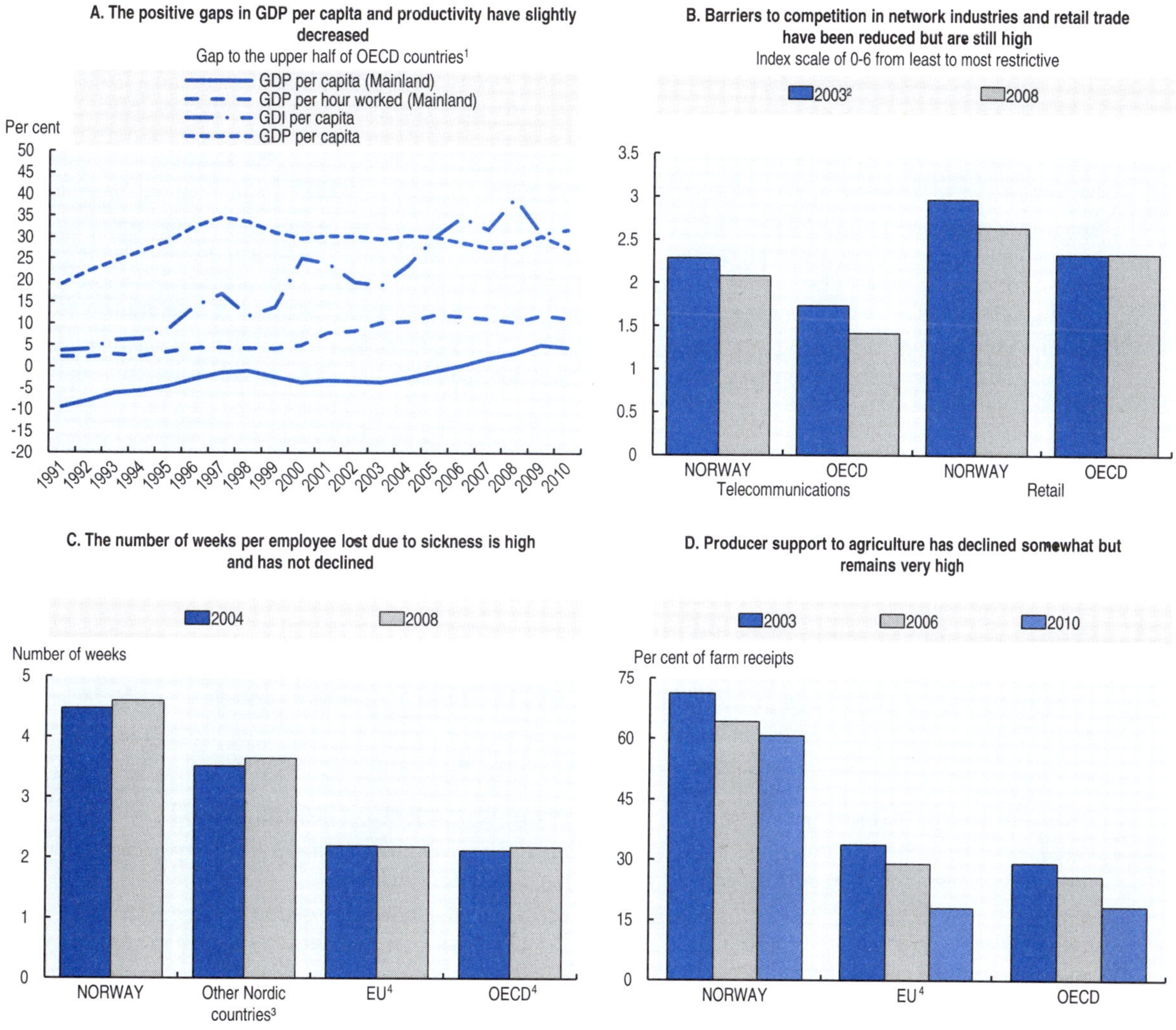

1. Percentage gap with respect to the simple average of the highest 17 OECD countries in terms of GDP per capita, GDP per hour worked and GDI per capita (in constant 2005 PPPs). GDP per capita (Mainland) excludes petroleum production and shipping. While total GDP overestimates the sustainable income potential, mainland GDP slightly underestimates it since returns on the financial assets the petroleum fund holds abroad are not included.
2. The OECD average excludes Chile, Estonia, Israel and Slovenia.
3. Average of Denmark, Finland and Sweden.
4. Average of European countries in the OECD. EU and OECD averages exclude Chile, Estonia, Israel and Slovenia in Panel C.

Source: Chart A: OECD, *National Accounts and Economic Outlook No. 90 Databases*; Chart B: OECD, *Product Market Regulation Database*; Chart C: OECD (2010), *Sickness, Disability and Work: Breaking the Barriers: A Synthesis of Findings across OECD Countries*; Chart D: OECD, *Producer and Consumer Support Estimates Database*.

StatLink http://dx.doi.org/10.1787/888932565604

POLAND

Priorities supported by indicators

Reduce public ownership and lower barriers to entrepreneurship (2007, 2009, 2011)

Recommendations: Boost the privatisation process. Reduce state interference in privatised companies, and shorten the time needed for setting up a new firm.

Actions taken: Privatisation has been slow but has accelerated since 2009 in part to curb the rising debt-to-GDP ratio. In 2009, the government created a one-stop shop for start-ups, and a new law was voted in 2011 aimed at cutting red tape further so as to lower barriers to entrepreneurship.

Reform the tax and benefit system (2007, 2009, 2011)

Recommendations: Reduce the tax wedge and tighten access to early retirement schemes.

Actions taken: Between 2007 and 2009, personal income taxes and social security contribution rates were cut and a child tax credit introduced. In 2008, the government significantly tightened eligibility criteria for the general early retirement scheme. Partially diverting pension contributions from the second fully-funded pension pillar to the first PAYGO (notional accounts) pillar in 2011 will most likely improve long-term fiscal sustainability at the cost of further reducing already very low future replacement rates.

Improve the efficiency of the education system (2007, 2009, 2011)

Recommendations: Improve provision of free pre-school education for those aged three to five. Introduce tuition fees in public higher-education institutions (HEIs) along with a more accessible system of means-tested grants and student loans with income-contingent repayment. Reinforce quality assessment and the transparency of promotion criteria for professors in tertiary education.

Actions taken: A law promoting attendance in public pre-schools for 5 year-old children was passed in 2009, but its implementation was delayed to 2013. A 2011 law requires HEIs to fill research and teaching vacancies competitively.

Other key priorities

Upgrade transport and communication infrastructure (2007, 2009, 2011)

Recommendations: Enhance transport and communication infrastructure.

Actions taken: Transport infrastructure is being upgraded with the help of EU structural funds.

Reform housing policies (2009, 2011)

Recommendations: Make the release of zoning plans by municipalities mandatory, introduce compulsory escrow accounts to protect buyers' advances, and further relax rent controls.

Actions taken: In 2010, the government lifted rent restrictions, reduced tenants' legal protection and generalised the lower 8.5% tax rate on rental income to curb the informal rental market.

Promote competition in professional services and telecommunications (2007)

Recommendations: Simplify regulations in professional services and facilitate third-party access to the network segment (including broadband Internet) in telecommunications.

Actions taken: No action taken for professional services. The telecom regulator became more independent from the government in 2009, through both a fixed five-year term appointment for its president and the establishment of conditions for its dismissal.

POLAND

- Convergence in GDP per capita has accelerated, but the shortfall relative to the upper half of the OECD countries remains large primarily due to a labour productivity gap.
- In key priority areas, the tax wedge has been lowered considerably, helping prop up labour demand during the crisis. Eligibility criteria for early retirement and disability pension schemes have been tightened and barriers to entrepreneurship reduced. However, improving the efficiency of education and reducing barriers to foreign ownership remain unaddressed priorities, and the privatisation of majority stakes in State-owned firms needs to be expedited.
- In other areas, temporary measures aimed at alleviating the consequences of the crisis include an increase in working time flexibility and job subsidies, and more emphasis given to active labour market policies, the latter being part of a long-term effort to move towards flexicurity.

Performance and policy indicators

A. The large gaps in GDP per capita and productivity continue to narrow

Gap to the upper half of OECD countries[1]

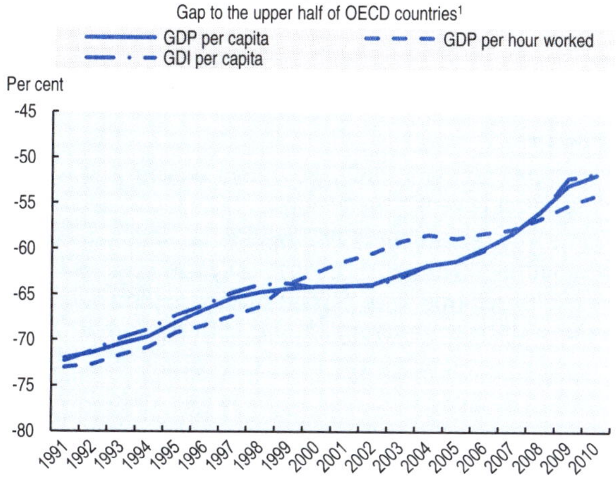

B. State control and barriers to entrepreneurship have been reduced but are still comparatively high

Index scale of 0-6 from least to most restrictive

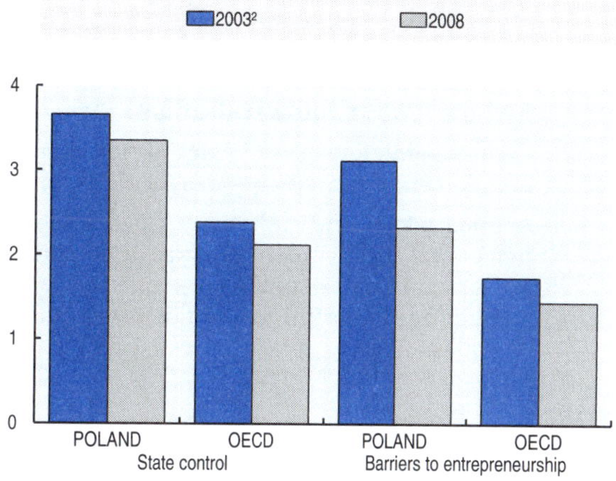

C. Tertiary educational attainment is catching up

Percentage of population aged 25-34

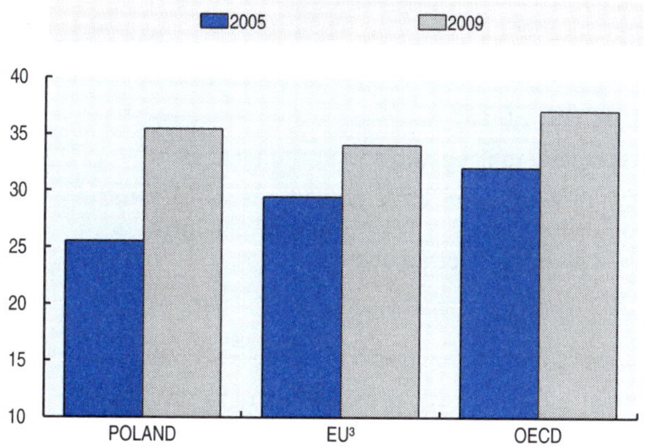

D. The average tax wedge on labour income[4] has been lowered but remains relatively high

Percentage of total labour compensation

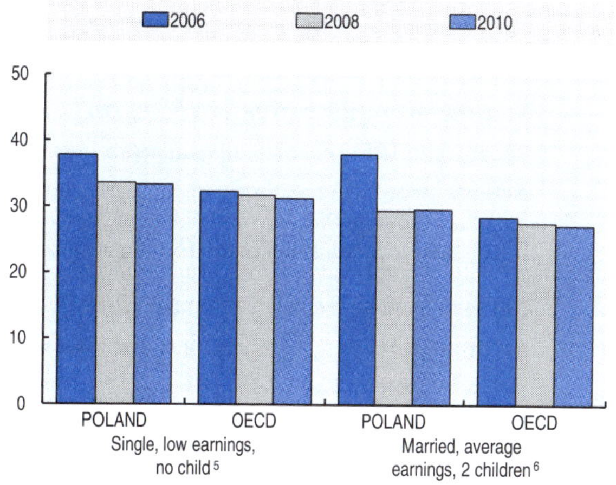

1. Percentage gap with respect to the simple average of the highest 17 OECD countries in terms of GDP per capita, GDP per hour worked and GDI per capita (in constant 2005 PPPs).
2. The OECD average excludes Chile, Estonia, Israel and Slovenia.
3. Average of European countries in the OECD.
4. Labour taxes include personal income tax and employee plus employer social security contributions and any payroll tax less cash transfers.
5. Low earnings refer to two-thirds of average earnings.
6. At 100% of the average worker earnings for the first earner. Average of three situations regarding the wage of the second earner (0%, 33% and 67% of average earnings).

Source: Chart A: OECD, *National Accounts and Economic Outlook No. 90 Databases*; Chart B: OECD, *Product Market Regulation Database*; Chart C: OECD (2011), *Education at a Glance*; Chart D: OECD, *Taxing Wages Database*.

StatLink http://dx.doi.org/10.1787/888932565642

PORTUGAL

Priorities supported by indicators

Improve secondary and tertiary education attainment (2007, 2009, 2011)

Recommendations: Improve outcomes and equity by reducing school-year repetition and enhancing teacher and school accountability. Further expand vocational education and training (VET).

Actions taken: The authorities have expanded VET for youngsters and low-skilled adults (*Novas Oportunidades* programme) and since 2007 have introduced tertiary education reforms, comprising governance, degrees and adults enrolment. The compulsory education age was raised from 15 to 18 (2009). The government introduced (2007) and revised (2010) a national teacher performance evaluation system.

Strengthen competition in non-manufacturing sectors (2007, 2009, 2011)

Recommendations: Reduce barriers to competition in network industries, retail and professional services.

Actions taken: The authorities unbundled energy networks, eased regulation of large outlets (2009, 2010), eliminated the state's special rights in privatised companies (2011) and presented a roadmap for phasing out regulated energy tariffs (2011). In 2011 they also announced plans to carry out privatisations in network sectors and liberalise regulated professions.

Reduce labour market dualism (2007, 2009, 2011)

Recommendations: Ease job protection on regular contracts and reduce unemployment benefit (UB) duration and replacement rates for older workers, while better covering the young.

Actions taken: The authorities relaxed legislation on regular contracts (2009), mainly by reducing procedural inconveniences and notice periods for individual dismissals. In 2011 they introduced legislation to lower severance payments for new hires, with reforms to be carried further in 2012 by expanding the definition of fair dismissal and making UB less generous, along with extended eligibility.

Other key priorities

Simplify the tax system and broaden tax bases (2007, 2009, 2011)

Recommendations: Improve tax collection and substantially curb tax expenditures for all types of taxes.

Actions taken: The tax administration has made steady progress in electronic tax filing and payment, sped up the handling of tax disputes (2009) and started a broad updating of dwellings' taxable values (2011). The 2012 Budget contains major base-broadening reforms in consumption and income taxes.

Reduce administrative burdens on business (2009, 2011)

Recommendations: Lower administrative burdens, especially in licensing and at the local level.

Actions taken: The authorities have continued to simplify administrative procedures at the central and local levels (*Simplex* and *Simplex Autárquico* programmes). In 2011 the government introduced legislation to abolish licensing for some services, to be extended to other sectors.

Reform public administration (2007)

Recommendations: Restructure the administration, assess performance and increase staff mobility.

Actions taken: The authorities restructured central administration (PRACE programme) and implemented performance assessment in 2009. In 2011 they started a new round of central government streamlining, to be extended to local governments in 2012-13, and announced reforms to promote mobility.

PORTUGAL

- GDP per capita relative to the upper half of OECD countries has declined over the past decade. This trend decline has been mainly accounted for by a relative fall in labour utilisation, but lower productivity alone explains the large gap in income levels.
- Against the background of the recession and the euro area sovereign debt crisis, Portugal negotiated an EU/IMF financial assistance programme, under which certain structural reforms are being implemented. In priority areas, substantial progress has been made since 2007 in improving educational attainment, reducing administrative burdens on business and reforming employment protection, although more efforts are needed to address labour market dualism. The areas of unemployment benefits and tax base broadening have witnessed less progress.
- In other areas, a major pension reform was implemented in 2007-08. Labour market support measures introduced during the crisis, and mostly withdrawn in 2010, included targeted reductions in non-wage costs, expansions in short-time working schemes and job-search, training and income support for the unemployed.

Performance and policy indicators

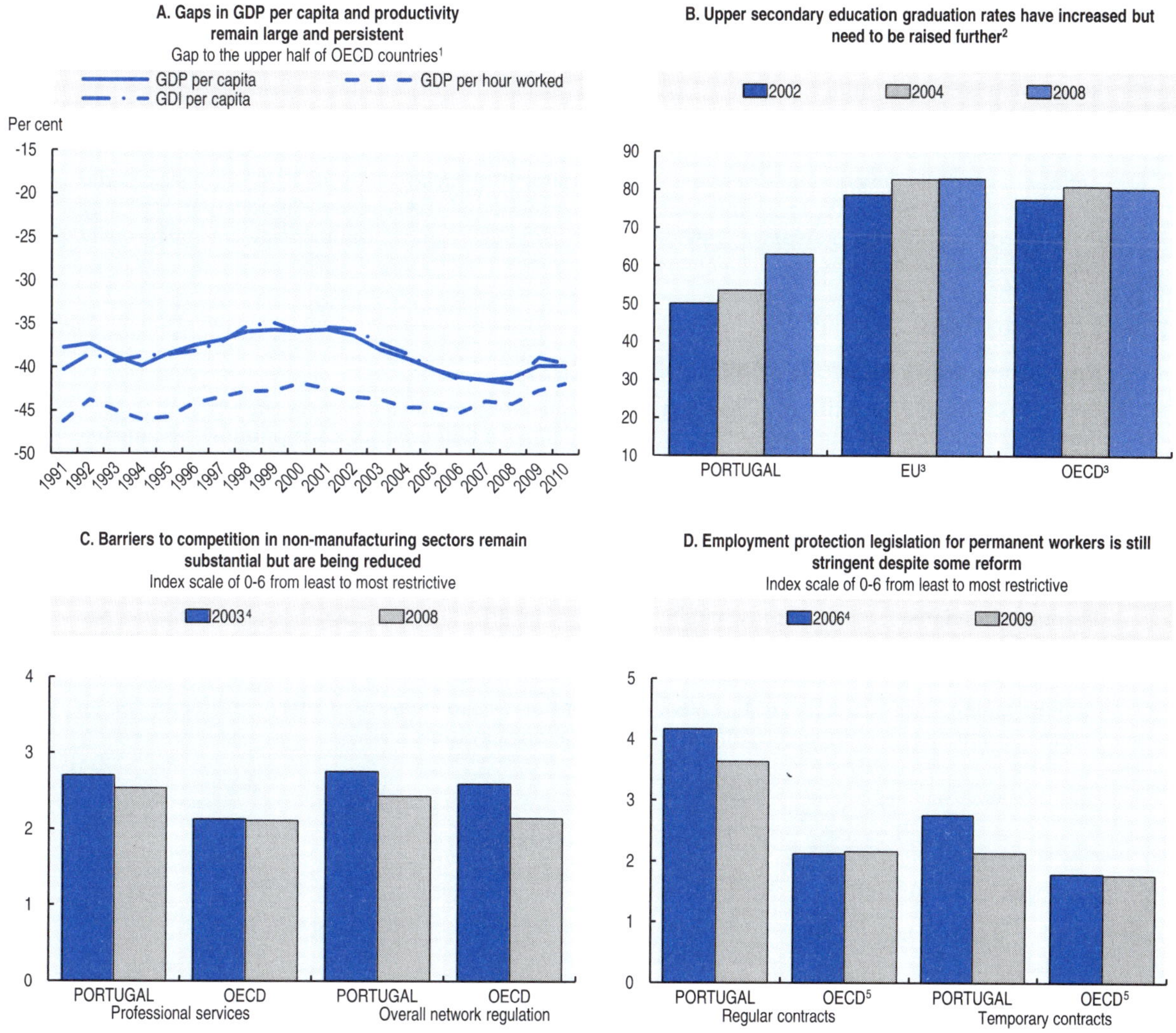

1. Percentage gap with respect to the simple average of the highest 17 OECD countries in terms of GDP per capita, GDP per hour worked and GDI per capita (in constant 2005 PPPs).
2. First-time graduation rates for single year of age at upper secondary level.
3. Average of European countries in the OECD. EU and OECD averages exclude Australia, Austria, Belgium, Estonia, France and the Netherlands.
4. The OECD average excludes Chile, Estonia, Israel and Slovenia.
5. Years 2006 and 2008.

Source: Chart A: OECD, *National Accounts and Economic Outlook No. 90 Databases*; Chart B: OECD (2011), *Education at a Glance*; Chart C: OECD, *Product Market Regulation Database*; Chart D: OECD, *Employment Database*.

StatLink http://dx.doi.org/10.1787/888932565661

RUSSIAN FEDERATION

Priorities supported by indicators

Lower barriers to trade and foreign direct investment (2011)

Recommendations: Discontinue discriminatory trade measures introduced during the crisis. Reduce tariff levels and dispersion. Shorten the list of strategic sectors in which foreign acquisitions require prior government approval.

Actions taken: The narrowing in March 2011 of the list of activities of strategic importance performed by non-state-owned banks removed the need for prior government approval for foreign acquisitions in this sector. Tariffs for selected agricultural products were reduced in response to the food price shock resulting from the drought in the summer of 2010.

Reduce state control over economic activity (2011)

Recommendations: Reduce the list of strategic enterprises. Increase the use of regulatory alternatives to direct interventions.

Actions taken: No action taken.

Raise the effectiveness of innovation policy (2011)

Recommendations: Continue the reforms in the state science sector. Monitor and regularly review the outcome of special projects. Support private-sector innovation activities through universally applied fiscal incentives and legislative framework, avoiding "picking winners".

Actions taken: The government's new innovation strategy "Innovative Russia-2020" emphasises the importance of private sector innovation activity. The creation of the Skolkovo "innovation city" may facilitate innovation, but its special legal and tax regimes go against the principles of universally applied rules and incentives.

Other key priorities

Raise the quality of public administration (2011)

Recommendations: Continue with efforts to simplify regulations and procedures and reduce bureaucratic interference in private sector activities. Reduce potential for corruption by minimising the need for subjective decision-making by bureaucrats.

Actions taken: An April 2011 legislative act requires that all draft legislation be subject to regulatory impact analysis in order to identify the provisions that create unjustified obstacles to investment.

Reform the healthcare system (2011)

Recommendations: Further increase public funding of health care and enhance the efficiency of the health care system. Focus prevention efforts on changing lifestyles. Encourage a shift from hospital to primary care. Improve the incentives for providers to deliver high-quality care.

Actions taken: Since 1 January 2011, citizens have got the right to choose a primary care doctor and an insurance company within the mandatory health insurance system.

RUSSIAN FEDERATION

- The rapid narrowing of the per capita income gap relative to the upper half of OECD countries was interrupted in 2009, as Russian Federation was relatively hard-hit by the global crisis. Income convergence has resumed but the gap with best-performing OECD countries remains large, mainly reflecting shortfalls in productivity.
- Progress has been made across most priority areas, such as easing FDI restrictions and improving innovation and healthcare policies. Little has been done to lower barriers to trade or reduce state control over economic activity.
- Outside priority areas, the decision to remove government officials from the board of state-owned enterprises was a step forward in improving corporate governance of these enterprises.

Performance and policy indicators

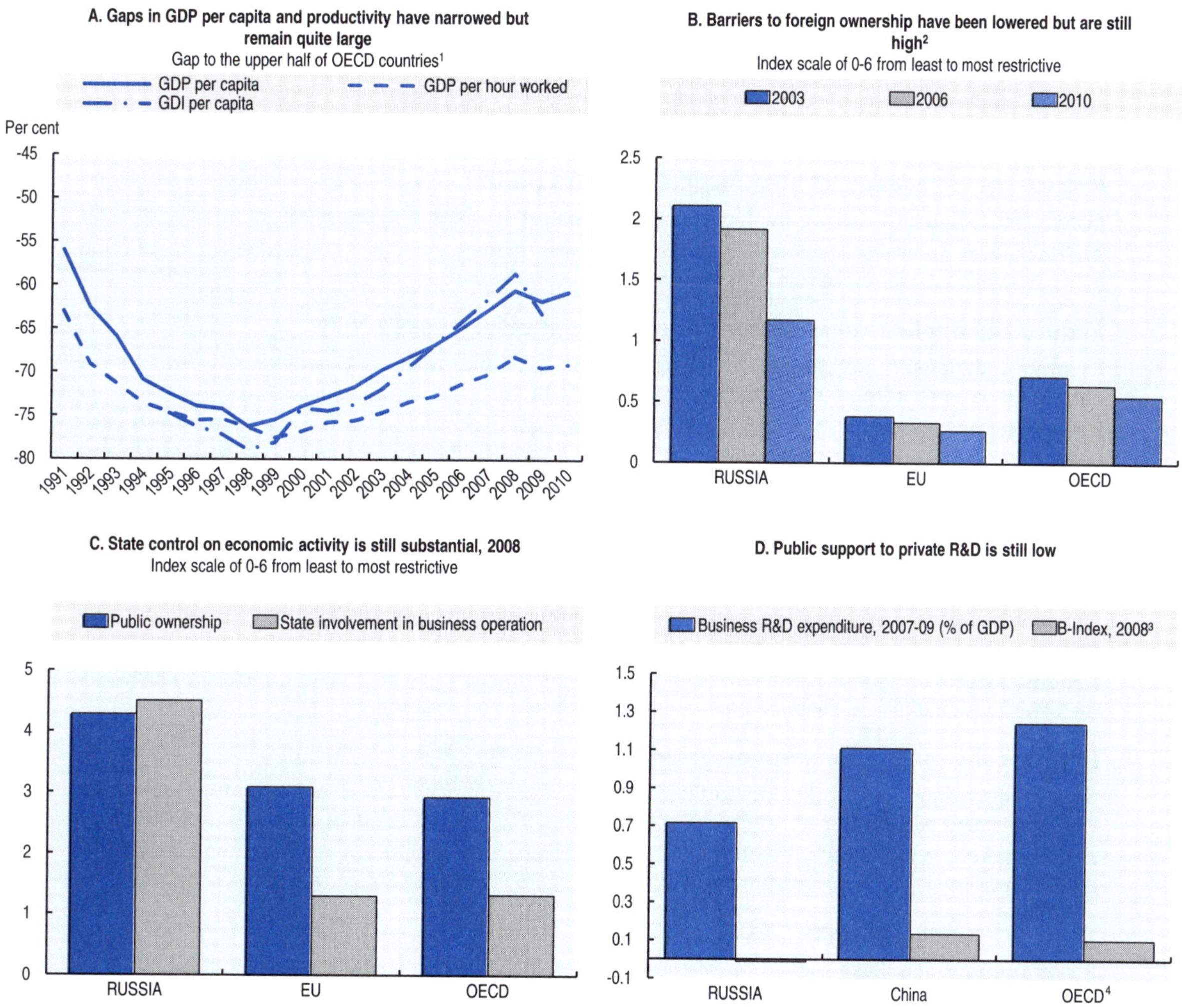

1. Percentage gap with respect to the simple average of the highest 17 OECD countries in terms of GDP per capita, GDP per hour worked and GDI per capita (in constant 2005 PPPs).
2. The OECD FDI regulatory restrictiveness index looks only at statutory restrictions and does not assess the manner in which they are implemented.
3. Measures the generosity of tax incentives to invest in R&D, on the basis of the pre-tax income necessary to cover the initial cost of one dollar R&D spending and pay corporate taxes on one dollar of profit. A value of zero on the chart would mean that the tax concession for R&D spending is just sufficient to offset the impact of the corporate tax rate. Average of SMEs and large firms.
4. Excluding Estonia and Slovenia for the B-Index.

Source: Chart A: World Bank (2011), *World Development Indicators (WDI)* and ILO (2011), *Key Indicators of the Labour Market (KILM) Databases*; Chart B: *http://www.oecd.org/investment/index*; Chart C: *Product Market Regulation Database*; Chart D: OECD, *Main Science and Technology Indicators Database*.

StatLink http://dx.doi.org/10.1787/888932565680

SLOVAK REPUBLIC

Priorities supported by indicators

Improve funding and effectiveness of the education system (2007, 2009, 2011)

Recommendations: Foster integration of Roma children, adapt vocational training to labour market needs, extend tuition fees to full-time students and introduce student loans with income-contingent repayments.

Actions taken: Since 2009, public funding of universities relies more on output indicators. In 2011 the authorities plan to reassess early tracking and reform the accreditation of tertiary study programmes.

Reduce regulatory barriers to competition (2009, 2011)

Recommendations: Reduce administrative burdens on corporations, resume the privatisation process in network industries, and abolish compulsory chamber membership for liberal professions.

Actions taken: In 2010, the points of single contact have been extended to liberal professions and will be developed further in 2011.

Eliminate barriers to female labour force participation (2009, 2011)

Recommendations: Shorten the duration of parental leave entitlements in favour of childcare subsidies and remove fiscal disincentives to work for second earners.

Actions taken: Since 2011, working parents are eligible for childcare subsidies.

Reduce the tax wedge for low-income workers (2007)

Recommendations: Curb the growth of the minimum cost of labour and introduce an in-work benefit.

Actions taken: An in-work benefit (employee bonus) was introduced in 2009 for workers on regular job contracts with salaries close to the minimum wage.

Reduce the implicit taxes on continued work at older ages (2007)

Recommendations: Index the retirement age to life expectancy and make pension adjustments for earlier and later retirement more actuarially neutral.

Actions taken: Access to early retirement has been tightened and a major pension reform is also envisaged for 2011 that would increase the retirement age in line with gains in life expectancy and introduce an automatic stabilisation mechanism to adjust pensions to demographic changes.

Other key priorities

Improve activation policies (2009, 2011)

Recommendations: Strengthen the capacity of the public employment service (PES), tighten conditionality requirements for jobseekers, expand training measures and target job creation subsidies more narrowly.

Actions taken: The government is discussing the reorganisation of active labour market policies and the introduction of private service providers for placement and training.

Improve the innovation support framework (2011)

Recommendations: Reduce administrative burdens on start-ups, facilitate access to venture capital and ICT, encourage collaboration between R&D institutions and improve the quality of public R&D funding.

Actions taken: In co-operation with the European Investment Fund, the government will launch the JEREMIE initiative, an EU programme providing funding to innovative SMEs by 2013.

Reform housing markets (2007, 2009)

Recommendations: Ease regulation of the private rental market, speed up resolution of tenancy disputes, strengthen competition in construction, and better target housing subsidies.

Actions taken: The government allocated state funds previously used to support construction of owner-occupied housing to rental housing projects in 2009 and 2010.

Strengthen the judicial and law enforcement systems (2007)

Recommendations: Improve accountability in the justice system by disseminating performance indicators and court statistics. Make greater use of transparent and open procedures for public procurement.

Actions taken: The 2011 Public Procurement Act will make electronic auctions gradually compulsory for most contracts and makes evaluation of tenders public.

SLOVAK REPUBLIC

- GDP per capita continues to converge relative to the upper half of OECD countries, notwithstanding some recent crisis-related setback. While hourly productivity increased continuously and more rapidly than in the best-performing OECD countries, substantial gaps remain in both productivity and labour utilisation levels.
- Among priority areas, measures have been taken to raise work incentives, increase educational attainment and strengthen competition in network industries. However, only limited action has been taken in other areas such as increasing female labour force participation, enhancing inclusiveness in the education system and removing regulatory barriers in the housing market.
- In other areas, the introduction of a short-time work scheme and of flexible working time accounts helped prevent layoffs during the crisis, and the latter measure was made permanent through the Labour Code Reform in 2011.

Performance and policy indicators

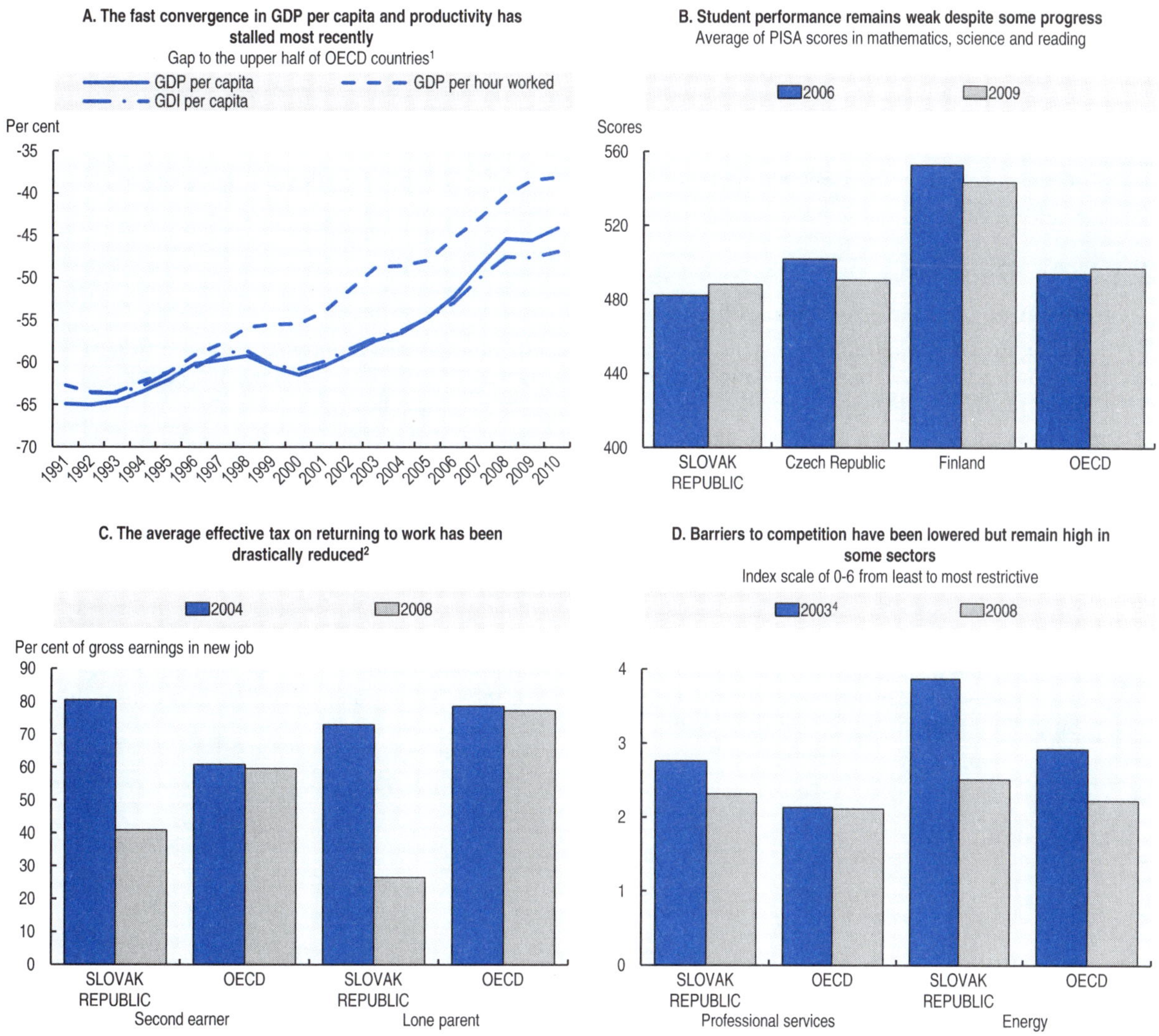

1. Percentage gap with respect to the simple average of the highest 17 OECD countries in terms of GDP per capita, GDP per hour worked and GDI per capita (in constant 2005 PPPs).
2. Taking into account childcare fees and changes of taxes and benefits in case of a transition to a job paying, two-thirds of average worker earnings.
3. The OECD average excludes Chile, Estonia, Israel, Italy, Mexico, Turkey and Slovenia.
4. The OECD average excludes Chile, Estonia, Israel and Slovenia.

Source: Chart A: OECD, *National Accounts and Economic Outlook No. 90 Databases*; Chart B: OECD, *PISA 2009 Database*; Chart C: OECD, *Benefits and Wages Database*; Chart D: OECD, *Product Market Regulation Database*.

StatLink http://dx.doi.org/10.1787/888932565699

SLOVENIA

Priorities supported by indicators

Reduce state involvement in the economy (2011)

Recommendations: Facilitate new entry in network industries by reducing state ownership and boosting competition. Devise a rigorous and transparent regime for determining which state assets should remain in public hands.

Actions taken: A draft strategy on the management of state assets was sent to the government in June 2011.

Ease employment protection legislation (2011)

Recommendations: Further reduce notice periods and administrative burdens on individual dismissals and relax the conditions under which individual dismissals are legitimate.

Actions taken: No action taken since the "mini-jobs" bill was rejected by referendum in April 2011.

Raise the statutory retirement age and reduce disincentives to work at older ages (2011)

Recommendations: Increase the statutory retirement age and limit access to early retirement. Introduce greater financial incentives to deferred retirement. Give more weight to inflation in the pension benefit indexation formula.

Actions taken: No action taken since new pension legislation was rejected by referendum in June 2010.

Other key priorities

Improve tertiary education outcomes (2011)

Recommendations: Implement policies to increase completion rates in tertiary education. Introduce tuition fees in public higher education institutions, along with student loans with income-contingent repayment. Tie access to student benefits to adequate progress in studies.

Actions taken: In March 2011, the government adopted the National Higher Education Programme 2011-20, which was later backed by Parliament in May 2011 and included proposals to recover part of costs from students who extend their studies beyond normal study durations.

Reform wage bargaining (2011)

Recommendations: Rather than postponing them, abolish the remaining steps of the horizontal equalisation of public sector wages, which resulted in disproportionate public sector wage increases in the past. Ensure the minimum wage is indexed to inflation for a while.

Actions taken: The authorities introduced a freeze on 2011 public sector wages. The minimum wage was increased by 23% in early 2010, while allowing gradual implementation (with employees' consent) by 2012 for firms facing economic difficulties.

SLOVENIA

- After some steady narrowing prior to the crisis, the income gap relative to the upper half of OECD countries has widened again. The labour productivity shortfall almost entirely explains this gap.
- In key priority areas, some progress has been made in the management of state-owned assets, while attempts to reform the pension system and ease employment protection legislation have failed.
- In other areas, to mitigate the labour market impact of the crisis, a short-time work scheme and subsidies for compensating temporarily laid off workers were introduced and later phased out. In addition, active labour market policies have been scaled up, eligibility conditions for unemployment benefits relaxed and benefit levels increased.

Performance and policy indicators

A. Convergence in GDP per capita and productivity has stalled recently

Gap to the upper half of OECD countries[1]

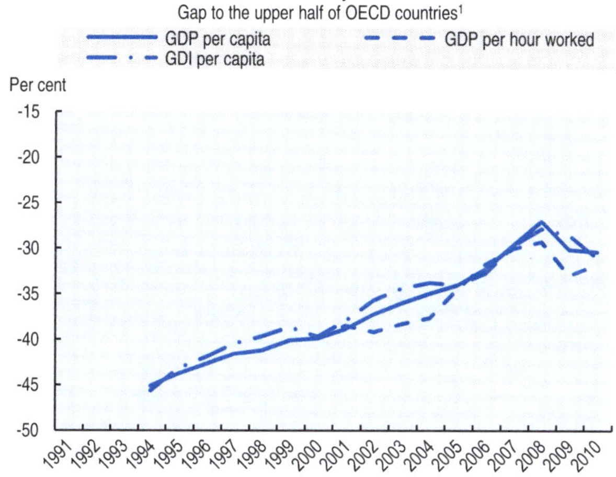

B. Implicit taxes on continued work at older ages are among the highest in the OECD, 2009[2]

Percentage of average worker earnings

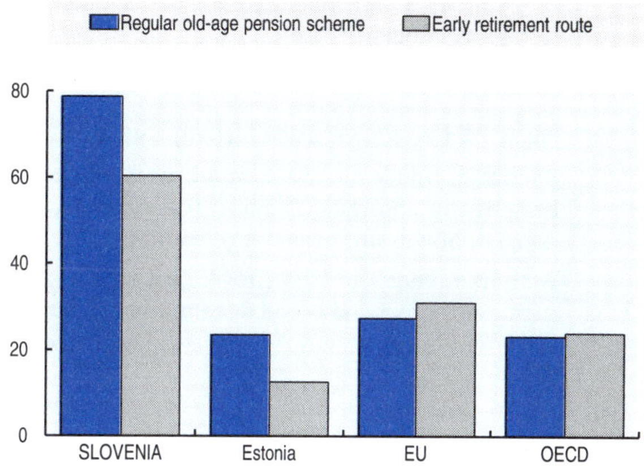

C. Employment protection legislation for regular workers is comparatively stringent, 2008

Index scale of 0-6 from least to most restrictive

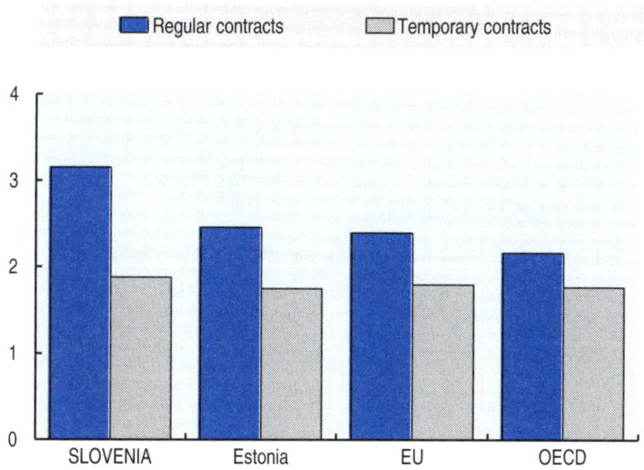

D. Tertiary education completion rates remain relatively low[3]

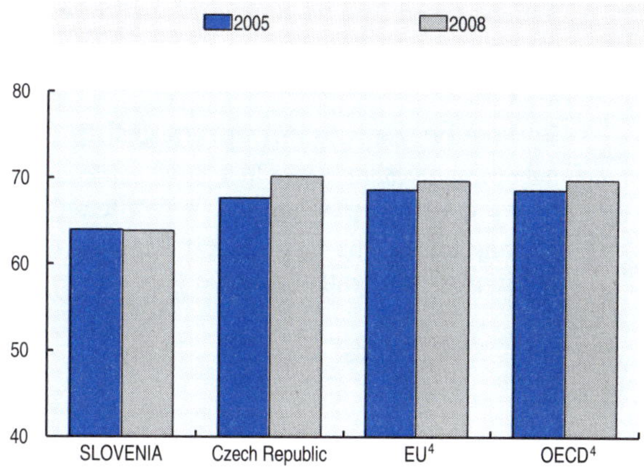

1. Percentage gap with respect to the simple average of the highest 17 OECD countries in terms of GDP per capita, GDP per hour worked and GDI per capita (in constant 2005 PPPs).
2. Implicit taxes on continued work for five more years embedded in the regular old-age pension scheme for 60 year olds and in "early retirement route" (as defined in Duval, 2003) for 55 and 60 year-olds.
3. Completion rates in tertiary-type A education represent the proportion of those who enter a tertiary-type A programme and graduate from at least a first tertiary-type A programme.
4. Average of European countries in the OECD. In 2005, EU and OECD averages exclude Chile, Greece, Ireland, Israel, Korea, Luxembourg, Spain and Turkey; and Canada, Estonia, Hungary, Italy in 2008.

Source: Chart A: OECD, *National Accounts and Economic Outlook No. 90 Databases*; Chart B: Duval, R. (2003), "The Retirement Effects of Old-Age Pension and Early Retirement Schemes in OECD Countries", OECD *Economics Department Working Papers*, No. 370, OECD Publishing and OECD calculations; Chart C: *Employment Database*; Chart D: OECD (2010 and 2008), *Education at a Glance*.

StatLink http://dx.doi.org/10.1787/888932565718

SOUTH AFRICA

Priorities supported by indicators

Raise the quality of education and reduce its dispersion (2011)

Recommendations: Improve teacher training. Phase out school fees. Improve the provision of textbooks and reading materials, and upgrade school infrastructure.

Actions taken: Improved workbooks in literacy and numeracy for grades 1-6 were rolled out beginning in January 2011. A strategic framework for teacher training was launched in 2011, and funding for bursaries for trainee teachers sharply increased, with further increases planned for 2012-14. Increased funding was allocated in the 2011-12 Budget for improving school infrastructure, with further increases to follow in 2012-14.

Enhance competition in network industries (2011)

Recommendations: Rule out granting state-owned enterprises exemptions from competition laws. Move towards separating generation, transmission and distribution of electricity. Strengthen the independence and resources of the telecoms regulator. Unbundle the divisions of the state-owned transport conglomerate Transnet and move towards privatisation of the units where feasible.

Actions taken: No action taken.

Reform the wage bargaining system (2011)

Recommendations: Weaken administrative extension of collective bargains in sectors covered by bargaining councils. Provide for indicative guidelines for wage bargains at a centralised level consistent with inflation targets and preserving employment prospects of labour market outsiders.

Actions taken: The New Growth Path strategy through 2020 endorsed by the Cabinet in October 2010 includes a proposed broad development pact on wages, prices and executive bonuses to help ensure a sufficient employment response to faster economic growth.

Other key priorities

Strengthen policies to tackle youth unemployment (2011)

Recommendations: Provide for age differentiation of minimum wages in sectors where these are set by the state. Implement a wage subsidy, possibly via the expansion of the learnership programme. Intensify placement assistance.

Actions taken: The New Growth Path Strategy commits to new funding for employment services and to changes in the functioning of labour centres in order to improve information about job and training opportunities.

Reduce barriers to entrepreneurship (2011)

Recommendations: Introduce systematic regulatory impact assessment for all new regulation, and review existing legislation with a view to reducing administrative burdens.

Actions taken: The institutional framework for conducting regulatory impact assessments is being put in place within the National Treasury.

SOUTH AFRICA

- The large GDP per capita and productivity gaps with the upper half of OECD countries have narrowed over the past ten years, and additional income convergence took place thanks to terms of trade gains. A large part of the GDP per capita gap is explained by low labour utilisation.
- In priority areas, efforts have been made to enhance the quality of education and the wage bargaining system. By contrast, little has been done to increase competition in network industries, and labour market reforms have been timid given the scale of the unemployment problem.
- In other areas, the main labour market measures taken during the crisis included the expansion of public works programmes and the introduction of a training layoffs scheme.

Performance and policy indicators

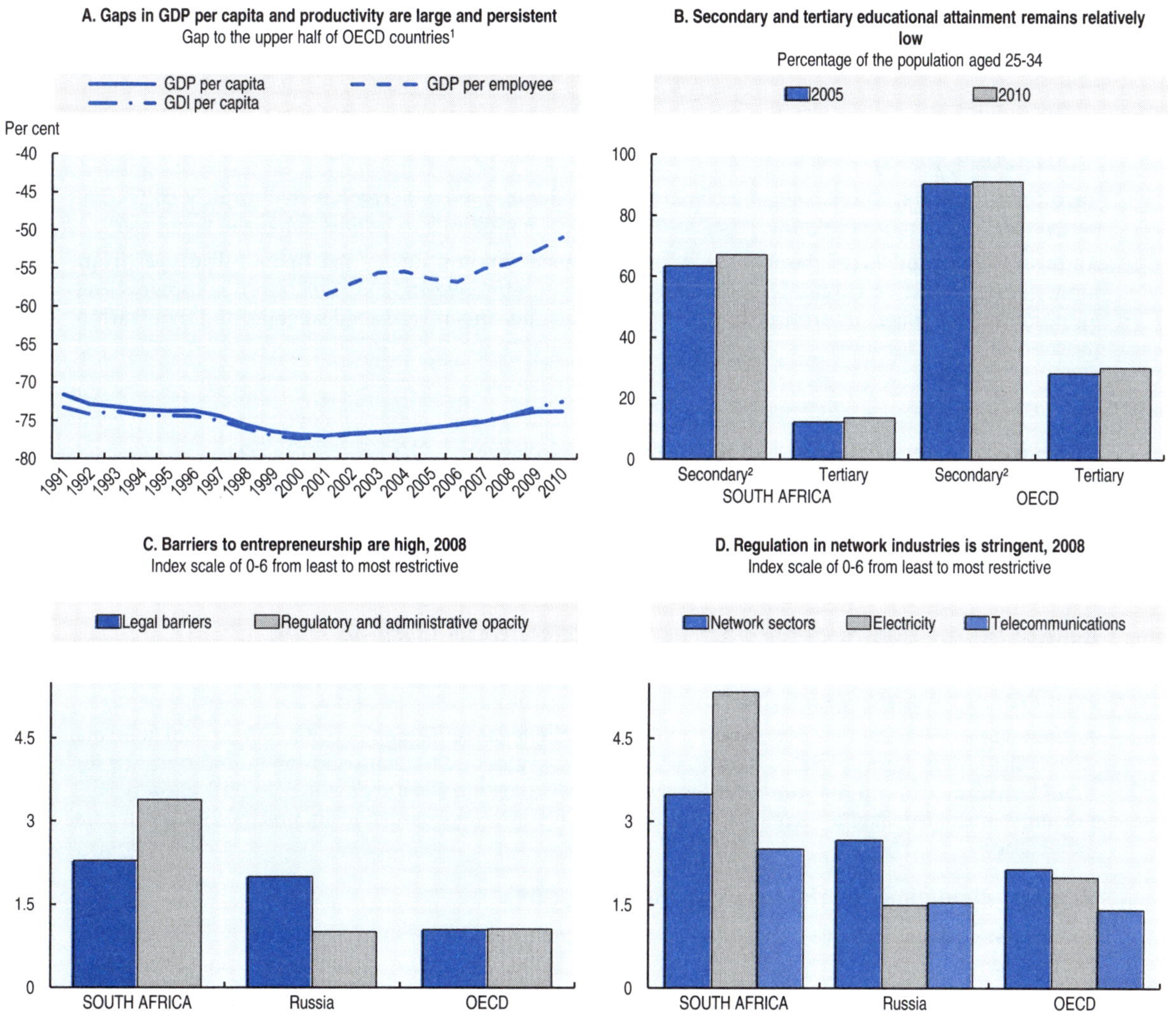

1. Percentage gap with respect to the simple average of the highest 17 OECD countries in terms of GDP per capita, GDP per employee and GDI per capita (in constant 2005 PPPs).
2. Secondary educational attainment measures the share of the population aged 25-34 that has reached at least lower secondary education.

Source: Chart A: World Bank (2011), *World Development Indicators (WDI) Database* and *Statistics South Africa*; Chart B: Samir *et al.* (2008), "Projection of Population by Level of Education Attainment, Age and Sex for 120 Countries for 2005-50", *International Institute for Applied Systems Analysis Interim Reports*; Charts C and D: *Product Market Regulation Database*.

StatLink http://dx.doi.org/10.1787/888932565794

SPAIN

Priorities supported by indicators

Improve educational attainment in secondary education (2007, 2009, 2011)

Recommendations: Lower grade repetition by focusing grade advancement criteria on key competencies and improve education outcomes by strengthening accountability and independence of schools.

Actions taken: Measures were legislated in 2011 to facilitate the transition of academically-weak pupils from lower secondary to vocational upper secondary education, introduce nation-wide testing, adapt vocational schools' curricula to local businesses' needs and ease access of graduates from vocational schools to tertiary education. Skill requirements for new teaching staff were raised in 2009.

Ease employment protection legislation for permanent workers (2007, 2009, 2011)

Recommendations: Lower severance pay for workers on permanent contracts.

Actions taken: The 2010 labour market reform should make it easier for firms to have dismissals accepted as justified, potentially reducing dismissal costs. It promotes contracts with lower severance pay.

Make wages more responsive to economic and firm-specific conditions (2007, 2009, 2011)

Recommendations: Abolish legal extensions of collective wage agreements. Simplify collective bargaining, giving more room for wages and other work conditions to be decided at the firm level.

Actions taken: The 2010 labour market reform eased the conditions for firms to opt out from higher-level collective bargaining outcomes. A reform, effective in 2011, facilitated company-level agreements on wage determination and working time and introduced accelerated arbitration procedures.

Other key priorities

Strengthen competition in the retail distribution sector (2007, 2009, 2011)

Recommendations: Eliminate barriers to the establishment of large surface outlets.

Actions taken: The national license requirement for large surface outlets was abolished in 2010, but regional governments may still require an authorisation under overriding reasons related to public interest.

Reduce the disincentives for older workers to continue working (2007, 2011)

Recommendations: Lengthen required contribution periods in the pension system and phase out extended benefit payments for older unemployed or partially retired workers.

Actions taken: The 2011 pension reform increased the legal retirement age to 67 years for workers with contribution records of less than 38.5 years and lengthened the contribution period required for a full pension. It raised discounts on early retirement pensions, reduced subsidies for early partial retirement and foresaw a revision of the pension system parameters in line with changes in life expectancy.

Remove distortions in the housing market (2009)

Recommendations: Remove barriers to the development of the rental market and provide housing support for low-income households through cash benefits rather than subsidies for social housing.

Actions taken: Legislation equalising the tax treatment of rented and owner-occupied housing has been in force since 2011. Procedures to evict tenants breaching contractual obligations were accelerated end-2009. The government cut subsidies for social housing in 2010.

SPAIN

- The GDP per capita gap relative to the upper half of OECD countries has persisted and is especially marked in labour utilisation. The recent improvement in productivity reflects labour shedding in low-productivity activities, notably in residential construction.
- Among key priority areas, progress has been made in reducing dismissal costs for workers on permanent contracts, making wages more responsive to firm-specific conditions and reducing disincentives to work in the pension system. Less has been achieved to reduce early school drop-outs and ease regulation of retailing.
- In other areas, in order to cushion the labour market crisis the government introduced temporary subsidies for new hires and training programs targeted mostly at young workers, lowered barriers for placement of the unemployed by private agencies and permanently increased resources in the public employment services.

Performance and policy indicators

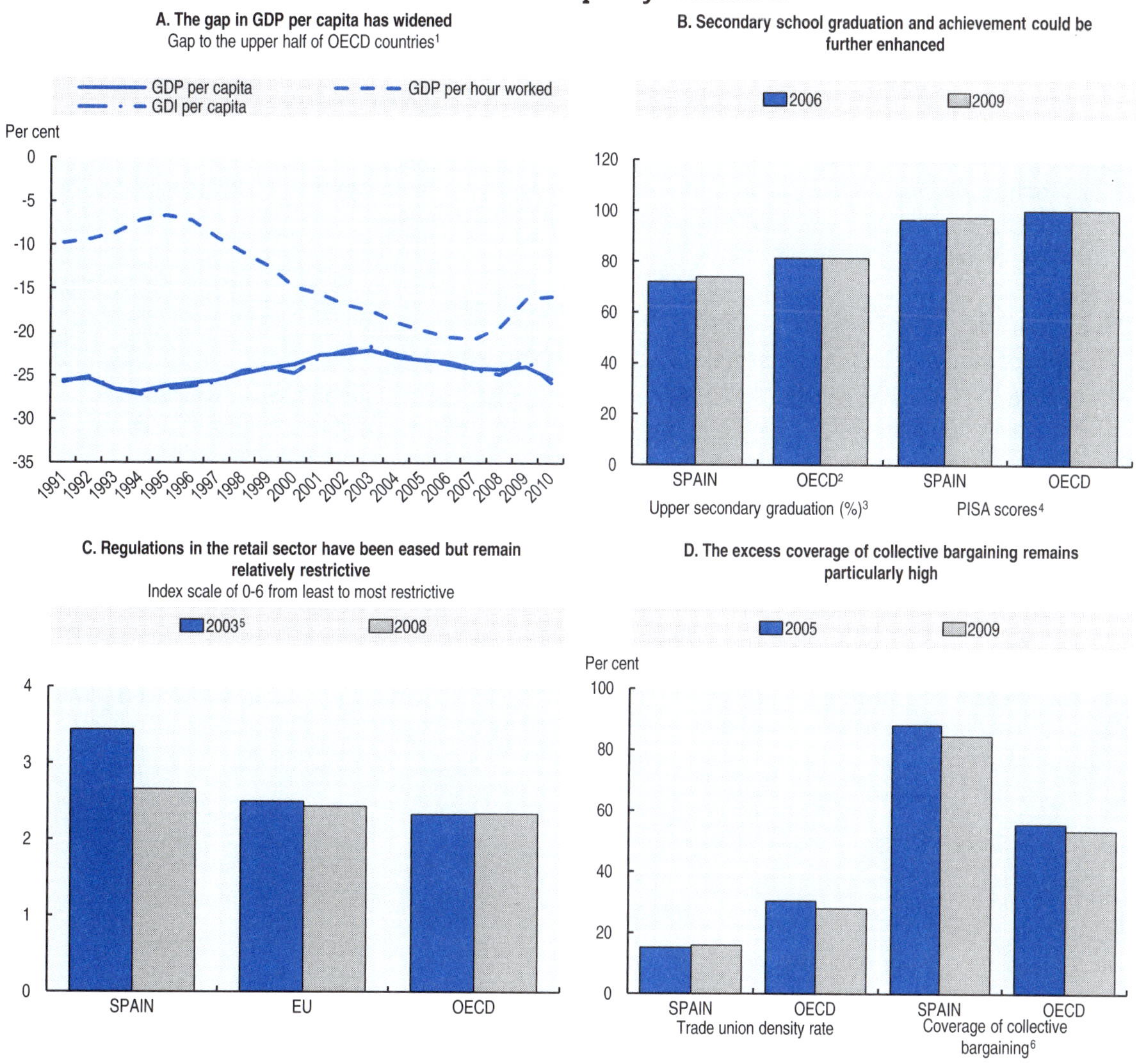

1. Percentage gap with respect to the simple average of the highest 17 OECD countries in terms of GDP per capita, GDP per hour worked and GDI per capita (in constant 2005 PPPs).
2. Average of OECD countries excluding Australia, Austria, Belgium, Estonia, France and the Netherlands.
3. First-time graduation rates for single year of age at upper secondary level.
4. Average score of student performance in mathematics, science and reading. Index OECD = 100.
5. Average of European countries in the OECD. EU and OECD averages exclude Chile, Estonia, Israel and Slovenia.
6. For Spain, data refer to 2004 and 2008.

Source: Chart A: OECD, *National Accounts and Economic Outlook No. 90 Databases*; Chart B: OECD (2011), *Education at a Glance* and OECD, *PISA 2009 Database*; Chart C: OECD, *Employment Database*; Chart D: OECD estimates and J. Visser, Amsterdam Institute for Advanced Labour Studies (2011), *ICTWSS Database on Institutions, Coordination, Trade Unions, Wage Setting and Social Pacts* (version 3.0).

StatLink http://dx.doi.org/10.1787/888932565243

SWEDEN

Priorities supported by indicators

Reform sickness and disability benefit schemes (2007, 2009, 2011)

Recommendations: Further improve gate-keeping to sickness and disability benefits. Limit the inflows of youth into these schemes.

Actions taken: Various measures have been taken as part of the comprehensive 2007 reform programme, including stricter eligibility requirements and time limits for sickness benefits in 2007, the introduction of greater financial incentives for the disabled to take up jobs in 2009 and the phasing out of temporary disability benefits in 2010.

Reduce marginal taxes on labour income (2007, 2009, 2011)

Recommendations: Cut income taxes for earnings above average levels by further raising the threshold for the state income tax or reducing its rate, while shifting some of the tax burden towards property and consumption taxes.

Actions taken: In 2009, the lower threshold for the state income tax was raised and social security contributions were cut. The in-work tax credit was expanded in 2009 and 2010.

Reform employment protection legislation (2007, 2009, 2011)

Recommendations: Reduce job protection on regular contracts, for instance by easing procedures for dismissals or, as a second best option, by lengthening the trial period.

Actions taken: No significant action.

Other key priorities

Reduce housing market distortions (2007, 2009, 2011)

Recommendations: Continue to ease rent regulation, boost competition in the construction sector, simplify the land planning process and reverse the housing taxation cut implemented in 2008.

Actions taken: Outright ownership of owner-occupied apartments was introduced for new apartment buildings in 2009, which should enlarge the rental market. New regulations, entering into force in 2011, require municipal housing companies to follow market principles.

Improve the efficiency of the education system (2007, 2009, 2011)

Recommendations: Improve the performance of secondary and vocational education. Reduce the average age of entry into tertiary education and shorten completion times.

Actions taken: The government introduced teacher certification in 2008 and gradually increased the use of tests in compulsory education. It reformed admission criteria to encourage earlier entry into university in 2010 and introduced tuition fees for students from outside the European Economic Area in 2011.

SWEDEN

- After having widened somewhat, the income gap *vis-à-vis* leading OECD economies has narrowed most recently, reflecting a rebound in productivity growth. Employment rates are high, but average hours worked are low. The remaining GDP per capita gap reflects mainly a productivity shortfall.
- Among key priorities, progress has been made in raising labour market participation through reforms of the sickness and disability benefit schemes and cuts in marginal taxes on labour income, as well as in improving the performance of the education system. By contrast, little has been achieved in terms of reforming employment protection legislation and reducing distortions in the housing market.
- In other areas, large additional spending on active labour market programmes and the extension of access to the education system helped mitigate the labour market impact of the crisis, and these measures are still in place.

Performance and policy indicators

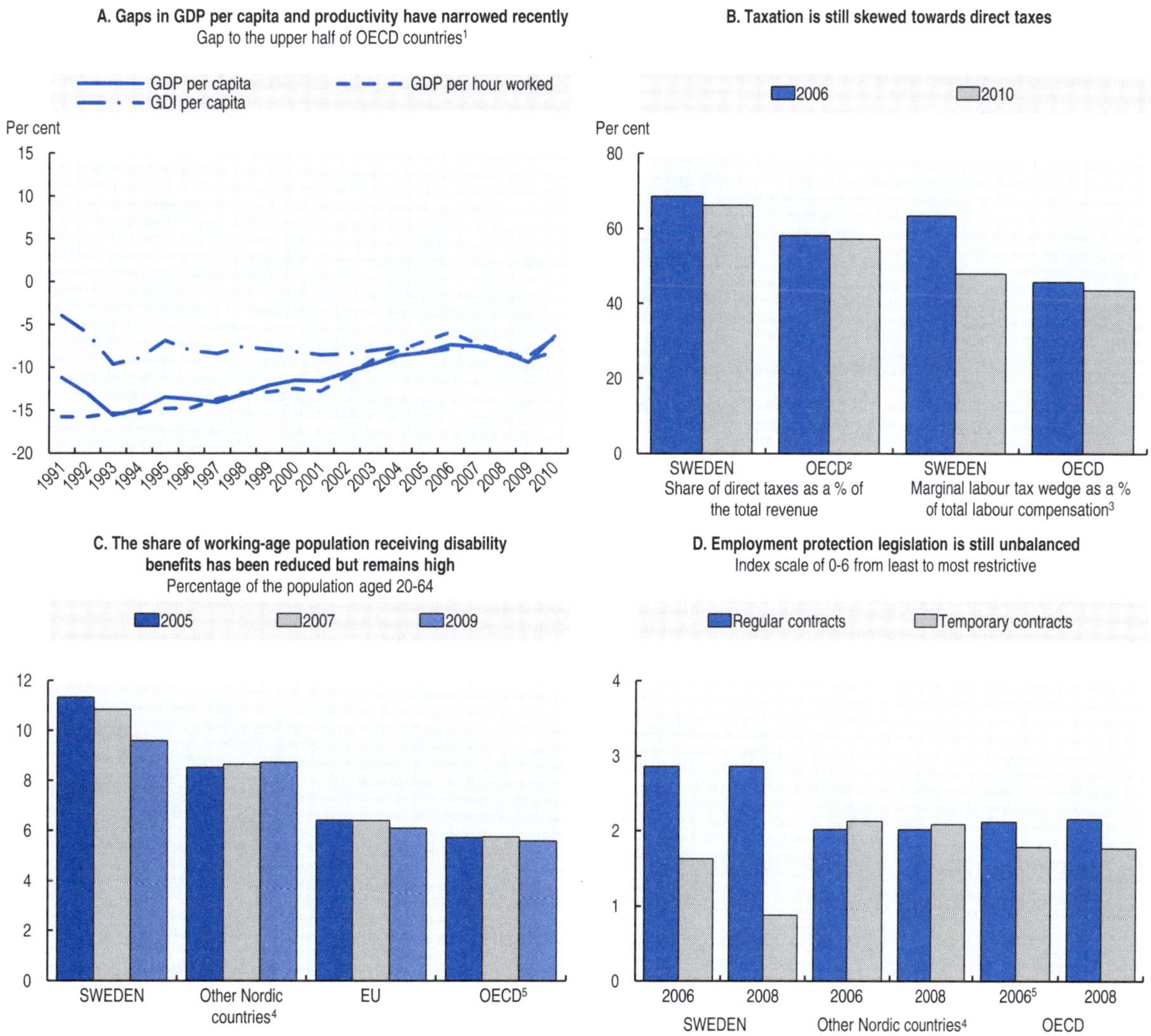

1. Percentage gap with respect to the simple average of the highest 17 OECD countries in terms of GDP per capita, GDP per hour worked and GDI per capita (in constant 2005 PPPs).
2. Data refer to 2009 for Australia, the Netherlands and Poland.
3. Labour taxes include personal income tax and employee plus employer social security contributions and any payroll tax less cash transfers. Evaluated at 100% of average earnings for a single person with no child.
4. Average of Denmark, Finland and Norway.
5. The OECD average excludes Chile, Iceland and Turkey.

Source: Chart A: OECD, *National Accounts and Economic Outlook No. 90 Databases*; Chart B: OECD, *Taxing Wages and Tax Databases*; Chart C: OECD (2010), *Sickness, Disability and Work: Breaking the Barriers: A Synthesis of Findings across OECD Countries*; Chart D: OECD, *Employment Database*.

StatLink http://dx.doi.org/10.1787/888932565737

SWITZERLAND

Priorities supported by indicators

Remove barriers to competition in network industries (2007, 2009, 2011)

Recommendations: Reduce further state control, improve competitors' access to the network and strengthen the sector regulators' powers.

Actions taken: Competitors' access to the network was improved in fixed line telephony in 2007 and in electricity transmission in 2008. The independent electricity commission took up work in 2008. The scope of the legal monopoly for letter delivery has been gradually reduced.

Reduce producer support to agriculture (2007, 2009, 2011)

Recommendations: Lower trade barriers and subsidies to producers and decouple subsidies from production. Reform land law.

Actions taken: The government eliminated most export subsidies in 2007 and milk production quotas in 2010. Producer support is being shifted to some extent to less distortive direct income support.

Facilitate full-time labour force participation of women (2007, 2009, 2011)

Recommendations: Improve provision of pre-school education and childcare at affordable prices. Move from joint to individual tax assessment of spouses' incomes.

Actions taken: The central government decided in 2010 to continue co-funding of childcare facilities to some extent until 2014. In 2009, Parliament approved a tax allowance for childcare expenses and many cantons have agreed to start compulsory schooling at four years. Legislation reducing differences in taxation between main and second income earners came into effect in 2008.

Other key priorities

Increase the efficiency of the health care system (2007, 2009, 2011)

Recommendations: Do away with the mixed hospital funding. Allow insurers more freedom to contract with individual providers. Widen the compensation of insurers for differences in risk characteristics.

Actions taken: 2007 legislation increased co-payment on branded drugs when a cheaper generic equivalent is available. Hospital funding based on diagnosis-related groups is being introduced by 2012.

Improve access to tertiary education (2009, 2011)

Recommendations: Introduce loans with income contingent repayments while allowing universities to raise fees. Review the mix of vocational and academic education content within upper secondary vocational tracks.

Actions taken: A 2009 law co-ordinates the policy of the Confederation and the cantons towards tertiary academic education, and introduces an independent accreditation agency and cost benchmarking across tertiary academic institutions. Regional governments are considering widening student loans somewhat.

Remove non-tariff trade barriers (2007)

Recommendations: Products conforming to EU standards should be accepted.

Actions taken: The government introduced the "Cassis de Dijon" principle in 2010, eliminating remaining technical barriers for over 80% of the imports from the EU, and facilitated domestic approval of foreign pharmaceuticals that are lawfully introduced abroad.

SWITZERLAND

- Real GDP per capita has been growing over the past five years *vis-à-vis* the best performing countries notably on account of expanding labour utilisation. While the productivity gap has stopped widening, it remains substantial.
- Among priority areas, considerable progress has been made in reducing non-tariff barriers to trade. Network industries have been opened up to competition but the gap relative to best practice remains large. There remains wide scope for lowering protection of domestic agricultural production, reducing the cost of health care provision and facilitating full-time female labour force participation.
- In other areas, parliament has approved in 2011 legislation to address the Too-Big-To-Fail problem of financial intermediaries with systemic risks.

Performance and policy indicators

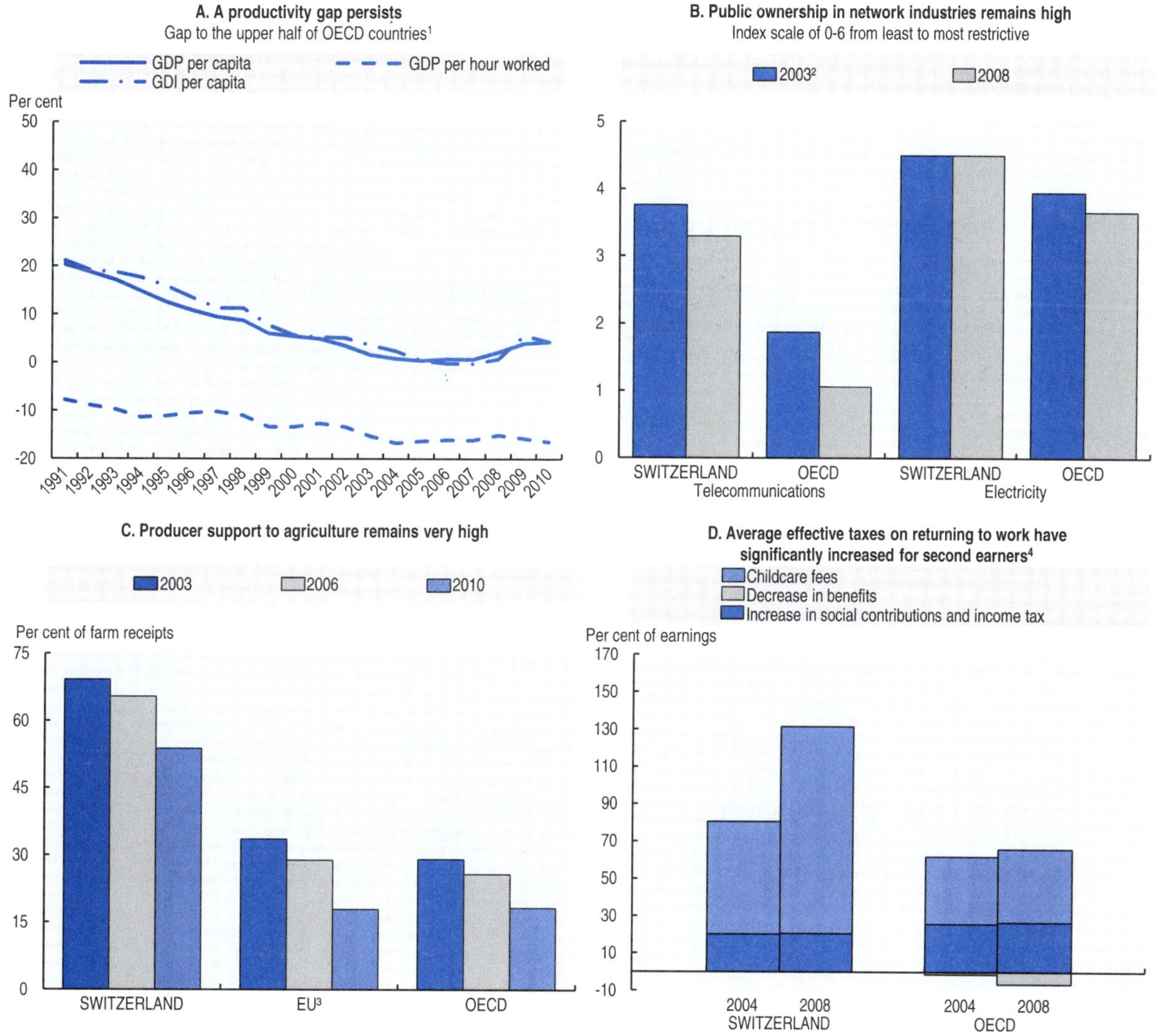

1. Percentage gap with respect to the simple average of the highest 17 OECD countries in terms of GDP per capita, GDP per hour worked and GDI per capita (in constant 2005 PPPs).
2. The OECD average excludes Chile, Estonia, Israel and Slovenia.
3. Average of European countries in the OECD.
4. Based on implicit tax on returning to work, defined as the cost of childcare, reductions in income-related benefits and increases in social contributions and personal income taxes, all relative to earnings in the new job. Measured for second earner with income equal to two-thirds of average earnings. The OECD average excludes Chile, Estonia, Israel, Italy, Mexico, Turkey and Slovenia.

Source: Chart A: OECD, *National Accounts and Economic Outlook No. 90 Databases*; Chart B: OECD, *Product Market Regulation Database*; Chart C: OECD, *Producer and Consumer Support Estimates Database*; Chart D: OECD, *Benefits and Wages Database*.

StatLink http://dx.doi.org/10.1787/888932565129

TURKEY

Priorities supported by indicators

Improve educational achievement (2007, 2009, 2011)

Recommendations: Increase the availability of high-quality education and finance this by broadening the tax base. Revise the curricula according to labour market needs. Fund schools on a per-pupil basis and give them greater managerial responsibility and accountability. New universities should be adequately funded.

Actions taken: An *Action Plan to Strengthen Links Between Vocational Education and Employment* was issued in 2010, with 37 priorities, including establishing a national skills classification system, revising vocational school curricula according to new skill groups, and closer co-operation with employers on new vocational courses.

Reduce the minimum cost of labour (2007, 2009, 2011)

Recommendations: Limit the growth of the official minimum wage and differentiate it across regions. Reduce social security contributions and make at least part of the temporary cuts granted during the crisis permanent.

Actions taken: In 2008 employers' social security contribution rates were reduced from 19.5 to 14.5%. Contributions were also cut for the early years of employment of young and female workers (valid until 2015) and in labour-intensive sectors in selected provinces.

Reform employment protection legislation (2007, 2009, 2011)

Recommendations: Ease job protection in the formal sector by reforming severance payments and liberalising temporary work. Allow more flexible labour contracts on a voluntary basis.

Actions taken: In 2009, a reform authorising manpower agencies to offer temporary work services was vetoed by the President. In 2011, restrictive conditions for establishing temporary work contracts were partly simplified.

Other key priorities

Simplify product market regulations (2007, 2009, 2011)

Recommendations: Simplify product market regulations, in particular the sectoral licensing rules. Encourage greater competition in network industries in particular by facilitating new entries in electricity generation and rail transportation.

Actions taken: The licensing of food producers was centralised in the Ministry of Agriculture as a regulatory streamlining measure. Permits concerning environmental issues were also consolidated into a single "environmental permit" administered electronically. Privatisation resumed in the electricity distribution sector after the crisis.

Reduce incentives for early retirement (2007, 2009, 2011)

Recommendations: Reduce incentives for early retirement by making benefits more actuarially neutral, and by establishing a health insurance contribution for young retirees. Remove retiring workers' entitlement to severance payments (in new labour contracts).

Actions taken: No action taken.

TURKEY

- The income gap *vis-à-vis* the upper half of OECD countries narrowed in the 2000s but remains very large owing to low productivity and labour utilisation levels. The strong catch-up has mainly been driven by productivity gains.
- In key priority areas, enterprise creation has been simplified, foreign direct investment has been stimulated, privatisations have reduced the scope of public ownership, and an action plan for vocational education has been launched. Reforms to reduce labour costs and enhance labour market flexibility have started but remain very limited so far.
- Growth-enhancing initiatives in other areas included an overhaul of the industrial investment incentives system, with the introduction of a single and more transparent framework of regional and sectoral investment incentives.

Performance and policy indicators

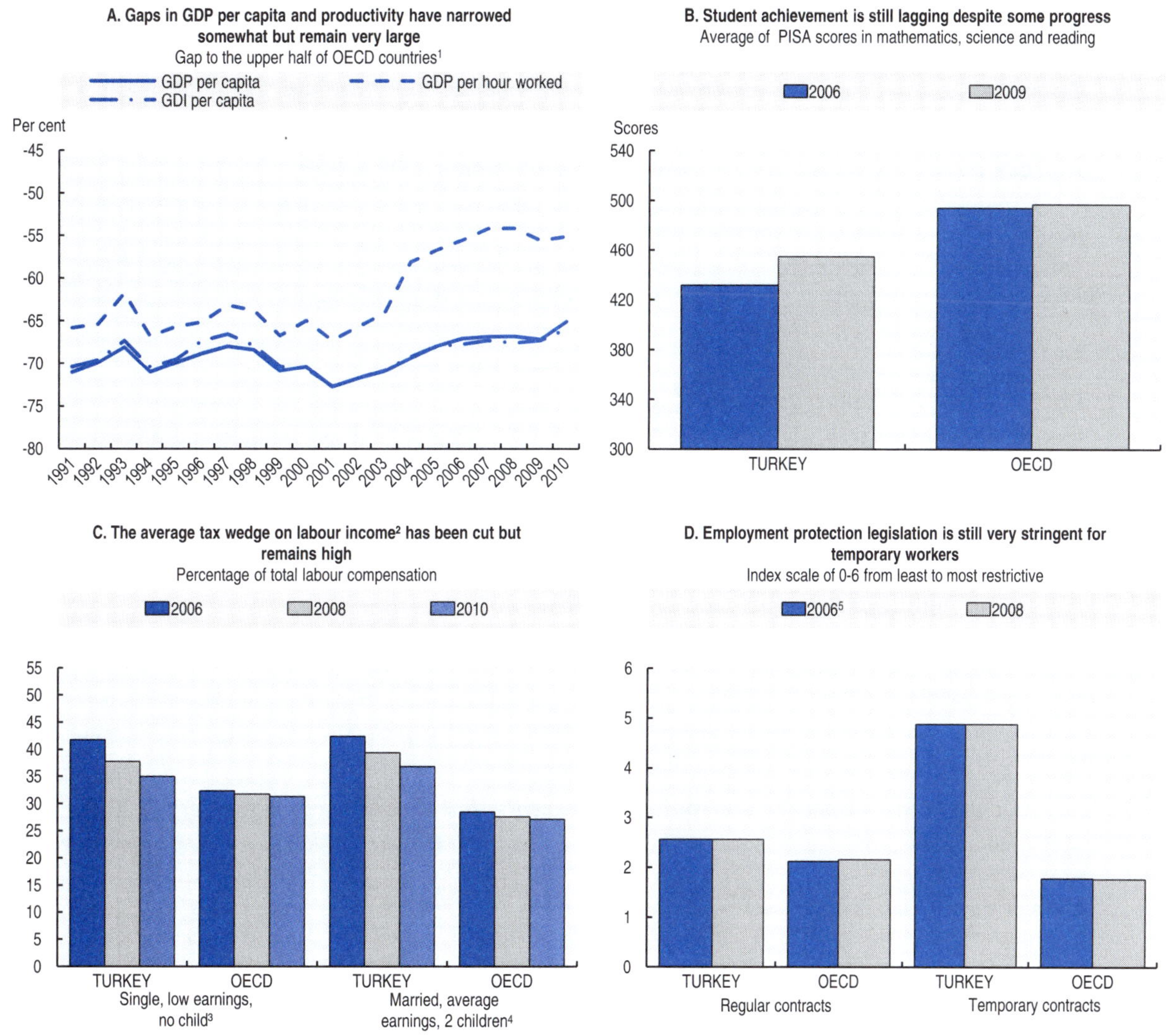

1. Percentage gap with respect to the simple average of the highest 17 OECD countries in terms of GDP per capita, GDP per hour worked and GDI per capita (in constant 2005 PPPs).
2. Labour taxes include personal income tax and employee plus employer social security contributions and any payroll tax less cash transfers.
3. Low earnings refer to two-thirds of average earnings.
4. At 100% of the average worker earnings for the first earner. Average of three situations regarding the wage of the second earner (0%, 33% and 67% of average earnings).
5. OECD average excludes Chile, Estonia, Israel and Slovenia.

Source: Chart A: OECD, *National Accounts and Economic Outlook No. 90 Databases*; Chart B: OECD, *PISA 2009 Database*; Chart C: OECD, *Taxing Wages Database*; Chart D: OECD, *Employment Database*.

StatLink http://dx.doi.org/10.1787/888932565756

UNITED KINGDOM

Priorities supported by indicators

Reform of disability benefit schemes (2007, 2009, 2011)

Recommendations: Extend the Pathway to Work scheme to all new and existing claimants. Limit inflows into the incapacity benefit scheme by early monitoring of the health status of applicants.

Actions taken: The Pathway to Work scheme was incrementally extended between 2008 and 2010, and was replaced by the new Work Programme in 2011 without major changes in coverage and monitoring. From 2011 all remaining claimants will be reassessed using the Work Capability Assessment.

Improve educational achievements of young people (2007, 2009, 2011)

Recommendations: Focus on core literacy and numeracy skills. Increase resources for disadvantaged students and improve targeting to students that are at risk of dropping out. Expand vocational programmes and ensure that they provide relevant skills.

Actions taken: In 2011 the government introduced a pupil premium for disadvantaged students and increased the number of apprenticeships. The (well-functioning) Education Maintenance Allowance was abolished in 2011 and replaced by a smaller targeted bursary programme administered by schools.

Improve public infrastructure, especially for transport (2007, 2009, 2011)

Recommendations: Preserve infrastructure investment from government spending restraint. Introduce a national roads pricing scheme to mitigate congestion.

Actions taken: Investment in infrastructure increased substantially over the review period, but under the government's fiscal plans, spending on public investment is set to fall sharply.

Other key priorities

Reform land planning regulations (2009, 2011)

Recommendations: Make the land planning system more flexible and predictable and provide incentives for local communities to release land for building, while continuing to protect the environment.

Actions taken: The 2011 draft National Planning Policy Framework simplifies the planning process and the New Homes Bonus should incentivise local communities to allow development.

Strengthen public sector efficiency (2007, 2009, 2011)

Recommendations: Improve efficiency in publicly-funded services. In the healthcare sector, contain compensation for some highly-paid National Health Service (NHS) personnel, reinforce competition among providers and consistency in the allocation of responsibility across government bodies.

Actions taken: An ongoing reform to delegate responsibilities for purchasing hospital care to General Practitioners (GPs) may increase efficiency.

Improve work incentives for low-paid lone parents and second income earners (2007)

Recommendations: Lower marginal effective tax rates and childcare costs for lone parents to improve work incentives.

Actions taken: The childcare element of the Working Tax Credit was increased 2009 and 2010. In 2013 the Universal Credit will replace a number of in-work benefits and tax credits, reducing complexity and improving work incentives for lone parents and second earners.

UNITED KINGDOM

- The gap in GDP per capita relative to the upper half of OECD countries continues to widen. Labour utilisation remains high, but GDP per hour worked is low in an international context and has fallen.
- Among key priority areas, progress has been made on lowering the number of disability benefit recipients and improving work incentives for second earners, while little has been achieved in terms of enhancing public sector efficiency and educational outcomes.
- In other areas, the introduction of the Flexible New Deal in 2009 is likely to have cushioned the crisis-driven increase in youth unemployment. The Universal Credit legislated in 2011 that will be rolled out from 2013 will simplify the social benefits system and increase work incentives.

Performance and policy indicators

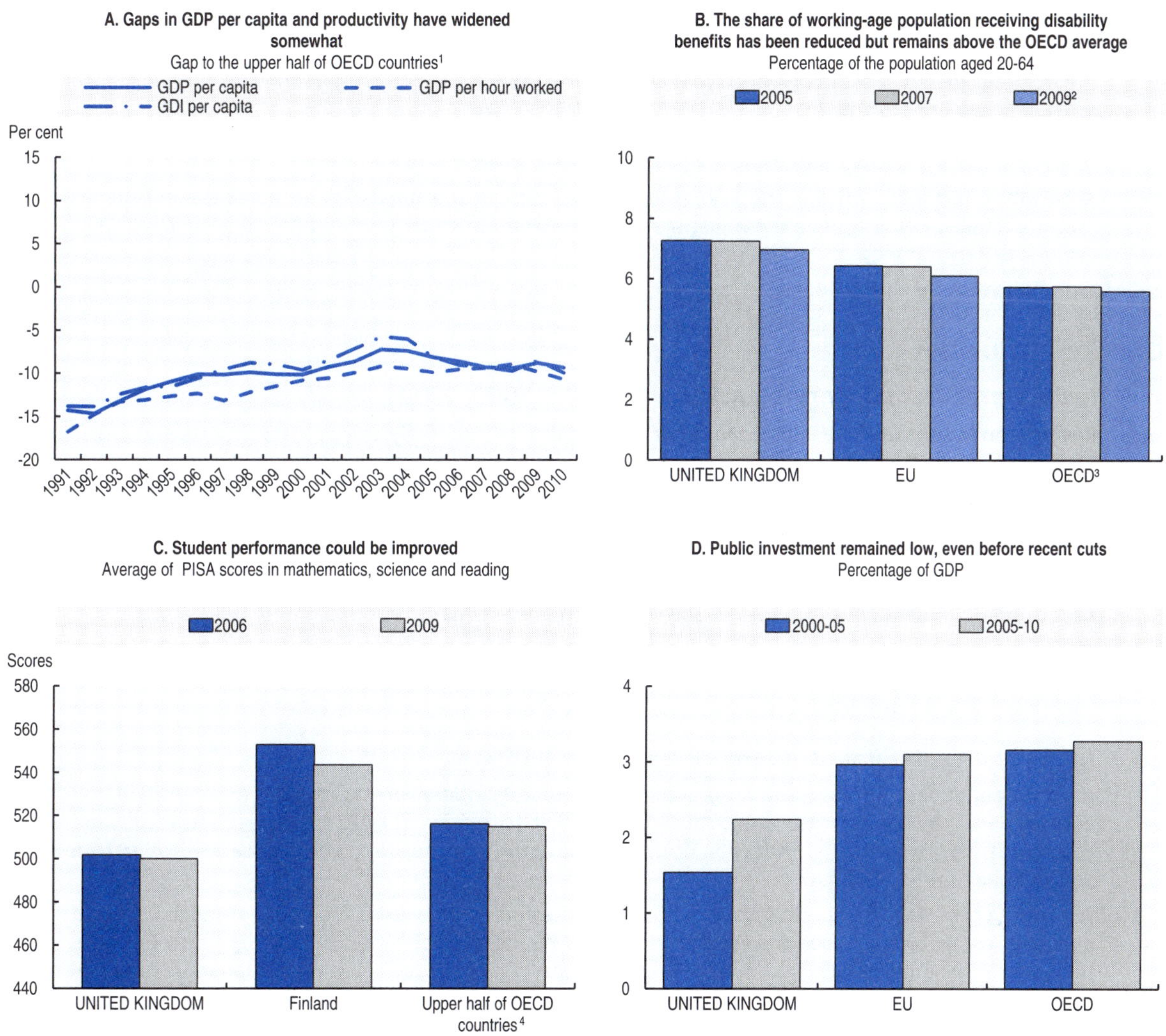

1. Percentage gap with respect to the simple average of the highest 17 OECD countries in terms of GDP per capita, GDP per hour worked and GDI per capita (in constant 2005 PPPs).
2. For the United Kingdom, data refer to 2008.
3. Excluding Chile, Iceland and Turkey.
4. Upper half of OECD countries in terms of PISA scores in mathematics, science and reading.

Source: Chart A: OECD, *National Accounts and Economic Outlook No. 90 Databases*; Chart B: (OECD 2010), *Sickness, Disability and Work: Breaking the Barriers: A Synthesis of Findings across OECD Countries*; Chart C: OECD, *PISA 2009 Database*; Chart D: *Economic Outlook No. 90 Database*.

StatLink http://dx.doi.org/10.1787/888932565338

UNITED STATES

Priorities supported by indicators

Improve primary and secondary education (2007, 2009, 2011)

Recommendations: Improve teacher education. Strengthen schools' accountability for student progress.

Actions taken: The Race to the Top fund encouraged states to adopt education standards, improve student assessment, and strengthen teacher evaluations through competitive grants awarded in 2010. Such reforms are included in the Administration's proposed overhaul of the Elementary and Secondary Education Act.

Improve the efficiency of the health care sector (2007, 2009, 2011)

Recommendations: Make health insurance compulsory. Introduce means-tested subsidies to purchase health insurance. Limit the tax exclusion for employer-provided health insurance. Reduce Medicare costs.

Actions taken: The 2010 health reform makes health insurance coverage compulsory, provides means-tested subsidies for their purchase, and creates an organisation to test Medicare provider-payment reforms.

Improve the efficiency of the tax system (2007, 2009, 2011)

Recommendations: Broaden the tax base by phasing out the mortgage-interest deduction on owner-occupied housing once the housing market recovery is under way and limiting the health tax exclusion. Rely more on consumption-based taxes.

Actions taken: No action taken.

Other key priorities

Reduce producer support to agriculture (2007, 2009, 2011)

Recommendations: Reduce support for agricultural producers, notably dairy price supports and tariffs on imported ethanol and sugar.

Actions taken: A backward action has been taken as the Food, Conservation and Energy Act of 2008 provided new incentives for the local production of cellulosic bio-fuels.

Strengthen policies to promote social mobility (2011)

Recommendations: Reduce childhood poverty and improve equality of opportunity in education.

Actions taken: Grants have been made available to the lowest performing schools. The Pell Grant programme was expanded in the 2010-11 academic year to make college more affordable for students from low-income households.

Improve and streamline financial regulation (2009)

Recommendations: Improve and streamline the regulatory framework to make it more unified and comprehensive. Systemically important financial institutions should be subject to strict and conservative prudential standards. Housing financing should be gradually turned over to a well-regulated private sector.

Actions taken: The 2010 Dodd-Frank overhaul of the financial system created a financial system oversight council, established the Federal Reserve as regulator of all systemically important financial institutions, slightly reduced the number of regulatory agencies, and created a consumer financial protection bureau. The Act also introduced an orderly resolution regime.

Reform disability benefits (2007)

Recommendations: Tighten eligibility criteria for the disability insurance system.

Actions taken: No action taken.

UNITED STATES

- After some reduction during much of the 2000s, the positive GDP per capita gap relative to the upper half of OECD countries has increased somewhat since 2008. This pick-up reflects higher labour productivity growth than in the other countries partly offset by a decline in relative labour utilisation.
- Among key priority areas, solid progress has been made in financial regulation and health care, although further reforms are likely to be required to contain growth in health care expenditures. Some progress has also been made in education and social mobility, but an Administration overhaul of federal education remains stalled in Congress. Backward steps have been taken in agriculture.
- In other areas, extensions of unemployment benefit duration, set to expire at the end of 2011, have cushioned income losses for the unemployed and supported economic activity during the recession as well as the subsequent recovery.

Performance and policy indicators

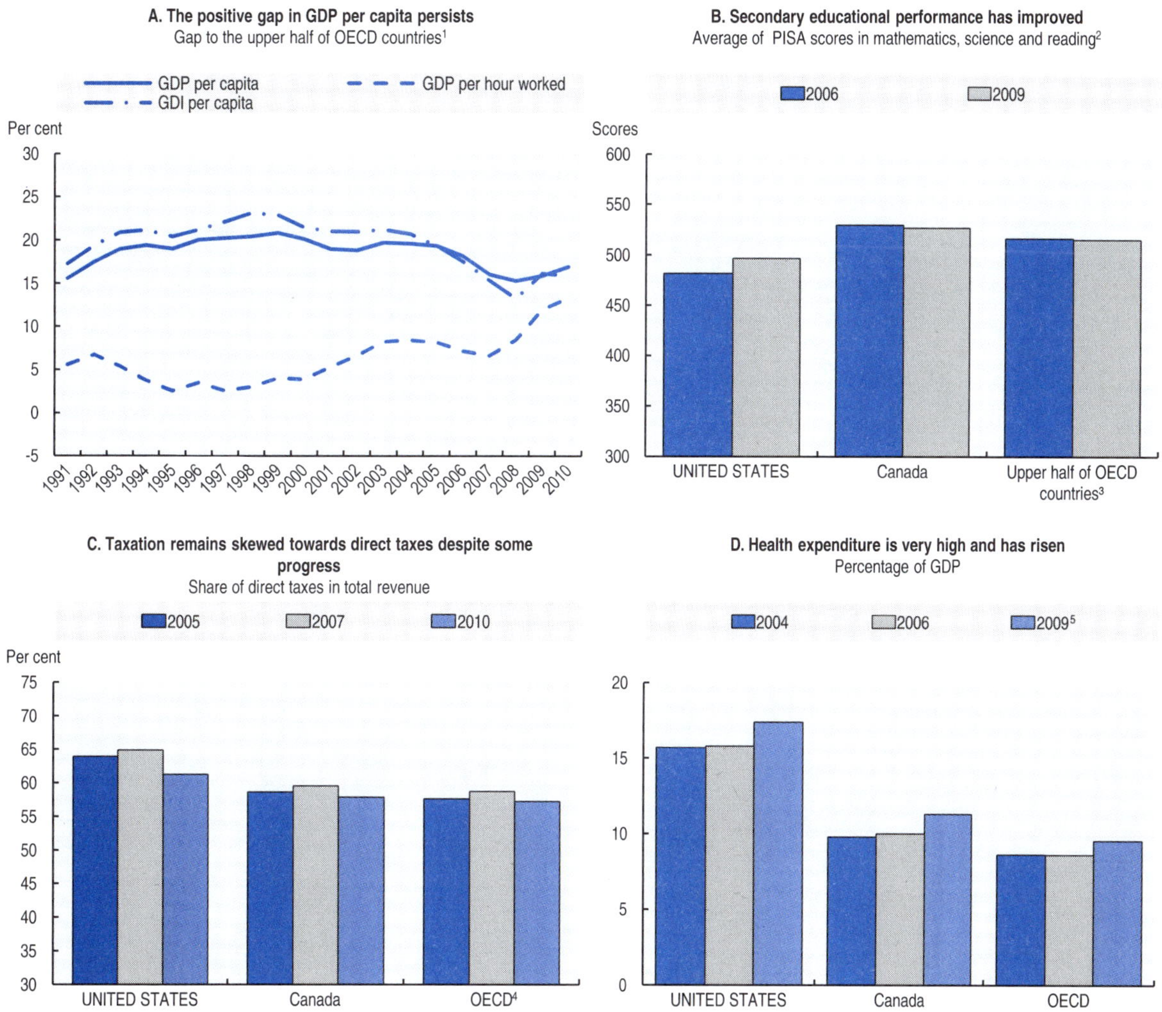

1. Percentage gap with respect to the simple average of the highest 17 OECD countries in terms of GDP per capita, GDP per hour worked and GDI per capita (in constant 2005 PPPs).
2. Due to data availability, reading score is not included in the average of PISA scores for the United States in 2006.
3. Upper half of OECD countries in terms of PISA scores in mathematics, science and reading.
4. Data refer to 2009 for Australia, the Netherlands and Poland.
5. 2010 for Canada.

Source: Chart A: OECD, *National Accounts and Economic Outlook No. 90 Databases*; Chart B: OECD, *PISA 2009 Database*; Chart C: OECD, *Tax Revenue Database*; Chart D: OECD (2011), *Health Database*.

StatLink http://dx.doi.org/10.1787/888932565775

Economic Policy Reforms 2012
Going for Growth
© OECD 2012

PART I

Chapter 3

Structural policy indicators

Note: Users of the data must be aware that they may not longer fully reflect the current situation in fast reforming countries.

Figure 3.1. **Cost of labour**

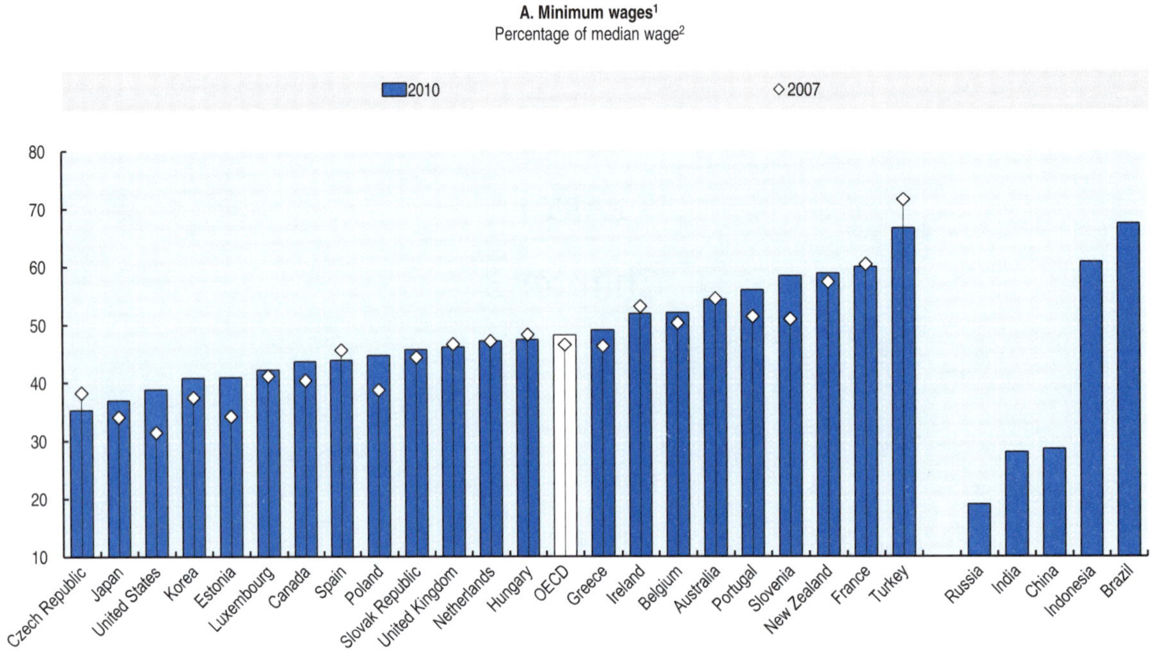

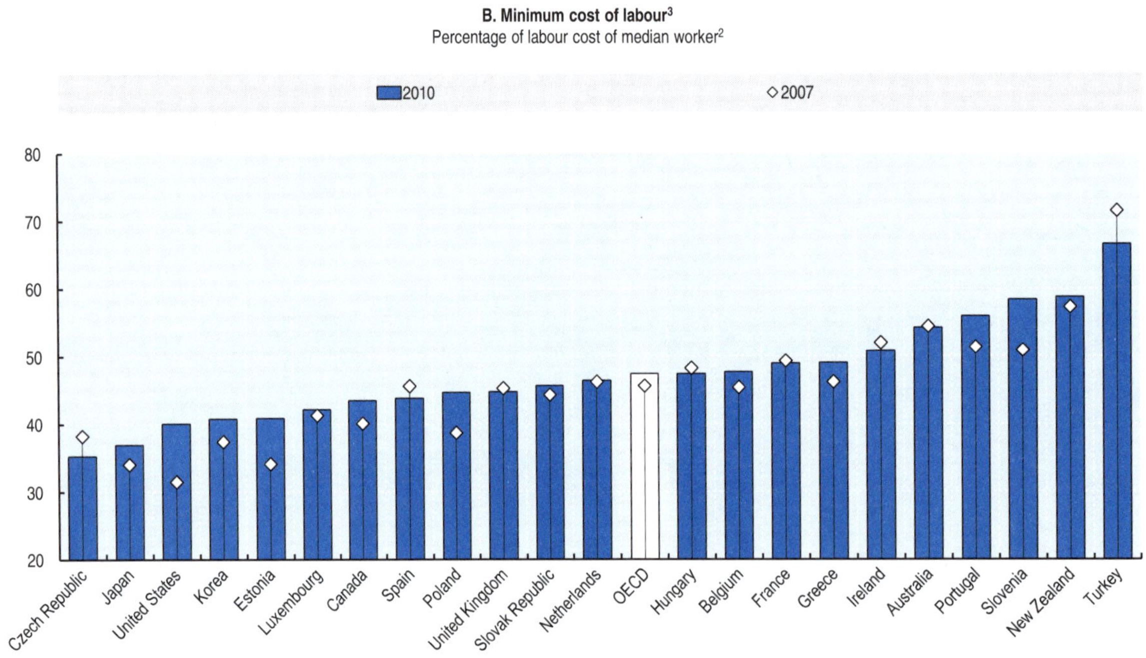

Note: Users of the data must be aware that they may no longer fully reflect the current situation in fast reforming countries.

1. Missing countries do not have a national statutory minimum wage except for Mexico, Chile and Israel for which data are not available.
2. Exactly half of all workers have wages either below or above the median wage for the OECD countries. For the non-OECD countries: percentage of minimum to average wage for Brazil (2010), China (2010), Indonesia (2011) and the Russian Federation (2011); of minimum to average manufacturing sector wage for India (2004).
3. The cost of labour is the sum of the wage level and the corresponding social security contribution paid by employers.

Source: Chart A: OECD (2011), *OECD Employment Outlook Database*; China Ministry of Human Resources and Social Security; *Instituto Brasileiro de Geografia e Estatística (Censo Demográfico)*; *International Labour Organization (ILO) Database*; Statistics Indonesia; Russia Federal State Statistics Service and OECD (2007), *OECD Employment Outlook 2007* (Box 1.3); Chart B; OECD (2011), *OECD Employment Outlook and Taxing Wages Databases*.

StatLink http://dx.doi.org/10.1787/888932565813

Figure 3.2. **Net income replacement rates for unemployment**[1]

Percentage of earnings

A. Short-term (first year)[2]

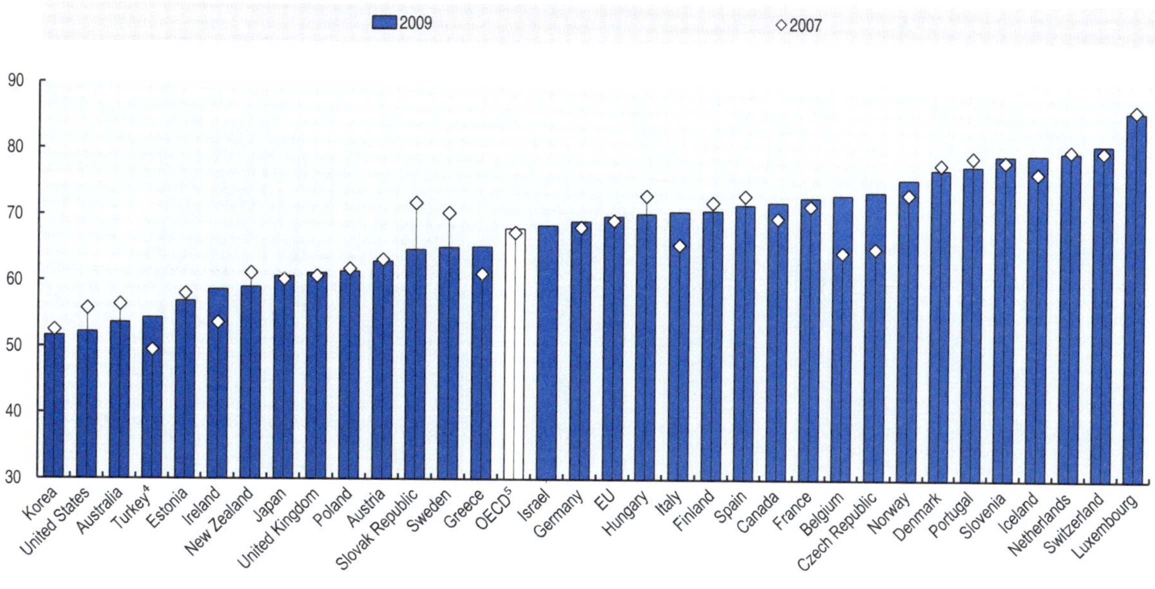

B. Long-term (after 5 years)[3]

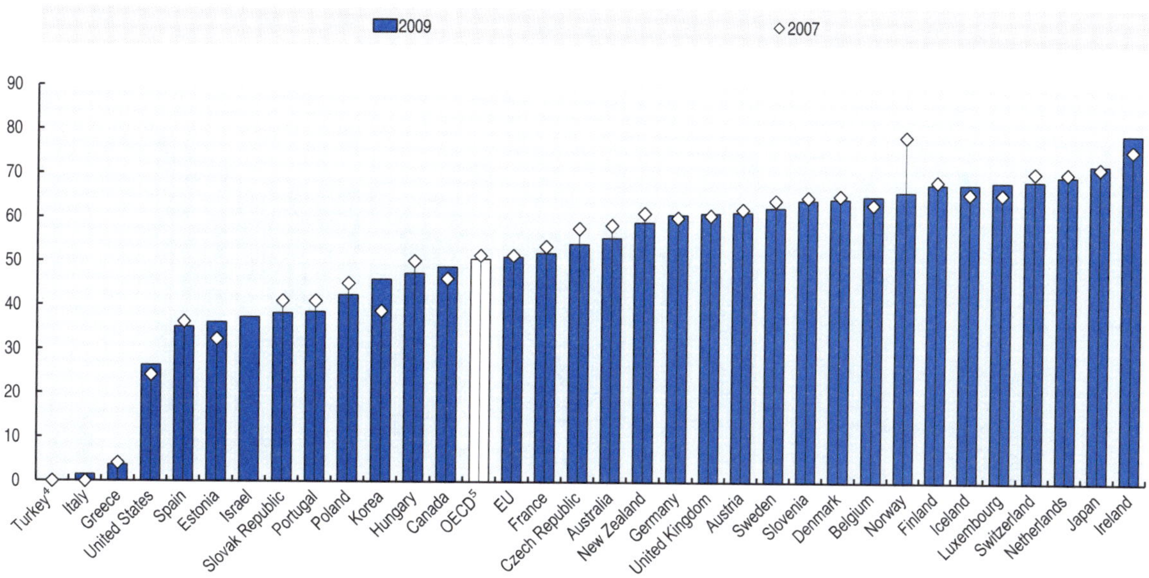

Note: Users of the data must be aware that they may no longer fully reflect the current situation in fast reforming countries.

1. Average of replacement rates for unemployed persons who earned 67% and 100% of average worker earnings.
2. Initial phase of unemployment but following any waiting period. No social assistance "top-ups" are assumed to be available in either the in-work or out-of-work situation. Any income taxes payable on unemployment benefits are determined in relation to annualised benefit values (*i.e.* monthly values multiplied by 12) even if the maximum benefit duration is shorter than 12 months.
3. After tax and including unemployment benefits, social assistance, family and housing benefits in the 60th month of benefit receipt. Values for Turkey are equal to zero in 2007 and 2009 and for Italy in 2007.
4. For Turkey, the average worker earnings (AW) value is not available. Calculations are based on average production worker earnings (APW).
5. The OECD average excludes Chile and Mexico.

Source: OECD (2011), *Benefits and Wages Database*.

StatLink http://dx.doi.org/10.1787/888932565832

Figure 3.3. **Average tax wedge on labour**[1]

Percentage of total labour compensation

A. At 67% of average worker earnings, single person without children

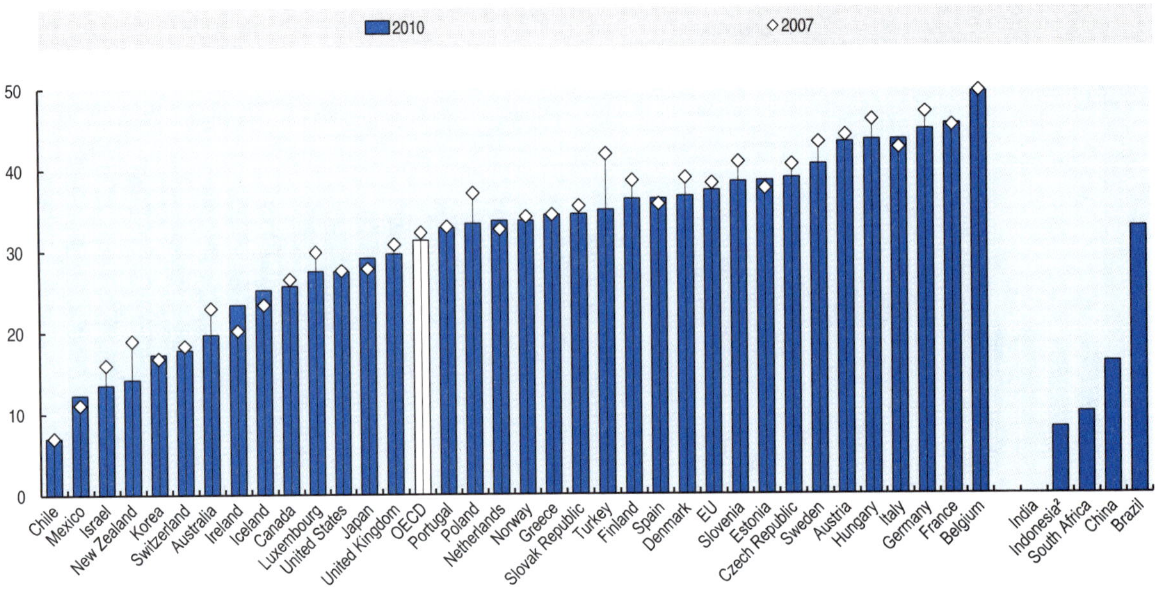

B. At 100% of average worker earnings, couple with two children[3]

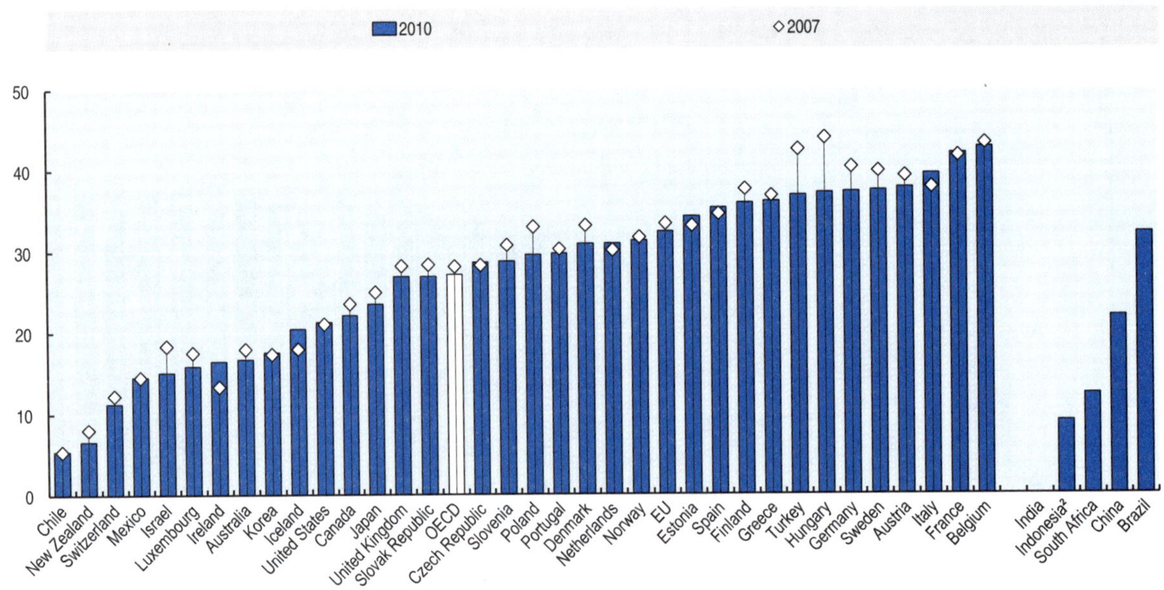

Note: Users of the data must be aware that they may no longer fully reflect the current situation in fast reforming countries.

1. Measured as the difference between total labour compensation paid by the employer and the net take-home pay of employees, as a ratio of total labour compensation. It therefore includes both employer and employee social security contributions. The value for India is equal to zero in 2010. For India, the data refer to employees in the 95% of companies in the manufacturing sector with less than ten employees. In firms with over 10 employees, the tax wedge would be no more than 5%. In China, a significant portion of the labour force are not covered by the social security system and their tax wedge would be significantly lower than the figure report here.
2. Data refer to 2009 for Indonesia.
3. Couple with two children, at 100% of average worker earnings for the first earner. Average of three situations regarding the wage of the second earner (0%, 33% and 67% of average worker earnings)

Source: OECD (2011), *Taxing Wages Database*; Gandullia, L., N. Iacobone and A. Thomas (2012), "Modelling the Tax Burden on Labour Income in Brazil, China, India, Indonesia and South Africa", *OECD Economics Department Working Papers*, OECD Publishing, forthcoming.

StatLink http://dx.doi.org/10.1787/888932565851

Figure 3.4. **Marginal tax wedge on labour**[1]

Percentage of total labour compensation

A. At 100% of average worker earnings, single person without children

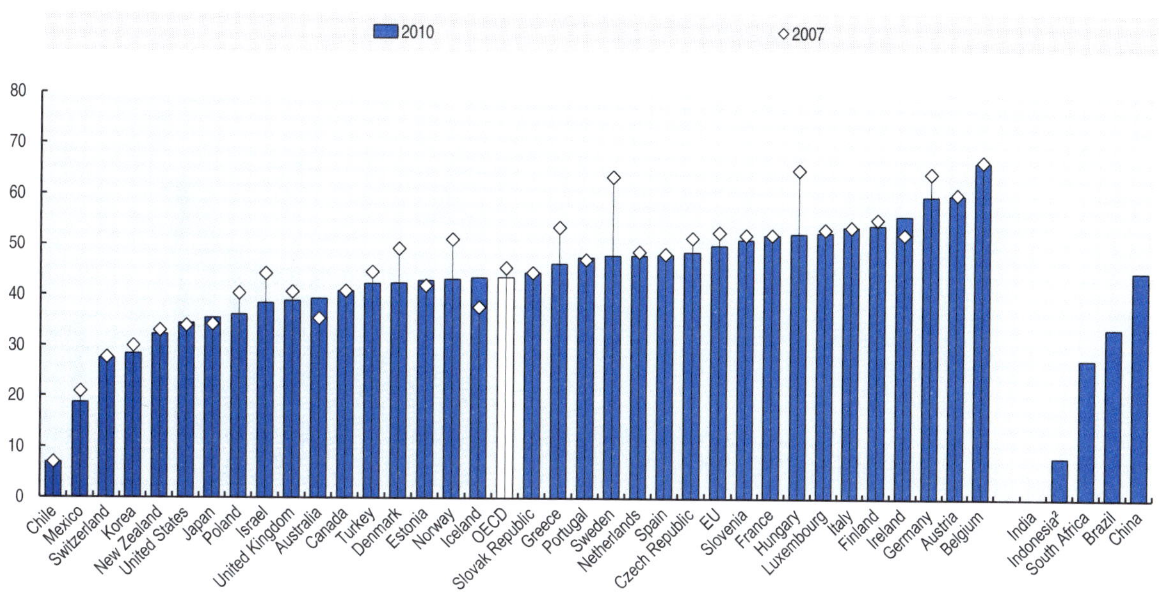

B. At 167% of average worker earnings, single person without children

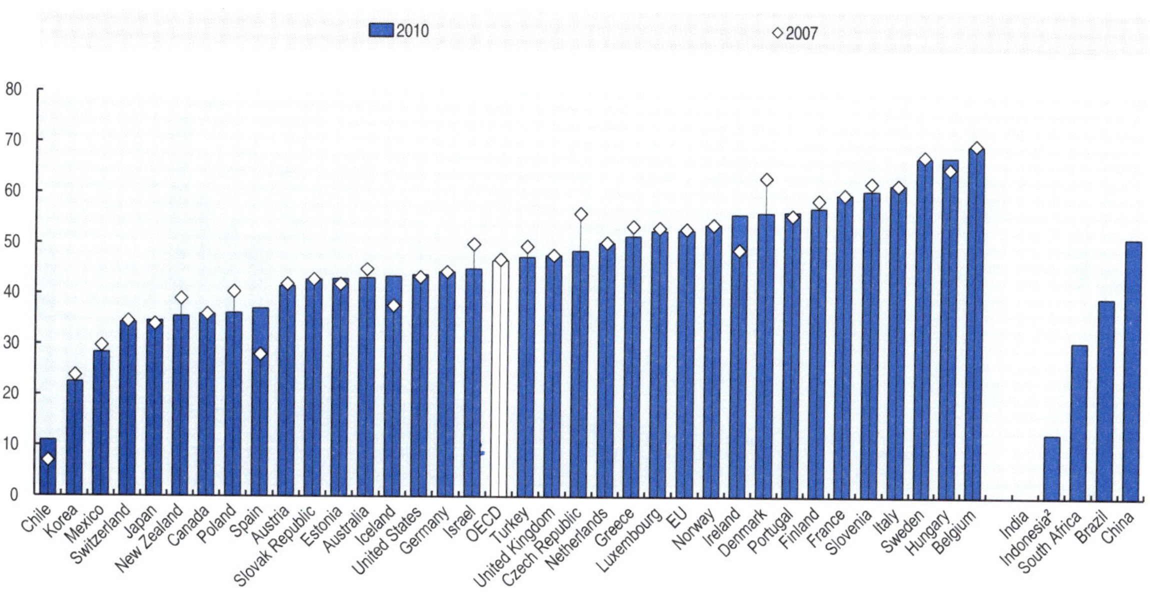

Note: Users of the data must be aware that they may no longer fully reflect the current situation in fast reforming countries.

1. Measured as the difference between the change in total labour compensation paid by employers and the change in the net take-home pay of employees, as a result of an extra unit of national currency of labour income. The difference is expressed as a percentage of the change in total labour compensation. The value for India is equal to zero in 2010. For India, the data refer to employees in the 95% of companies in the manufacturing sector with less than ten employees. In firms with over 10 employees, the tax wedge would be no more than 5%. In China, a significant portion of the labour force are not covered by the social security system and their tax wedge would be significantly lower than the figure report here.
2. Data refer to 2009 for Indonesia.

Source: OECD (2011), *Taxing Wages Database*; Gandullia, L., N. Iacobone and A. Thomas (2012), "Modelling the Tax Burden on Labour Income in Brazil, China, India, Indonesia and South Africa", *OECD Economics Department Working Papers*, OECD Publishing, forthcoming.

StatLink http://dx.doi.org/10.1787/888932565870

Figure 3.5. **Implicit taxes on continued work at older ages**

Percentage of average worker earnings

A. Implicit tax on continued work: early retirement[1]

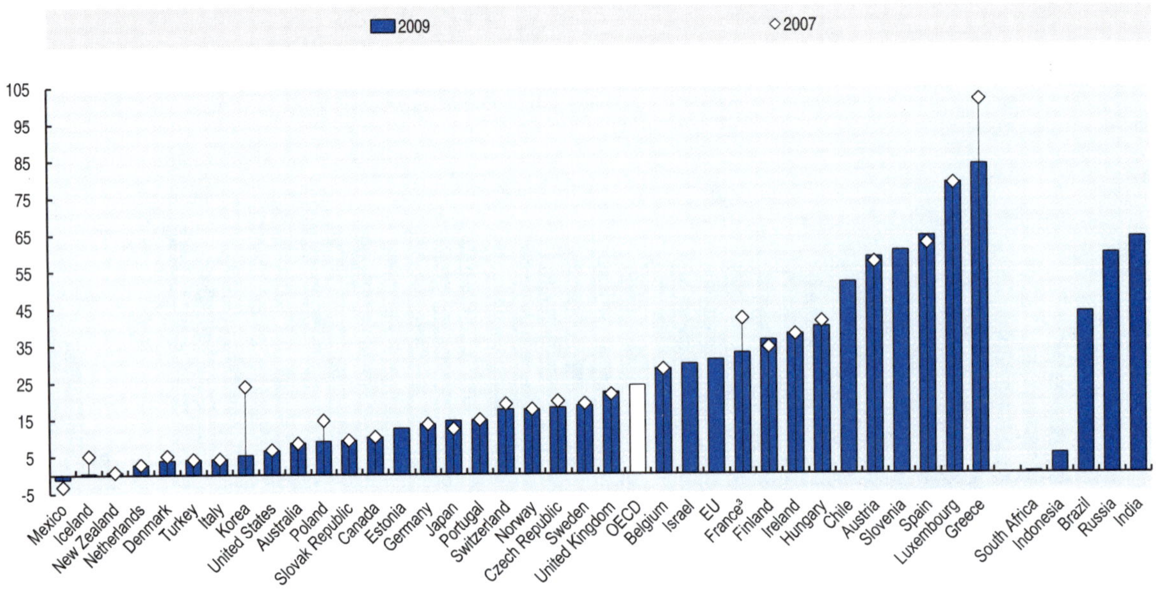

B. Implicit tax on continued work: old-age pensions[2]

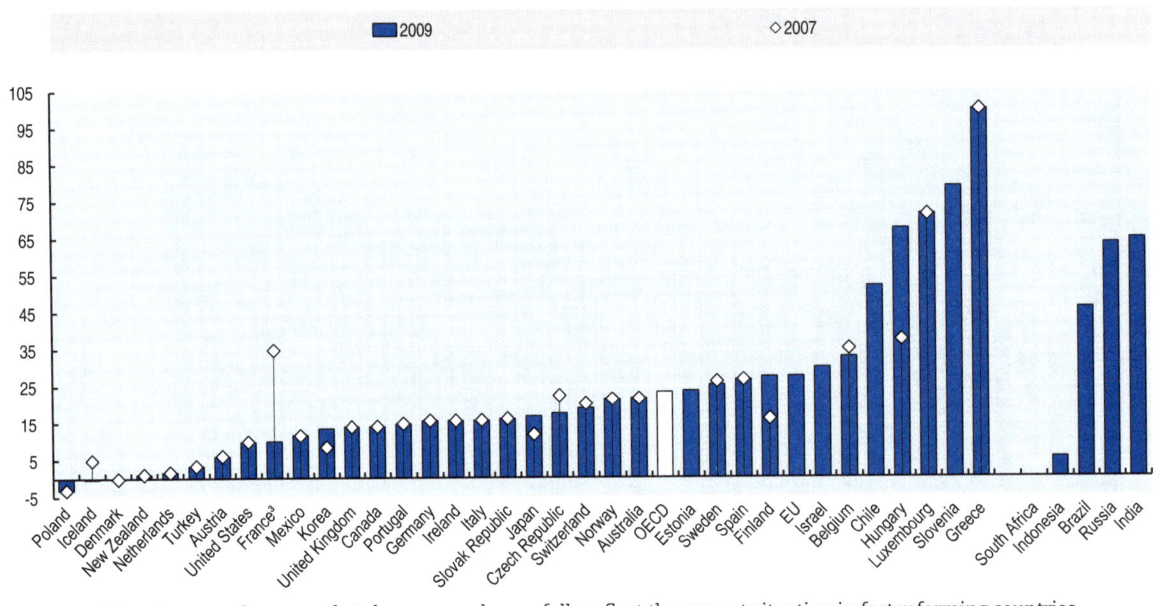

Note: Users of the data must be aware that they may no longer fully reflect the current situation in fast reforming countries.

1. Average for 55 and 60 year-olds workers of implicit tax on continued work for five more years in "early retirement route", as defined in Duval (2003).
2. Implicit tax on continued work in regular old-age pension system, for 60 year olds. The value for South Africa is equal to zero in 2009.
3. For France, year 2010.

Source: Duval, R. (2003), "The Retirement Effects of Old-Age Pension and Early Retirement Schemes in OECD Countries", *OECD Economics Department Working Papers*, No. 370, OECD Publishing and OECD calculations.

StatLink http://dx.doi.org/10.1787/888932565889

Figure 3.6. **Average tax wedge – single parent *versus* second earner**

Percentage

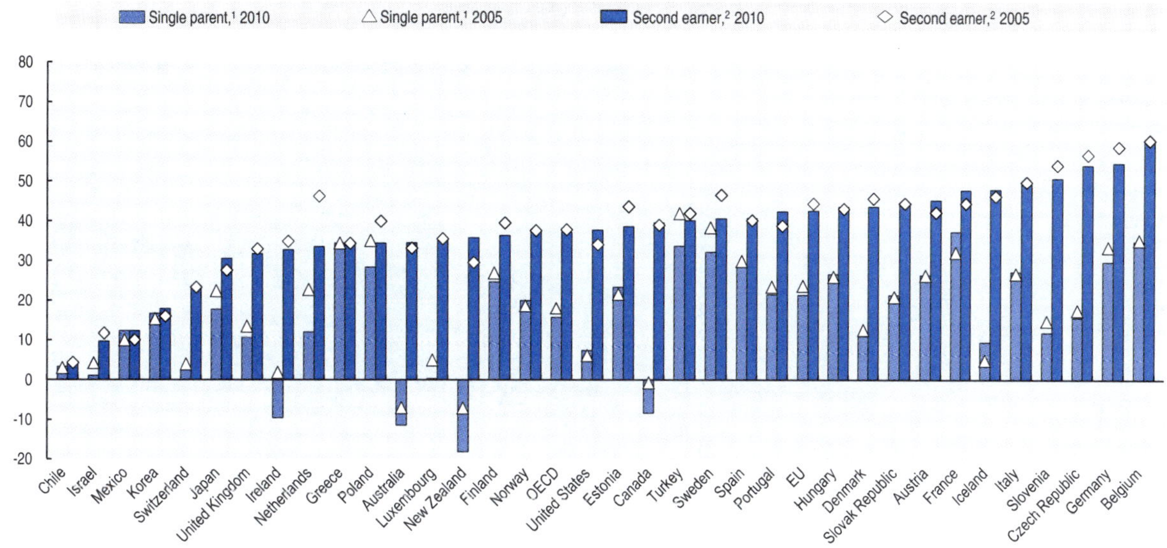

Note: Users of the data must be aware that they may no longer fully reflect the current situation in fast reforming countries.

1. Single parent earning 67% of the average wage.
2. Family with two children where the primary earner earns 100% of the average wage and the secondary earner earns 67% of the average wage.

Source: OECD (2011), Taxing Wages models.

StatLink http://dx.doi.org/10.1787/888932565908

Figure 3.7. **Public expenditure on childcare services**[1]

Percentage of GDP

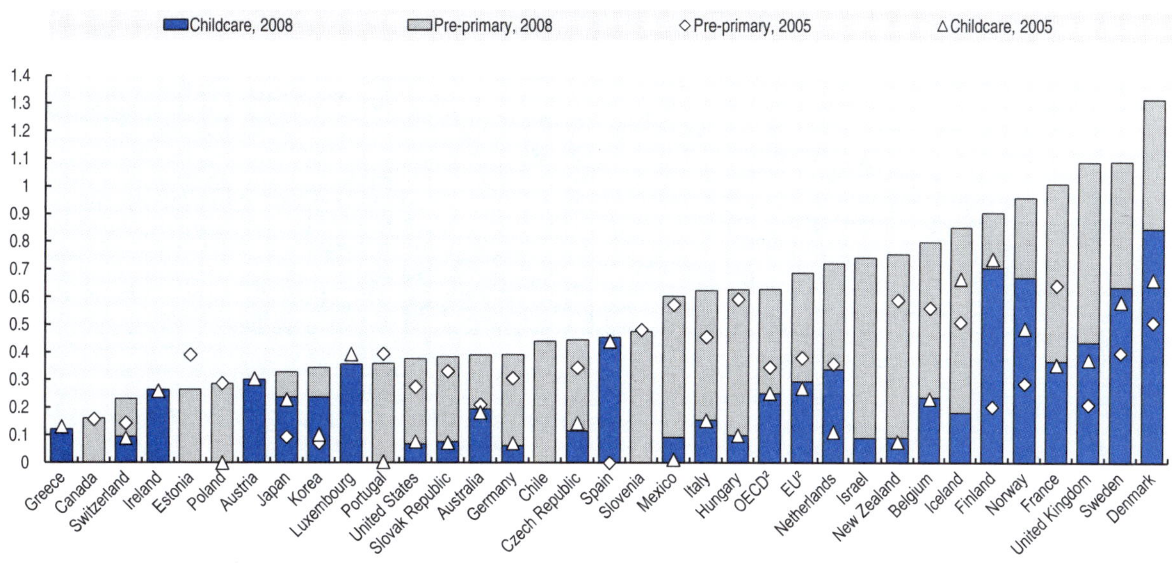

Note: Users of the data must be aware that they may no longer fully reflect the current situation in fast reforming countries.

1. Childcare expenditure cover children under 3 years-old enrolled in childcare and children between 3 and 5 years-old enrolled in pre-school. Childcare refers to formal day-care services, such as day care centres and family day care. Pre-school includes kindergartens and day-care centres which usually provide an educational content as well as traditional care for children (ISCED 0 under UNESCO's classification system).
2. EU is the average of European countries in the OECD. OECD and EU averages exclude Turkey. Data are missing for Chile and Israel in 2005; Greece, Ireland and Austria for pre-primary in 2005 and 2008; Luxembourg for pre-primary in 2005 and Spain for pre-primary in 2008; Canada and Slovenia for childcare in 2005 and 2008; Poland for childcare in 2008. Corresponding OECD and EU averages (where relevant) do not include these countries.

Source: OECD (2011), *Social Expenditure Database, www.oecd.org/els/social/expenditure.*

StatLink http://dx.doi.org/10.1787/888932565927

Figure 3.8. **Implicit tax on returning to work**[1]

Net transfers and childcare fees for households with two children aged 2 and 3, 2008

A. Second earner taking up employment[2]

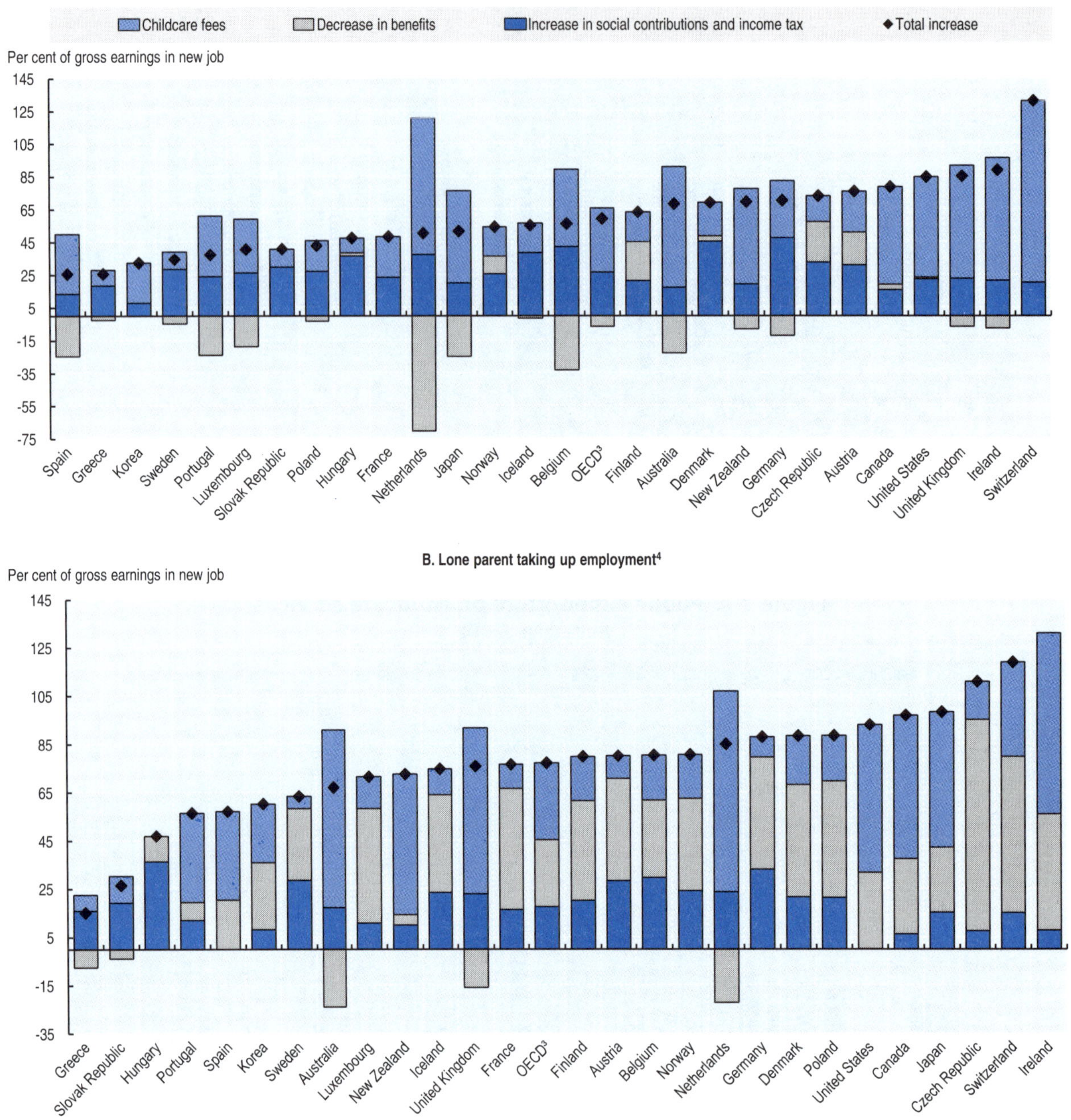

Note: Users of the data must be aware that they may no longer fully reflect the current situation in fast reforming countries.

1. Taking into account childcare fees and changes of taxes and benefits in case of a transition to a job paying two-thirds of average worker earnings.
2. Second earner taking up employment at 67% of average wage and the first earner earns 100% of average wage.
3. The OECD average excludes Chile, Estonia, Israel, Italy, Mexico, Turkey and Slovenia.
4. Lone parent taking up employment at 67% of average wage.

Source: OECD (2011), *Benefits and Wages Database.*

StatLink http://dx.doi.org/10.1787/888932565946

Figure 3.9. **Net costs of childcare**

Percentage of average wage, 2008

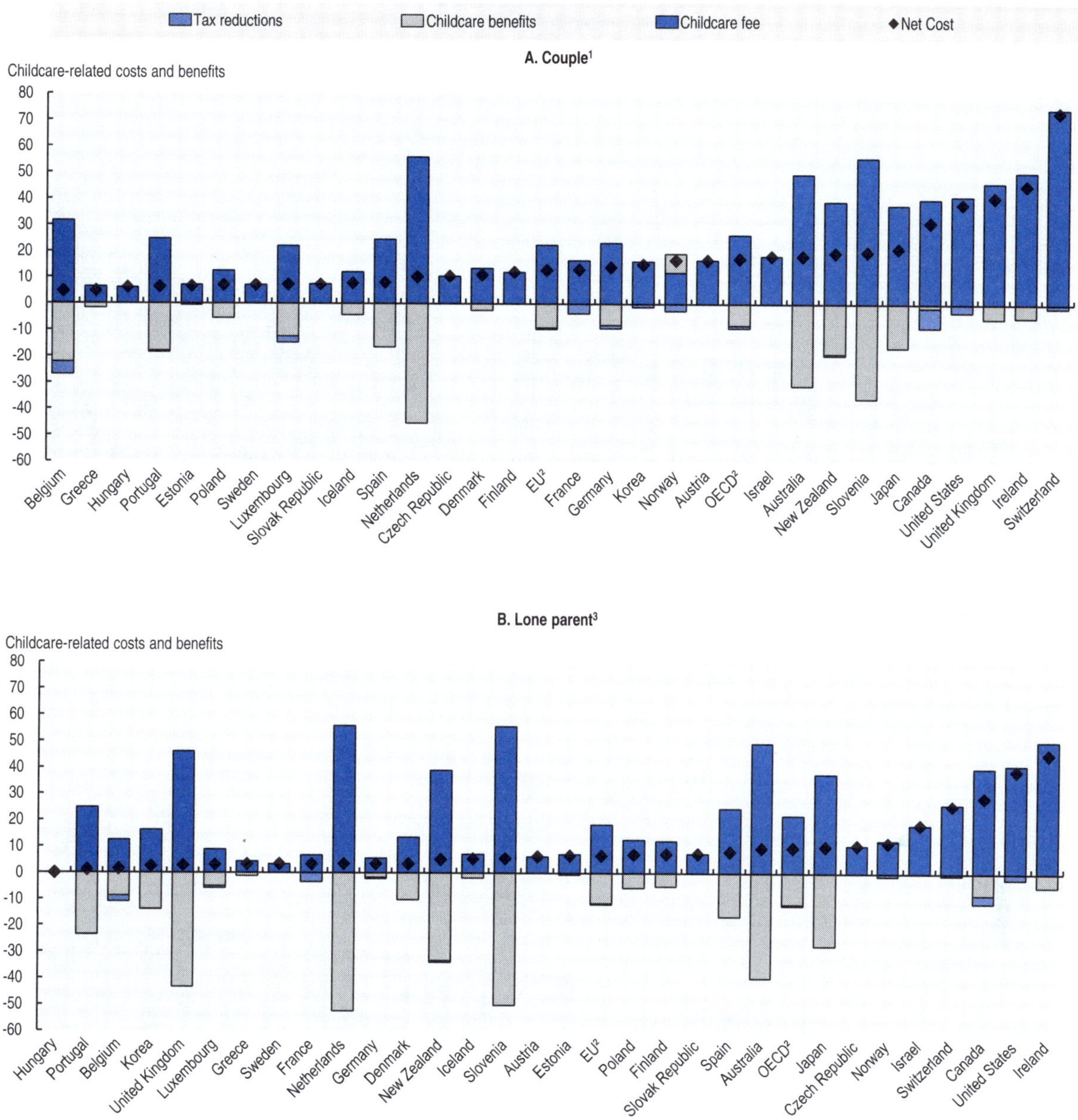

Note: Users of the data must be aware that they may no longer fully reflect the current situation in fast reforming countries.

1. Couple where the first earner earns 100% of the average wage and the second earns 67% of the average wage. For Canada and the United Kingdom, childcare benefits refer to childcare benefits and other benefits.
2. EU and OECD averages exclude Chile, Italy, Mexico and Turkey.
3. Lone parent earning 67% of the average wage. For Canada and the United Kingdom, childcare benefits refer to childcare benefits and other benefits.

Source: OECD, Tax-benefit models, *www.oecd.org/els/social/workincentives*.

StatLink http://dx.doi.org/10.1787/888932565965

Figure 3.10. **Income support for disability and sickness**

A. Per cent of population aged 20-64 years-old receiving disability benefits[1]

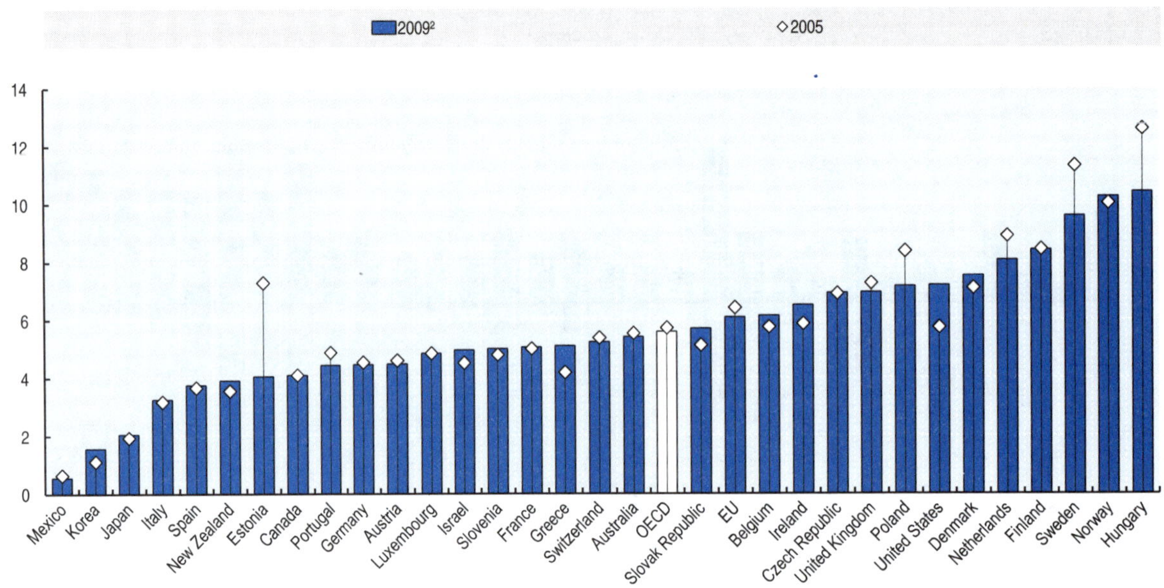

B. Number of weeks lost due to sickness leave

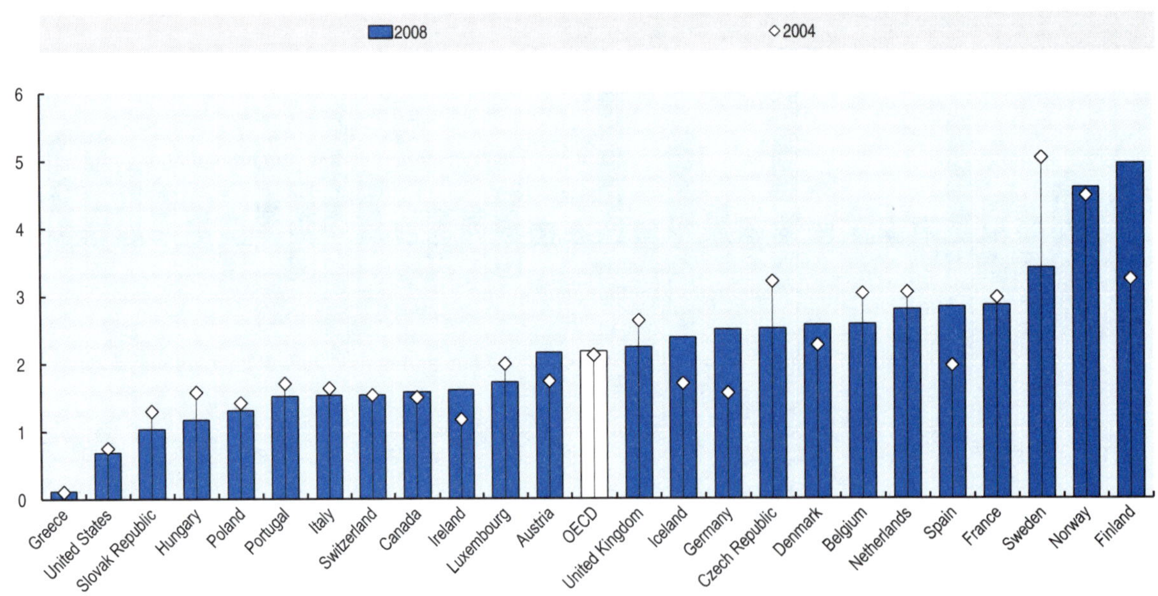

Note: Users of the data must be aware that they may no longer fully reflect the current situation in fast reforming countries.

1. Disability benefits include benefits received from schemes to which beneficiaries have paid contributions (contributory), programmes financed by general taxation (non-contributory) and work injury schemes.
2. The last available year is 2005 for Luxembourg; 2007 for Canada, France, Italy, Spain and Poland; 2008 for Australia, Austria, Belgium, the United Kingdom, Greece, Ireland, Japan, Korea, Slovenia; 2010 for Denmark, Estonia, Hungary, Israel and Portugal.

Source: OECD (2010), *Sickness, Disability and Work: Breaking the Barriers – A Synthesis of Findings across OECD Countries*; estimates of the percentage of population aged 20-64 years-old receiving disability benefits have been updated (unpublished data).

StatLink http://dx.doi.org/10.1787/888932565984

Figure 3.11. **Employment Protection Legislation (EPL)**

Index scale of 0-6 from least to most restrictive

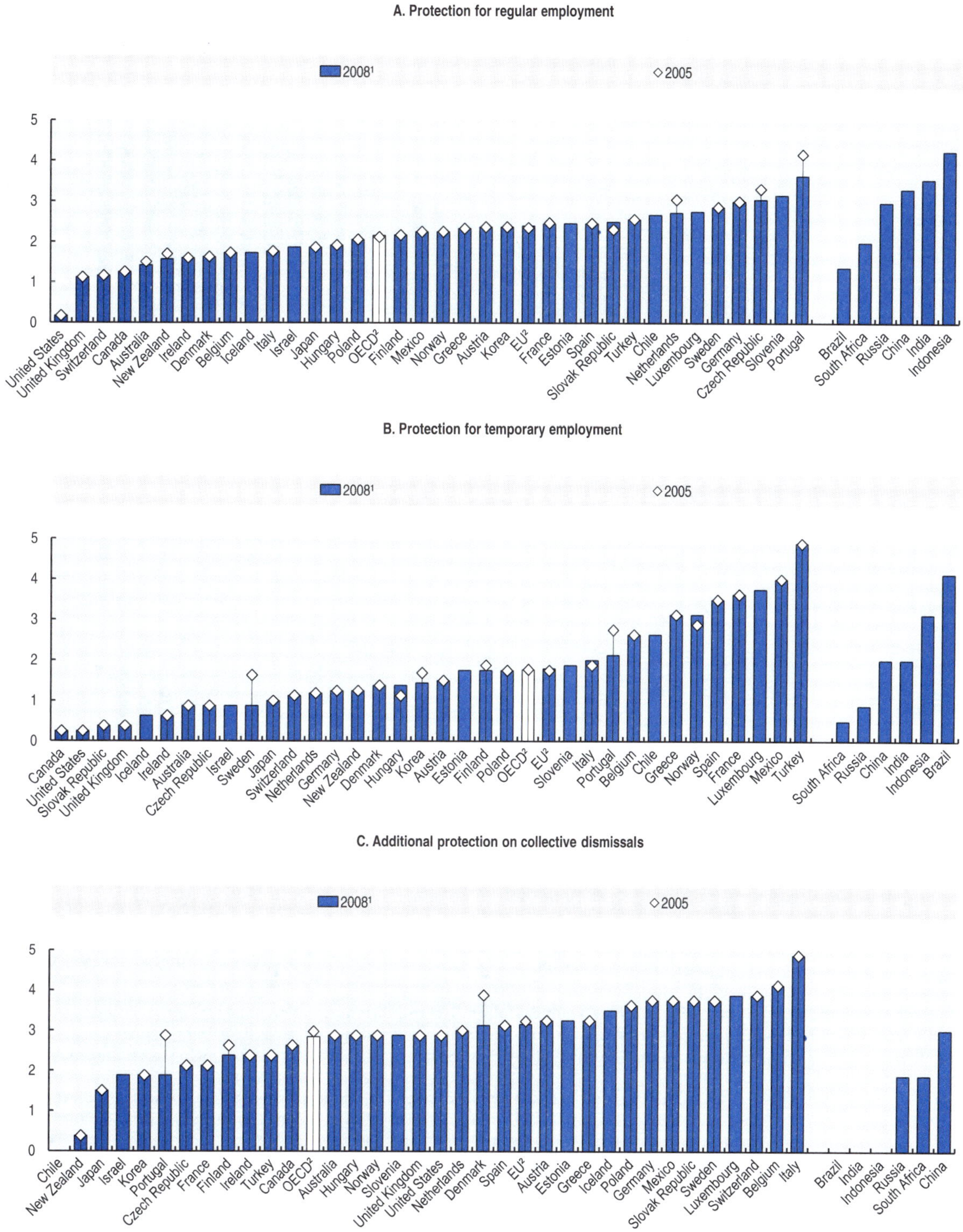

Note: Users of the data must be aware that they may no longer fully reflect the current situation in fast reforming countries.

1. 2009 for France and Portugal. In Panel C, values for Brazil, India and Indonesia are equal to zero in 2008.
2. In 2005, OECD and EU averages exclude Chile, Estonia, Iceland, Israel, Luxembourg and Slovenia.

Source: OECD (2011), *OECD Employment Database*.

StatLink http://dx.doi.org/10.1787/888932566003

Figure 3.12. **Coverage rates of collective bargaining agreements and trade union density rates**[1]

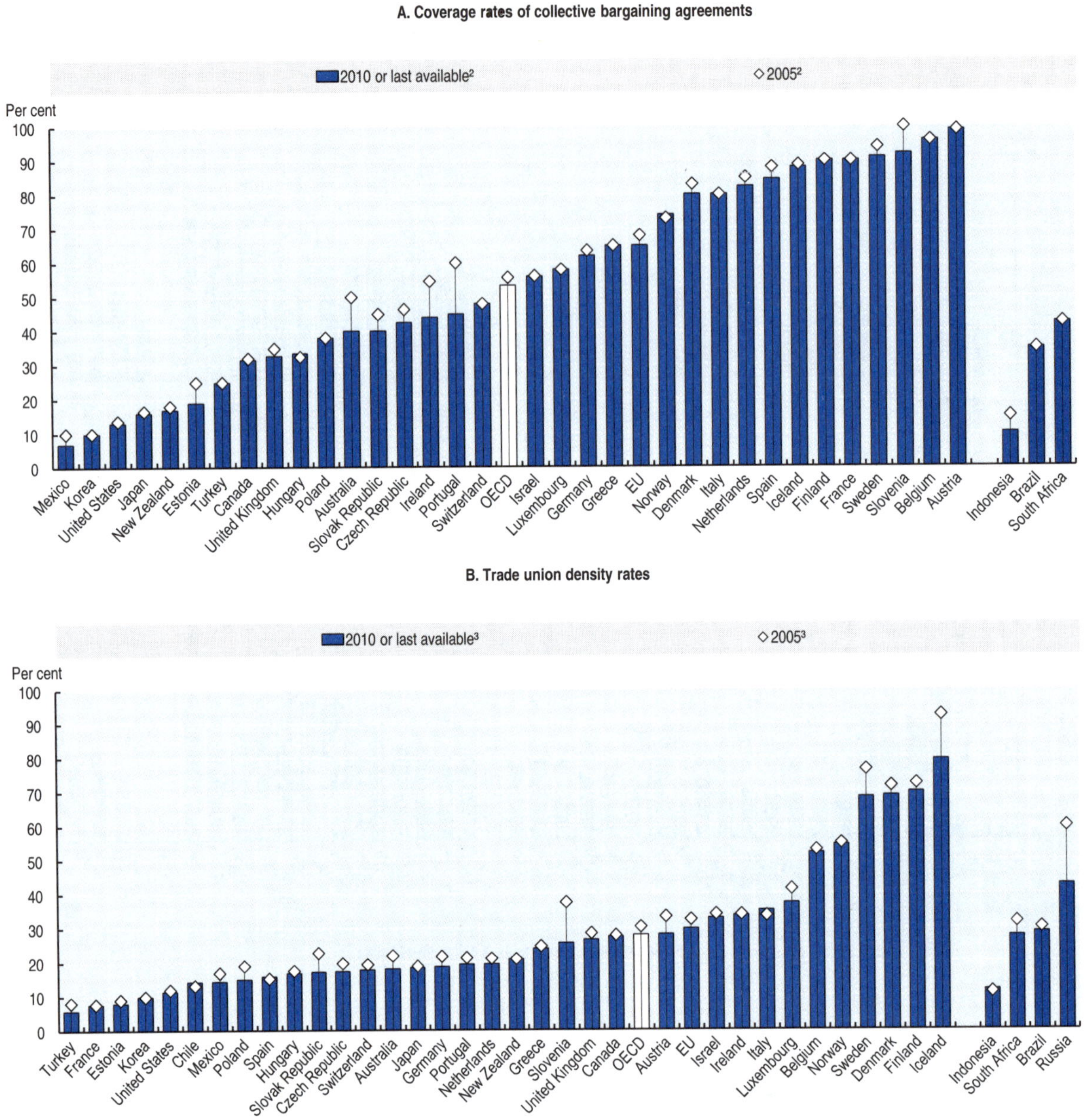

Note: Users of the data must be aware that they may no longer fully reflect the current situation in fast reforming countries.

1. The coverage rate is measured as the percentage of workers who are covered by collective bargaining agreements, regardless of whether or not they belong to a trade union. The union density rate is the percentage of workers belonging to a trade union. The rates refer to wage and salary workers.
2. For 2010, the last available year is 2009 for Canada, the Czech Republic, Estonia, Germany, Hungary, Italy, Portugal, the Slovak Republic, Slovenia and the United Kingdom; 2008 for Belgium, Brazil, France, Greece, Iceland, Indonesia, Ireland, Japan, Korea, Luxembourg, Mexico, the Netherlands, Norway, Poland, South Africa, Spain, Sweden and Switzerland; 2007 for Australia, Denmark, Finland and New Zealand; 2006 for Israel and Turkey. For 2005, data refer to 2006 for Korea, Switzerland and the Slovak Republic; 2004 for Spain; 2003 for Brazil, Indonesia, Luxembourg and New-Zealand; 2002 for Austria, Belgium, Denmark, France, Iceland, Ireland, Mexico and Turkey; 2001 for Australia and Chile; 2000 for Israel.
3. For 2010, the last available year is 2009 for Belgium, Chile, the Czech Republic, Denmark, Ireland, Korea, the Netherlands, Norway, Slovenia, Spain, Switzerland and Turkey; 2008 for Brazil, France, Greece, Hungary, Iceland, Luxembourg, the Russian Federation, the Slovak Republic and South Africa; 2007 for Indonesia and Israel. For 2005, data refer to 2006 for Israel; 2003 for Slovenia; 2002 for Iceland and 2001 for the Russian Federation.

Source: OECD estimates and J. Visser, Amsterdam Institute for Advanced Labour Studies (2011), ICTWSS *Database on Institutions, Coordination, Trade Unions, Wage Setting and Social Pacts (version 3.0).*

StatLink http://dx.doi.org/10.1787/888932566022

Figure 3.13. **Product market regulation**

Index scale of 0-6 from least to most restrictive

A. Restrictiveness of economy-wide product market regulation

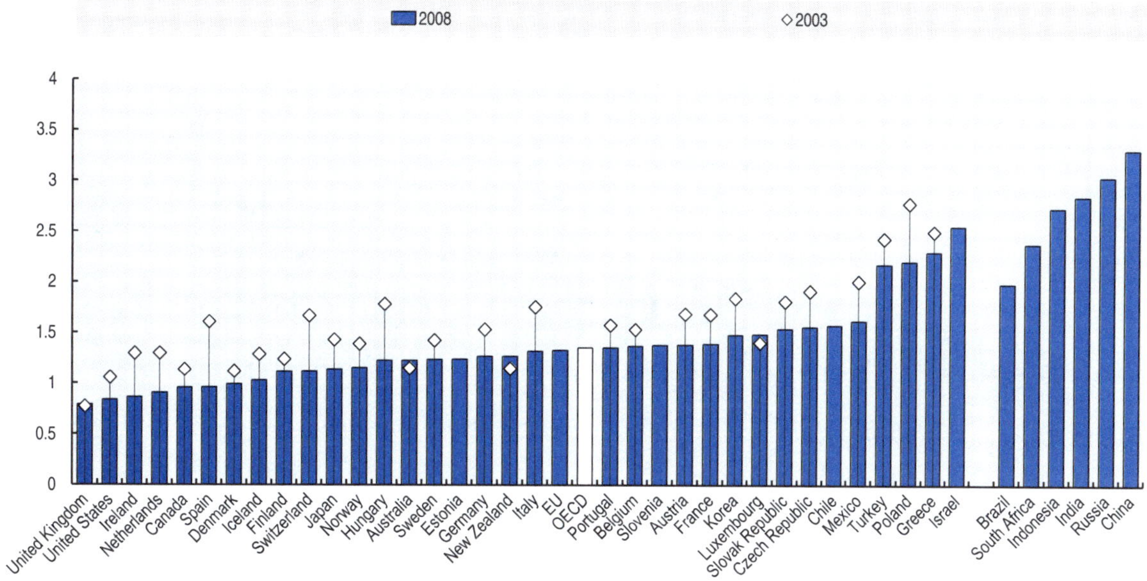

B. Restrictiveness of overall administrative regulation[1]

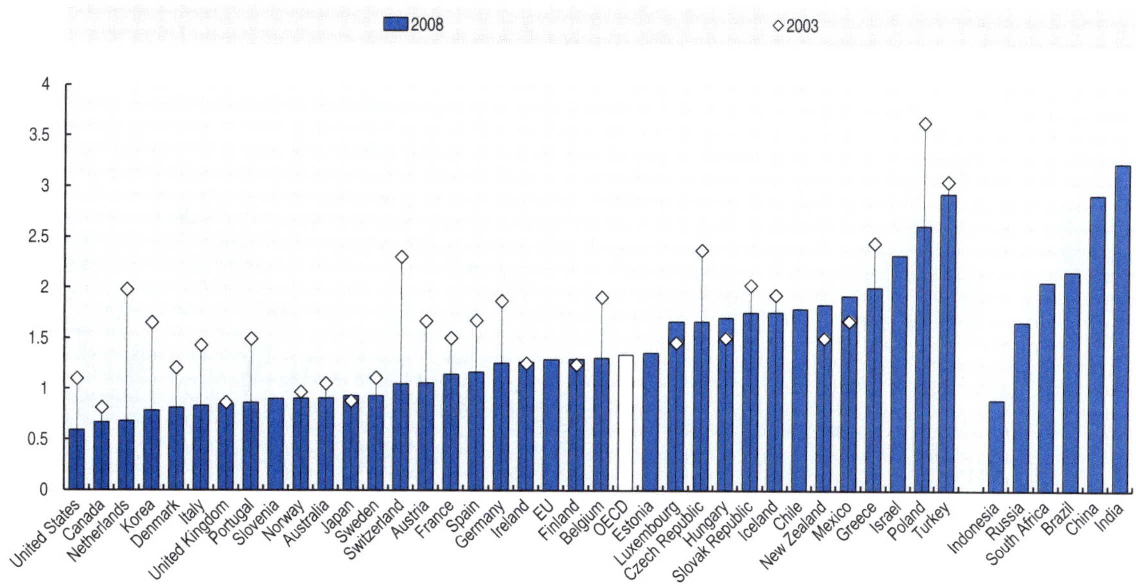

Note: Users of the data must be aware that they may no longer fully reflect the current situation in fast reforming countries.

1. Simple average of regulatory and administrative opacity and administrative burdens on start-ups under the product market regulation domain "barriers to entrepreneurship".

Source: OECD (2011), *Product Market Regulation Database*; Woefl, A. *et al.* (2010), "Product Market Regulation: Extending the Analysis Beyond OECD Countries", *OECD Economics Department Working Papers*, No. 799, OECD Publishing.

StatLink http://dx.doi.org/10.1787/888932566041

Figure 3.14. **State control of business operations**

Index scale of 0-6 from least to most restrictive

A. Extent of public ownership[1]

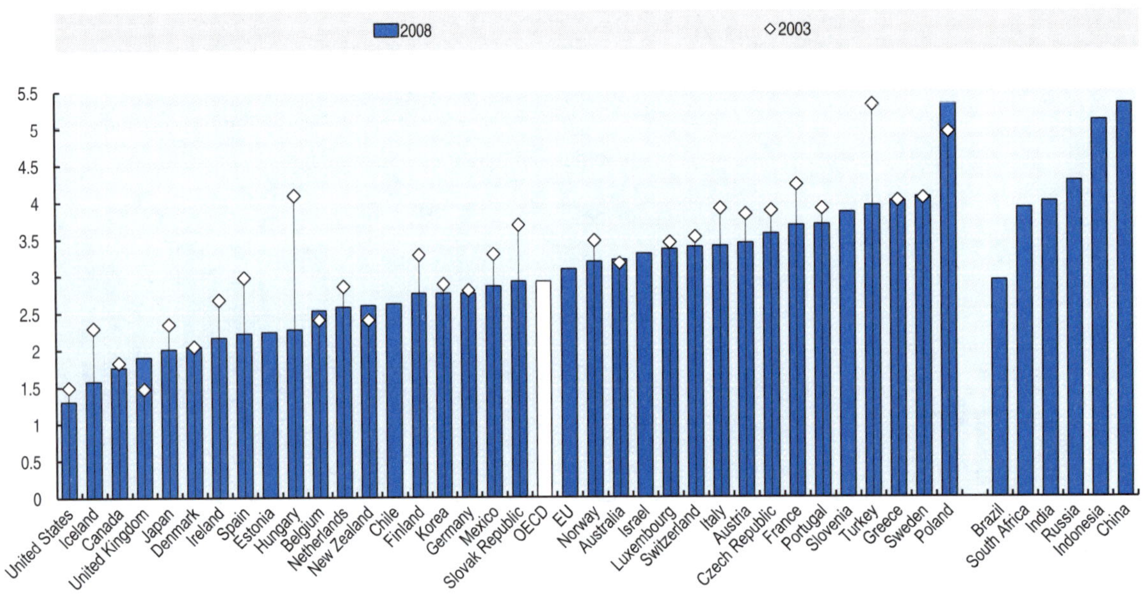

B. State involvement in business operations[2]

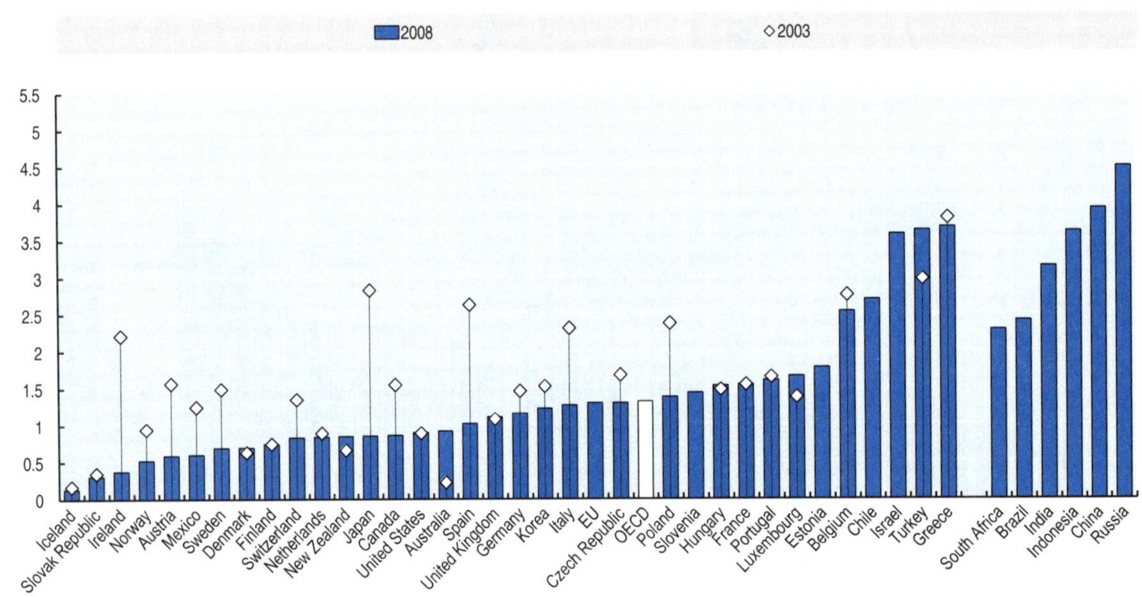

Note: Users of the data must be aware that they may no longer fully reflect the current situation in fast reforming countries.

1. Covers scope of public enterprise and government's involvement in network sectors as well as the direct state control over business enterprises (via voting rights or legislative bodies).
2. Concerns the involvement of the state in business operations via price controls and the use of command-and-control regulation.

Source: OECD (2011), *Product Market Regulation Database*; Woefl, A. *et al.* (2010), "Product Market Regulation: Extending the Analysis Beyond OECD Countries", *OECD Economics Department Working Papers*, No. 799, OECD Publishing.

StatLink http://dx.doi.org/10.1787/888932566060

Figure 3.15. **Administrative burdens on start-ups**

Index scale of 0-6 from least to most restrictive

A. Administrative burdens for corporations and sole proprietor firms[1]

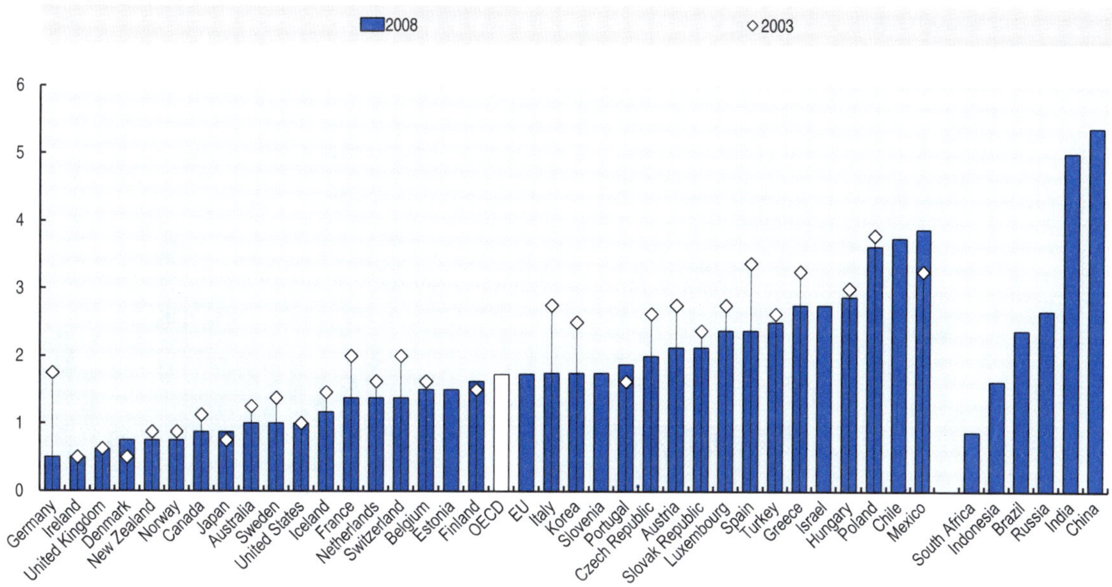

B. Sector-specific administrative burdens[2]

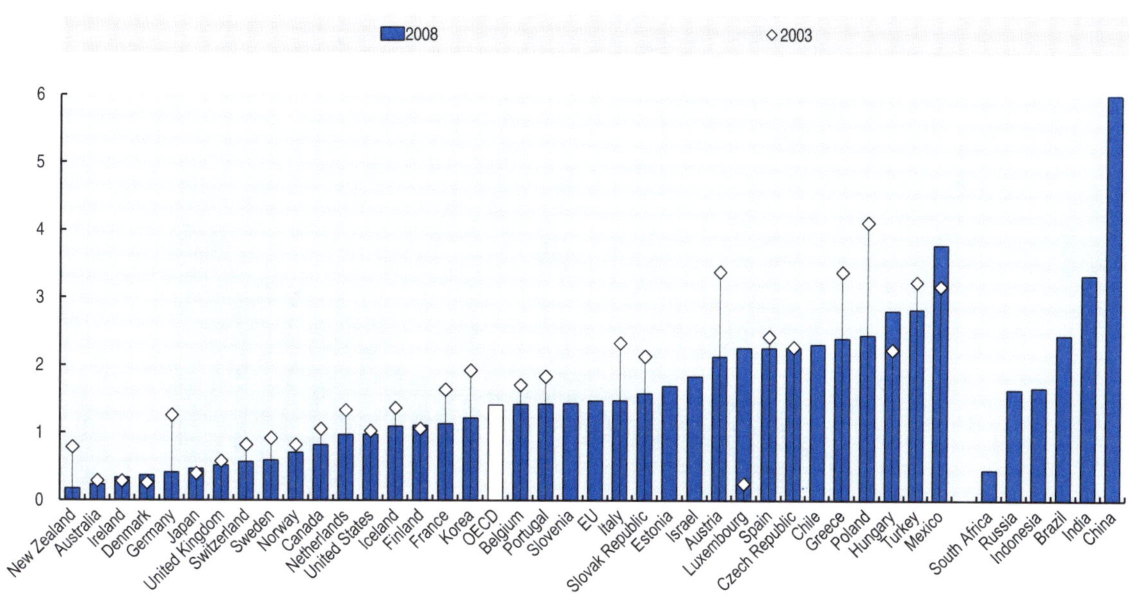

Note: Users of the data must be aware that they may no longer fully reflect the current situation in fast reforming countries.

1. Simple average of administrative burdens for corporations and for sole proprietor firms under the product market regulation sub-domain "administrative burdens on start-ups".
2. This index refers to administrative burdens in the road transport and retail distribution sectors.

Source: OECD (2011), *Product Market Regulation Database*; Woefl, A. *et al.* (2010), "Product Market Regulation: Extending the Analysis Beyond OECD Countries", *OECD Economics Department Working Papers*, No. 799, OECD Publishing.

StatLink http://dx.doi.org/10.1787/888932566079

Figure 3.16. **Barriers to entry**

Index scale of 0-6 from least to most restrictive

A. Legal barriers to entry in industries

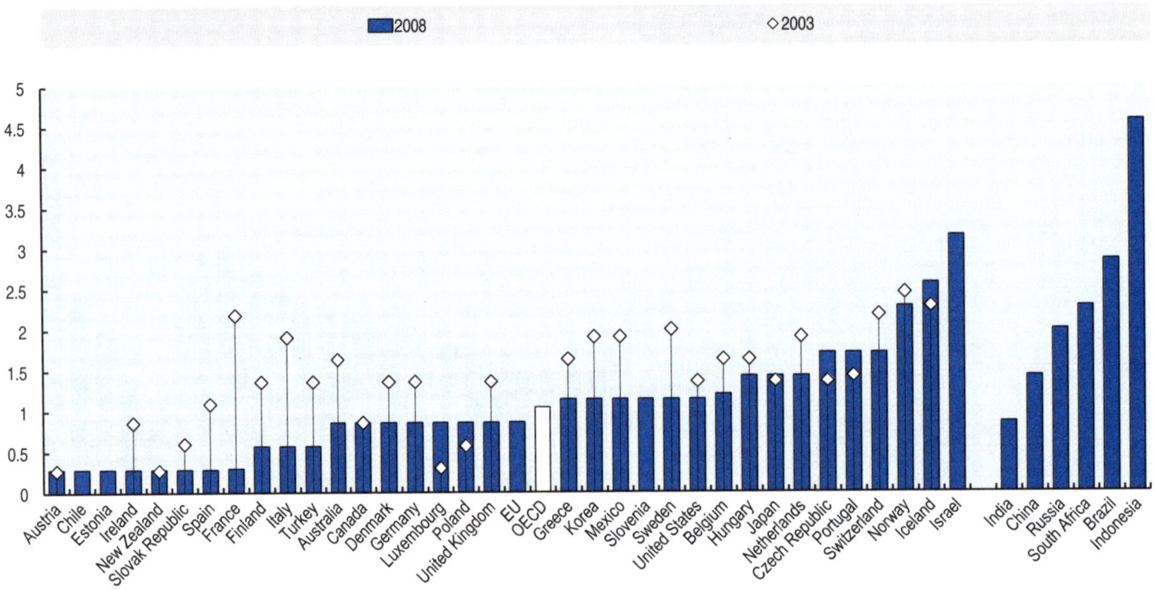

B. Complexity of regulatory procedures[1]

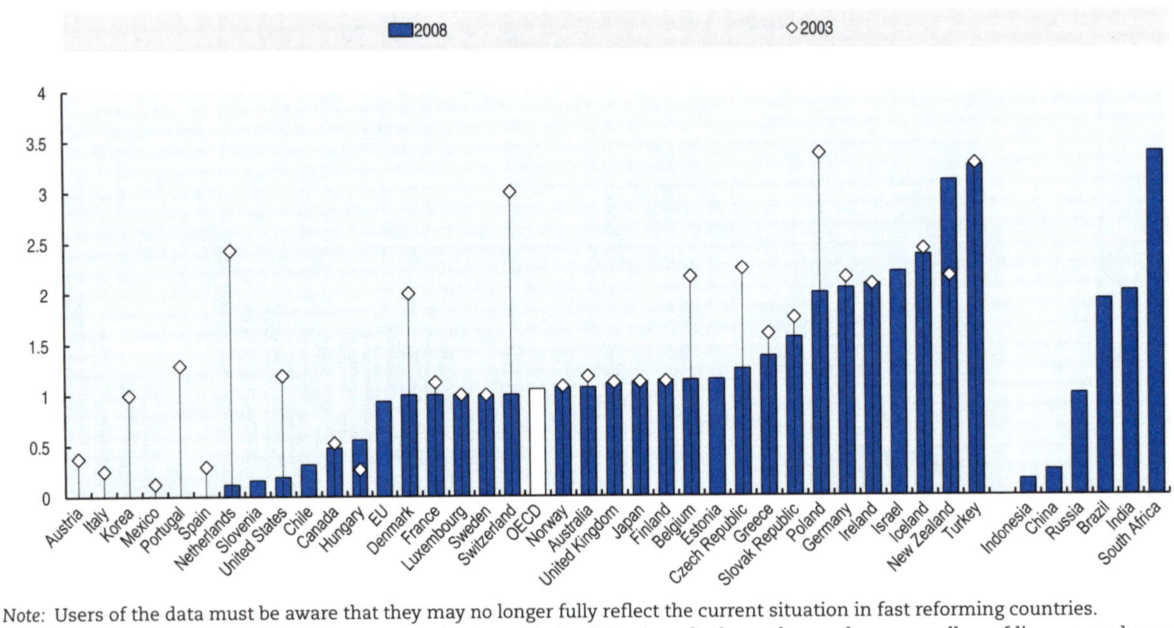

Note: Users of the data must be aware that they may no longer fully reflect the current situation in fast reforming countries.

1. Concerns complexity of government communication and simplification of rules and procedures as well as of licences and permits system. Values for Austria, Italy, Korea, Mexico, Portugal and Spain are equal to zero in 2008.

Source: OECD (2011), *Product Market Regulation Database*; Woefl, A. *et al.* (2010), "Product Market Regulation: Extending the Analysis Beyond OECD Countries", *OECD Economics Department Working Papers*, No. 799, OECD Publishing.

StatLink http://dx.doi.org/10.1787/888932566098

Figure 3.17. Barriers to foreign direct investment[1]

Index scale of 0-6 from least to most restrictive

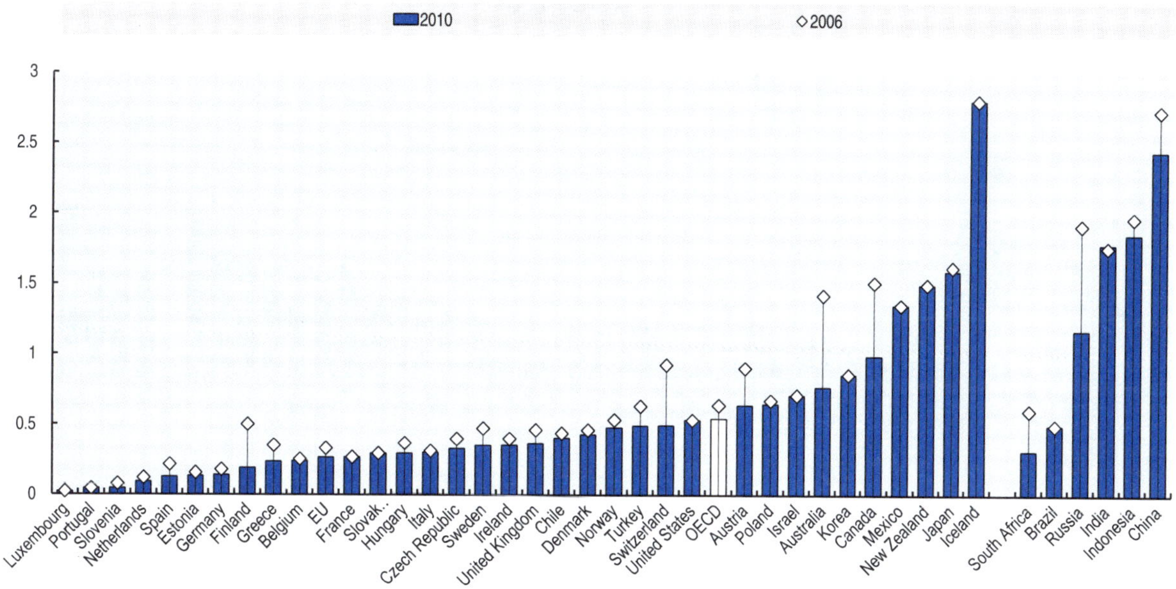

Note: Users of the data must be aware that they may no longer fully reflect the current situation in fast reforming countries.

1. The OECD FDI regulatory restrictiveness index looks only at statutory restrictions and does not assess the manner in which they are implemented.

Source: OECD, the OECD FDI Regulatory Restrictiveness Index (FDI Index), *www.oecd.org/investment/index*.

StatLink http://dx.doi.org/10.1787/888932566117

Figure 3.18. Restrictiveness of external trade tariffs[1]

Index scale of 0-6 from least to most restrictive

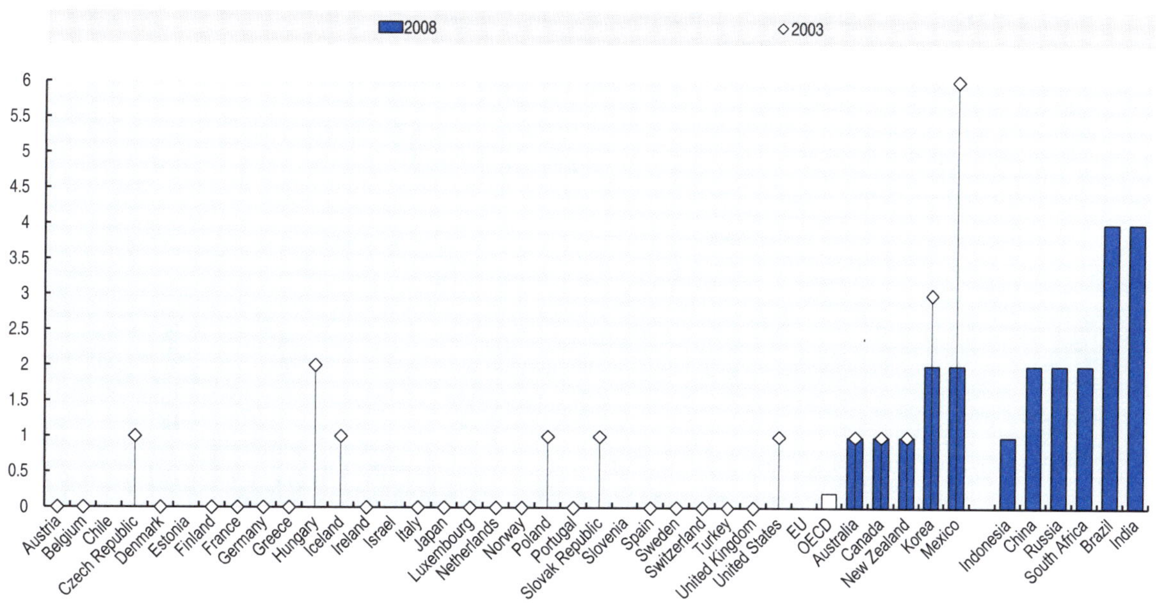

Note: Users of the data must be aware that they may no longer fully reflect the current situation in fast reforming countries.

1. Values are equal to zero in 2008 for the EU average and for all OECD countries except Australia, Canada, Korea, Mexico and New Zealand.

Source: OECD (2011), *Product Market Regulation Database*; for methodology see Woefl, A. *et al.* (2010), "Product Market Regulation: Extending the Analysis Beyond OECD Countries", *OECD Economics Department Working Papers*, No. 799, OECD Publishing. Tariffs reflect the simple average of effectively applied tariffs. See World Trade Organization's (WTO), *Integrated Database (IDB)*.

StatLink http://dx.doi.org/10.1787/888932566136

Figure 3.19. **Sectoral regulation in the transport sector**

Index scale of 0-6 from least to most restrictive

A. Airlines sector[1]

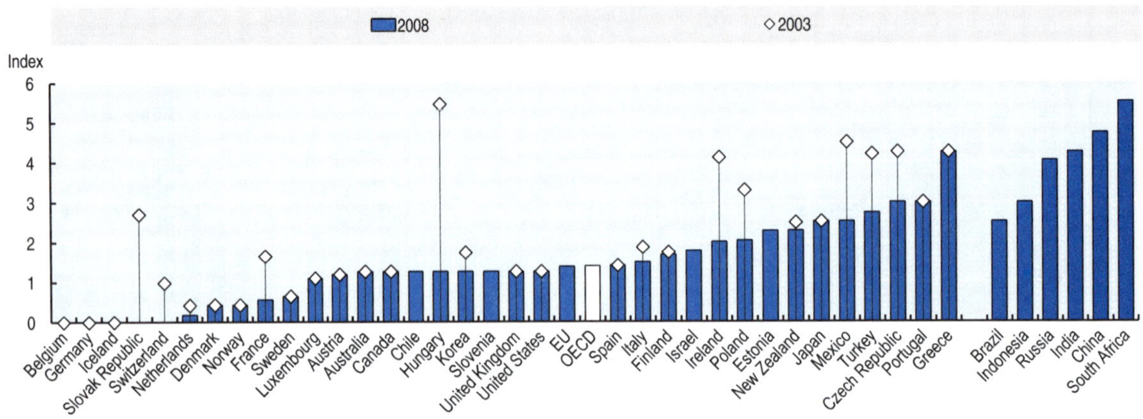

B. Rail sector

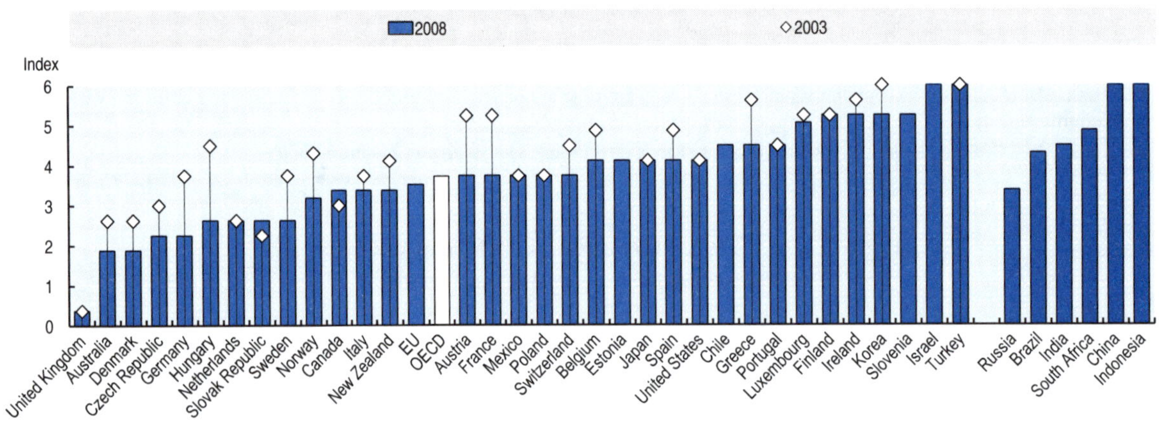

C. Road sector[2]

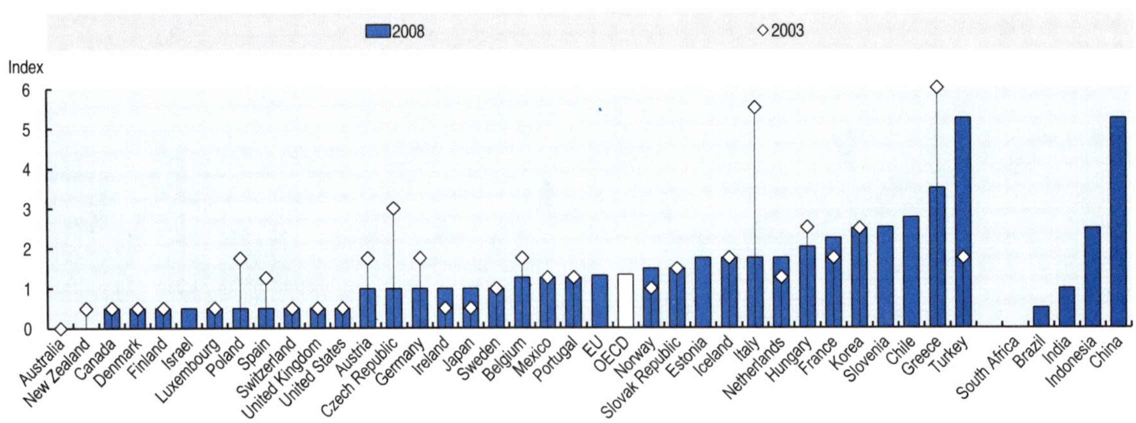

Note: Users of the data must be aware that they may no longer fully reflect the current situation in fast reforming countries.

1. Values for Belgium, Germany, Iceland, Switzerland and the Slovak Republic are equal to zero in 2008.
2. Values for Australia, New Zealand and South Africa are equal to zero in 2008.

Source: OECD (2011), *Product Market Regulation Database*.

StatLink http://dx.doi.org/10.1787/888932566155

Figure 3.20. **Sectoral regulation in the energy sector**

Index scale of 0-6 from least to most restrictive

A. Electricity sector

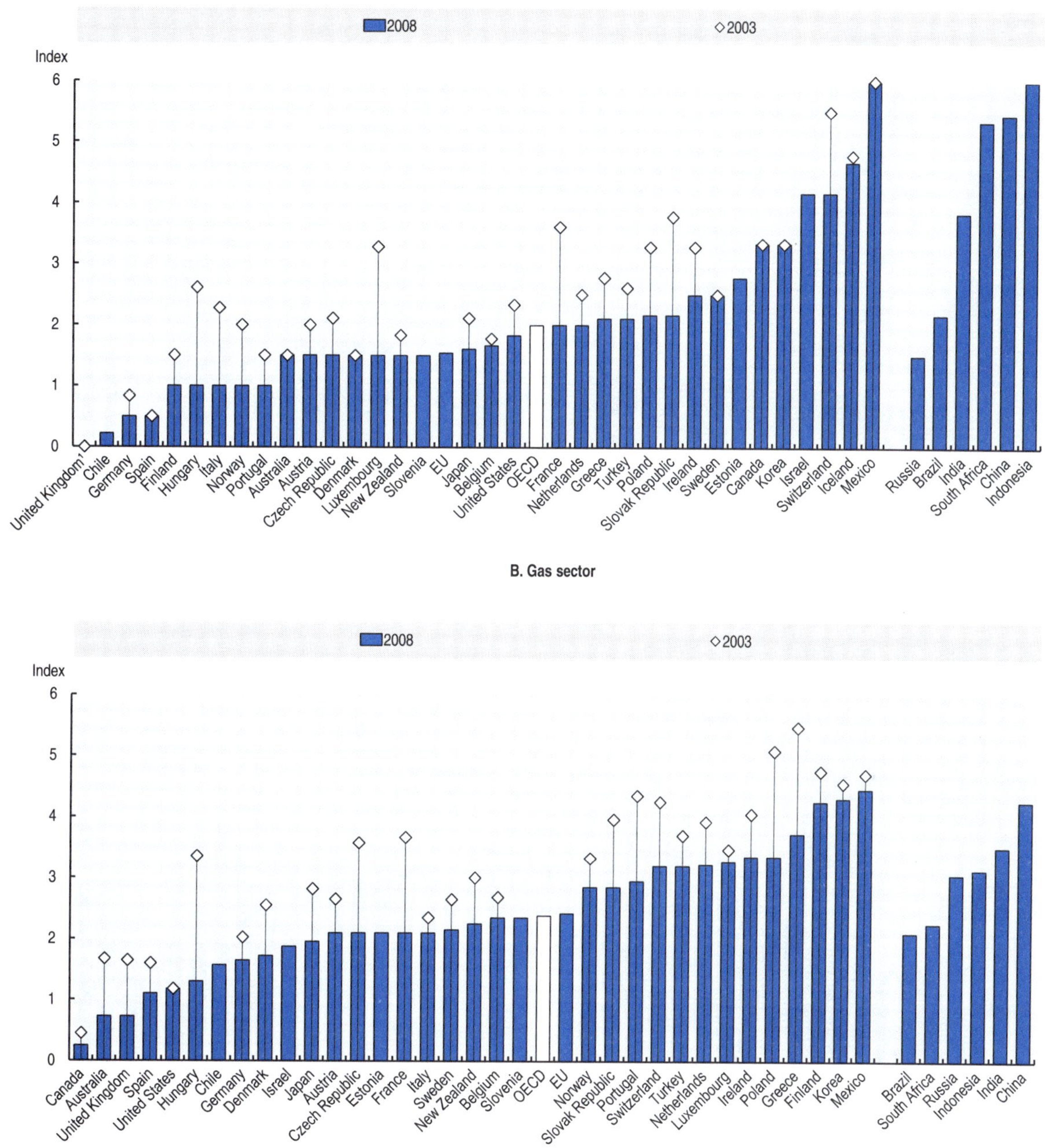

Note: Users of the data must be aware that they may no longer fully reflect the current situation in fast reforming countries.

1. The value for the United Kingdom is equal to zero in 2008.

Source: OECD (2011), *Product Market Regulation Database*.

StatLink http://dx.doi.org/10.1787/888932566174

Figure 3.21. Sectoral regulation in the post and telecommunications sector

Index scale of 0-6 from least to most restrictive

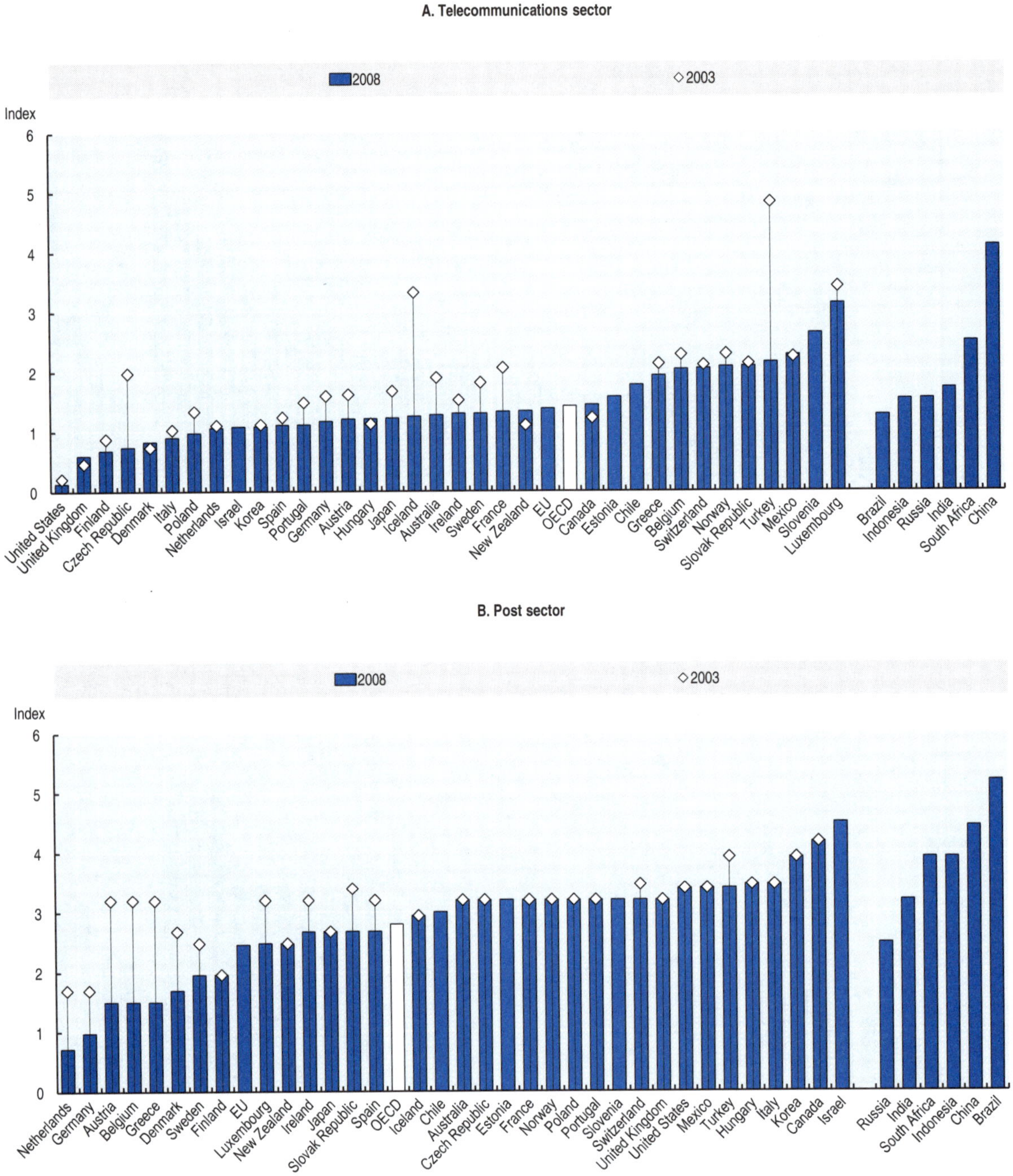

Note: Users of the data must be aware that they may no longer fully reflect the current situation in fast reforming countries.

Source: OECD (2011), *Product Market Regulation Database.*

StatLink http://dx.doi.org/10.1787/888932566193

Figure 3.22. **Sectoral regulation in retail and professional services**

Index scale of 0-6 from least to most restrictive

A. Retail sector

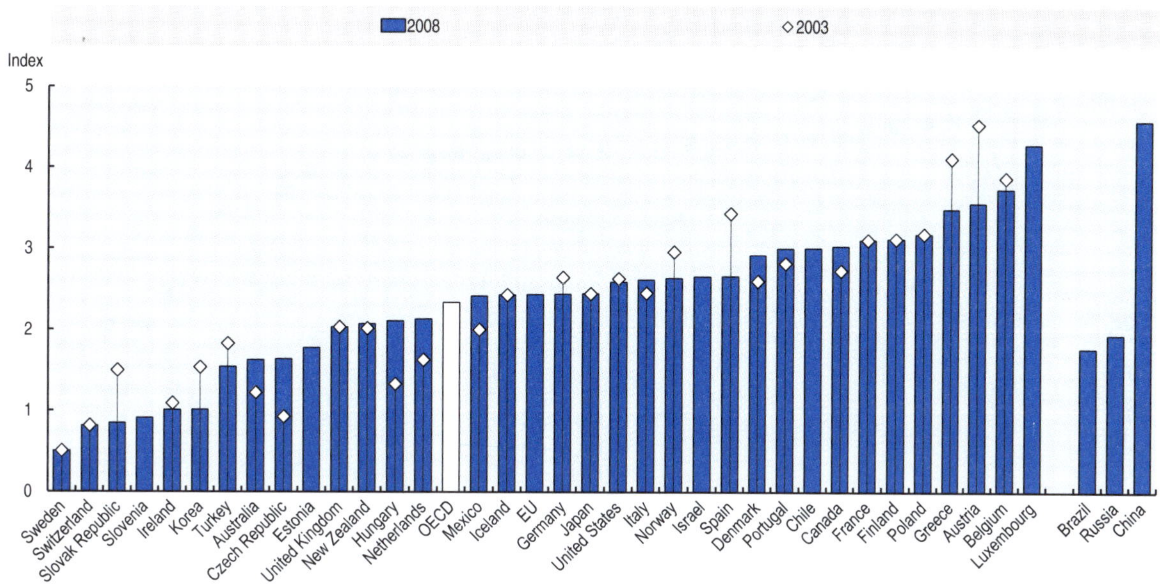

B. Professional services

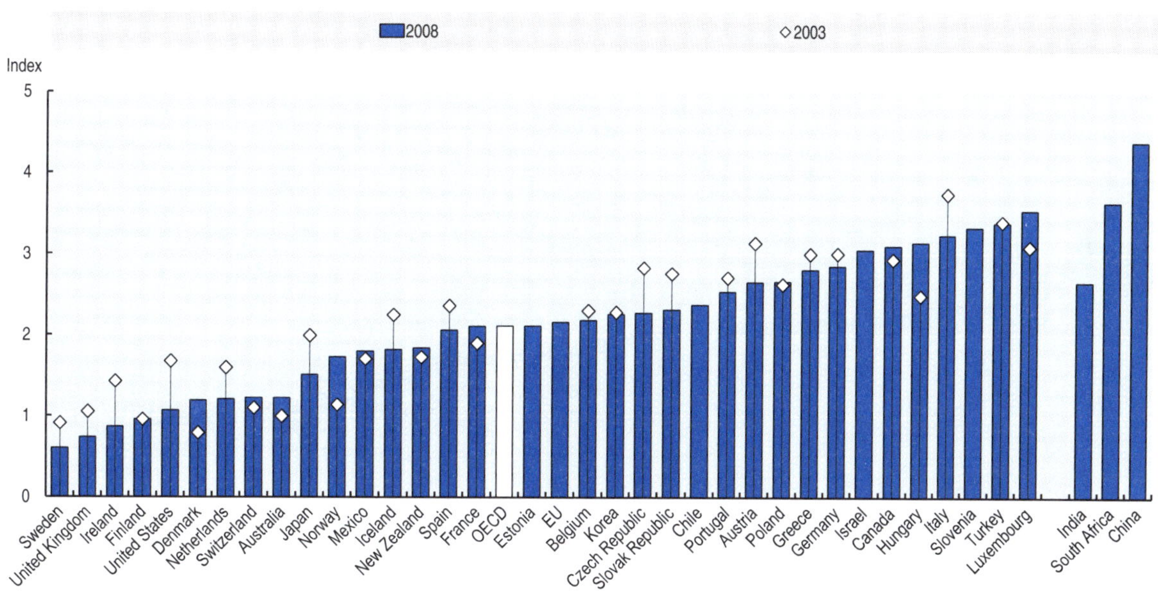

Note: Users of the data must be aware that they may no longer fully reflect the current situation in fast reforming countries.

Source: OECD (2011), *Product Market Regulation Database*.

StatLink http://dx.doi.org/10.1787/888932566212

Figure 3.23. **Educational attainment, 2009**

Percentage of population aged 25-34 and 45-54

A. Upper secondary education

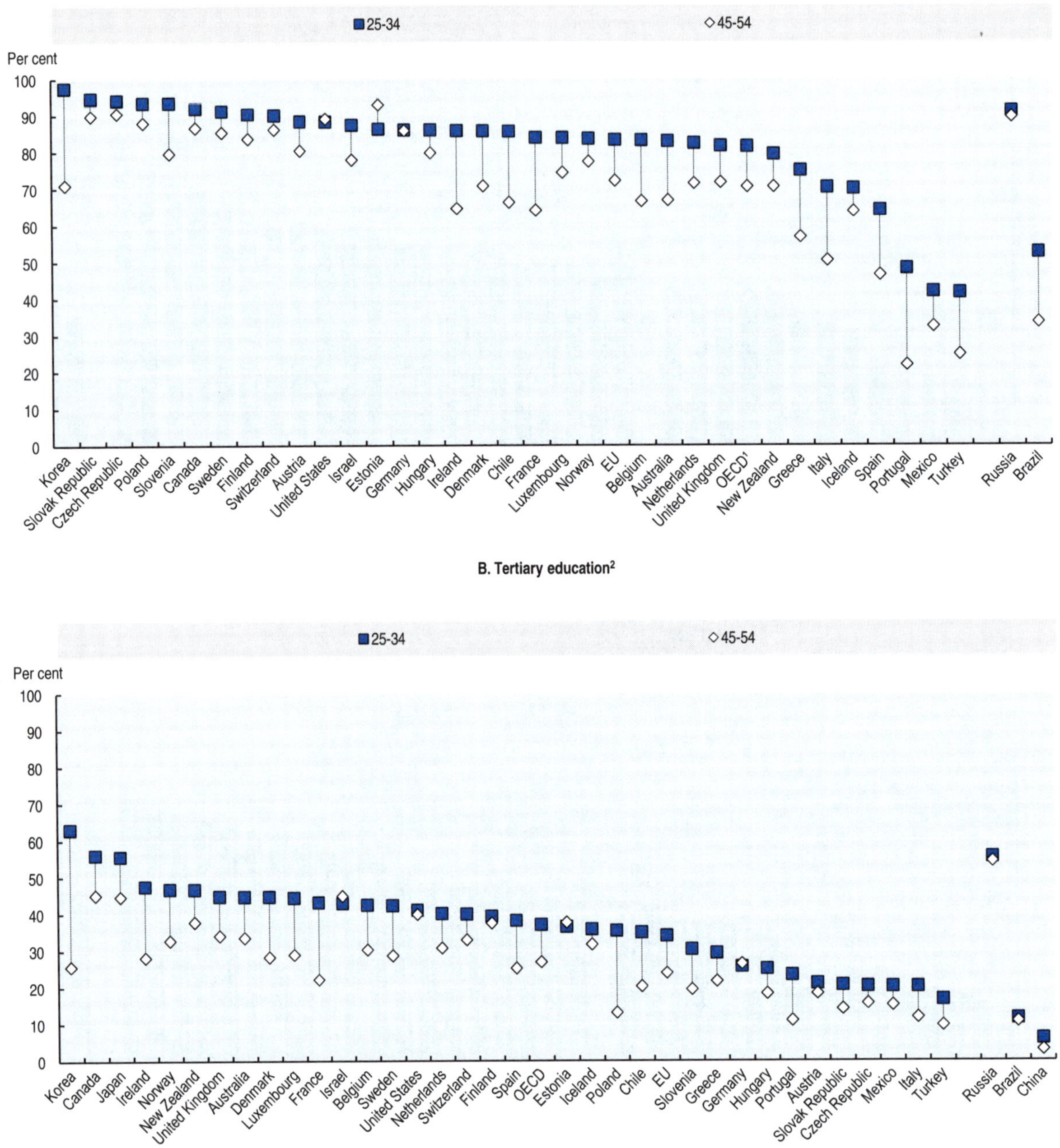

Note: Users of the data must be aware that they may no longer fully reflect the current situation in fast reforming countries.

1. Data are missing for Japan.
2. The reference year is 2000 for China and 2002 for the Russian Federation.

Source: OECD (2011), *Education at a Glance 2011: OECD Indicators.*

StatLink http://dx.doi.org/10.1787/888932566231

Figure 3.24. **Graduation rates in upper secondary and tertiary education**[1]

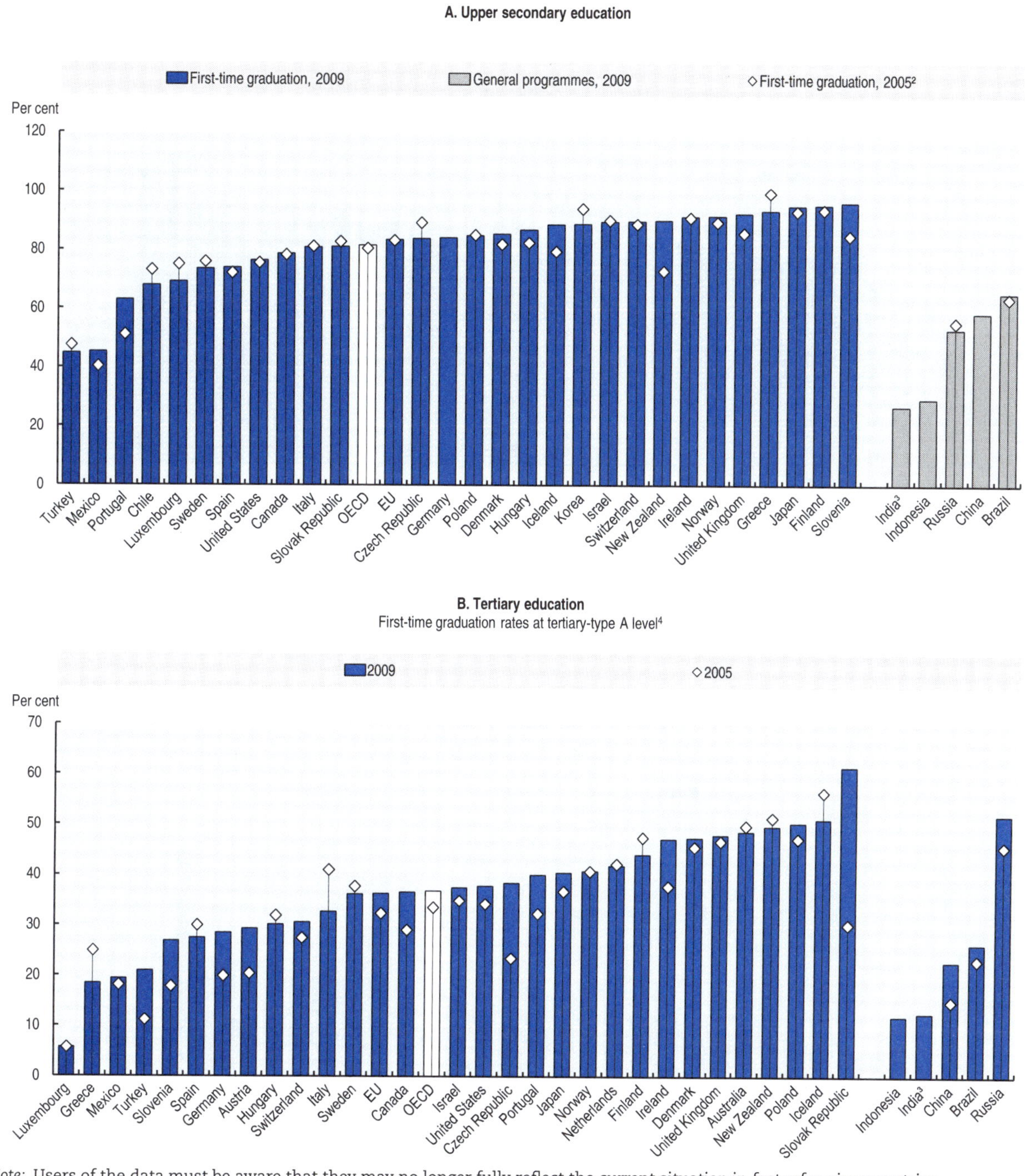

Note: Users of the data must be aware that they may no longer fully reflect the current situation in fast reforming countries.

1. Data refer to 2010 for China; 2008 for Canada, Greece, India, Portugal and Switzerland in Panel A and data refer to 2008 for Australia, Canada, Greece and Luxembourg in Panel B.
2. For Brazil and the Russian Federation, data for 2005 refer to general programmes.
3. Data for upper secondary education in India are defined as 19 year olds who completed upper secondary education; data for tertiary education refer to 24 year olds and over who graduated.
4. Tertiary graduates are those who obtain a tertiary-type A qualification (ISCED 5A). For Brazil, Indonesia and the Russian Federation, data refer to first degree graduation in years 2006 and 2009.

Source: OECD (2011), *Education at a Glance 2011: OECD Indicators*; China Statistical Yearbook and India National Sample Survey (2007/8).

StatLink http://dx.doi.org/10.1787/888932566250

Figure 3.25. **Educational achievement**

Average of PISA scores in reading, mathematics and science[1, 2]

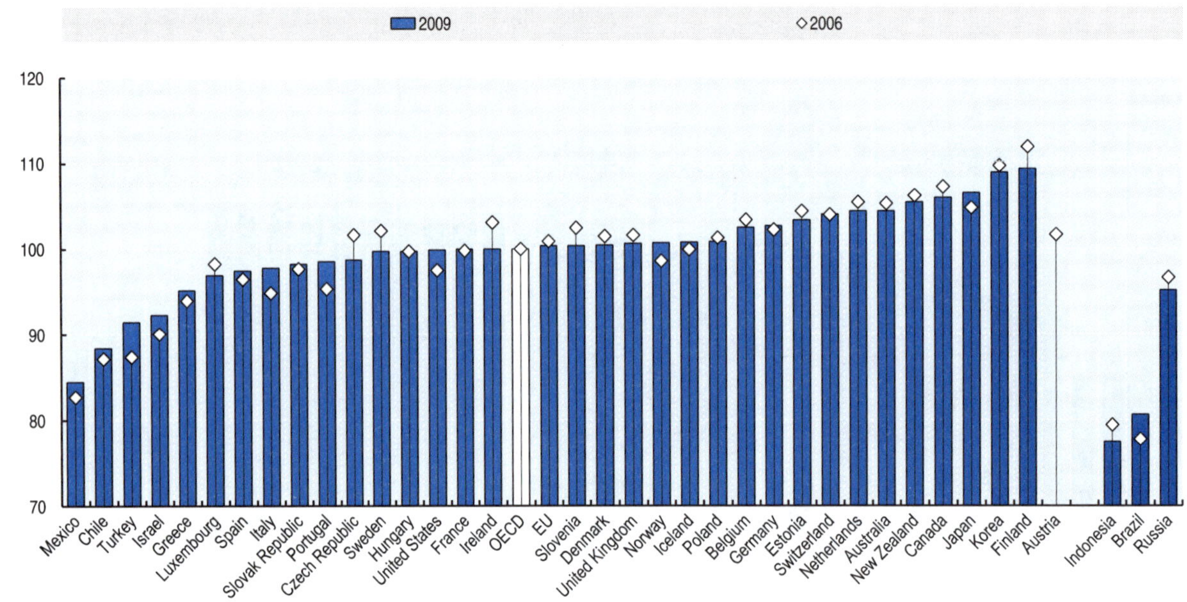

Note: Users of the data must be aware that they may no longer fully reflect the current situation in fast reforming countries.

1. PISA is the Programme for International Student Assessment. OECD = 100.
2. For the United States, average of PISA scores in mathematics and science in 2006. Data for Austria is not available in 2009.

Source: OECD (2010), *PISA 2009 Database.*

StatLink http://dx.doi.org/10.1787/888932566269

Figure 3.26. **Health expenditure**

Percentage of GDP

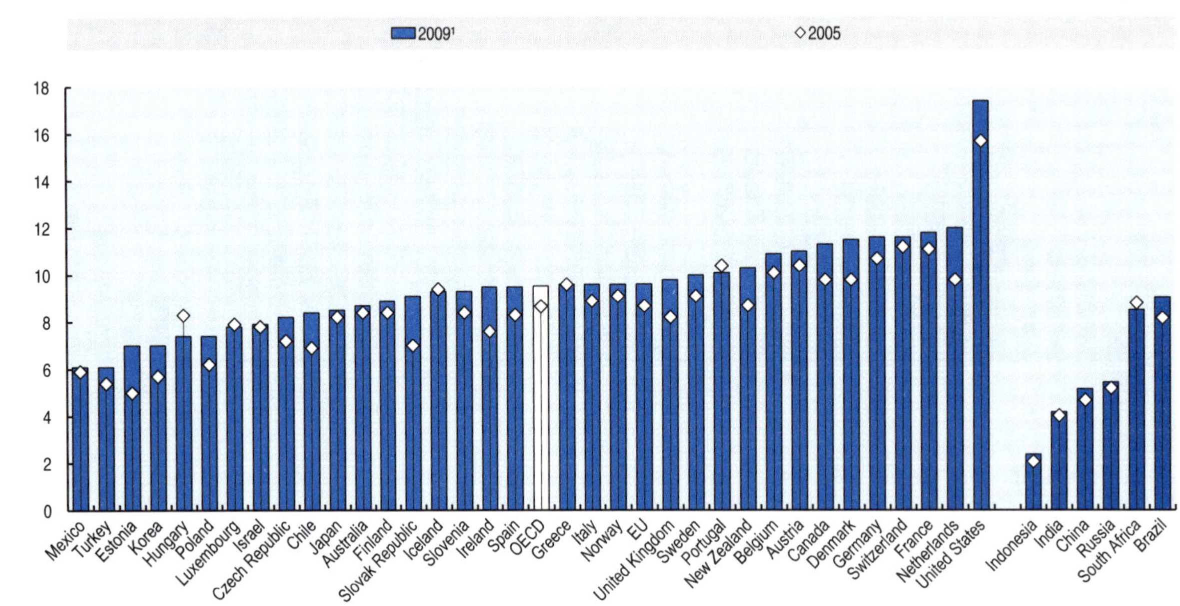

Note: Users of the data must be aware that they may no longer fully reflect the current situation in fast reforming countries.

1. The last available year is 2007 for Greece; 2008 for Australia, Portugal and Turkey; 2010 for Canada, Finland, Iceland, Italy, Korea, Mexico and Switzerland.

Source: OECD (2011), *Health Database*; World Bank (2011), *World Development Indicators Database* and China Statistical Yearbook 2011.

StatLink http://dx.doi.org/10.1787/888932566288

Figure 3.27. **Producer support estimate to agriculture**

Percentage of farm receipts

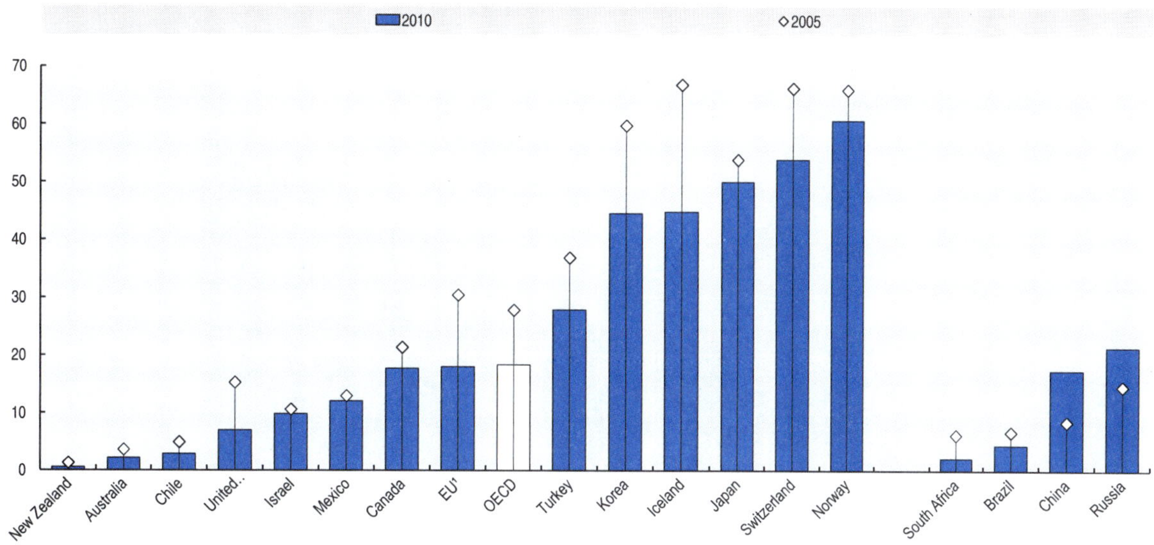

Note: Users of the data must be aware that they may no longer fully reflect the current situation in fast reforming countries.

1. EU is the aggregate of European countries in the OECD.

Source: OECD (2011), *Producer and Consumer Support Estimates Database.*

StatLink http://dx.doi.org/10.1787/888932566307

Figure 3.28. **Public investment**

Percentage of GDP

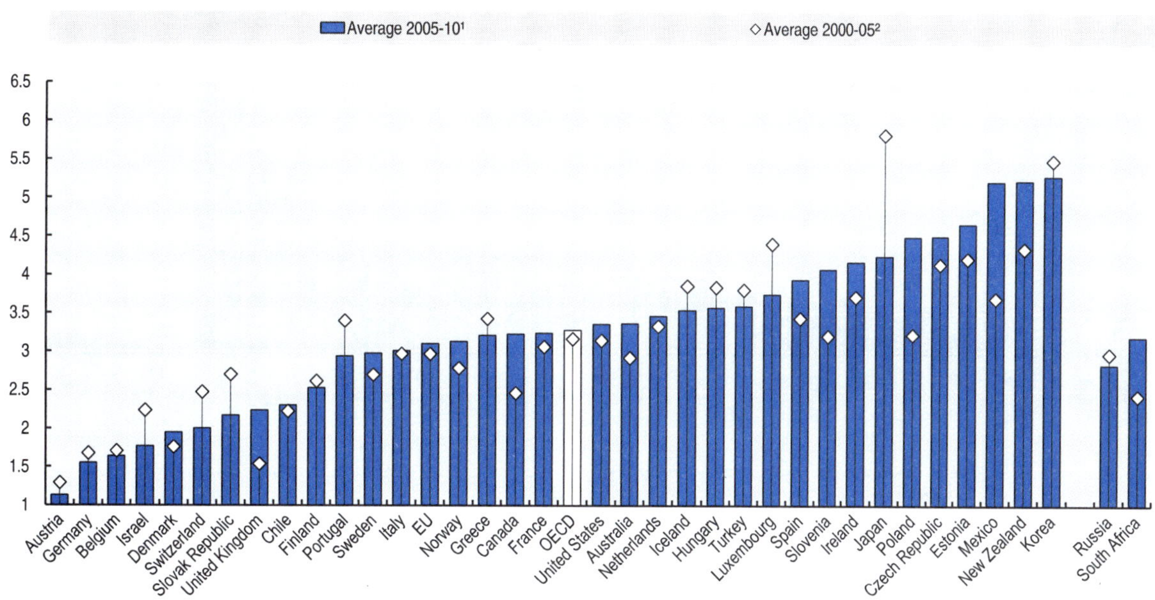

Note: Users of the data must be aware that they may no longer fully reflect the current situation in fast reforming countries.

1. Average 2005-09 for Chile and the Russian Federation.
2. Average 2002-05 for the Russian Federation.

Source: OECD (2011), *OECD Economic Outlook*, Vol. 2011/2.

StatLink http://dx.doi.org/10.1787/888932566326

Figure 3.29. **Infrastructure**

A. Rail density, 2009[1]
Km per 100 square km, less forest area

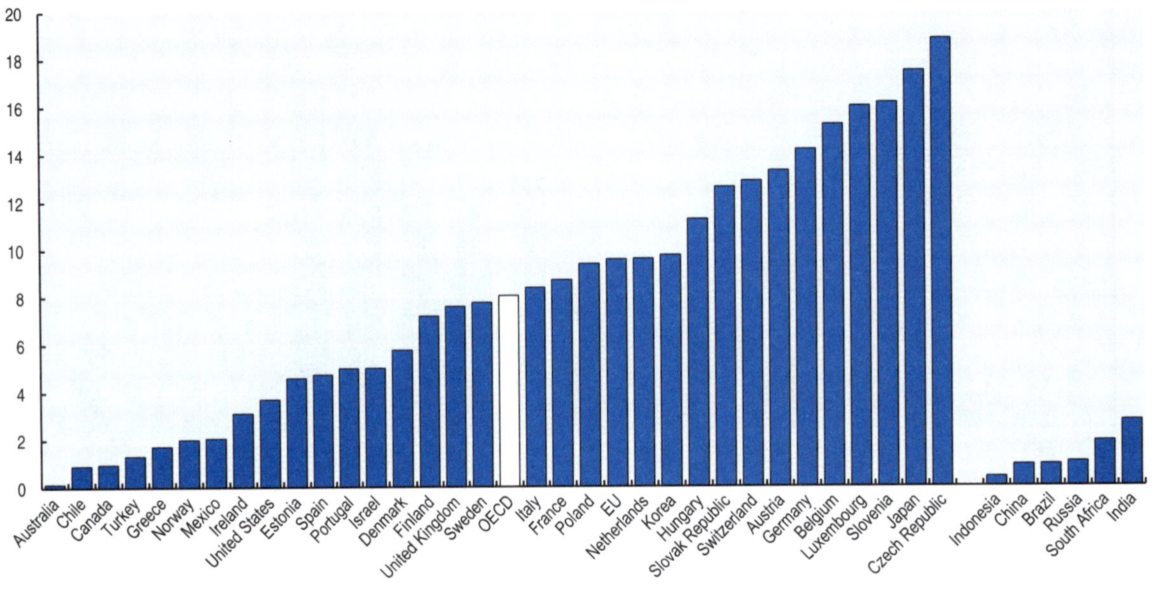

B. Road density, 2008[2]
Km per square km, less forest area

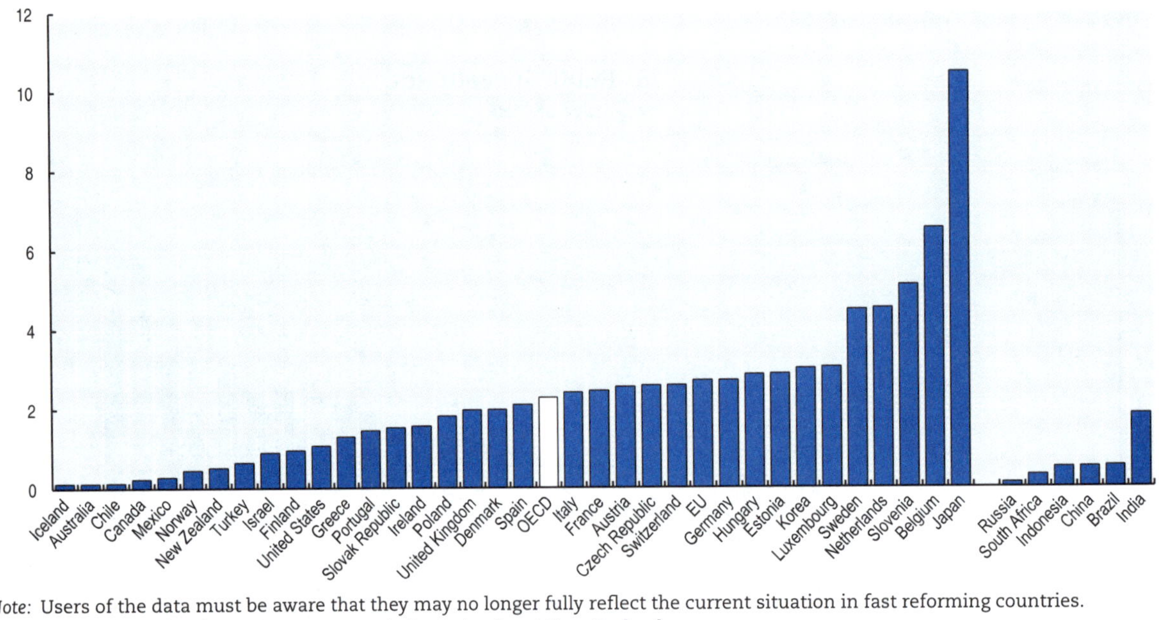

Note: Users of the data must be aware that they may no longer fully reflect the current situation in fast reforming countries.

1. 2008 for Indonesia. The OECD average excludes Iceland and New Zealand.
2. 2000 for Chile and Spain; 2004 for Brazil and Luxembourg; 2005 for Italy and Portugal; 2006 for Turkey; 2007 for Japan, the Russian Federation and Spain.

Source: World Bank (2011), *World Development Indicators (WDI)*.

StatLink http://dx.doi.org/10.1787/888932566345

Figure 3.30. **Financial support for private R&D investment**

A. Direct public funding of business R&D

Percentage of GDP

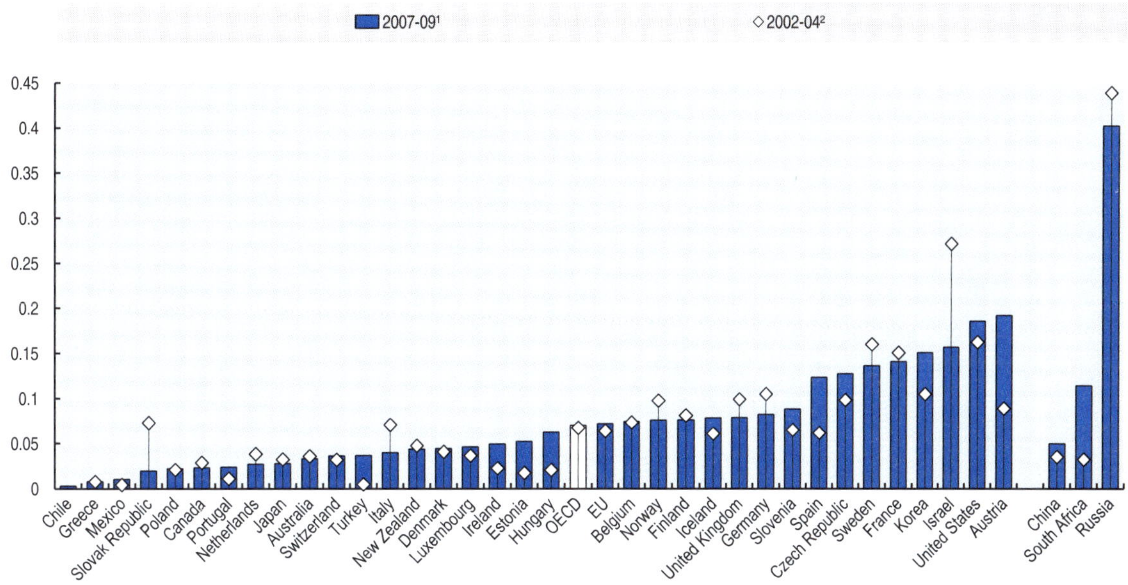

B. Rate of tax subsidies for one dollar of R&D[3]

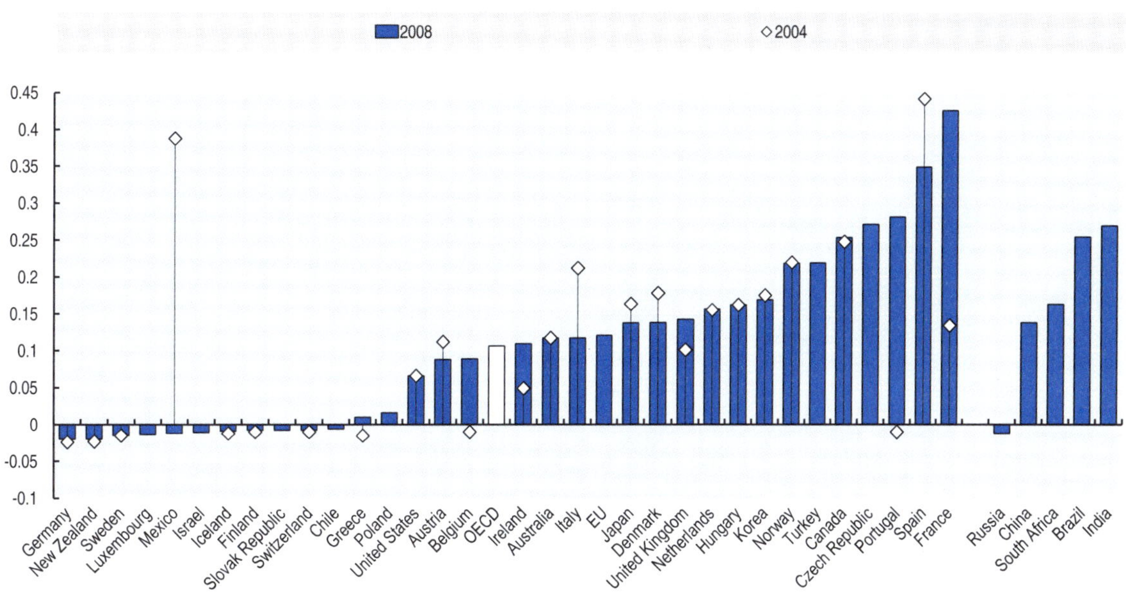

Note: Users of the data must be aware that they may no longer fully reflect the current situation in fast reforming countries.

1. 2007 for Greece, Mexico and New Zealand; 2008 for Switzerland.
2. 2003 for New Zealand; 2004 for Switzerland.
3. Measures the generosity of tax incentives to invest in R&D, on the basis of the pre-tax income necessary to cover the initial cost of one dollar R&D spending and pay corporate taxes on one dollar of profit (B-index). A value of zero on the chart would mean that the tax concession for R&D spending is just sufficient to offset the impact of the corporate tax rate. Average over small and medium enterprises and large firms.

Source: OECD (2011), *Science, Technology and R&D Statistics Database*; OECD (2009), *OECD Science, Technology and Industry Scoreboard.*

StatLink http://dx.doi.org/10.1787/888932566364

PART II

Thematic studies

Economic Policy Reforms 2012
Going for Growth
© OECD 2012

PART II

Chapter 4

Can structural reforms kick-start the recovery? Lessons from 30 years of OECD reform[1]

Not much is known about the short-term effects of structural reforms whose benefits are expected in the long term. It has been argued that some reforms could be detrimental at the current juncture, for instance if they further weakened aggregate demand. This chapter presents new empirical analysis drawn from 30 years of reform data from OECD countries. It shows that, while their benefits usually take time to fully materialise, structural reforms seldom involve significant losses and often deliver gains already in the short run. At the same time, though, some of them, such as unemployment benefit and job protection reforms, have smaller or even negative effects in depressed economies. Current conditions of wide remaining spare capacity, constrained macroeconomic policies and impaired fiscal positions in most OECD countries would put a premium on reforms that offer comparatively strong short-term gains in terms of facilitating the jobs recovery:

- *In all countries, there is a case for sheltering resources devoted to active labour market policies from ongoing fiscal consolidation efforts. Strengthening job-search assistance and training can help job seekers find new jobs more quickly and ensure that those at risk of discouragement remain attached to the labour market.*
- *Growth-friendly tax reforms that shift the tax burden away from labour taxes could help strengthen the jobs content of a recovery, while also helping fiscal consolidation insofar as they are implemented in a way that raises tax revenue.*
- *A well-designed package of labour and product market reforms could help alleviate the potential transition costs of certain individual reforms. Supporting reforms with a well-functioning financial system and an effective communication strategy is another key for maximising short-term gains.*

Summary and conclusions

This chapter attempts to shed light on how the impact of structural reform varies across different types of reform as well as over time, identifying the horizon over which their full effects materialise, and investigating how such effects may depend on a country's economic conditions. These issues are especially important in the current economic context; indeed at a time when spare capacity remains high in many OECD countries and macroeconomic policies are constrained (Chapter 1), there is a premium on reforms that would help kick-start the recovery.

The benefits of structural reforms – typically aimed at increasing labour productivity or employment – often take time to materialise, and their short and long-term impacts may differ. Many long-term gains can involve transition costs, due for instance to the disappearance of firms and associated layoffs in the wake of product market liberalisation, or because it takes time for capital to find new productive uses and for workers to find new jobs when reforms involve reallocation (Blanchard and Giavazzi, 2003). On the other hand, some structural reforms can boost growth quickly; for instance, if they improve confidence and increase expected future income gains, they can immediately stimulate consumption and investment. Likewise, forward-looking financial markets can incorporate healthier longer-term economic prospects – and therefore the effects of reforms – into asset prices, thereby further stimulating near-term activity.

This chapter draws on new OECD empirical analysis of the short-term effects of product market, labour market and taxation reforms to highlight a number of lessons for policy:

- The benefits from reforms often take time to materialise.
- Concerns about possible negative short-term effects of structural reforms seem exaggerated, however. Some structural reforms appear to boost growth fairly quickly, while usually very few if any have short-term costs.
- Because reforms do not turn out to have noticeable deflationary effects, the analysis does not support the need for significant monetary and fiscal accommodation to speed up the gains from reforms.
- Cyclical conditions matter for the short-term effects of reforms. There is some evidence that in "bad times", certain labour market reforms (of unemployment benefit systems and job protection in particular) can make the economic situation temporarily worse. In still depressed economies, such reforms would therefore be more quickly beneficial if carried out only once the labour market shows clear signs of recovery.
- In view of wide remaining spare capacity, constrained macroeconomic policies and impaired fiscal positions in most OECD countries, policy priority should be given to reforms that offer comparatively strong short-term gains, especially in terms of strengthening the jobs recovery:
  - There is a case for sheltering resources devoted *to active labour market policies* (ALMPs) from ongoing fiscal consolidation efforts in all OECD countries. Strengthening ALMPs,

particularly on training and job search, can help job seekers find new jobs more quickly and ensure that those at risk of discouragement remain attached to the labour market.

  - *Growth-friendly tax reforms* that shift the tax burden away from labour towards consumption, the environment, and – as housing markets allow – immovable property appear to reduce unemployment relatively quickly, particularly for young people, and also stimulate private investment.
  - To encourage the job content of the recovery, there is case for *product market reforms* that ease entry barriers in certain services, especially retail trade and professional services. This is especially the case in continental and southern European countries.
  - A well designed *package* of labour and product market reforms would deliver the largest gains and alleviate the transitional costs of certain individual reforms – for instance, liberalising product markets alongside job protection or unemployment benefit reforms can mitigate possible real wage declines associated with the latter.

- The short-term impact of structural reforms will be stronger if an effective communication strategy and a strong and well-regulated banking sector foster confidence and induce households and firms to spend against future reform-driven income gains.
- Some reforms can help fiscal consolidation by strengthening public budgets, either directly or indirectly via higher output and employment. For example, unemployment benefit and pension reforms directly improve fiscal balances, while gradually delivering employment gains that further raise tax revenue and reduce public spending. Expectations of enhanced long-term debt sustainability can reduce government borrowing costs and thereby help stimulate the economy.

The broad driving factors of the short-term effects of reforms

The demand and supply effects of reforms

Structural reforms are typically aimed at increasing labour productivity or employment over the long run (see Chapter 1 and past *Going for Growth* editions). However, their effects may not materialise immediately, depending in part on their short-term impact on aggregate demand in relation to supply and the macroeconomic policy response.

Demand channels…

Structural reforms may affect aggregate demand in several ways. One such channel is the "*multiplier effect*" associated with their impact on the fiscal balance.[2] Unfinanced costly reforms are likely to have more positive short-run effects on demand than revenue-raising reforms. For example, absent any offsetting schemes, increasing spending on ALMPs is likely to stimulate aggregate demand in the short run, whereas reducing unemployment benefits is likely to depress it. The multiplier effects of costly reforms are likely to be higher when such reforms are associated with spending increases or revenue reductions that fall mainly on domestic goods, such as increases in government spending on education and infrastructure. Likewise, the demand effect of revenue-raising reforms depends on whether and how the revenue is spent. For example, the potential negative effect of a cut in unemployment benefits on disposable income will be attenuated by simultaneously introducing offsetting fiscal measures (*e.g.* a tax cut for low income earners).

The positive or negative impacts of reforms on demand also depend on how they affect *confidence, income andwealth*:

- Positive *confidence, income and wealth effects* may result from reform-driven changes in future incomes. The positive effects of structural reforms on future income may be incorporated into household's perceptions of permanent income. They may also be reflected into forward-looking asset prices, and therefore in household wealth.[3] In turn, higher asset prices may ease credit constraints via improved collateral, thereby further boosting consumption and investment. In this regard, a well-functioning financial sector is instrumental for bringing forward the gains from reforms, since it allows households and firms to borrow against future income or collateral.[4]
- *Permanent income effects* should most often be positive but reform design also plays a role. For instance, a pension reform that cuts future replacement rates may reduce aggregate consumption in the short run insofar as some households seek to save more to make up for reduced retirement income in the future. By contrast, a pension reform that increases the minimum or standard retirement age may stimulate consumption as households expect to work over a longer time horizon and hence can reduce saving while maintaining their future living standards (Kerdrain *et al.*, 2010).
- Negative *confidence* effects may arise from households' perception of higher income insecurity in the wake of certain reforms, leading to higher *precautionary savings* and lower demand. For instance, reducing job protection might adversely affect households' consumption by increasing labour turnover and job insecurity, even if such reform does not trigger higher overall unemployment and increases exit rates from unemployment.

Positive demand effects are more likely insomuch as an effective communication strategy gives households and firms clear and timely information about reform implementation and its expected benefits. Clear communication can reduce the risk of reform-driven increases in precautionary savings and induce economic agents to spend in anticipation of future incomes. Also, announcing reforms (*e.g.* product market liberalisation) in advance can trigger immediate response by firms, accelerating the upside adjustment in investment and output even before the reform is actually implemented.[5] A related argument can be made about reform credibility. Reforms that are introduced with broad political support and strong government commitment will solicit a greater and faster response of the economy as they are less likely to be rolled back.

The short-term demand effects of structural reforms might also depend on countries' degree of openness. Greater trade openness can dampen any demand impact of reforms on the economy because imports will change while exports will be unaffected. Furthermore, insofar as reforms reduce domestic prices and thereby improve external price competitiveness, the associated boost to aggregate demand will be larger for smaller, more open economies.

... and supply channels

The effects on supply, and in particular on productivity, are typically long term. However, the time it takes to reap such benefits may differ across reform areas depending on a number of factors:

- *Measures to stimulate knowledge and innovative activities*, such as education reforms and innovation policies, require a long time to deliver their full benefits.[6] It also takes time for product market liberalisation to encourage firms to adopt new technology.

- Reforms that raise productivity through *reallocation* of production factors may also payoff only gradually. One example is the productivity impact of job protection (Bassanini *et al.*, 2009). Another is rental housing market liberalisation that promotes workers' mobility, leading to labour reallocation across firms, industries and geographical areas.
- Reforms that reduce *inefficiencies* in firms and industries can have a more immediate positive impact on labour productivity. Efficiency-enhancing public sector reforms that succeed in reducing slack in certain publicly-run industries or state-owned enterprises may fall into this category. Similarly, the productivity gains associated with trade liberalisation and product market reform are likely to materialise more quickly in industries where incumbents are relatively inefficient.

... which result in a priori-ambiguous effects of reforms

New OECD analysis based on a theoretically coherent but simplified economic model illustrates how the short-term effects of reforms depend on whether the demand or the supply channels dominate (Cacciatore *et al.*, 2012). Short-term effects depend in particular on the relative impact of reforms on lay-offs *versus* job creation. For example:

- *Job protection reforms* are predicted to increase lay-offs more quickly than they boost job creation, and thereby temporarily result in higher unemployment.
- Temporary labour market slack can also follow *product market liberalisation*. Labour shedding is immediate, while it may take time before new firms are created and the displaced workers find a new job.
- *Unemployment benefit reforms* appear to reduce unemployment even in the short run, because they increase job creation without affecting job losses.

Model-based results need to be interpreted with care though, as the analysis cannot feature all possible demand channels, and in particular the potential increases in precautionary savings associated with certain reforms. This effect would result in more negative or less positive short-run effects, for instance in the case of unemployment benefit reforms to the extent that the latter increase income insecurity.

... which reform packages can help turn unequivocally positive

The OECD model-based analysis points to sizeable gains from undertaking structural reforms simultaneously in different areas (Cacciatore *et al.*, 2012). Combining product market, job protection and unemployment benefit reforms appears to have the potential to boost GDP, employment and wages immediately, in contrast with the effects of some of these reforms in isolation. In particular, reducing entry barriers in product markets in parallel to labour market reforms alleviates the real wage losses that would result from the latter alone. More broadly, compared with individual reforms, a broad package yields larger income and employment gains, the expectation of which gives an immediate boost to aggregate demand and job creation. Keeping in mind that model-based simulations are necessarily stylised, Figure 4.1 illustrates that the short-term gains associated with a broad reform package can be substantial.

The role of macroeconomic policies

Structural reforms that change the output gap – defined as the difference between the level of current (observed) output and the level of "potential" (unobservable) *post-reform* output – and inflation should in principle trigger a macroeconomic policy response. In

Figure 4.1. **The sizeable short-term economic gains from an ambitious package of structural reforms**

Model simulation of the short-term impact of a reform package combining a decline in entry barriers, a reduction in the unemployment benefit replacement rate and a relaxation of job protection in a hypothetical "rigid" economy (gaps with respect to no reform)

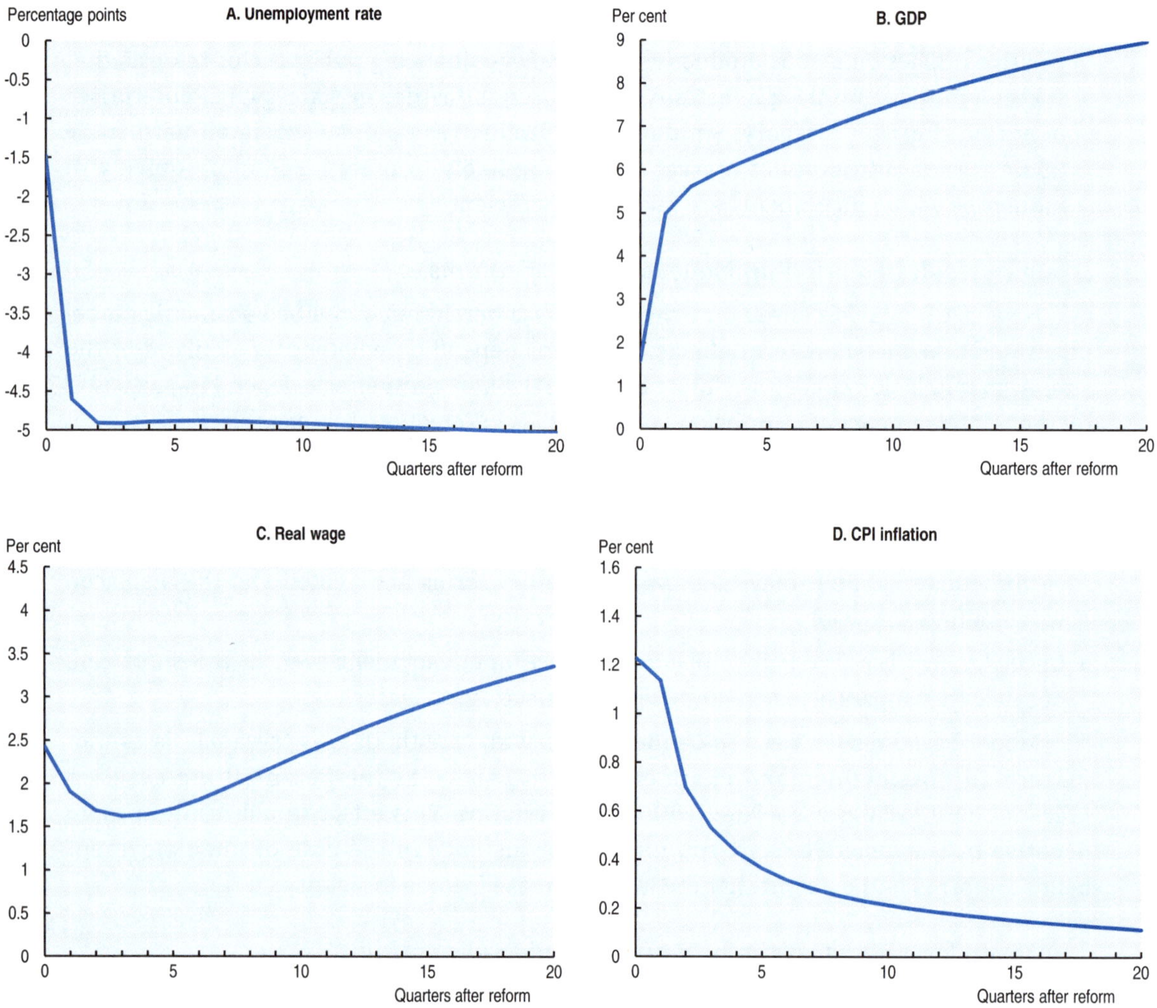

Note: The size of the simulated reform corresponds to a reduction in the value of each policy parameter from a hypothetical "rigid" economy to a hypothetical "flexible" economy (calculated as an average of "flexible" OECD countries). The composition of the basket of benchmark OECD countries is slightly different across policy parameters. See Cacciatore *et al.* (2012) for details.

Source: Cacciatore, M., R. Duval and G. Fiori (2012), "Short-term Pain or Gain? A DSGE Model-based Analysis of the Short-term Effects of Structural Reforms in Labour and Product Markets", *OECD Economics Department Working Papers*, OECD Publishing, forthcoming.

StatLink http://dx.doi.org/10.1787/888932566383

particular, when reforms raise supply more than demand and hence create economic slack, expansionary monetary and fiscal policies can strengthen their short-term effects. Otherwise, the gains from reforms would come through more gradually as the excess supply in goods or labour markets puts downward pressure on price and wage inflation. In practice, however, model-based analysis does not support the need for such macroeconomic policy support because it does not find structural reforms to have noticeable deflationary effects (Cacciatore *et al.*, 2012). This suggests that in practice monetary authorities may not face the so-called "paradox of toil" (Eggertsson, 2010).[7] This hypothetical situation might arise when, because already-low interest rates cannot fall below zero, a reform-driven increase in supply lowers prices, raises the real interest rate and thereby ultimately depresses rather than stimulates the economy.

The finding that structural reforms do not generally call for much macroeconomic easing naturally extends to fiscal policy. Structural reforms may even have positive feedback effects on the economy via their effect on public finances and long-term interest rates. Indeed reforms that reduce fiscal sustainability concerns and therefore the perception of sovereign risk (*e.g.* pension reforms, reductions in government consumption through enhanced efficiency of public spending in health or education) may lead to a decline in interest rate *premia* which in turn may boost short-term growth, *ceteris paribus* (Giavazzi and Pagano, 1990).[8]

The short-term effects of structural reforms in practice: New evidence from 30 years of reform in OECD countries

Given existing uncertainties regarding the short-term impact of reforms, the OECD has conducted new empirical analysis to shed light on the actual dynamic effects of past product market, labour market and tax reforms on aggregate output and labour utilisation. The analysis first identifies a broad range of structural reform "shocks" that were implemented OECD countries during the 30 years prior to the recent financial crisis and then estimates their economic effects over a five-year horizon (for methodological details, see Box 4.1). This section summarises the main results of the analysis and attempts to interpret them in light of the underlying channels of transmission discussed above.

Box 4.1. **Methodology: an overview**

Based on roughly 30 years of data from 30 OECD countries prior to (but not including) the recent crisis, the analysis involved the following steps:

- Structural reform "shocks" were identified from the cross-country time-series variation in existing OECD policy indicators in the following areas: unemployment benefit systems, labour taxes, job protection, ALMPs, product market regulation, administrative extensions of bargaining agreements and the tax structure (for details, see Table 1 in Bouis *et al.*, 2012).
- For each reform, the average impact in the five years following its implementation was estimated for: *i)* overall GDP, as well as employment and unemployment; *ii)* various components of aggregate demand, in particular private consumption and investment, in order to better identify the components driving the aggregate effects; and *iii)* specific population groups (young people, prime-aged, women and seniors), as these are likely to behave differently in the labour market and thus to be differently affected by structural reforms. An attempt was also made to estimate whether the short-term impact of a reform depends on the other policy and institutional features of the country considered. For example, do the short-term effects of labour market reforms differ across countries depending on whether their product market regulation is more or less conducive to strong competition?
- The analysis then explored whether the short-term impact of a reform shock depends on cyclical conditions in that country when the reform was implemented. For example, did the differences in the short-term effects of labour market reforms across countries depend on whether labour markets were tight or slack (*i.e.* on the unemployment gap, measured as the difference between the actual and "structural" levels of unemployment)?

Labour market and welfare reforms

The analysis suggests that the short-term effects of labour market and welfare reforms are mostly positive or null. There is no evidence of aggregate costs of these reforms – although there may have been distributional consequences which go beyond the scope of this paper (see Chapter 5 on the income distribution effects of labour market policies and institutions). The main findings can be summarised as follows:

- *Unemployment benefit* reforms are found to deliver fairly quick positive impacts on labour utilisation, contrary to fears that they may weaken consumption in the short run. The estimated increase in employment following an 8 percentage point reduction in the initial replacement rate – corresponding to the median reform over the three decades considered in the study – reaches almost 0.5 percentage points on average after three years (Figure 4.2, Panel A). This finding echoes the model-based predictions mentioned

Figure 4.2. **Unemployment benefit reforms can have a fairly quick positive impact on labour utilisation**

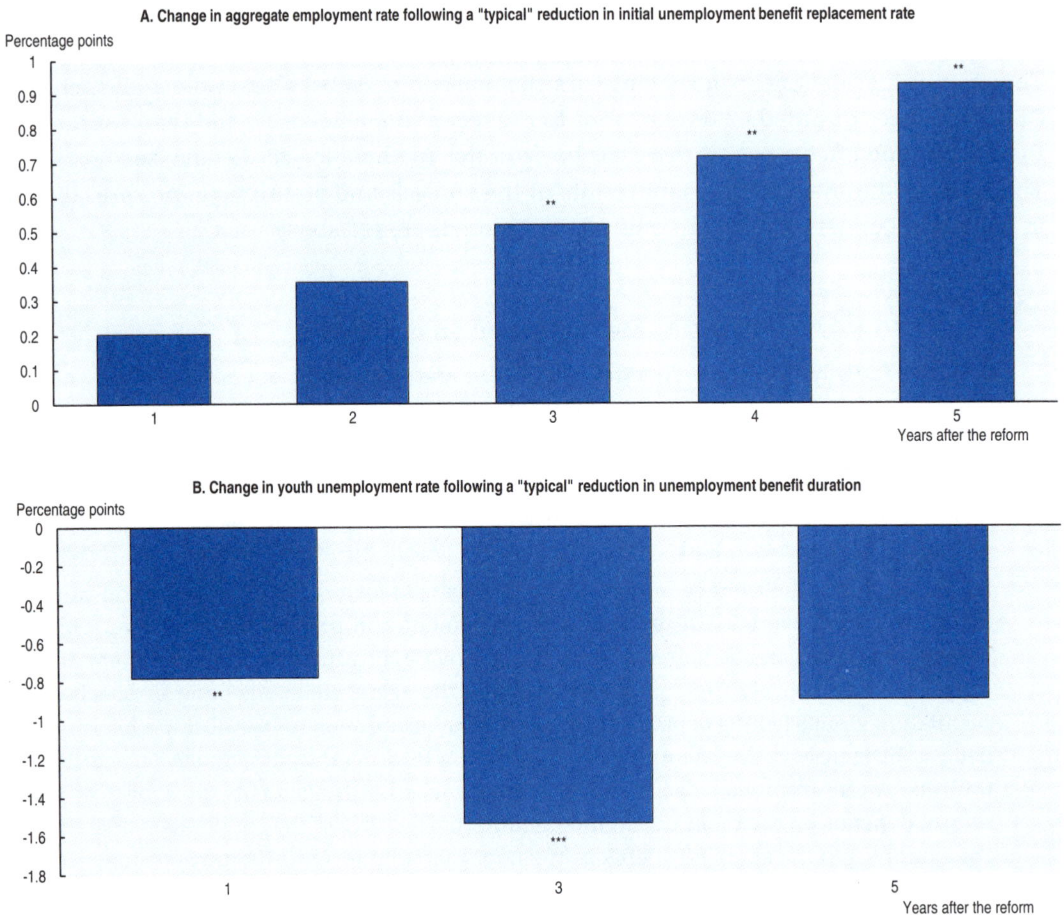

Note: *** and ** represent statistical significance at the 1 and 5% levels, respectively. The simulation is based on the median-sized reform observed in the estimation sample. In Panel B, the impact of the reform is estimated controlling for the initial unemployment benefit replacement rate.

Source: Bouis, R. et al. (2012), "The Short-term Effects of Structural Reforms: an Empirical Analysis", *OECD Economics Department Working Papers*, OECD Publishing, forthcoming.

StatLink http://dx.doi.org/10.1787/888932566402

above (see also Cacciatore *et al.*, 2012), and could reflect the fact that lower unemployment benefits boost job creation by increasing jobseekers' incentives to actively look for a job and return to work (see *e.g.* Bassanini and Duval, 2006) but do not increase job destruction. Reductions in benefit duration are found to be followed by quick declines in unemployment particularly for young people (Figure 4.2, Panel B). As an illustrative example, the estimates suggest that a decrease in benefit duration similar to that implemented in Denmark in 2001 – corresponding approximately to the median reform over the past three decades – may reduce the unemployment rate of young people by more than 1½ percentage points after three years in the average OECD country. Consistent with their employment effects, benefit reforms are also found to be associated with stronger investment and output growth.

- At the same time, however, unemployment benefit reforms seem to have negative short-term effects on specific groups of the labour force, in particular older workers. For instance, reducing unemployment benefit duration seems to be associated with a reduction in senior employment. Where older age groups are over-represented among the long-term unemployed, this effect may be driven by labour force withdrawal – possibly coupled with a move to early retirement in countries where this has been possible.
- Short-run employment gains associated with unemployment benefit reforms are found to be stronger where job protection is weak. This result could suggest that stringent job protection might prevent labour demand, in particular firms' hiring decisions, from responding fully to the potential increase in effective labour supply arising from unemployment benefit reforms.
- Based on a handful of reform experiences, it seems that *reducing job protection on regular contracts* has no significant effects on aggregate employment, consistent with priors. Still, there is tentative evidence that job protection reforms may reduce unemployment in the short run, especially for certain marginal categories of the labour force such as young people and women, who may enjoy better relative job prospects from a relaxation of regular contract provisions.
- *Reducing job protection on temporary contracts*, a frequent reform in OECD countries over the past three decades, is found to reduce employment in the years following the reform. The initial decrease in the overall employment rate is 0.2 percentage points, reaching 2 percentage points after five years (Figure 4.3). This broadly confirms previous analysis, including by the OECD, which highlighted the weaknesses of *two-tier reforms of job protection, i.e.* reforms aimed at reducing job protection on temporary contracts while maintaining stringent provisions for regular workers.[9] As well as having negative employment effects, these reforms are also associated with lower GDP, consumption, and investment growth rates.
- *Strengthening active labour market policies (ALMPs)* through better job search services and stronger enforcement of conditionality *vis-à-vis* jobseekers could in principle reduce unemployment by facilitating short-run job creation. Such gains are difficult to identify empirically because ALMPs reforms can only be measured by changes in expenditures, and the latter are driven more by cyclical conditions than by institutional changes. The analysis attempted to address this issue by removing the cyclical component from the associated policy indicators and by focusing on those public spending categories which are

less sensitive to the economic cycle. The corresponding results suggest that, indeed, increases in spending on employment incentives (Figure 4.4), as well as on training, increase employment in the short term – particularly among women as regards training measures.

Figure 4.3. **The failure of two-tier job protection reforms to raise employment**

Change in aggregate employment following a "typical" reduction in job protection on temporary contracts

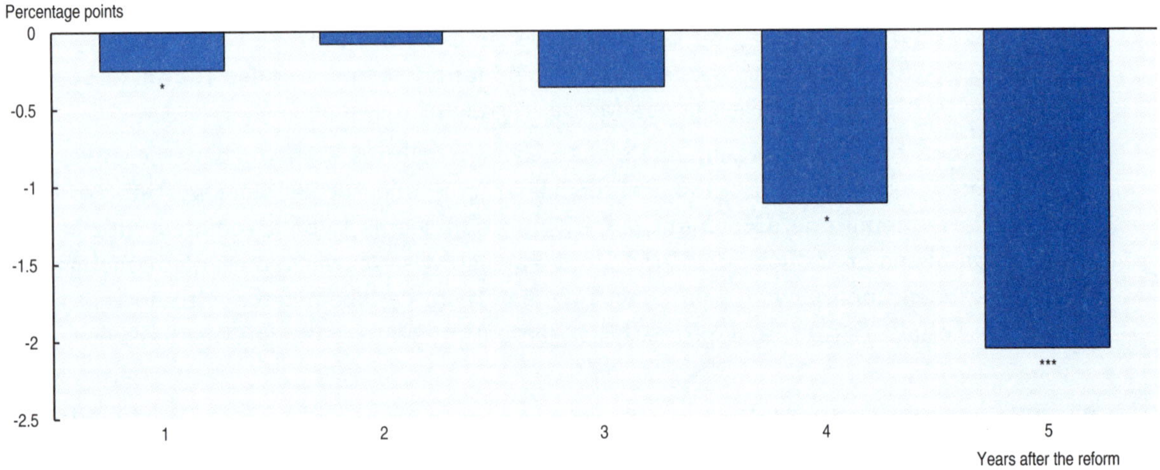

Note: *** and * represent statistical significance at the 1 and 10% levels, respectively. The simulation is based on the median-sized reform observed in the estimation sample.

Source: Bouis, R. *et al.* (2012), "The Short-term Effects of Structural Reforms: an Empirical Analysis", *OECD Economics Department Working Papers*, OECD Publishing, forthcoming.

StatLink http://dx.doi.org/10.1787/888932566421

Figure 4.4. **How strengthening active labour market policies can help strengthen the jobs recovery**

Change in aggregate employment rate following a "typical" increase in public spending on ALMP employment incentives

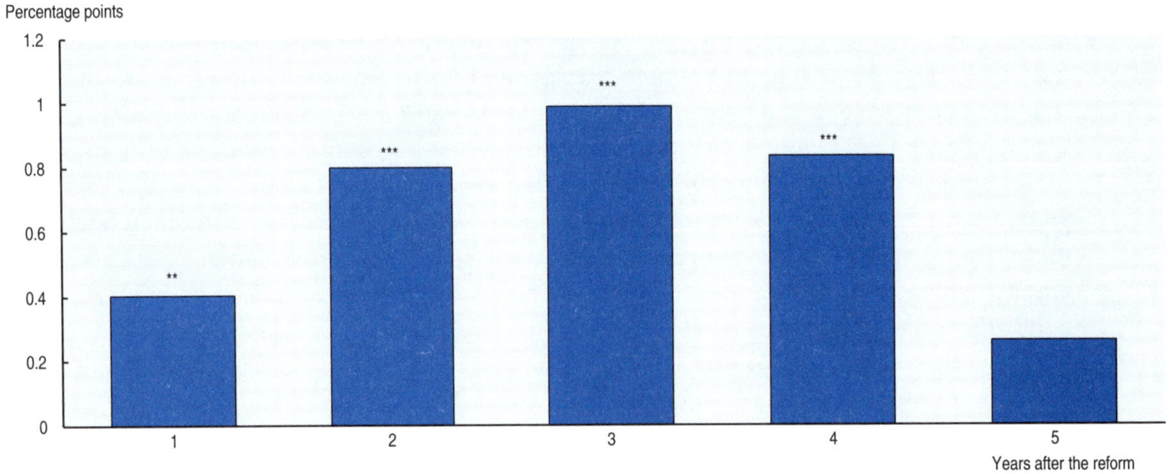

Note: *** and ** represent statistical significance at the 1 and 5% levels, respectively. The simulation is based on the median-sized reform observed in the estimation sample.

Source: Bouis, R. *et al.* (2012), "The Short-term Effects of Structural Reforms: an Empirical Analysis", *OECD Economics Department Working Papers*, OECD Publishing, forthcoming.

StatLink http://dx.doi.org/10.1787/888932566440

- *Reducing administrative extensions of collective agreements* increases firms' freedom to set working conditions and wage policies and can increase labour demand, in particular for low-productivity workers and "outsiders" who may otherwise be priced out of the labour market. Empirical evidence confirms this by showing that past reductions in administrative extensions of collective agreements have reduced unemployment, particularly for females.[10] For example, taken at face value, the results suggest that reducing "excess" coverage of collective bargaining (a measure of the degree of administrative extension)[11] in Portugal to the level prevailing in Germany – a reduction equivalent to the median reform over the past three decades – might lower female unemployment by almost 0.5 percentage point after three years.

Tax reforms

Economic theory and empirical evidence suggest that shifting the tax burden away from more mobile and elastic bases such as capital and labour can deliver quick and substantial short-term gains. This is especially true for tax cuts targeted at women and low-skilled workers, whose labour supply tends to be more responsive to tax changes.[12] A growth-friendly way to offset the budgetary impact of such cuts is to shift the burden towards taxes on less mobile and responsive bases, such as consumption, immovable property, or the environment,[13] as often recommended among *Going for Growth* reform priorities (Chapters 1 and 2). New empirical results based on past reform experiences across OECD countries broadly confirm this prior:

- *Reducing the share of direct taxes in overall tax revenue* appears to quickly reduce unemployment, particularly for young people. In the short run, such reforms also trigger stronger labour force participation by female and young people, although these effects are eventually found to fade away after three years. Moreover, private investment growth appears to rise in the wake of such tax reforms. This is consistent with the view that shifting the tax burden away from labour and capital makes the tax structure more investment-friendly.
- *Reducing the labour tax wedge* (*i.e.* the difference between the salary costs of a single "average worker" to the employer and the net income the worker receives)[14] is found to raise senior employment in the short run, driven by increased participation. However, there seems to be no effect on aggregate employment, perhaps suggesting that it takes a longer time to materialise.

Product market reforms

Product market reforms are advocated to boost long-run labour productivity and labour utilisation; empirical evidence of their beneficial effects is abundant.[15] Short-run effects are less straightforward to predict and are likely to depend on the nature of the reform, whether it applies to economy-wide regulation or is sector-specific and (in the latter case) on the sector that is subject to reform. For instance, product market reforms can entail transitory costs in terms of job losses (Cacciatore *et al.*, 2012). Such transitory costs are likely to arise especially in the aftermath of liberalisation of mature industries with limited growth potential and large incumbents, *e.g.* postal services in a number of high-income OECD countries.

The new empirical analysis finds that product market liberalisation of network industries[16] reduced investment and GDP growth in the near term, possibly reflecting capital spending cuts in the wake of past privatisation episodes.[17] At the same time, such reforms are found to have boosted labour force participation in the medium term (Figure 4.5), especially for women. Product market reforms are also more likely to boost short-run employment when they lift supply constraints in sectors where there is pent-up demand, such as the removal of entry barriers for new firms in retail trade and professional services. In particular, country-specific evidence strongly suggests that product market reforms that make it easier to create a firm and recruit workers in retail trade bring relatively quick employment gains (see *e.g.* Bertrand and Kramarz, 2002, for evidence from France).

Figure 4.5. **Product markets reforms typically encourage labour force participation**

Change in aggregate labour force participation following a "typical" product market reform

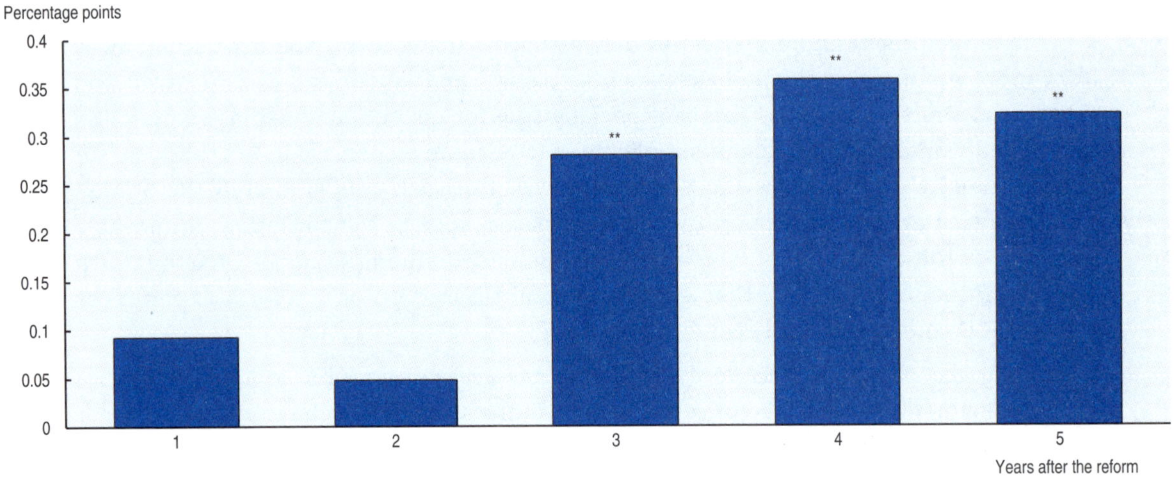

Note: ** represents statistical significance at the 5% level. The simulation is based on the median-sized reform observed in the estimation sample.

Source: Bouis, R. *et al.* (2012), "The Short-term Effects of Structural Reforms: an Empirical Analysis", *OECD Economics Department Working Papers*, OECD Publishing, forthcoming.

StatLink http://dx.doi.org/10.1787/888932566459

The role of macroeconomic conditions

So far, this empirical section has presented the average short-term impact of past reforms. However, this impact may vary depending *inter alia* on prevailing macroeconomic conditions. Indeed, the short-term positive effects of unemployment benefit and job protection reforms turn out to be stronger during "good" times, and weaker – and in some cases even negative – during "bad" times. For example, the analysis suggests that a "typical" reduction in the initial unemployment benefit replacement rate would bring about a 0.5 percentage point employment gain after three years in "normal" times – *i.e.* when there is no slack in the economy, as indicated by a zero unemployment gap – but the same reform could lead to employment losses in very depressed labour markets (Figure 4.6). This asymmetric effect may reflect the fact that while raising incentives for the unemployed to look harder for a job might increase outflows from unemployment when the labour market is tight, it could be ineffective and even counter-productive when labour demand is particularly weak. Likewise, a "typical" decline in job protection on regular contracts appears to raise employment over the medium term in "good" times, but to reduce it in "bad" times.

Figure 4.6. **Unemployment benefit reforms become ineffective when the economy is depressed**

Change in aggregate employment following a "typical" reduction in initial unemployment benefit replacement rate: the influence of economic conditions

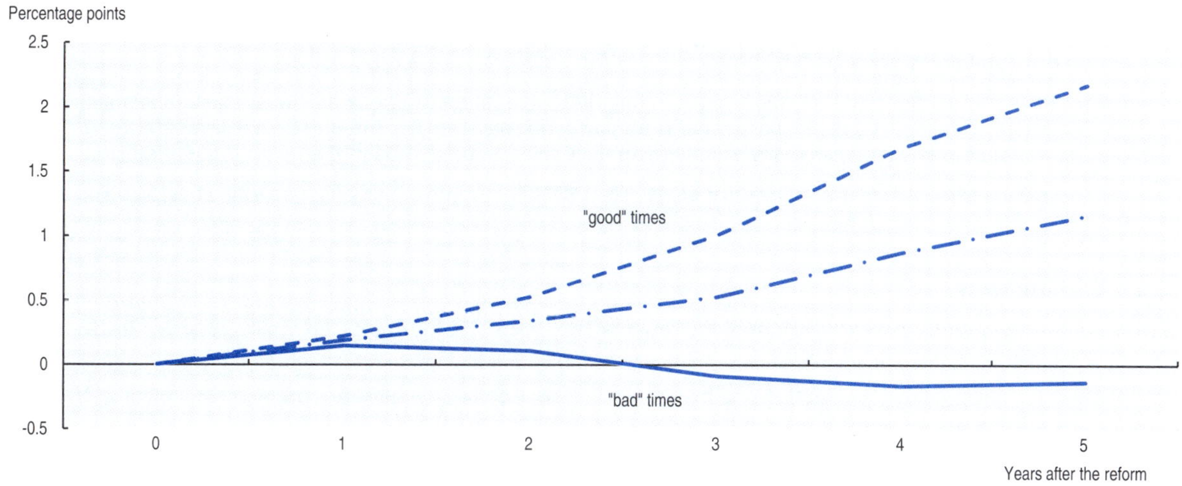

Note: The lower line corresponds to the impact of the reform during "bad" times, while the upper line represents the impact during "good" times, corresponding to the minimum and maximum levels of the unemployment gap, respectively, as observed across the sample (*i.e.* across all countries and time). The central broken line represents the impact of the reform when the unemployment gap equals its median value. The unemployment gap is calculated as the difference between the structural rate of unemployment and the observed level of unemployment in the estimation sample.

Source: Bouis, R. *et al.* (2012), "The Short-term Effects of Structural Reforms: an Empirical Analysis", *OECD Economics Department Working Papers*, OECD Publishing, forthcoming.

StatLink http://dx.doi.org/10.1787/888932566478

Notes

1. This chapter is based on analysis in Bouis *et al.* (2012) and Cacciatore *et al.* (2012).
2. The fiscal multiplier measures by how much output or aggregate demand increases (decreases) in response to a given change in the fiscal balance. For a review of the factors that influence the size of fiscal multipliers, see Sutherland *et al.* (2010).
3. In the absence of credit constraints and under perfect information about the future income gains from reforms, there is no distinction between permanent income and wealth effects.
4. Angeloni *et al.* (2003); Mishkin (2007).
5. Adjémian *et al.* (2007).
6. These reforms may still have demand effects if unfinanced, as discussed above.
7. This model-based conclusion needs to be taken with care, though, because it does not incorporate the potential negative short-term effects of reforms arising though increases in precautionary savings. Moreover, the model assumes away the possibility of impaired banks and ill-functioning credit channels.
8. For recent empirical work based on historical episodes of fiscal contractions, see Sutherland *et al.* (2012) and Chapter 3 of IMF (2010).
9. See de Serres *et al.* (2012) for a recent assessment and various editions of the *OECD Employment Outlook* (for instance OECD, 2010). This result is consistent with Blanchard and Landier (2002) and Bentolila *et al.* (2010), who argue that *two-tier reforms of job protection* may in fact increase the equilibrium unemployment *rate* by increasing unemployment *turnover*.
10. These results are in line with recent OECD empirical work in de Serres *et al.* (2012).
11. The "excess coverage" of collective bargaining is taken as a *de facto* measure of the degree of administrative extension, as it is defined as the difference between the percentage of workers who are covered by collective bargaining agreements regardless of whether they belong to a trade union (the union coverage rate) and the percentage of workers belonging to a trade union (the union density rate).

12. See OECD (2011) for recent evidence.
13. See *e.g.* Arnold *et al.* (2011).
14. This measure is based on *National Accounts* and includes consumption taxes.
15. For recent evidence on the productivity effects of product market reforms, see *e.g.* Bourlès *et al.* (2010) and for their (aggregate) employment effects see *e.g.* Alesina *et al.* (2005).
16. The analysis relies on product market regulation reforms in network industries (telecoms, electricity, gas, post, rail, air passenger transport, and road freight). Indeed, data unavailability on a time-series basis makes it impossible to analyse the dynamic impact of economy-wide reforms.
17. However this finding is at odds with other recent OECD empirical analysis (Kerdrain *et al.*, 2010).

Bibliography

Adjémian, S. *et al.* (2007), "Variantes en Univers Incertain", Économie et Prévision, Special Issue "*Développements récents des DSGE*".

Alesina, A. *et al.* (2005), "Regulation and Investment", *Journal of the European Economic Association*, Vol. 3/4, pp. 791-825.

Angeloni, I. *et al.* (2003), "The Output Composition Puzzle: A Difference in the Monetary Transmission Mechanism in the Euro Area and United States", *Journal of Money, Credit, and Banking*, Vol. 35, No. 6, pp. 1265-1306.

Arnold, B. *et al.* (2011). "Tax Policy for Economic Recovery and Growth", *The Economic Journal*, Vol. 121/550, pp. F59-F80.

Bassanini, A. and R. Duval (2006), "Employment Patterns in OECD Countries: Reassessing the Role of Policies and Institutions", *OECD Economics Department Working Papers*, No. 486, OECD Publishing.

Bassanini, A., L. Nunziata, and D. Venn (2009), "Job Protection Legislation and Productivity Growth in OECD Countries", *Economic Policy*, Vol. 24, No. 58, pp. 349-402, April.

Bentolila, S. *et al.* (2010), "Two-tier Labor Markets in the Great Recession: France vs. Spain", *IZA Discussion Paper Series, No. 5340.*

Bertrand, M. and F. Kramarz (2002), "Does Entry Regulation Hinder Job Creation? Evidence from the French Retail Industry", *Quarterly Journal of Economics*, Vol. 117/4, pp. 1369-1413.

Blanchard, O. and A. Landier (2002), "The Perverse Effects of Partial Labour Market Reform: Fixed-Term Contracts in France", *Economic Journal*, Vol. 112/480, June, pp. F214-F244.

Blanchard, O. and F. Giavazzi (2003), "Macroeoconmic Effects of Regulation and Deregulation in Goods and Labor Markets", *Quarterly Journal of Economics*, Vol. 118/3, pp. 879-907.

Bouis, R. *et al.* (2012), "The Short-term Effects of Structural Reforms: an Empirical Analysis", *OECD Economics Department Working Papers*, OECD Publishing, forthcoming.

Bourlès, R. *et al.* (2010), "Do Product Market Regulations in Upstream Sectors Curb Productivity Growth?: Panel Data Evidence for OECD Countries", *OECD Economics Department Working Papers*, No. 791, OECD Publishing.

Cacciatore, M., R. Duval and G. Fiori (2012), "Short-term Pain or Gain? A DSGE Model-based Analysis of the Short-term Effects of Structural Reforms in Labour and Product Markets", *OECD Economics Department Working Papers*, OECD Publishing, forthcoming.

Eggertsson, G. (2010), "The Paradox of Toil", *Federal Reserve Bank of New York Staff Reports*, No. 433, February.

Giavazzi, F. and M. Pagano (1990), "Can Severe Fiscal Contractions be Expansionary? Tales of Two Small European Countries", *NBER Working Paper*, No. 3372, pp. 75-111.

IMF (International Monetary Fund) (2010), "Will it Hurt? Macroeconomic Effects of Fiscal Consolidation", *World Economic Outlook*, October, IMF.

Kerdrain, C., I. Koske and I. Wanner (2010), "The Impact of Structural Policies on Saving, Investment and Current Accounts", *OECD Economics Department Working Papers*, No. 815, OECD Publishing.

Mishkin, F. (2007), "Housing and the Monetary Transmission Mechanism", *NBER Working Paper*, No. 13518.

OECD (2010), *OECD Employment Outlook 2010: Moving Beyond the Job Crisis*, OECD Publishing.

OECD (2011), *Taxation and Employment*, OECD Tax Policy Studies, No. 21, OECD Publishing.

de Serres, A. F. Murtin, and C. De la Maisonneuve (2012), "Policies to Facilitate the Return to Work", *OECD Economics Department Working Papers*, OECD Publishing, forthcoming.

Sutherland, D. *et al.* (2010), "Counter-cyclical Economic Policy", *OECD Economics Department Working Papers*, No. 760, OECD Publishing.

Sutherland, D. *et al.* (2012), "Fiscal Consolidation", *OECD Economics Department Working Papers*, No. 932, OECD Publishing.

Economic Policy Reforms 2012
Going for Growth
© OECD 2012

PART II

Chapter 5

Reducing income inequality while boosting economic growth: Can it be done?

This chapter identifies inequality patterns across OECD countries and provides new analysis of their policy and non-policy drivers. One key finding is that education and anti-discrimination policies, well-designed labour market institutions and large and/or progressive tax and transfer systems can all reduce income inequality. On this basis, the chapter identifies several policy reforms that could yield a double dividend in terms of boosting GDP per capita and reducing income inequality, and also flags other policy areas where reforms would entail a trade-off between both objectives.

Summary and conclusions

In many OECD countries, income inequality has increased in past decades. In some countries, top earners have captured a large share of the overall income gains, while for others income has risen only a little. There is growing consensus that assessments of economic performance should not focus solely on overall income growth, but also take into account income distribution. Some see poverty as the relevant concern while others are concerned with income inequality more generally. A key question is whether the type of growth-enhancing policy reforms advocated for each OECD country and the BRIICS in *Going for Growth* might have positive or negative side effects on income inequality. More broadly, in pursuing growth and redistribution strategies simultaneously, policy makers need to be aware of possible complementarities or trade-offs between the two objectives.

This chapter sheds new light on this issue, following up on recent OECD work (OECD, 2011). It first highlights differences in income inequality across the OECD and the factors driving them, such as cross-country differences in wage and non-wage income inequality, as well as in hours worked and inactivity. The chapter then provides new analysis of the policy and non-policy determinants of overall income inequality, assessing separately the drivers of labour income inequality and the redistributive role of tax and transfer systems. In each case, the analysis identifies "win-win" policies that can both reduce inequality and promote economic growth, and also highlights policies that may entail trade-offs between the two policy goals.

OECD countries can be divided into five groups according to their patterns of inequality. For example, in five English-speaking countries (Australia, Canada, Ireland, New Zealand and the United Kingdom) and the Netherlands wages are rather dispersed and the share of part-time employment is high, driving inequality in labour earnings above the OECD average. Means-tested public cash transfers and progressive household taxes reduce overall income inequality, but it remains above the OECD average. At the other end of the scale, four Nordic countries and Switzerland all have comparatively low labour income inequality because wage dispersion is narrow and employment rates are high. Cash transfers tend to be universal and are thus less redistributive. Income inequality for this group is considerably below the OECD average.

This chapter also presents new empirical analysis which shows that although technological change and globalisation have played a role in widening the distribution of labour income, the marked cross-country variation is likely due to differences in policies and institutions. This leads to the following conclusions about policies and institutions:

- Education policies matter. Policies that increase graduation rates from upper secondary and tertiary education and that also promote equal access to education help reduce inequality.
- Well-designed labour market policies and institutions can reduce inequality. A relatively high minimum wage narrows the distribution of labour income, but if set too high it may reduce employment, which dampens its inequality-reducing effect. Institutional

arrangements that strengthen trade unions also tend to reduce labour earnings inequality by ensuring a more equal distribution of earnings. Job protection reforms that make permanent and temporary contracts more even in their provisions lower income inequality through smaller wage dispersion and also possibly *via* higher employment.

- Removing product market regulations that stifle competition can reduce labour income inequality by boosting employment. The empirical evidence for the link between product market reform and the dispersion of earnings is rather mixed.
- Policies that foster the integration of immigrants and fight all forms of discrimination reduce inequality.
- Tax and transfer systems play a key role in lowering overall income inequality. Three quarters of the average reduction in inequality they achieve across the OECD is due to transfers. However, the redistributive impact of cash transfers varies widely across countries, reflecting both the size and progressivity of these transfers. In some countries (*e.g.* Australia, the United Kingdom to a lesser extent), cash transfers are small in size but highly targeted on those in need. In some others (*e.g.* France or Germany), large transfers redistribute income mainly over the life-cycle rather than across individuals, and their progressivity is often low.
- Of the various types of taxes, the personal income tax tends to be progressive, while social security contributions, consumption taxes and real estate taxes tend to be regressive. But progressivity could be strengthened by cutting back tax expenditures that benefit mainly high-income groups (*e.g.* tax relief on mortgage interest). In addition, removing other tax reliefs – such as reduced taxation of capital gains from the sale of a principal or secondary residence, stock options and carried interest – would increase equity and allow a growth-enhancing cut in marginal labour income tax rates. It would also reduce tax avoidance instruments for top-income earners.

These findings, combined with past OECD and other work on the gross domestic product (GDP) per capita effects of policies and institutions – which underpins the growth-enhancing reform recommendations made in *Going for Growth* – highlight the existence of both complementarities and trade-offs between reducing inequality and promoting economic growth:

- Many policies entail a double dividend as they reduce income inequality while at the same time boosting long-run GDP per capita. Examples include facilitating the accumulation of human capital, making educational potential less dependent on personal and social circumstances, reducing labour market dualism or promoting the integration of immigrants and fostering female labour market participation. Concerning taxation, reducing tax expenditures, for instance for investing in housing, contributes to equity objectives while also allowing a growth-friendly cut in marginal tax rates.
- By contrast, several policies may entail a trade-off between reducing income inequality and raising GDP per capita. For instance, administrative extensions of collective wage agreements may reduce wage earnings dispersion among workers, but if they set labour costs at too-high levels for some employers they may harm competition and productivity and possibly reduce employment. Shifting the tax mix to less-distorting taxes – in particular away from labour and corporate income taxes towards consumption and real estate taxes – would improve incentives to work, save and invest, but could undermine equity. Cash transfers targeted to lower incomes can be used to ease this trade off.

- Finally, some policies aimed at boosting GDP per capita have an uncertain impact on income inequality. For instance, avoiding too-high and long-lasting unemployment benefits may raise employment over the long run but also widen the distribution of income among workers, with an ambiguous net effect on inequality. The same holds as regards keeping minimum wages at moderate levels.

Understanding inequality

How does one measure income inequality? According to a report by the Stiglitz-Sen-Fitoussi Commission (Stiglitz *et al.*, 2009), the most comprehensive income concept is household disposable income that has been adjusted for publicly-provided in-kind transfers, such as public spending on education and health care. This measure, referred to here as "adjusted household disposable income" is shaped by various factors illustrated in Figure 5.1. All these factors can vary and shape inequality as follows:[1]

- *Individual labour income.* The dispersion of individual labour income amongst the working-age population reflects both the wage dispersion for full-time employees and the labour income dispersion of other groups who make up the working-age population (part-time workers and the self-employed, as well as the unemployed and people not looking actively for a job).[2]
- *Household labour income.* Working-age families differ in size and composition, affecting the total labour income of households.
- *Household market income.* It includes both household labour and capital income.[3]
- *Household disposable income.* Household disposable income covers all households and income sources, after taxes and cash transfers.
- *Household adjusted disposable income.* It adjusts household disposable income for in-kind transfers (*e.g.* public spending on health, education and social housing).

Figure 5.1. **From individual labour earnings to adjusted household disposable income**

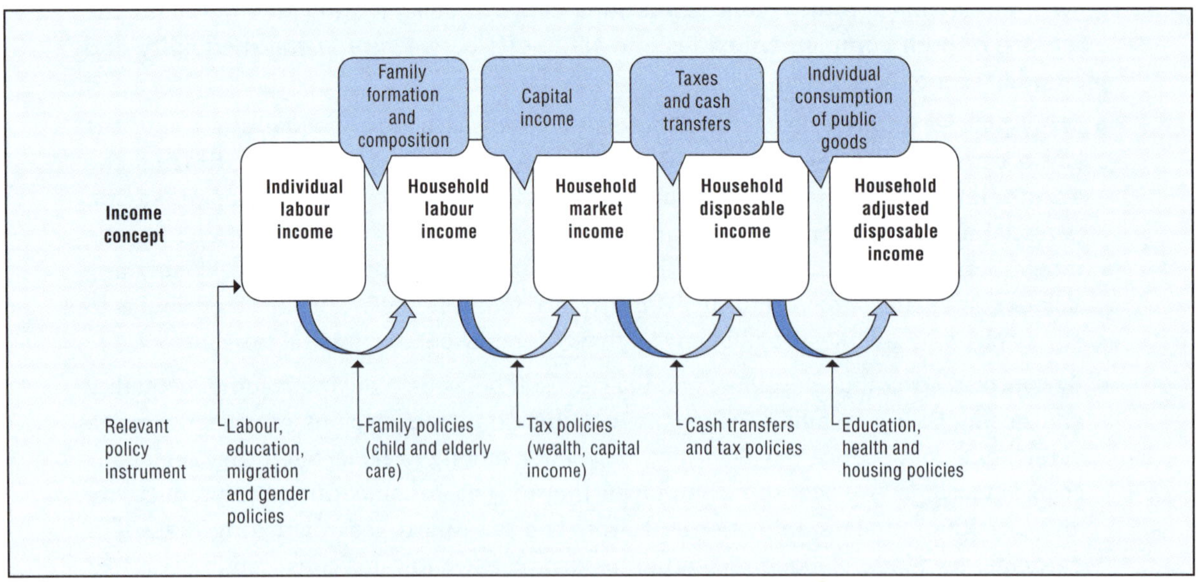

The rest of this chapter covers three of these five income concepts – household labour income, household market income and household disposable income – since these are the most relevant for the build-up of inequality and the most responsive to structural reforms, while the measurement of the redistributive impact of in-kind benefits is difficult.[4] Due to data availability constraints, the chapter focuses on inequality at a given point in time, while the issue should ideally also be looked at from a life-time perspective, taking into account the role of social mobility.

The dispersion of household labour and market income differs across countries

The dispersion of household labour income is driven by four factors: *i)* the dispersion of hourly earnings among those who have a full-time job; *ii)* the share of part-time workers; *iii)* the non-employment rate; and *iv)* household formation. Countries differ widely in the dispersion of earnings among full-time workers, with Chile, the United States and Portugal being the most unequal countries and Belgium, Denmark and Switzerland being the most equal ones (Figure 5.2). Inequality is higher in all countries when extending the analysis to part-time workers or the entire working age population (*i.e.* also including the unemployed and the inactive), reflecting the large income differentials between these groups and full-time workers. This effect is particularly large for countries where part-time workers make up a sizable share of total employment (*e.g.* Australia, Germany, Japan, the United Kingdom) and where unemployment and inactivity rates are high (*e.g.* Belgium, Chile, Hungary, Italy). Accounting for household size and composition reveals a more

Figure 5.2. **Labour income inequality varies across countries and depends on the population group considered**

Gini index, 2008

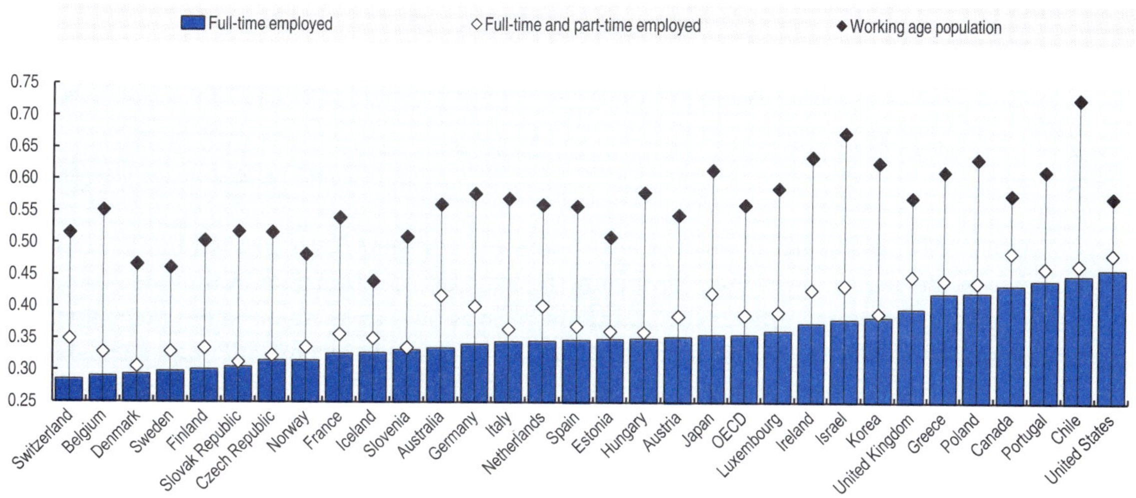

Note: The Gini index is a measure of inequality that ranges from zero (perfect equality) to one (where one individual receives all earnings). The group of employed individuals includes both dependent and self-employed individuals. The working age population includes all persons aged 15 to 64 except for students and people above the country's statutory retirement age. The Gini coefficients take into account labour earnings only; the precise data for labour earnings differs across countries. 2007 for France, Korea and the United States, 2009 for Australia and Japan. The value for the OECD is calculated as an unweighted average across all OECD countries for which data are available.

Source: Panel Study of Income Dynamics (PSID) for the United States; Household Income and Labour Dynamics in Australia Survey (HILDA) for Australia; National Socioeconomic Characterization Survey (CASEN) for Chile; Korean Labour and Income Panel Study (KLIPS) for Korea; Luxembourg Income Study (LIS) for Israel; Japan Household Panel Survey (JHPS) for Japan; Swiss Household Panel (SHP) for Switzerland; and European Union Statistics on Income and Living Conditions (EU-SILC) for the other countries.

StatLink http://dx.doi.org/10.1787/888932566497

complex picture (OECD, 2008a). Working household members often combine their income, which narrows the dispersion of income because of the ensuing economies of scale in consumption, whereas the inclusion of dependents in households widens it.

Incorporating capital income, which is more concentrated than labour earnings, increases inequality among households. Even so, given its smaller overall size, capital income is not a major determinant of total household market income dispersion (Figure 5.3). Labour market income accounts for around 75% of the dispersion on average in the OECD, *versus* just 25% for self-employment and capital income combined.

Figure 5.3. **Labour income inequality is the main contributor to the dispersion in household market income**

Contributions to the concentration coefficient of market income, working age population, in the late 2000s

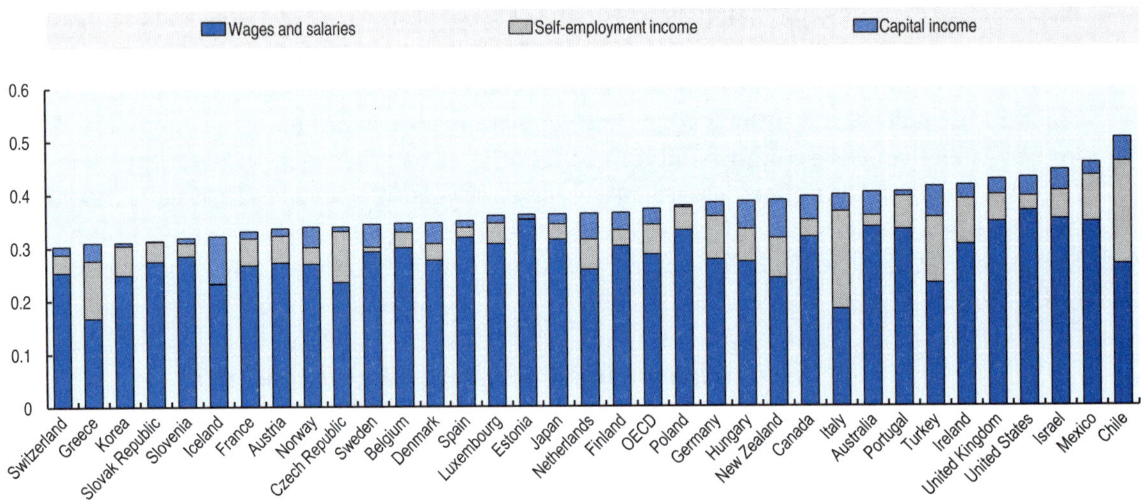

Note: Contributions to overall household market income inequality are derived by multiplying the concentration coefficients of each income source by their weight in total market income. The data for Greece, Hungary, Mexico and Turkey are net of taxes. Data for France and Ireland refer to the mid-2000s.

Source: OECD Income Distribution and Poverty, *OECD Social Expenditure Statistics (Database).*

StatLink http://dx.doi.org/10.1787/888932566516

OECD-wide, inequality in income *after* taxes and transfers, as measured by the Gini index, was about 25% lower than for income *before* taxes and transfers in the late 2000s, while poverty measured after taxes and transfers was 55% lower than before taxes and transfers.[5] That said, the distribution of household disposable income still varies widely across countries (Figure 5.4). Indeed even after taxes and transfers, the Gini index ranged from below 0.25 in Slovenia (little inequality) to 0.5 in Chile (high inequality). Percentile ratios provide a measure of income inequality at specific points of the income distribution and are an intuitive way to gauge the width of the income distribution. In around 2008, the income of the 90th (*i.e.* richest) centile of households was three times higher than the income of the 10th (*i.e.* poorest) centile of households in several Eastern European and Nordic countries (Figure 5.4). But this ratio stood above 6 for Chile, Israel,[6] Mexico and Turkey. Also, cross-country differences in the share of top income earners (99th centile) in total income are very wide, ranging from 4.5% for Sweden to 18.1% for the United States (Box 5.1).

Figure 5.4. **The divide between the rich and the poor is quite pronounced in some countries**

Household disposable income: Gap between the 10th and the 90th centile and the Gini index in the late 2000s

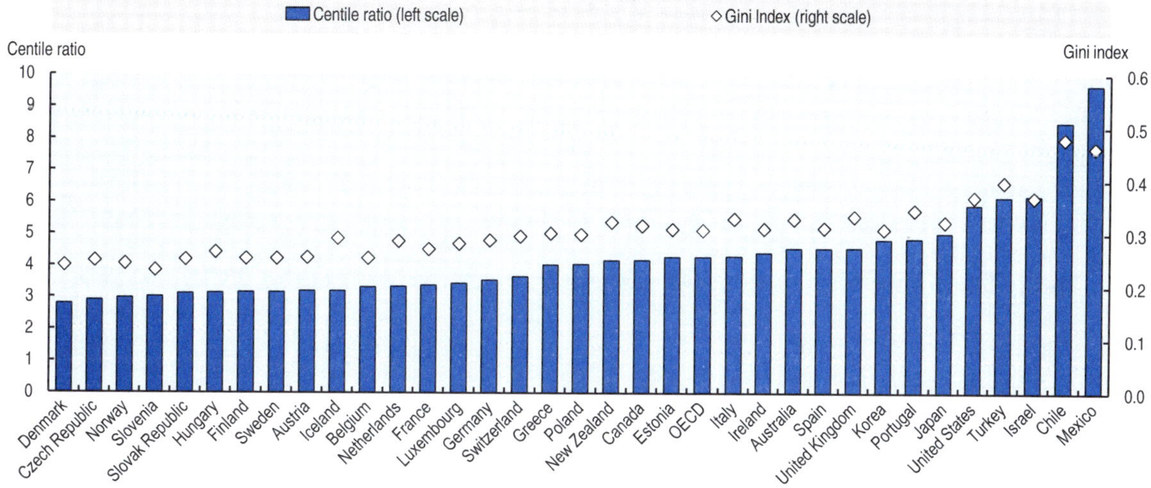

Note: Data for France and Ireland refer to the mid-2000s instead of the late 2000s.

Source: OECD Income Distribution and Poverty, *OECD Social Expenditure Statistics (Database).*

StatLink http://dx.doi.org/10.1787/888932566535

Box 5.1. **Why are top earners getting a growing share of the cake?**

Rising income inequality is often shaped by the increasing concentration of income at the top end of the income distribution (Hoeller, 2012). In the United States, for example, the top 1% of the population received 18% of pre-tax income in 2008, up from 8% in 1980. While the share in total income of the top earners has also risen in most other OECD countries (Figure 5.5), countries vary considerably both in the extent of this increase and in when it started. Despite a growing interest in the rise in top incomes, there is still substantial disagreement about the causes and their relative importance. Some of the more prominent explanations include the following:

Changes in taxation

- Tax rates for high earners have come down considerably over time – this may have boosted the income that top earners declare to the tax authorities. Studies suggest that in a country with a top marginal tax rate of 50%, a cut in the marginal tax rate by 1% would boost taxable income by 1%.
- Tax regimes may influence the mix of compensation, tilting it towards lower taxed forms of compensation, and thereby boost disposable income, particularly at the top (Goolsbee, 2000; Piketty and Saez, 2003; Roine *et al.*, 2009). For example, capital gains are often taxed at a lower rate than other income and, in a few countries, they are not taxed at all. Stock options also benefit from preferential tax treatment in many OECD countries (OECD, 2006a) and the same is likely to hold for carried interest arrangements.

Globalisation, technological change and the market for talent

- New information technologies, together with globalisation, have widened the market for "stars", boosting top incomes in the sports and entertainment industries (Rosen, 1981; Gordon and Dew-Becker, 2008).
- The skill requirements and responsibilities of top managers have become more complex, largely owing to stronger competition associated with deregulation and globalisation (*e.g.* Murphy and Zabojnik, 2004; Garicano and Rossi-Hansberg, 2006; Cuñat and Guadalupe, 2009). Moreover, the stability of top management positions has declined while the outside options of top managers have improved, raising

Box 5.1. **Why are top earners getting a growing share of the cake?** *(cont.)*

their bargaining power. Outside options which include jobs overseas may explain why the top income shares of some countries influence those of others. For example, the top income share in the United States has been found to have a considerable influence on the share in Canada, while those in the United Kingdom and Australia influence the one in New Zealand (Saez and Veall, 2005; Atkinson and Leigh, 2008).

- Globalisation has also led to a sharp increase in the market capitalisation of large multi-national companies, with the rise in executive pay closely following the rise in company size (Gabaix and Landier, 2008).

Figure 5.5. **Share of the top 1% of earners in total taxable income, 1980 and 2008**

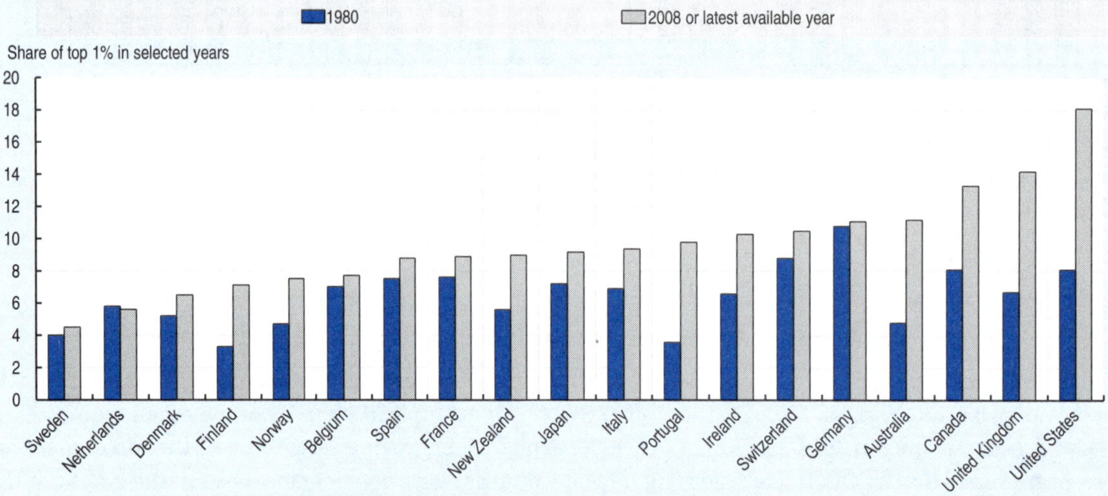

Note: The pre-tax income data exclude capital gains for all countries except Australia and Finland. The data are based on tax returns.

Source: Alvaredo, F. et al. (2011), *The Top Incomes Database*, *www.parisschoolofeconomics.eu/en/news/the-top-incomes-database-new-website/*; Matthews, S. (2011), "Trends in Top Incomes and their Tax Policy Implications", *OECD Taxation Working Papers*, No. 4, OECD Publishing.

StatLink http://dx.doi.org/10.1787/888932566554

Classifying countries by their inequality patterns

Five groups of countries with similar inequality patterns were identified using a cluster analysis (Figure 5.6).[7] The five groups are listed below, starting with those that have the lowest dispersion of household disposable income:

i) A group – which includes four Nordic countries plus Switzerland – is characterised by below-average inequality thanks to little wage dispersion, in particular at the upper end, combined with a high employment rate. However, the share of part-time employment is above average in all these countries (except Sweden), contributing to inequality in labour income. Cash transfers are often universal and household taxes tend to be largely proportional to household income, implying only moderate redistribution through the tax and transfer system. Overall, both the dispersion in disposable income and the poverty rate are well below the OECD average.

ii) In a group of eight European countries (Belgium, the Czech Republic, Estonia, Finland, France, Italy, the Slovak Republic and Slovenia), inequality originating from the labour market is slightly below the OECD average. Wages are little dispersed in international comparison but inequality in labour earnings is driven by a low employment rate (in

Figure 5.6. **Country groups with similar patterns of inequality**[1]

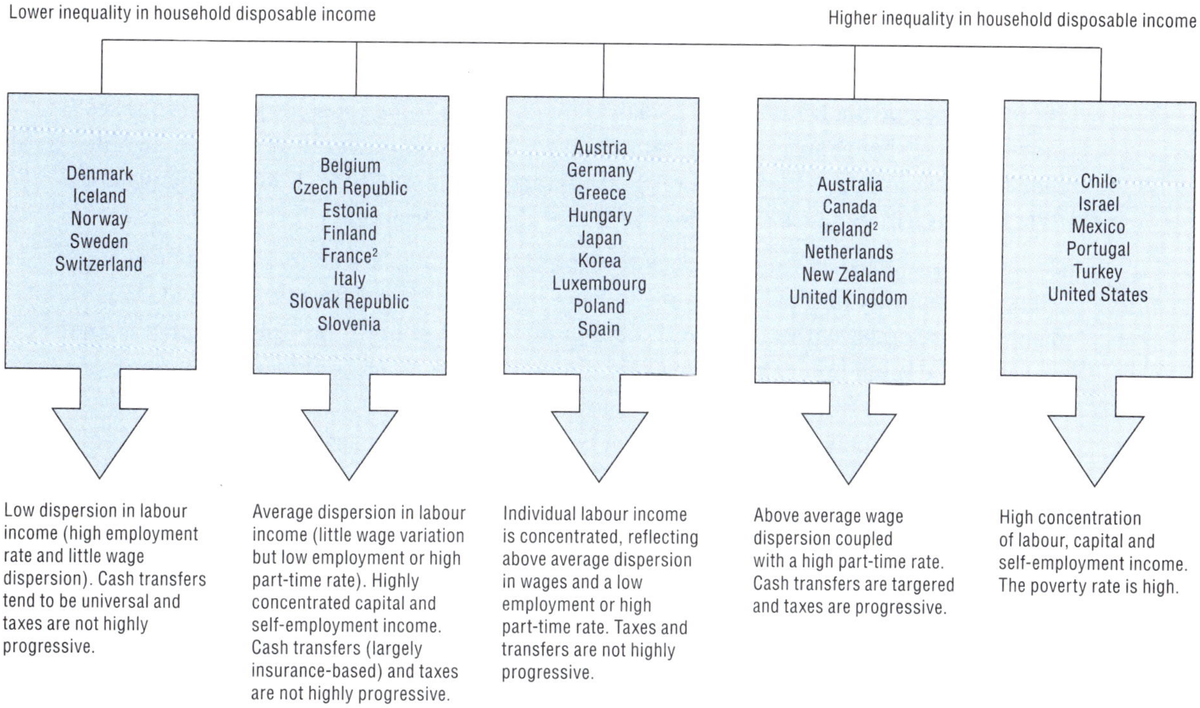

1. Country groups are derived from a cluster analysis of a set of 12 core income inequality indicators, with standardised values and unsquared Euclidean distance to measure differences between groups. Various alternative scenarios have been run. They suggest that the two groups to the right are very stable. The dividing lines between the three groups to the left are less sharp.
2. For France and Ireland, mid-2000s (instead of end-2000s) data have been used for the cluster analysis.

Source: Hoeller, P. *et al.* (2012), "Less Income Inequality and More Growth – Are they Compatible? Part 1. Mapping Income Inequality Across the OECD", *OECD Economics Department Working Papers*, No. 924, OECD Publishing.

particular for Belgium, France, Italy and the Slovak Republic). The high concentration of self-employment or capital income brings inequality in household market income close to the OECD average (except for the Slovak Republic and Slovenia). However, the size of tax and cash transfer systems as a share of GDP is large, reducing household disposable income inequality to or below the OECD average.

iii) In a group of seven other continental European countries (Austria, Germany, Greece, Hungary, Luxembourg, Poland and Spain) plus Japan and Korea, inequality originating from the labour market is at or above the OECD average. However, the underlying causes vary. The wage dispersion is wide in all these countries but in Germany it is mainly at the lower end of the wage distribution, while in Hungary and Poland, wage dispersion arises more at the upper end of the income distribution. The employment rate is also low in Greece, Hungary, Korea, Luxembourg, Poland and Spain, while the share of part-time employment is high in Austria and Japan. In some of these countries (in particular Greece and Korea), an important redistribution of labour earnings occurs within families. Cash transfers tend to have little redistributive impact since they are small in size (Korea) or largely insurance-based and thus not highly progressive (Austria, Germany, Greece, Hungary, Japan, Poland and Spain). Overall, both the dispersion in household disposable income and the poverty rate are close to the OECD average.

iv) Five English-speaking countries (Australia, Canada, Ireland, New Zealand and the United Kingdom) and the Netherlands all have a large share of part-time employment, driving inequality in labour earnings. On the other hand, the employment rate is above the OECD average in all these countries except Ireland. While small in size (for all countries except the Netherlands), cash transfers tend to be more targeted and taxes more progressive than in the other OECD countries, and therefore have a sizable redistributive impact. Household disposable income inequality is, however, above the OECD average in all these countries except for the Netherlands.

v) Chile, Israel, Mexico, Portugal, Turkey and the United States are characterised by above average inequality originating from the labour market. This reflects a very wide wage dispersion coupled with a low employment rate (though here the United States is an exception). Capital and self-employment income also tend to benefit a small group of households. Cash transfers have little redistributive impact because they are small in size and often largely insurance-based. The size of tax systems is also small in most of these countries, although some embody more progressivity than on average in the OECD. Overall, both inequality in household disposable income and the poverty rate are well above the OECD average.

What drives inequality?

Technological change and globalisation partly explain recent trends in labour income inequality

Technological advances may affect labour income inequality as they can benefit higher-skilled workers more than others. For example, to the extent that medium-skilled workers focus on routine tasks that can also be accomplished by computers, technological change will reduce the demand for such workers. The opposite effect can be expected for highly-skilled and low-skilled workers who tend to focus respectively on abstract and manual non-routine tasks, both of which are harder to replace by machines. If the demand shifts are not offset by equal shifts in the composition of labour supply (*e.g.* by a large enough rise in tertiary education attainment), technological progress may reduce the earnings or employment of medium-skilled workers relative to both the low- and high-skilled ones. Indeed the data point to a polarisation of employment by skill level (*e.g.* Autor *et al.*, 2006, Goos *et al.*, 2009).

Globalisation may also widen inequality. A *first* channel through which this may happen is offshoring. The tasks that are relocated from richer to poorer countries are typically not skill intensive from the perspective of the skill-rich country, but they are from the perspective of the skill-poor country. As a result, offshoring makes labour demand more skill intensive in both poorer and richer countries, thus increasing inequality in both groups of countries (Feenstra and Hanson, 1996). *Second*, if firms differ in their profitability and low-income workers work disproportionately in low-productivity firms that are battered by import competition, trade may increase labour income inequality by lowering employment or the relative earnings of low-income workers (*e.g.* Egger and Kreickemeier, 2009; Helpman *et al.*, 2010). The implied positive link between globalisation and inequality is supported by a growing body of studies of individual firms, but it is more difficult to establish a robust link at the aggregate level.

Globalisation and technological change may also reinforce each other, thereby further raising inequality. On the one hand, technology may underpin globalisation and on the other, the increased competition that comes with globalisation may force firms to innovate. Innovation may raise labour income inequality both temporarily – since R&D is skill intensive (Dinopoulos and Segerstrom, 1999; Neary, 2003) – and permanently, provided it results in skill-biased technological change as discussed above (Acemoglu, 2002).

Labour income inequality is also influenced by structural policies

Structural policies in the areas of education, labour and product markets influence labour income inequality by affecting *i)* the employment rate and *ii)* the dispersion of earnings among those that have a job (see Koske *et al.*, 2012 for a detailed discussion). Policies that foster equity in education lower income inequality by reducing the dispersion of earnings. The same applies to policies that promote upper secondary or tertiary education, at least in countries with an already high share of upper secondary or tertiary graduates, respectively, among the working-age population. For many labour market policies, by contrast, the impact is less clear cut as they affect both the dispersion of earnings and the level of employment in sometimes conflicting ways, at least for some types of workers. Examples include increasing the minimum wage relative to the median wage, increasing the level of employment protection and increasing the generosity of unemployment benefits. One labour market reform that stands out as having a positive effect on both employment and earnings equality is lowering the gap of employment protection on temporary and permanent work. The impact of product market liberalisation on income inequality is ambiguous. While boosting employment, some types of product market reforms may widen the distribution of earnings. A rough quantification of the average size of the effects of selected structural policy reforms on the dispersion of earnings is provided in Table 5.1, based on the new OECD empirical analysis.

Table 5.1. **Policy experiments for reducing labour earnings inequality**

Policy experiment[1]	90/10 percentile ratio[2] falls by...
A rise in the share of the population with post-secondary education by 10 percentage points	≈ 0.04
A fall in job projection on regular work from the level observed in Germany (third-highest level) to that observed in Finland (about OECD average)	≈ 0.16
A rise in job projection on temporary work from the level observed in the United Kingdom (second-lowest level) to that observed in Finland (about OECD average)	≈ 0.08
A rise in union membership by 10 percentage points	≈ 0.01
A rise in the ratio of the minimum to the median wage from the level observed in the Czech Republic (third-lowest level) to that observed in Poland (about OECD average)	< 0.01

1. The policy experiments are roughly equivalent to the impact of a one standard deviation change in the policy variables of interest on the 90/10 percentile ratio.
2. One way to measure inequality is to look at the ratio between different income percentiles. The ratio between incomes at the top of the distribution (the 90th percentile) and at the bottom (the 10th percentile) is abbreviated as the 90/10 ratio. A fall in the 90/10 ratio means that inequality is falling. The average 90/10 percentile ratio in OECD countries is about 4.5 with a standard deviation across countries of 0.8 (see Hoeller *et al.*, 2012).

Source: Based on Table 1, specifications 3 (for the rise in the minimum wage) and 2 (for all other policy reforms) in Koske, I., J.-M. Fournier and I. Wanner (2012), "Less Income Inequality and More Growth – Are They Compatible? Part 2. The Distribution of Labour Income", *OECD Economics Department Working Papers*, No. 925, OECD Publishing.

Some countries rely heavily on taxes and transfers to influence distributional outcomes

Tax and transfer systems play a key role in lowering overall income inequality. Cash transfers – such as pensions, unemployment and child benefits – account for more than three quarters of the overall redistributive impact, and taxes for one quarter. However, there are large differences across the OECD in the size, composition and progressivity of taxes and cash transfers (Joumard *et al.*, 2012). On the transfer side, pensions account for the bulk of total transfers in most but not all countries (Figure 5.7). They primarily aim at redistributing income over the lifetime of individuals – those with higher incomes contribute more but will also receive higher pensions. Thus, pensions often redistribute comparatively less across different individuals. Other transfers are usually more progressive, although how much depends on their design, *e.g.* the relative portion of flat *versus* income-related benefits. In most countries, family and housing benefits are either universal or means-tested, thus involving more redistribution across individuals.

Figure 5.7. **Cash transfers vary greatly across countries, but less redistributive old age transfers account for the largest share**

Public cash transfers to households: level and composition,[1] 2007

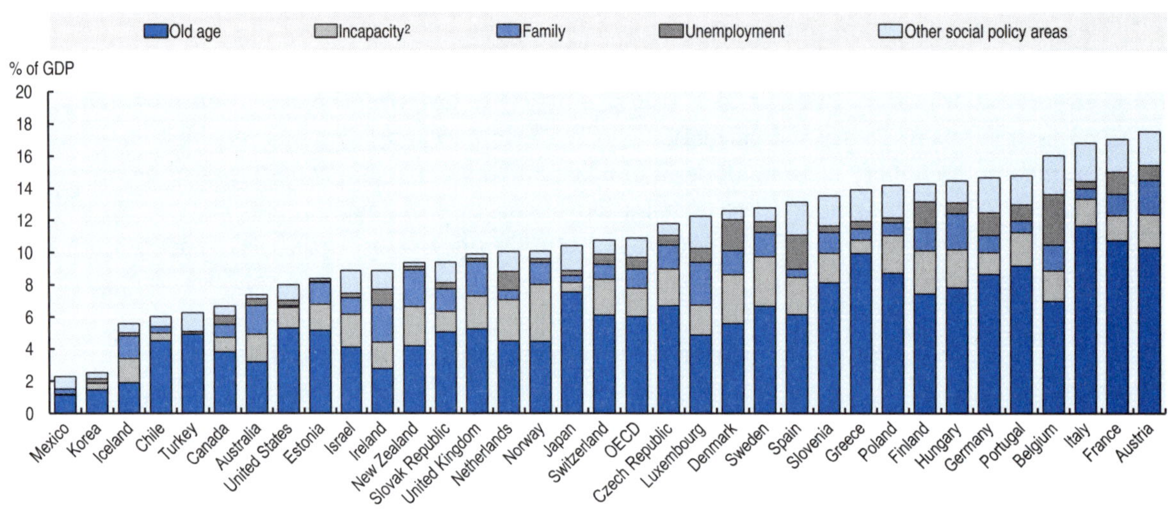

1. The data shown here exclude private mandatory spending which accounts for an important share of total social spending in some countries (in particular Chile, Germany and Switzerland). In addition, public cash transfers shown here may not fully account for those programmes and services provided, or co-financed, by local governments. Measurement gaps may be high, notably in federal countries such as Canada.
2. Incapacity-related spending covers expenditure on disability pensions and sick leave schemes (occupational injury and other sickness daily allowances).

Source: *OECD Social Expenditure Statistics (Database)*.

StatLink http://dx.doi.org/10.1787/888932566573

The redistributive impact of taxes varies less across countries than the large differences in tax-to-GDP ratios would suggest. Indeed some high-tax countries show little progressivity, either because: *i)* the tax mix favours consumption taxes and social security contributions over more progressive personal income and wealth and inheritance taxes;[8] *ii)* the progressivity of tax schedules is limited (*e.g.* in the Nordic countries); or *iii)* statutory progressivity is weakened by tax expenditures that benefit high-income groups most.

Labour income tax schedules have become more progressive but tax expenditures hamper redistribution

Whether the tax and transfer system has become more or less redistributive over time across the OECD is unclear. The progressivity of statutory labour tax schedules (including social security contributions) has increased in the majority of countries since 2000 (Figure 5.8). Though there has been a steep decline in top marginal income tax rates, a number of countries have cut social security contributions, and introduced or strengthened in-work tax benefits, targeted at lower incomes, thus increasing the progressivity of labour taxes. By contrast, the use of tax expenditures which often benefit high-income groups most – such as tax breaks for health and child care, tertiary education, owner-occupied housing and retirement savings – has been growing (OECD, 2010b).

Figure 5.8. **The progressivity of statutory labour tax schedules has increased in the majority of countries**

Progressivity indicator based on net personal income tax schedules for single taxpayers without children, in 2000 and 2009

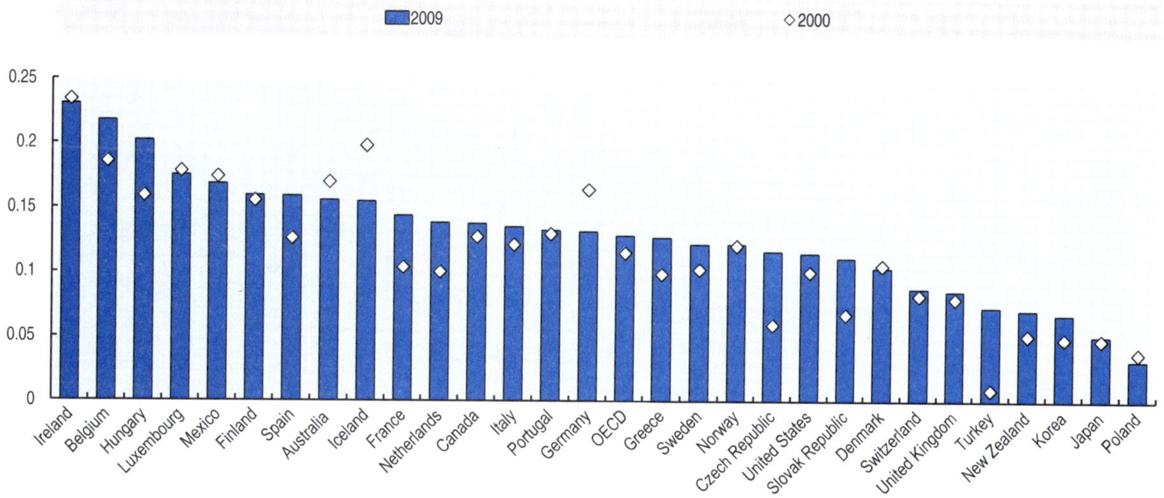

Note: Net personal income tax is defined as the sum of personal income tax and employee social security contributions net of standard cash transfers. Standard tax relief measures – including those linked to marital and family status and income level – are accounted for. Non-standard tax relief measures, *i.e.* those determined by reference to actual expenses incurred (such as the amount of interest paid on loans), are not included. The indicator for net personal tax progressivity is calculated as the difference between the average net personal tax rate at two income levels based on the assumption of a similar income dispersion across OECD countries. This difference is then divided by the difference between the two income levels.

Source: OECD (2009), *Taxing Wages 2008*, OECD Publishing; OECD estimates.

StatLink http://dx.doi.org/10.1787/888932566592

The taxation of capital income, wealth and inheritance has also been reduced in many countries, which has clearly reduced the redistributive impact of tax systems. Indeed, capital income tends to be increasingly concentrated in the upper income brackets, as do wealth and inheritance (Piketty, 2010; Fredriksen, 2012). Property taxes vary widely across countries. They largely consist of recurrent taxes on immovable property. These taxes, however, often absorb a larger share of the income of poorer households because they are often set as a payment for the benefits of local public services (*e.g.* waste collection) which do not increase fully in line with income.[9]

Policy trade-offs and complementarities between growth and income equality objectives

Despite a vast theoretical literature on the link between inequality and growth, no general consensus has emerged and the empirical evidence is rather inconclusive. A simple scatter plot of inequality and growth also shows no link (Figure 5.9). Still, specific structural reforms that aim at raising average living standards also influence the distribution of income. Table 5.2 provides a qualitative summary of the findings of new research on the GDP per capita and inequality effects of various structural reforms. It suggests that growth-enhancing policies can be divided into three broad categories (last two columns of Table 5.2): *i)* those that are likely to reduce labour income inequality; *ii)* those that are likely to raise it; and *iii)* those that seem to have an ambiguous effect.

Figure 5.9. **There is no simple link between inequality and growth**

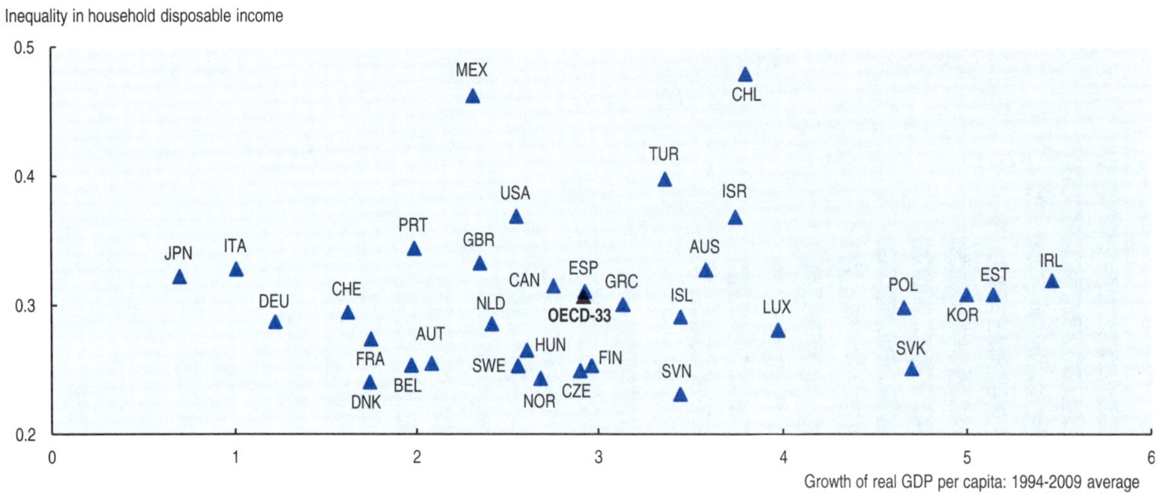

Note: Inequality in household disposable income is measured by the Gini index. The inequality measures refer to the late 2000s, except for France and Ireland for which they refer to the mid-2000s.

Source: OECD Income Distribution and Poverty, *OECD Social Expenditure Statistics (Database)*; *OECD Economic Outlook: Statistics and Projections (Database)*.

StatLink http://dx.doi.org/10.1787/888932566611

Growth-enhancing policy reforms that are likely to reduce income inequality

Improving the quality and reach of education

Reforms to increase human capital are important for improving living standards, and are also likely to reduce labour income inequality. New analysis shows that a rise in the share of workers with upper secondary education is associated with a decline in labour earnings inequality (Fournier and Koske, 2012). Examples of policy initiatives to raise upper secondary education attainment include *inter alia* enhanced accountability for schools, better teacher recruitment and training, and special support for pupils at risk of dropping out.

Encouraging more students to pursue tertiary studies may have a more ambiguous effect on earnings inequality. Such reforms tend to widen income dispersion by increasing the share of high-wage earners (the composition effect). On the other hand, new research suggests that this effect may be more than offset by a decline in the returns to tertiary education relative to the returns to lower levels of education (Koske *et al.*, 2012). Tuition

Table 5.2. **Some structural policies benefit both growth and equality but others may entail a trade-off**

A rise in:	Employment rate	Earnings equality[1]	Total labour income equality[2]	GDP per capita
The tertiary education graduation rate	~	+	+	+
The upper secondary graduation rate	~	+	+	+
Equity in education	~	+	+	+
The minimum wage (as share of the median wage)	0/–	+	~	0/–
Unionisation	~	+	+	~
Legal extensions of collective wage agreements	–	~	–	–
The overall level of employment protection legislation (EPL)	0/–	+	~	–
The gap between EPL on regular *versus* temporary work	–	–	–	–
The replacement rate and duration of unemployment benefits	–	+	~	–
Spending on active labour market policies	0/+	~	+	+
Anti-competitive product market regulation	–	0/+	~	–
The integration of immigrants	+	+	+	+
Anti-discrimination initiatives	+	+	+	+
Female labour force participation	+	+	+	+

1. The term "Earnings equality" refers to equality among those who earn an income from employment.
2. The term "Total labour income equality" refers to equality among the working-age population, thus accounting for both employment and earnings inequality effects.

Note: A plus symbol (+) denotes a significant rise in the variable, a minus symbol (–) a significant fall and a zero (0) no impact; 0/+ and 0/– mean that research is contradictory, *i.e.* some studies cannot find a significant effect while others find a positive/negative effect or studies cannot find an aggregate effect but find a significant effect on some parts of the population. ~ means that the sign of the effect is unknown because the empirical literature is inconclusive or because studies on the link are not available.

Source: The GDP per capita effects are based on the findings of previous OECD and other studies or deducted from the employment rate effect (*e.g.* Barnes, S., *et al.* (2011), "The GDP Impact of Reform: A Simple Simulation Framework", *OECD Economics Department Working Papers*, No. 834, OECD Publishing; Bouis, R. and R. Duval (2011), "Raising Potential Growth After the Crisis: A Quantitative Assessment of the Potential Gains from Various Structural Reforms in the OECD Area and Beyond", *OECD Economics Department Working Papers*, No. 835, OECD Publishing. The earnings and employment effects are taken from new OECD analysis reported in Koske, I. *et al.* (2012) and the studies cited therein.

fees that make students share at least part of the cost of tertiary education could lower disposable income inequality (as the current financing of education is regressive), provided they are accompanied by flanking measures so that the poor are not excluded from tertiary education.[10]

Promoting equity in education

Raising social mobility by making educational outcomes less dependent on personal and social circumstances should boost GDP per capita by enhancing entrepreneurship, the overall quality and allocation of human capital and, ultimately, productivity. At the same time, a more equitable distribution of educational opportunities has been shown to result in a more equitable distribution of labour income (*e.g.* De Gregorio and Lee, 2002). Examples of reforms include postponing early tracking, strengthening links between school and home to help disadvantaged children learn, and providing early childhood care and basic schooling for all. The latter may yield large positive returns over an individual's entire lifetime, particularly for the most disadvantaged (Chetty *et al.*, 2011; OECD, 2006b).

Reducing the gap between employment protection on temporary and permanent work

If employment protection[11] is much stricter for regular than for temporary contracts, workers at the margin of the labour market – such as young people – risk getting trapped in a situation where they move between temporary work and unemployment without getting into permanent work. This can have adverse implications for human capital and career progression (OECD, 2004) and, ultimately, income equality and economic growth. New OECD analysis finds that low-income workers on temporary contracts earn less than workers with similar characteristics on permanent contracts (Fournier and Koske, 2012). This is not the case for higher-income workers. Tentative evidence on the size of the effect illustrated in Table 5.1 suggests, for example, that reducing protection for permanent work from the level observed in Germany (third-highest level) to that observed in Finland (which is about OECD average) while increasing protection for temporary work from the level observed in the United Kingdom (second-lowest level) to that observed in Finland (which is about OECD average) would reduce the 90/10 percentile ratio by about 0.24 (which is about 7% of the average 90/10 percentile ratio in OECD countries). More even job protection for temporary and permanent contracts is also likely to reduce the income gap between immigrants and non-immigrants, as previous studies have shown that immigrants suffer disproportionately from contract-related labour market dualism (Causa and Jean, 2007).

Increasing spending on active labour market policies

High social benefits can reduce the incentives for work and employment. Active labour market policies may limit these adverse effects by better matching jobs with skills and enhancing job search support and monitoring. Existing empirical evidence suggests indeed that active labour market policies raise employment (Bassanini and Duval, 2006). This should entail positive effects for both GDP per capita and labour income equality. Programme design is key to reaping such gains, however (Martin and Grubb, 2001).

Promoting the integration of immigrants

Better integration of immigrants in the labour market can both reduce inequality and raise GDP per capita through higher labour force participation. Targeted policies, such as language courses, and transparent systems of recognising foreign qualifications should help to close the gap between immigrants and non-immigrants' labour market performance.

Improving labour market outcomes of women

Women tend to take on more caring responsibilities than men, meaning they work fewer hours and thus take home less pay. Arguably, their higher labour supply elasticity should lead women to be taxed at a lower rate than men. Since this is not feasible in practice, policies to improve the availability of formal care for children and the elderly can serve as an alternative solution. Such policies should help to reduce gender differences in working hours and – at least to the extent that hourly wages are little affected – pay, and at the same time improve long-run living standards through higher participation rates.

Fighting discrimination

Since at least part of the earnings gap between immigrants and non-immigrants and between men and women is likely to be due to discrimination (Koske *et al.*, 2012), more effective legal rules (*e.g.* legal action against those who engage in discriminatory practices) could also help.

Taxing in a way that allows equitable growth

Taxes do not only affect the distribution of income; they also affect GDP per capita by influencing labour use and productivity, or both (Johansson *et al.*, 2008). Some tax reforms appear to be win-win options – improving growth prospects while narrowing the distribution of income. Many, however, may imply trade-offs between these objectives. Following the same approach as for labour market, product market and education policies discussed above (Table 5.2), these complementarities and trade-offs are drawn out in Table 5.3.

Table 5.3. **The impact of tax reforms on growth and equality**

Tax policies	Income equality	GDP per capita	Comments
Increasing total tax revenues	+ (in general)	–	• The impact of taxes on income distribution depends on the level of taxation, the tax mix and the use of tax revenues, but if tax systems are progressive overall, equality is enhanced. • Taxes dampen incentives to work, save and invest and are thus detrimental to growth. But some taxes have a less adverse effect than others.
Changing the tax mix while keeping total tax revenues constant			
Moving from personal income tax to consumption taxes	–	+	• Personal income tax tends to be progressive while consumption tax is regressive. • Personal income tax reduces work and saving incentives. A shift from direct to indirect taxes would raise GDP per capita.
Moving from labour income to property and capital taxes: • to wealth, inheritance and capital income taxes, such as capital gains taxes; • to real estate taxes.	 ~ –	 + +	• Wealth and inheritance taxes tend to be progressive. • The distributive impact depends on the relative progressivity of income *versus* wealth and inheritance taxes. • Real estate taxes are often less progressive than the personal income tax and can even be regressive. • Property taxes are among the least harmful for growth. Moving from income to property taxes tends to improve incentives to work and invest, and thus raise output, at least in the short and medium-term.
Cutting tax expenditures and marginal rates	+ (in most cases) – (for in-work tax credits)	+	• Most tax expenditures benefit high-income groups (in-work tax credits and other tax expenditures targeted at low-income groups are the exception). Cutting tax expenditure would narrow the distribution of disposable income. • Cutting marginal rates improves incentives to work, save and invest, and thus lifts GDP per capita.
Increasing the progressivity of taxes (revenue-neutral)			
Personal income tax: • increase in top rates; • above measure combined with expanded EITC schemes or tax free allowances.	+ {+ +}	~ –} +}	• In-work tax credits narrow the income distribution and raise incentives to work. • On the other hand, higher top rates may reduce working hours and productivity by undermining incentives to work, invest and innovate. • The GDP per capita impact is thus ambiguous.

Note: + means more equality or higher GDP per capita; – means less equality or lower GDP per capita; ~ means ambiguous effect.
Source: Joumard, I., M. Pisu and D. Bloch (2012), "Less Income Inequality and More Growth – Are They Compatible? Part 3. Income Redistribution *via* Taxes and Transfers across OECD Countries", *OECD Economics Department Working Papers*, No. 926, OECD Publishing.

The findings in Table 5.3 and in the literature suggest some policy options that could promote growth and reduce inequality:

- *Re-assess tax expenditures that benefit mainly high-income groups* (*e.g.* tax relief on mortgage interest). Cutting back such tax expenditures is likely to be beneficial both for long-term GDP per capita, allowing a reduction in marginal tax rates, and for a more equitable distribution of income. Lowering tax expenditures would also reduce the complexity of the tax system, and thus tax compliance and collection costs.

- *Reduce distortions in taxing capital income.* Tax relief – such as reduced taxation for capital gains from the sale of a principal or secondary residence – often distorts resource allocation without boosting aggregate savings and growth, and benefits mainly high-income groups. Specific tax relief may also provide tax avoidance instruments for top-income earners. In particular, there is little justification for tax breaks for stock options and carried interest. Raising such taxes would increase equity and allow a growth-enhancing cut in marginal labour income tax rates.

Growth-enhancing policy reforms that are likely to raise income inequality

Increasing the flexibility of wage determination

Extending collective wage agreements to firms that are not party to the original settlement may make labour costs too high for some employers. This can hamper productivity through lower competitive pressures from the entry of new firms, and can also reduce employment (Murtin *et al.*, 2012). However, new OECD evidence suggests that unions compress the distribution of labour earnings. To the extent that administrative extensions have a similar effect, their overall impact on income inequality is ambiguous, reflecting offsetting effects on employment and the dispersion of labour earnings.

Shifting the tax mix from personal and corporate income taxes towards real estate and consumption taxes

Personal and corporate income taxes, as well as social security contributions, are the most distortive taxes as they have sizable adverse effects on labour use, productivity and capital accumulation. Shifting the tax mix away from such taxes and towards recurrent taxes on immovable property (the least distortive) and consumption taxes should thus raise living standards (Johansson *et al.*, 2008). However, there is likely to be a trade-off with the income distribution objective since personal income taxes are progressive while real estate and consumption taxes are at best neutral in a lifetime perspective and in most cases tend to be regressive. Targeted transfers can reduce the severity of this trade-off.

Growth-enhancing policy reforms that have an ambiguous effect on income inequality

Avoiding too high and long-lasting unemployment benefits

If unemployment benefits are too high or long-lasting, they risk reducing job-search incentives and raising wages above market-clearing levels. This lowers employment with negative effects on GDP per capita and labour income equality. In the short run, these adverse income distribution effects are likely to be dominated by the direct inequality-reducing impact of the income support for the unemployed.[12]

Liberalising product markets

A wide range of studies illustrate the large beneficial effects of product market liberalisation on productivity (*e.g.* Bourlès *et al.*, 2010; Conway *et al.*, 2006), but the impact on labour income inequality is uncertain. Product market liberalisation generally raises employment (*e.g.* Bassanini and Duval, 2006; Griffith *et al.*, 2007), but this inequality-reducing effect could potentially be offset by a wider dispersion of earnings, though the evidence on the latter link is far from conclusive (*e.g.* Guadalupe, 2007; Koske *et al.*, 2012).

Lowering minimum labour costs

Minimum wages that are set too high can limit the job market opportunities for young and low-skilled workers. Under such circumstances, lowering relative labour costs may boost the employment of these marginal groups in the labour market (Neumark and Wascher, 2007). Greater employment in turn raises GDP per capita and reduces labour income inequality. However, existing studies, including new OECD analysis (Koske *et al.*, 2012), suggest that a fall in the minimum wage risks widening the dispersion of wages at the bottom of the distribution among those who are already employed, so that the impact on labour income inequality among the working age population is ambiguous. The employment effect of a lower minimum wage is likely to be smaller when the initial level of minimum labour costs is already low, which increases the likelihood that labour income inequality will rise.

Moving from income to wealth or inheritance taxes

Shifting taxes from income to wealth or inheritance would raise GDP per capita, since property taxes are among the least distortive taxes. As personal income, wealth and inheritance taxes all tend to be progressive, the distributional impact would depend on the relative progressivity of each tax but may be broadly neutral.

Notes

1. OECD (2011) provides more detail on the five main income concepts shown in Figure 5.1, and also discusses changes over time.
2. When examining inequality in individual labour earnings, the unemployed and people not looking actively for a job are assigned zero income.
3. As the focus of the first three income concepts is on market income, the population covered is the working-age population.
4. The determinants of inequality for each of the five income concepts are discussed in greater detail in a series of *OECD Economics Department Working Papers*, in particular Hoeller *et al.* (2012), Koske *et al.* (2012) and Joumard *et al.* (2012).
5. The poverty rate is defined as the share of the population whose equivalised household disposable income is below 50% of the median income.
6. The statistical data for Israel are supplied by and under the responsibility of the relevant Israeli authorities. The use of such data by the OECD is without prejudice to the status of the Golan Heights, East Jerusalem and Israeli settlements in the West Bank under the terms of international law.
7. The cluster analysis is performed on a set of 12 variables: the Gini index for individual labour earnings for the working age population, the ratio of the 9th to 5th deciles for wage earnings of full-time employees, the ratio of the 5th to 1st deciles for wage earnings of full-time employees, the share of part-time employment in total employment, the non-employment rate, the Gini index for household labour earnings (working age population), the Gini index for household market income for the working age population, the concentration ratio for transfers, the concentration ratio for taxes, the Gini index for household disposable income for the whole population, the income ratio of the 5th to the 1st quintile for household disposable income adjusted for in-kind public services and the poverty rate.
8. Consumption taxes tend to be regressive because lower-income households consume a larger share of their income. To mitigate this regressive impact, many OECD countries apply reduced rates and exemptions for goods and services that account for a large share of poorer households' consumption basket. The evidence, however, suggests that such tax reliefs benefit high-income groups most and may thus not be an effective redistributive tool (Dalsgaard, 2000; OECD, 2010a).
9. The regressive nature of recurrent taxes on immovable property may partly fade in a lifetime perspective. Indeed, the elderly are often income-poor but wealth-rich and property taxes based

on real estate values absorb a large share of their income. In contrast, working-age households tend to have higher income and lower wealth and property taxes absorb a lower share of their income.

10. For example, this could be achieved by combining tuition fees with student loans and linking repayment to income. Empirical evidence suggests that any negative effect of tuition fees on participation rates can be fully offset through improvements in the financial support for students (OECD, 2008b; Heller, 1999).

11. Employment protection refers both to regulations concerning hiring (*e.g.* rules favouring disadvantaged groups, conditions for using temporary or fixed-term contracts, training requirements) and firing (*e.g.* redundancy procedures, mandatory notification periods and severance payments, special requirements for collective dismissals and short-time work schemes).

12. In addition, the adverse effects on labour income inequality that stem from lower employment may potentially be offset – at least partially – by a more compressed income distribution (if unemployment benefits are progressive or lower-income workers are more likely to receive them).

Bibliography

Acemoglu, D. (2002), "Technical Change, Inequality, and the Labor Market", *Journal of Economic Literature*, Vol. 40, No. 1.

Atkinson, A.B. and A. Leigh (2008), "Top Incomes in New Zealand 1921-2005: Understanding the Effects of Marginal Tax Rates, Migration Threat, and the Macroeconomy", *Review of Income and Wealth*, Vol. 54, No. 2, pp. 149-165.

Autor, D.H., L.F. Katz and M.S. Kearney (2006), "The Polarization of the US Labour Market", *American Economic Review*, Vol. 96, No. 2, pp. 189-194.

Bassanini, A. and R. Duval (2006), "Employment Patterns in OECD Countries: Reassessing the Role of Policies and Institutions", *OECD Economics Department Working Papers*, No. 486, OECD Publishing.

Bourlès, R. *et al.* (2010), "Do Product Market Regulations in Upstream Sectors Curb Productivity Growth: Panel Data Evidence for OECD Countries", *OECD Economics Department Working Papers*, No. 791, OECD Publishing.

Causa, O. and S. Jean (2007), "Integration of Immigrants in OECD Countries: Do Policies Matter?", *OECD Economics Department Working Papers*, No. 564, OECD Publishing.

Chetty, R. *et al.* (2011), "How Does Your Kindergarten Classroom Affect Your Earnings? Evidence from Project Star", *Quarterly Journal of Economics*, Vol. 126, No. 4.

Conway, P. *et. al.* (2006), "Regulation, Competition and Productivity Convergence", *OECD Economics Department Working Papers*, No. 509, OECD Publishing.

Cuñat, V. and M. Guadalupe (2009), "Globalization and the Provision of Incentives inside the Firm: The Effect of Foreign Competition", *Journal of Labor Economics*, Vol. 27, No. 2, pp. 179-212.

Dalsgaard, T. (2000), "The Tax System in Mexico – A Need for Strengthening the Revenue-Raising Capacity", *OECD Economics Department Working Papers*, No. 233, OECD Publishing.

Dinopoulos, E. and P. Segerstrom (1999), "A Schumpeterian Model of Protection and Relative Wages,"*American Economic Review*, Vol. 89, No. 3, pp. 450-472.

Egger, H. and U. Kreickemeier (2009), "Firm Heterogeneity and the Labor Market Effects of Trade Liberalization", *International Economic Review*, Vol. 50, No. 1, pp. 187-216.

Feenstra, R.C. and G.H. Hanson (1996), "Foreign Investment, Outsourcing and Relative Wages", *NBER Working Paper*, No. 5121, National Bureau of Economic Research.

Fournier, J.-M. and I. Koske (2012), "Equality and Growth – Are They Compatible? Part 7. The Drivers of Labour Earnings Inequality – An Analysis Based on Conditional and Unconditional Quantile Regressions", *OECD Economics Department Working Papers*, No. 930, OECD Publishing.

Fredriksen, K. (2012), "Less Income Inequality and More Growth – Are They Compatible? Part 6. The Distribution of Wealth", *OECD Economics Department Working Papers*, No. 929, OECD Publishing.

Gabaix, X. and A. Landier (2008), "Why Has CEO Pay Increased So Much?", *Quarterly Journal of Economics*, Vol. 123, No. 1, pp. 49-100.

Garicano, L. and E. Rossi-Hansberg (2006), "Organization and Inequality in a Knowledge Economy", *Quarterly Journal of Economics*, Vol. 121, No. 4, pp. 1383-1435.

Goolsbee, A. (2000), "Taxes, High-Income Executives, and the Perils of Revenue Estimation in the New Economy", *American Economic Review*, Vol. 90, No. 2, pp. 271-275.

Goos, M., A. Manning and A. Salomons (2009), "The Polarization of the European Labor Market", *American Economic Review Papers and Proceedings*, Vol. 99, No. 2, pp. 58-63.

Gordon, R. and I. Dew-Becker (2008), "Controversies about the Rise of American Inequality: A Survey", *NBER Working Papers*, No. 13982, National Bureau of Economic Research.

Gregorio, J. De and J. Lee (2002), "Education and Income Inequality: New Evidence from Cross-Country Data", *Review of Income and Wealth*, Vol. 48, No. 3, pp. 395-416.

Griffith, R., R. Harrison and G. Macartney (2007), "Product Market Reforms, Labour Market Institutions and Unemployment", *Economic Journal*, Vol. 117.

Guadalupe, M. (2007), "Product Market Competition, Returns to Skill, and Wage Inequality", *Journal of Labor Economics*, Vol. 25, No. 3, pp. 439-474.

Heller, D.E. (1999), "The Effects of Tuition and State Financial Aid on Public College Enrollment", *Review of Higher Education*, Vol. 23, No. 1, pp. 65-89.

Helpman, E., O. Itskhoki and S.J. Redding (2010), "Inequality and Unemployment in a Global Economy", *Econometrica, Vol. 78, No. 4*, pp. 1239-1283.

Hoeller, P. (2012), "Less Income Inequality and More Growth – Are They Compatible? Part 4. Top Incomes", *OECD Economics Department Working Papers*, No. 927, OECD Publishing.

Hoeller, P. *et al.* (2012), "Less Income Inequality and More Growth – Are They Compatible? Part 1. Mapping Income Inequality Across the OECD", *OECD Economics Department Working Papers*, No. 924, OECD Publishing.

Johansson, Å. *et al.* (2008), "Taxation and Economic Growth", *OECD Economics Department Working Papers*, No. 620, OECD Publishing.

Journard, I., M. Pisu and D. Bloch (2012), "Less Income Inequality and More Growth – Are They Compatible? Part 3. Income Redistribution *via* Taxes and Transfers across OECD Countries", *OECD Economics Department Working Papers*, No. 926, OECD Publishing.

Koske, I., Fournier, J.-M. and I. Wanner (2012), "Less Income Inequality and More Growth – Are They Compatible? Part 2. The Distribution of Labour Income", *OECD Economics Department Working Papers*, No. 925, OECD Publishing.

Martin, J.P. and D. Grubb (2001), "What Works and for Whom: A Review of OECD Countries' Experiences with Active Labour Market Policies", *Swedish Economic Policy Review*, Vol. 8, No. 2, pp. 9-56.

Murphy, K.J. and J. Zábojník (2004), "CEO Pay and Appointments: A Market-Based Explanation for Recent Trends", *American Economic Review*, Vol. 94, No. 2, pp. 192-196.

Murtin, F., de Serres, A. and A. Hijzen (2012), "The Ins and Outs of Unemployment: The Role of Labour Market Institutions", *OECD Economics Department Working Papers*, OECD Publishing, forthcoming.

Neary, J.P. (2003), "Presidential Address: Globalization and Market Structure", *Journal of the European Economic Association*, Vol. 1, No. 2-3, pp. 245-271.

Neumark, D. and W. Wascher (2007), "Minimum Wages and Employment", *IZA Discussion Papers*, No. 2570.

OECD (2004), *OECD Employment Outlook 2004*, OECD Publishing.

OECD (2006a), *The Taxation of Employee Stock Options*, OECD Tax Policy Studies, No. 11, OECD Publishing.

OECD (2006b), *Starting Strong II: Early Childhood Education and Care*, OECD Publishing.

OECD (2008a), *Growing Unequal? Income Distribution and Poverty in OECD Countries*, OECD Publishing.

OECD (2008b), *Tertiary Education for the Knowledge Society: Volume 1 and Volume 2*, OECD Publishing.

OECD (2010a), *OECD Economic Surveys: Czech Republic 2010*, OECD Publishing.

OECD (2010b), *Tax Expenditures in OECD Countries*, OECD Publishing.

OECD (2011), *Divided We Stand: Why Inequality Keeps Rising*, OECD Publishing.

Piketty, T. (2010), "On the Long-Run Evolution of Inheritance: France 1820-2050", *Paris School of Economics Working Paper*, May.

Piketty, T. and E. Saez (2003), "The Evolution of Top Incomes: A Historical and International Perspective", *American Economic Review*, Vol. 96, No. 2, pp. 200-205.

Roine, J., J. Vlachos and D. Waldenström (2009), "The Long-Run Determinants of Inequality: What Can We Learn from Top Income Data?", *Journal of Public Economics*, Vol. 93, No. 7-8, pp. 974-988.

Rosen, S. (1981), "The Economics of Superstars", *American Economic Review*, Vol. 71, No. 5, pp. 845-858.

Saez, E. and M.R. Veall (2005), "The Evolution of High Incomes in Northern America: Lessons from Canadian Evidence", *American Economic Review*, Vol. 95, No. 3, pp. 831-849.

Stiglitz, J., A. Sen and J.P. Fitoussi (2009), *Report by the Commission on the Measurement of Economic Performance and Social Progress*, Commission on the Measurement of Economic Performance and Social Progress.

Economic Policy Reforms 2012
Going for Growth
© OECD 2012

PART II

Chapter 6

Under shock: How to spread macroeconomic risks more fairly[1]

Macroeconomic crises and shocks often cause large and unforeseen income and employment losses. Such losses tend to be unevenly spread across the population, often with the greatest impact on the poor and the most vulnerable in society. This chapter presents new OECD analysis of the types of policies that have helped to protect the most vulnerable from these losses in a wide group of OECD and emerging countries. These policies include pro-competitive product markets, openness to trade and foreign direct investment (FDI), low tax wedges on labour, a strong fiscal situation, generous unemployment benefits, strong unions, minimum wages and job protection. Some of these policies and institutions also benefit growth and jobs, thereby providing obvious avenues for reform. But others may involve trade-offs between short-term protection and other longer-term economic objectives. Finally, the chapter classifies OECD and emerging economies into four broad groups according to whether their institutional arrangements facilitate risk sharing through strong social protection or swift reallocation of labour and capital.

Summary and conclusions

The recent global financial crisis has highlighted that macroeconomic shocks can cause large and unforeseen losses that are unevenly distributed across the population. As income and employment security is one key dimension of individual and social well-being,[2] effective and fair risk-sharing mechanisms – such as well-designed unemployment benefit systems or short-time work arrangements – are essential for improving social welfare. However, while risk sharing is highly desirable, some fair risk-sharing arrangements may have an economic cost by undermining people's incentives to work, save or invest. This chapter presents new analysis covering 40 OECD and BRIICS[3] countries over 30 years.[4] It examines how various macroeconomic risks have been shared within economies, and suggests reforms to improve risk-sharing and make it more economically efficient. The main findings are:

- Macroeconomic shocks – such as financial crises, large fiscal consolidations, commodity price shocks or exchange rate depreciations – have widely different effects across the population. Incomes of the poor have in general been most affected, suffering particularly strongly in bad times but also rising disproportionately in good ones. Adverse macroeconomic shocks have also typically led to relatively more job losses for young people than for other age groups. In the case of financial crises, both high-income households and the poor have been hurt severely. Some of these "distributional" effects of shocks are undesirable and should be reduced by risk-sharing mechanisms.
- Existing institutions shape the distributional effects of macroeconomic shocks within OECD countries and the BRIICS. Some of the institutions that improve risk-sharing are also good for growth or jobs, thereby providing obvious directions for reforms. Examples are well-designed short-time working schemes, competitive product markets, low taxes on labour, and prudent fiscal policy.[5] Others, such as high minimum wages or strict job protection, can come at a cost, and particular care is therefore needed in designing them.
- The analysis identifies two broad types of institutional set-ups for sharing income risk, namely "social protection" and "reallocation-facilitating" institutions. Social protection institutions include unemployment benefits, job protection, minimum wages and strong unions. Pro-competitive product market regulation and low tax wedges on labour are examples of institutions that help to share risk by enabling resources and workers to be reallocated more easily. Based on these two institutional set-ups, OECD and BRIICs countries are categorised into four broad groups:
  - *i)* Countries that provide income risk sharing mainly via social protection institutions, such as most countries of continental Europe.
  - *ii)* Countries that rely mainly on reallocation-facilitating institutions, such as English-speaking and Asian OECD countries.
  - *iii)* Countries where neither class of institutions are developed, typically OECD and non-OECD emerging economies.
  - *iv)* Countries that rely strongly on both types, mainly the Nordic countries.

These models reflect different social choices and development levels. However, in many countries the terms of the trade-off between income per capita and risk-sharing objectives could be improved, for instance by reducing the efficiency cost of certain existing insurance mechanisms (*e.g.* well-designed in-work benefits could be a substitute for to-high statutory minimum wages).

The new analysis leads to the following detailed policy conclusions:

- Increasing pro-competitive product market regulation seems to allow for more equitable risk sharing, as well as having permanent positive effects on output and employment. Anti-competitive product market regulation has particularly negative effects for young people and increases poverty in the wake of macroeconomic shocks.
- Trade and FDI openness is important for mitigating the negative effects of shocks on the poor and vulnerable. In contrast, capital account openness has amplified the negative distributional effects of certain shocks, and global financial integration more broadly may facilitate the spreading of large international shocks across borders (see also Ahrend and Goujard, 2011).
- Lowering high taxes on labour could not only permanently raise employment (see de Serres *et al.* 2012), but also mitigate the job losses incurred by young and older workers in the wake of certain macroeconomic shocks. Temporary, targeted reductions in tax wedges in particularly bad times may also be effective for this purpose.
- Strong macro-prudential regulation has also a social dimension, especially in countries with complex financial sectors. Financial development, and especially high lending and leverage, amplifies the inequitable effects of various shocks.
- Generous unemployment benefits, and in particular high payments at the beginning of the unemployment spell, can mitigate the negative impact of macroeconomic shocks on the poor. Countries with low replacement rates could temporarily increase them in the wake of large negative shocks, as was the case during the recent financial crisis. Such increases, however, may have detrimental long-term effects on employment if they become permanent and if they are not accompanied by effective activation policies that assist and oblige the unemployed to return to work.
- Strong labour unions play an important insurance role for people with lower incomes in the wake of certain shocks. Stronger union power also typically improves the labour market performance of prime-age groups at these times, though the price is greater youth unemployment.
- Minimum wages reduce wage inequality (OECD, 2011b), but can increase youth unemployment in the wake of numerous shocks. Group-specific minimum wages for young people would be one possible policy device to help them to better get through difficult times.
- Stricter job protection has provided some security for those with lower and middle incomes in the wake of negative shocks. It has also improved the labour market performance of workers with long job tenure (older workers) compared to those with shorter tenure or those entering the job market (young people).

Introduction: The social implications of the recent financial crisis

After two decades of what has often been described as the Great Moderation, the recent crisis has been a forceful reminder that economies are still at risk of being affected by – sometimes violent – shocks. The economic implications of such shocks can vary markedly across the population. For example, young people have been particularly badly hit by the recent financial crises, with their unemployment rate increasing twice as much as the overall rate across the OECD and the BRIICS (Figure 6.1, Panel A). Such dissimilar implications of macroeconomic shocks reflect in part the greater sensitivity of certain groups to general economic conditions, but they are also likely to depend on policies and institutions. For instance, during the recent financial crisis youth unemployment increased more in countries with higher statutory minimum wages (Figure 6.1, Panel B), and more rigorous analysis presented further below confirms that this was more than mere coincidence.

Figure 6.1. **Young people have been particularly badly hurt by the recent financial crisis, and especially so in countries with high minimum wages**

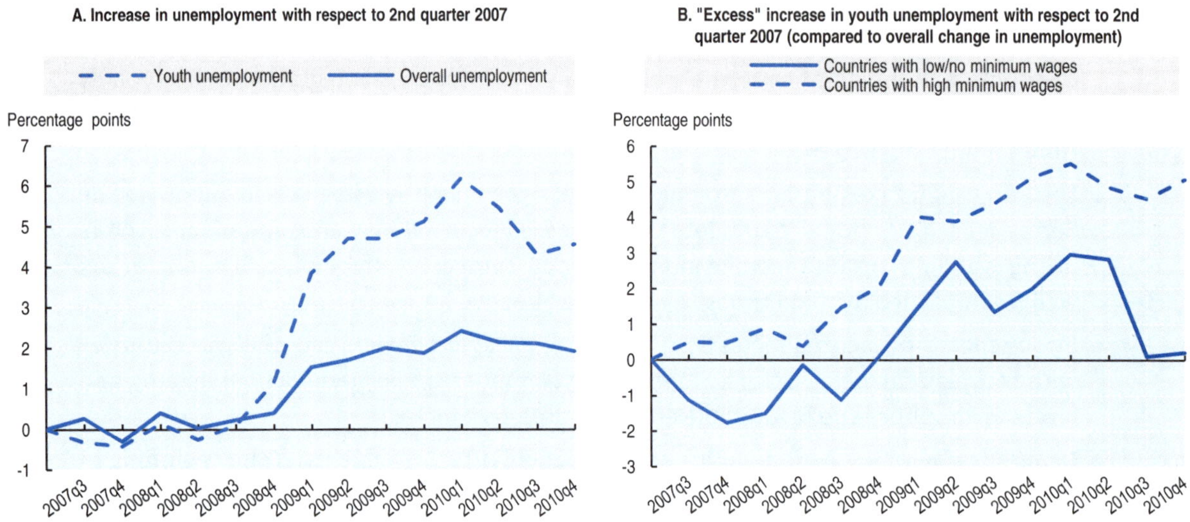

Note: In Chart B, OECD and BRIICS countries are classified by statutory minimum wage rates as a share of median wages, as reported in (OECD, 2011), *Economic Policy Reforms 2011: Going for Growth*, OECD Publishing. Countries with minimum wage rates below those of the median country (the sample includes countries with no statutory minimum wage) are classified as low/no minimum wage countries (Austria, Brazil, China, Czech Republic, Denmark, Estonia, Finland, Germany, Iceland, India, Italy, Japan, Norway, Russian Federation, South Africa, South Korea, Sweden, Switzerland, and the United States). Correspondingly, countries with minimum wage rates above the median are classified as high minimum wage countries (Australia, Belgium, Canada, France, Greece, Hungary, Ireland, Indonesia, Luxembourg, Netherlands, New Zealand, Poland, Portugal, Slovak Republic, Slovenia, Spain, Turkey and the United Kingdom). Chart B presents averages for the two country groups. Changes are shown with respect to the last pre-crisis quarter.

Source: International Labour Organisation (ILO) and OECD calculations.

StatLink http://dx.doi.org/10.1787/888932566630

Mechanisms for macroeconomic risk sharing

Macroeconomic risk sharing has two fundamental dimensions: The first dimension, international collective risk sharing, concerns the possibilities for a *country as a whole* to insure against or to export the impact of macroeconomic shocks. In practice, international risk-sharing devices are limited.[6] As it is impossible for a country to protect all citizens *fully* from macroeconomic shocks, there is a need to spread the residual impact across individuals, and there is no straightforward burden-sharing criterion to do so (Box 6.1).[7] The second dimension of risk sharing therefore covers national public and private mechanisms to share risk across individuals and shape the distributive impact of shocks. This chapter focuses on these mechanisms to share risk across individuals within a country. Examples include unemployment benefit systems or private insurance contracts.[8]

Risk-sharing mechanisms within countries typically differ in two ways: *i)* the type of provider (public, private market or private non-market); and *ii)* the object of protection

Box 6.1. **How should risk be shared?**

As most individuals dislike risk, limiting their exposure to risk matters for public policy. The importance of fairness in the way risk is shared across individuals has been recently highlighted by the public outcry over the perceived privatisation of benefits and the subsequent socialisation of losses from financial-sector driven increases in macroeconomic risk. In this respect, explicit and transparent *ex ante* risk-sharing institutions (*e.g.* deposit insurance) are likely to be perceived as much fairer than implicit and opaque *ex post* arrangements (*e.g. ad hoc* bank bail-outs). However, risk-sharing institutions are of little social use when the insurance they provide to some (*e.g.* to banks whose failure could damage the banking system and the wider economy) results in a build-up of aggregate macroeconomic risk.

Social preferences for how best to split large losses in economy-wide national income and wealth are likely to differ across countries. National choices will reflect a number of tradeoffs, especially between equity and economic efficiency, as many public risk-sharing devices do have a cost in the form of lower aggregate GDP.* Fairness would suggest that the larger share of the costs should be borne by those who either benefited most from the risk as long as no shock materialised, or by those who increased the likelihood of the risk occurring in the first place (such as large interconnected banks before the 2007 global financial crisis). Mitigating moral hazard risk, this would also be economically efficient. However, the amount of compensation that can be obtained from corporations or individuals is inevitably limited and typically insufficient to cover the costs of a macroeconomic shock. It is therefore also necessary to decide how the remaining risk should be distributed across the population, especially taking into account income. As poorer individuals have less scope for "self insurance" – using part of their wealth or borrowing capacity – good risk-sharing institutions should reduce income volatility especially for these people. There may also be a case for providing temporary protection to those who have little possibility of adjusting rapidly to the shock, such as single-parent households with young children or the elderly. Social costs are likely to be particularly high in the wake of large and infrequent shocks, so there is a case for stronger social protection in these circumstances. For example, *ad hoc* mechanisms can be useful where risk-sharing institutions are not well developed and where prudent fiscal behaviour prior to the shock means some fiscal action can be taken. During the recent recession, many OECD countries temporarily extended risk-sharing mechanisms – such as short-time working schemes – and the coverage, level and duration of unemployment benefits.

However, even with the best risk-sharing policies in place, in reality the outcomes may be sub-optimal. Powerful and politically well-represented groups – the financial sector, large voting groups (*e.g.* baby boomers) or labour-market "insiders", for example – may avoid bearing an adequate amount of risk. Other groups with high bargaining power, like farmers, may also avoid bearing their share of risk. Powerful groups may influence risk sharing either directly after a shock, or indirectly by shaping the design of the institutions – such as labour, product and financial market regulations – thereby affecting how the costs of macroeconomic shocks are spread across society.

* Even under well-functioning insurance markets shocks will usually have distributional effects, as individuals who opt for different degrees of protection will be affected differently.

(wage income, capital income, or wealth). An examination of risk-sharing options for a selection of macroeconomic shocks shows that private market mechanisms to insure wage income against job loss (or a broader range of risks) are very rare, and moral hazard limits the scope for progress (Ahrend *et al.*, 2011a).[9] Therefore, the essential providers of this protection in most OECD countries are government-sponsored unemployment insurance and social benefit systems. Other institutions, such as the strength of employment protection regulation or trade unions, also make a difference for income-risk sharing. In contrast to wage income, asset-derived income or wealth can to some degree be hedged in private markets.[10] Individuals' abilities to exploit these possibilities differ significantly, however, depending on their financial sophistication or wealth levels.[11]

In addition to the risk-sharing mechanisms provided by governments or private insurance markets, risk sharing within households or extended families can play a large role. This is especially so in the emerging economies, where wage-income risk is often taken care of through risk-sharing within the family and to some extent via informal labour markets. More generally, families (or extended families) allow individual members to pool income risk, and can adjust their labour in response to shocks. In particular, the ability of spouses to adjust their labour market participation and working hours – including in developed economies, when helped by strong childcare subsidies – has often offered valuable protection from household income losses (Attanasio *et al.*, 2005). Younger workers have the safety net of being able to shift between living with their parents and independently (Kaplan, 2010). In some countries, firms provide their workers with considerable protection from transitory downturns in the firm's performance (Guiso *et al.*, 2005). Such transitory economic shocks can also be mitigated through short-time working schemes, under which workers forced into shorter hours are partially compensated by employers or public unemployment insurance schemes (OECD, 2010).

How do public risk-sharing mechanisms work in practice? New evidence from OECD and BRIICS countries

In recent decades, an uneven exposure of households to macroeconomic shocks has often led to changes in income or wealth distribution. This section presents new empirical analysis (Box 6.2) of a broad range of macroeconomic shocks that occurred in OECD countries and the BRIICS during the 30 years prior to the recent financial crisis.

Box 6.2. **Methodology**

Based on roughly 30 years of data prior to (and not covering) the 2007 global financial crisis for 40 OECD and BRIICS countries, the analysis followed these steps:

- Various types of shocks – financial crises as well as commodity price, exchange rate, and fiscal shocks – were identified.
- For each type of shock, the average impact on incomes or jobs over the five-year period following its occurrence was compared across countries, for various income, wealth, age, gender and education groups. The analysis allowed for positive and negative shocks to have asymmetric impacts.
- The analysis then explored whether the impact of a shock on certain groups depended on the institutional features of the country considered. For example, knowing that financial crises have had particularly negative effects on labour market outcomes for the young, the research examined whether the strength of this effect differed across countries depending *e.g.* on the degree of pro-competitiveness of their product market regulation, the level of their statutory minimum wage, etc. For further details see Ahrend *et al.* (2011a).

The main results from this empirical analysis are as follows (for more detailed results see Table 6.1 and Ahrend *et al.*, 2011a, 2011b).

- Generally, those with lower incomes have been more exposed to macroeconomic fluctuations: they have suffered more from adverse economic shocks but have often also benefited more from favourable ones. One specific group of low-income workers – young people – experiences a disproportionately strong reduction in their job opportunities in the wake of almost any negative macroeconomic shock (for an example, see Figure 6.2, Panel A).

Table 6.1. **The distributional impact of macroeconomic shocks: Key OECD findings**

Financial crises have...	• Increased the income share of the middle classes, and reduced the income share of high-income earners. • Increased poverty. • Particularly weakened the labour market for young and old workers, women, and those without tertiary education.
Fiscal consolidations have...	• Increased inequality and poverty. • Particularly worsened the labour market for young and old workers.
Fiscal expansions have...	• Reduced inequality and poverty. • Increased the income share of the young and pensioners. • Particularly enhanced the labour market for young and old workers.
Exchange-rate devaluations have...	• Increased inequality. • Particularly worsened the labour market for young and old workers.
Exchange-rate appreciations have...	• Reduced inequality.
Commodity-price increases have...	• Decreased the income share of households with high capital income. • Decreased the income share of low-income households and increased poverty. • Particularly worsened the labour market for the young.
Commodity-price declines have...	• Reduced inequality.

Source: Ahrend, R., J. Arnold and C. Moeser (2011), "The Sharing of Macroeconomic Risk: Who Loses (and Gains) from Macroeconomic Shocks", *OECD Economics Department Working Papers*, No. 877, OECD Publishing.

- Financial crises in particular have tended to hurt high-income households and the poor (Figure 6.2, Panel B), but less so middle-income households. The larger impact on the poor may reflect their greater sensitivity to general economic conditions. In turn, the larger effect on high-income households may arise as capital income – which is concentrated in the higher income strata – as well as sectors with high labour incomes (*e.g.* banking) are hit particularly hard by financial crises. The negative effect on high-income earners appears to be restricted to countries with well-developed financial markets.
- Upward commodity-price shocks have increased inequality. Particularly strong income losses for lower-income households – though possibly just a reflection of their greater sensitivity to overall cyclical conditions – may be of particular concern as they come on

Figure 6.2. **Financial crises have disproportionally affected youth employment and increased poverty rates**

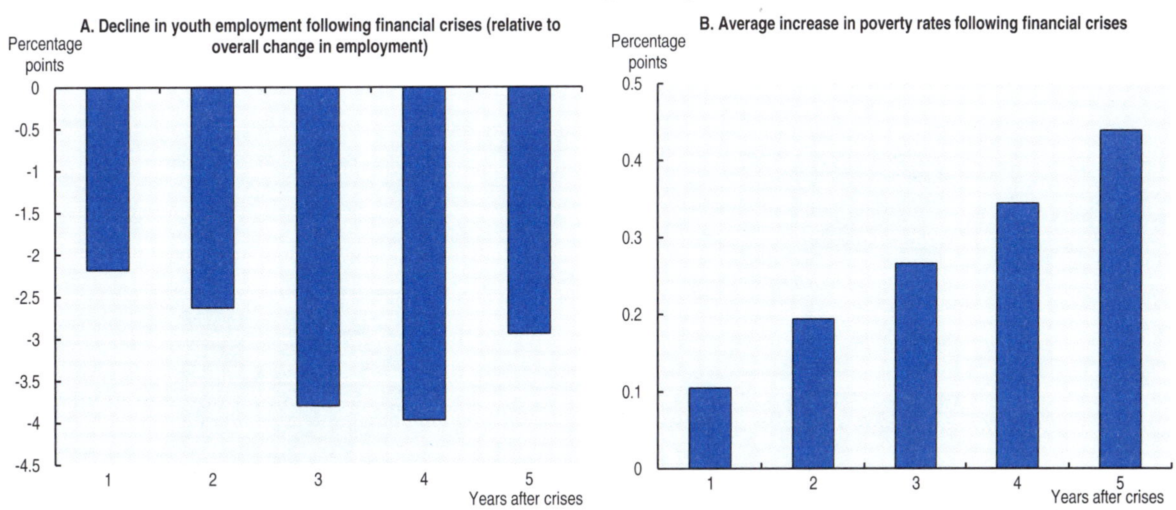

Source: Ahrend, R., J. Arnold and C. Moeser (2011), "The Sharing of Macroeconomic Risk: Who Loses (and Gains) from Macroeconomic Shocks", *OECD Economics Department Working Papers*, No. 877, OECD Publishing.

StatLink http://dx.doi.org/10.1787/888932566649

top of a reduction in their relative purchasing power when commodity prices go up. Indeed, commodity products (*e.g.* gasoline or energy) typically account for a larger share of the expenditures of low-income households, compared with more affluent ones.

- Older and low-income households have been particularly affected by large changes in the fiscal stance. While fiscal expansions have typically improved the income share of pensioners compared with workers, fiscal consolidations have particularly weakened the employment prospects of older workers. Similarly, the poor have generally benefited from fiscal expansions, while suffering more than others from fiscal consolidations. This may reflect the greater exposure of low income households to cuts in social transfers during fiscal consolidations, as well as more generous funding of public programmes aimed at helping the poor during times of fiscal expansion.

Macroeconomic shocks do not only affect the distribution of income, but also of wealth, through their impact on asset prices. As (net) wealth losses increase with leverage, more leveraged age groups are likely to suffer more. This implies that the 26-35 year-olds would be likely to lose a larger share of their wealth, as the available data show them to be the most leveraged age group with leverage decreasing gradually after the age of 35. Beyond leverage, portfolio composition also plays a role. Financial crises, for example, are often associated with large falls in house prices and comparatively less severe and shorter-lasting equity price declines.[12] Consequently, wealth effects from financial crises are larger for those whose asset portfolios primarily consist of housing. These tend to be households with low capital income, since the portfolios of those with sizeable capital income mostly consist of business assets and stocks (Figure 6.3).[13] Consequently, financial crises would be expected to destroy a comparatively smaller share of the wealth of richer households.[14] At first glance this may seem at odds with the aforementioned finding that higher incomes take a relatively stronger hit in the wake of financial crises. However, with capital income representing a much higher share of their total income, even a comparatively smaller impact on their wealth could translate into a larger impact on their income.

Figure 6.3. **Vulnerability of wealth varies across households due to a different composition of asset portfolios**

Composition of assets of households with high and low capital income

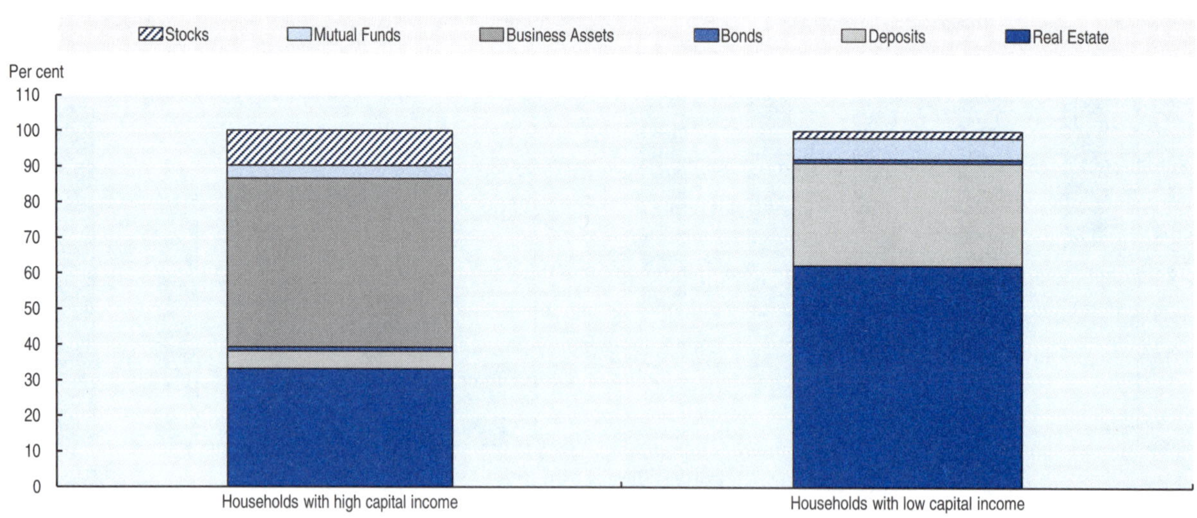

Note: Calculations based on gross wealth data for Canada, Italy, Sweden and the United States, averaged across these four countries.

Source: Ahrend, R., J. Arnold and C. Moeser (2011), "The Sharing of Macroeconomic Risk: Who Loses (and Gains) from Macroeconomic Shocks", *OECD Economics Department Working Papers*, No. 877, OECD Publishing. StatLink http://dx.doi.org/10.1787/888932566668

The role of institutions

So far, the analysis has presented the average impact of macroeconomic shocks across different OECD countries and the BRIICS. However, effects differ between countries according to their different institutional settings (see also Table 6.2 for a summary of results):

- *Generous unemployment benefits*, and in particular high payments during the first year of unemployment, reduce the negative impact of macroeconomic shocks on the poor (Figure 6.4). This finding suggests that, especially for countries with low replacement rates, temporary increases in unemployment benefits during the recent crisis helped to cushion the poor. At the same time, higher levels and a longer duration of unemployment benefits seem to amplify employment losses for young and older workers. Previous OECD evidence also points to adverse effects on unemployment over the longer term, unless there are effective activation strategies that assist and oblige the unemployed to return to work (Bassanini and Duval, 2006). This implies that crisis-related increases in the level or duration of unemployment benefits should only be temporary where they were already high before the crisis. By contrast, unemployment benefit coverage could be permanently extended to groups that were previously uninsured. If accompanied by effective activation mechanisms, this wider coverage would strengthen the effectiveness of social protection systems without undermining labour market performance.
- *Higher labour taxes* appear to have particularly worsened the employment performance of groups with a lower attachment to the labour market, such as young people, following adverse shocks. Therefore, lowering high tax wedges on labour income could not only permanently raise employment (Bassanini and Duval, 2006) but also mitigate the job losses incurred by young and older workers in bad times. In such situations, temporary, targeted reductions in tax wedges may also be an effective strategy (de Serres *et al.*, 2012).
- *Stronger labour unions* have played an important insurance function for lower income groups in the wake of certain shocks. Stronger union power has also typically improved the labour market performance of prime-age groups in the aftermath of shocks, but at the cost of greater youth unemployment.

Table 6.2. **How institutions affect the impact of adverse shocks on equality**

More developed welfare systems (*i.e.* larger government transfers) have...	• Reduced increases in poverty. • Reduced the negative income effects for young people.
More generous unemployment benefits have...	• Limited increases in poverty and income inequality. • Reduced negative income effects for older workers. • Decreased labour market performance for young people.
Higher tax wedges on labour have...	• Decreased labour market performance for young and older workers.
More stringent job protection has...	• Alleviated increases in poverty and sheltered the income of middle classes. • Improved labour market performance for older, and deteriorated labour market performance for younger workers.
More extensive use of minimum wages has...	• Decreased the labour market performance for young people and (for some shocks) for older workers.
Stronger unions have...	• Reduced increases in income inequality. • Improved labour market performance for prime-age workers while worsening it for young people.
More pro-competitive product market regulation has...	• Reduced increases in poverty and income inequality. • Improved labour market performance for young people.
Greater openness to trade/FDI has...	• Reduced the deterioration in the labour market performance for young people. • Reduced increases in income inequality.
Greater openness to capital flows has...	• Contributed to greater inequality.
Financial development has...	• Amplified declines in the income shares of low and high income people. • Reduced the deterioration in the labour market performance for young people.

Source: Ahrend, R., J. Arnold and C. Moeser (2011), "The Sharing of Macroeconomic Risk: Who Loses (and Gains) from Macroeconomic Shocks", *OECD Economics Department Working Papers*, No. 877, OECD Publishing.

Figure 6.4. **Generous unemployment benefits have mitigated crisis-driven increases in poverty**

Increase in poverty rates following financial crises

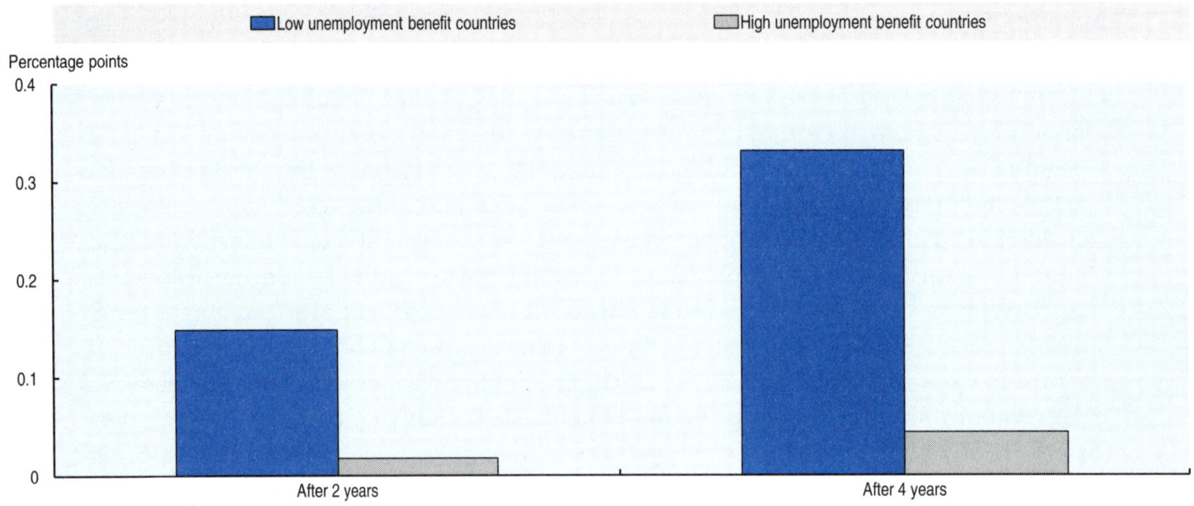

Source: Ahrend, R., J. Arnold and C. Moeser (2011), "The Sharing of Macroeconomic Risk: Who Loses (and Gains) from Macroeconomic Shocks", *OECD Economics Department Working Papers*, No. 877, OECD Publishing.

StatLink http://dx.doi.org/10.1787/888932566687

- *Stricter job protection* has also reduced shock-driven declines in the incomes of the lower and middle classes and mitigated increases in poverty (Figure 6.5, Panel A). At the same time, it has improved the post-shock labour-market performance of workers with long job tenure (older workers) compared to those with shorter tenure or just entering the job market, such as young people (Figure 6.5, Panel B).
- *Minimum wages* reduce wage inequality in general (OECD, 2011b), but they have worsened unemployment and employment performance for the young in the wake of numerous shocks. Reducing the minimum cost of labour for the young where it is currently high

Figure 6.5. **Stricter job protection has protected lower incomes, but weakened labour market performance of the young**

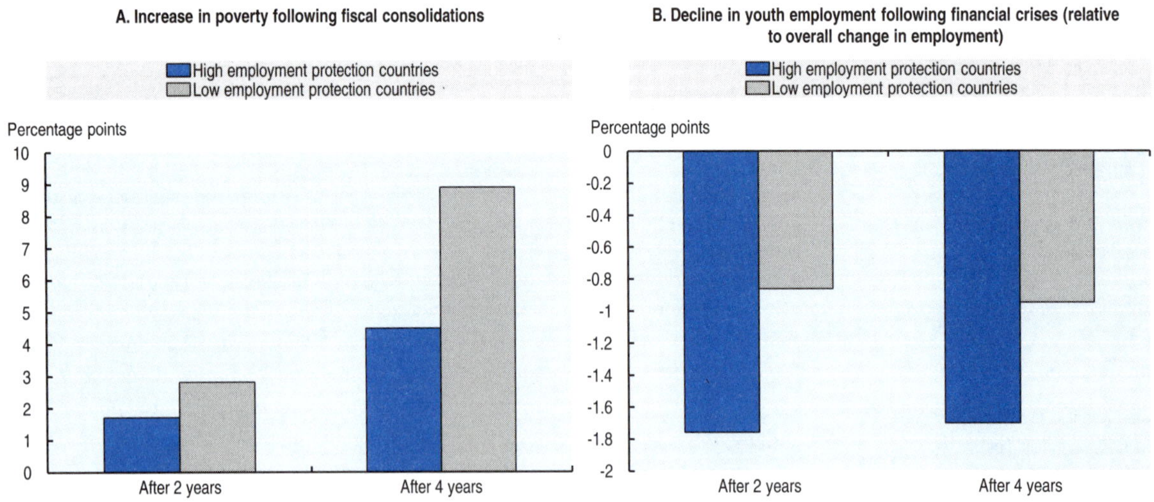

Source: Ahrend, R., J. Arnold and C. Moeser (2011), "The Sharing of Macroeconomic Risk: Who Loses (and Gains) from Macroeconomic Shocks", *OECD Economics Department Working Papers*, No. 877, OECD Publishing.

StatLink http://dx.doi.org/10.1787/888932566706

(mostly in a number of continental European countries) through group-specific minimum wages or targeted cuts in social security contributions could help them to better weather bad times.

- *Anti-competitive product market regulation* has amplified the adverse impacts of macroeconomic shocks on both poverty and labour market performance of young people (Figure 6.6). More competitive product markets may allow for quicker reallocation of resources across sectors and firms in the wake of adverse macroeconomic shocks (Arnold *et al.*, 2008), with greater turnover in labour markets improving the relative situation of young and poor people. More pro-competitive product market regulation would therefore appear to share risk more equitably, in addition to having permanent positive effects on output and employment, as identified in previous OECD work (*e.g.* Boulhol *et al.*, 2008; Bassanini and Duval, 2006; Conway *et al.*, 2007).

Figure 6.6. **More competitive product markets have dampened crisis-driven increases in youth unemployment**

Increase in youth unemployment following financial crises (relative to overall change in unemployment)

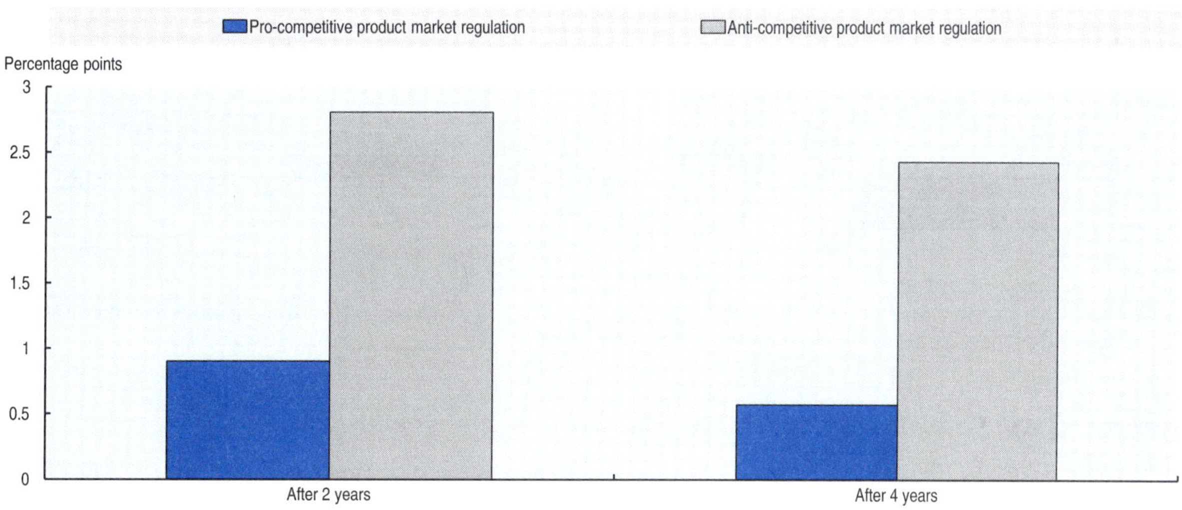

Source: Ahrend, R., J. Arnold and C. Moeser (2011), "The Sharing of Macroeconomic Risk: Who Loses (and Gains) from Macroeconomic Shocks", *OECD Economics Department Working Papers*, No. 877, OECD Publishing.

StatLink http://dx.doi.org/10.1787/888932566725

- *Financial account openness* has increased the impact of certain shocks on the more vulnerable. However, greater *FDI and trade openness* appears to reduce the adverse effects of shocks on weaker groups in society – such as the young or the poor – over and above the international insurance role they perform by exporting domestic shocks.[15] This confirms the importance of trade and FDI openness for shock mitigation, even though openness may also facilitate the spreading of a global shock or a shock affecting a large economy across borders.

- *A more developed financial sector* has long been found to benefit long-term growth, but new analysis shows that it also increases the negative impact of financial crises on youth employment, and more generally that it amplifies the inequitable effects of various shocks (Ahrend *et al.*, 2011b). This arises mainly as financial market sophistication allows for increased leverage, thereby amplifying credit cycles and the depth of financial crises. Similarly, exchange rate devaluations are found to have disproportionally harmed the poor where the financial sector (and specifically credit) was more developed (Figure 6.7). One explanation could be that financial development facilitates credit and overinvestment in non-tradables such as housing during periods of exchange-rate overvaluation. The larger economic adjustment required in the wake of the devaluation especially hurts the poor. These risks further strengthen the case for strong macro and micro-prudential regulation to counteract boom-bust episodes, especially in countries with complex financial sectors.

Figure 6.7. **Financial development has amplified the redistributive effects of shocks**

Change in inequality (GINI coefficient) following devaluation shocks

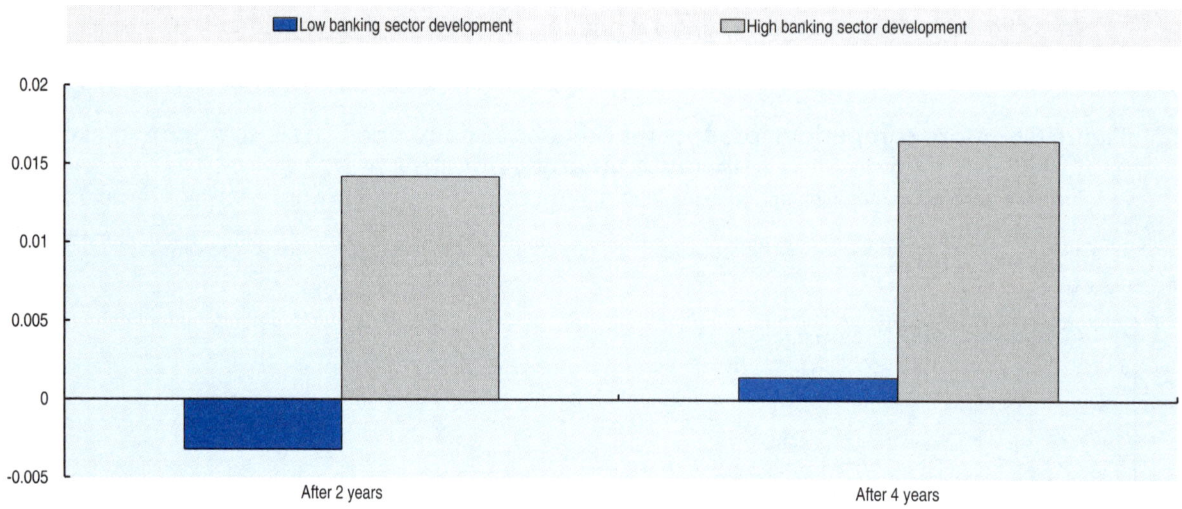

Source: Ahrend, R., J. Arnold and C. Moeser (2011), "The Sharing of Macroeconomic Risk: Who Loses (and Gains) from Macroeconomic Shocks", *OECD Economics Department Working Papers*, No. 877, OECD Publishing.

StatLink http://dx.doi.org/10.1787/888932566744

Summing up: Four broad country models of income risk sharing

Overall, the new empirical analysis highlights two broad types of institutions that facilitate income risk sharing:

i) "Social protection" institutions: these include unemployment benefits, stricter job protection, minimum wages or strong unions.

ii) "Reallocation-facilitating" institutions: examples include pro-competitive product market regulations and low tax wedges on labour. These work by helping to reallocate labour and capital rapidly following a shock.

On this basis, four broad groups of countries can be identified with respect to their income risk-sharing models (Figure 6.8). These country groups are likely to differ not only in the strength of their income risk-sharing mechanisms but also in terms of the associated costs:

- Countries that provide income risk sharing mainly via social protection institutions, namely the large majority of continental-European countries (Switzerland being the most notable exception) and (to a lesser degree) eastern-European countries. These countries are likely to provide a high degree of income protection for lower-income households. However, over the long term there may be a considerable cost in terms of weaker labour market performance for young people and other labour market outsiders, *i.e.* groups for whose members it is often particularly difficult to find stable employment.

Figure 6.8. **A stylised classification of risk-sharing models across the OECD and the BRIICS**

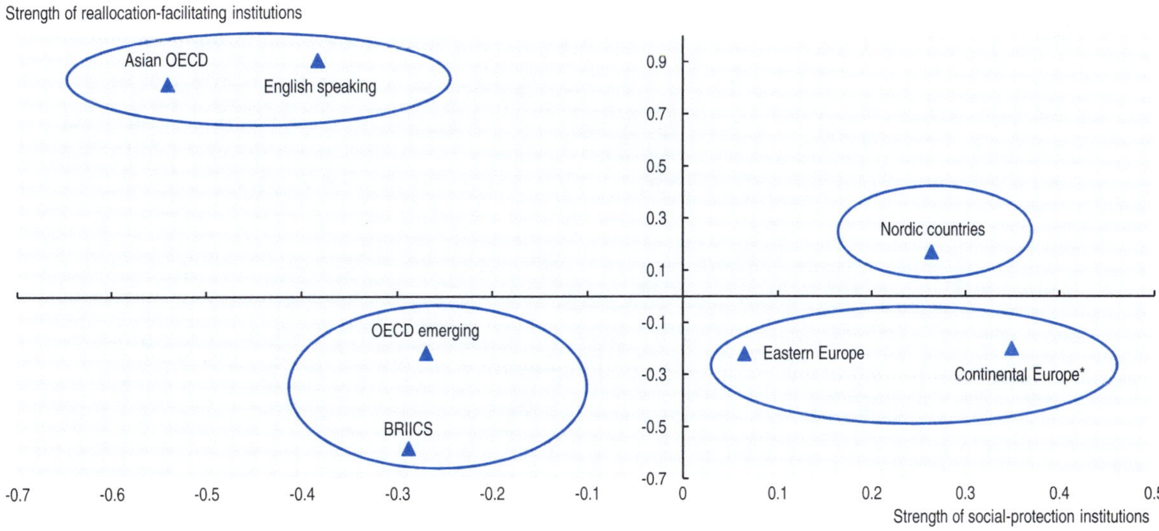

Note: The two axes show indicators of the development of reallocation-facilitating and social-protection institutions, respectively. The higher the value of an indicator, the stronger is the capacity of a country to prevent macroeconomic shocks from having distributional impacts. The indicator measuring the strength of reallocation-facilitating institutions is based on product market regulation and average tax wedges on labour, with lower tax wedges and more pro-competitive regulation resulting in higher indicator values. The indicator measuring the strength of social-protection institutions is based on unemployment benefits, employment protection legislation, statutory minimum wages, and the strength of trade unions, with higher values in these variables resulting in higher indicator values. Underlying variables have been normalised prior to aggregation.

* Excluding Switzerland.

Source: Ahrend, R., J. Arnold and C. Moeser (2011), "The Sharing of Macroeconomic Risk: Who Loses (and Gains) from Macroeconomic Shocks", *OECD Economics Department Working Papers*, No. 877, OECD Publishing.

StatLink http://dx.doi.org/10.1787/888932566763

- Countries that rely mainly on reallocation-facilitating institutions, such as English-speaking and Asian OECD countries. *Short-term* income risk sharing may be comparatively less developed in these countries.
- Countries where neither class of institutions are developed. These are typically OECD and non-OECD emerging economies, with eastern-European countries sharing some features with continental Europe and some with emerging economies. When neither class of institutions is developed – in part reflecting lower levels of economic development and therefore limited administrative capacity – households rely to a greater extent on risk sharing through family networks, "self-insurance" through savings, and, possibly, increased participation in the informal sector.
- Countries that rely strongly on both types of institutions, mainly the Nordic countries. Because they typically combine strong reallocation-facilitating institutions with well-developed social insurance and a strong fiscal position, these countries tend to provide a high degree of (relative) income protection to lower-income households in the wake of adverse macroeconomic shocks. Possible adverse effects of the Nordic model, such as on youth unemployment, seem to have been minimised in practice through other policies.[16]

Some policies and institutions are beneficial from both a risk-sharing and an efficiency perspective, thereby providing obvious directions for reforms. Examples are well-designed short-time working schemes, competitive product markets, low tax wedges on labour, and prudent fiscal policy, which spread risk more fairly and benefit long-term living standards. Other polices and institutions may entail trade-offs between long-term efficiency and short-term income risk sharing. While this does not allow for a ready comparison of the four models,[17] there may be room for improving the terms of the trade-offs in many countries by reducing the efficiency cost of certain existing risk-sharing institutions. For instance, in-work benefits might protect workers from the risk of income loss at a lower employment and economic cost than high minimum labour costs (OECD, 2006).

Any attempt at striking a more favourable balance between efficiency and risk-sharing objectives – *i.e.* reducing income risk at a lower economic cost – should also recognise the existence of economic and political-economy linkages across different risk-sharing mechanisms. For example, strong economy-wide trade unions that represent the whole working-age population may strengthen political support for risk-sharing devices that benefit *both* outsiders and insiders, such as higher public spending on active labour market policies (Elmeskov *et al.*, 1998). More broadly, each of the existing "models" may have some degree of internal coherence, making it difficult – and in some cases even unwarranted – to change certain specific policy settings in isolation. Each model may also reflect strong social preferences and different stages of development – looking at best practice within each grouping may be more sensible than all countries aspiring to the same model.

Notes

1. This chapter is based on Ahrend, Arnold and Moeser (2011a), "The Sharing of Macroeconomic Risk: Who Loses (and Gains) from Macroeconomic Shocks".
2. See OECD, 2011a.
3. Brazil, Russian Federation, India, Indonesia, China, South Africa.
4. The countries covered by the empirical analysis vary depending on data availability, with somewhat greater variation for BRIICS countries.
5. Well-designed short-time working arrangements should in particular include built-in incentives for workers and firms to withdraw from them once they have outlived their conjunctural purpose so as to avoid negative long-term effects on productivity and labour utilisation.
6. Individuals can also try to protect themselves against shocks internationally, for example by holding their wealth in foreign-currency denominated assets. However, such options are typically not available to the entire population of a country at the same time, so cannot provide a country with full protection.
7. For instance, when the government takes part of the risk it shifts costs on to current or future taxpayers and risk towards holders of existing government bonds.
8. Another option in principal available both to countries and individuals is to use saving and borrowing to smooth consumption.
9. A prominent example of moral hazard is unemployment insurance, which may discourage unemployed individuals from actively looking for a new job. Dealing with moral hazard is complex and in general only partially successful and/or costly, which may explain why in most countries instances of severe moral hazard are typically addressed by government-sponsored institutions, such as public unemployment insurance schemes.
10. For example, holding part of one's assets in foreign currency is a hedge against both wealth and capital income effects from *exchange-rate shocks*. Households in commodity-importing countries can, to some degree, hedge wealth against *commodity price shocks* by holding stocks of commodity companies. Households can protect their wealth or capital income against *inflation shocks* insofar as they can hold inflation-proof assets. See Ahrend *et al.* (2011a) for a more detailed discussion.
11. In addition, wealthier individuals would typically be expected to have more diversified income sources and wealth holdings, which may provide a greater degree of protection against macroeconomic shocks.

12. Reinhart and Rogoff (2008) document prolonged declines in housing prices, which averaged around 38% for 13 financial crises over the last 30 years. In contrast, equity price declines have been substantially more modest and short lived, with a complete recovery generally reached after three years.
13. Households with high capital income are defined as the top 33% earners of capital income in a given country before a shock.
14. Assuming that households with higher capital income are typically richer than households with lower capital income.
15. These results are consistent with findings in the literature that show long-term benefits for the poor from economic openness. For a survey of the literature, see Winters *et al.* (2004).
16. Adverse employment effects on young people may have traditionally been mitigated by generous financing for education and low requirements to qualify for unemployment benefits in Nordic countries. In turn, disincentive effects from unemployment benefits may have been limited by strong activation policies and social ethics. At the same time, such a "model" typically entails high costs of benefit systems and activation policies, with high marginal tax rates on the financing side, highlighting possible trade-offs between economic efficiency and risk-sharing (defined here as income distribution) considerations.
17. The trade-off between income levels and income risk is also explored in Bouis and Renne (2006).

Bibliography

Ahrend, R. and A. Goujard (2011), "*Drivers of Systemic Banking Crises: The Role of Bank-Balance-Sheet Contagion and Financial Account Structure*", *OECD Economics Department Working Papers,* No. 902, OECD Publishing.

Ahrend, R., J. Arnold and C. Moeser (2011a), "The Sharing of Macroeconomic Risk: Who Loses (and Gains) from Macroeconomic Shocks", *OECD Economics Department Working Papers,* No. 877, OECD Publishing.

Ahrend, R., C. Moeser and T. Monacelli (2011b), "How Institutions Shape the Distributive Impact of Macroeconomic Shocks: A DSGE Analysis", *OECD Economics Department Working Papers*, No. 884, OECD Publishing.

Arnold, J., G. Nicoletti and S. Scarpetta (2008), "Regulation, Allocative Efficiency and Productivity in OECD Countries: Industry and Firm-Level Evidence", *OECD Economics Department Working Papers*, No. 616, OECD Publishing.

Attanasio, O., H. Low and V. Sánchez-Marcos (2005), "*Female Labor Supply as Insurance against Idiosyncratic Risk*", *Journal of the European Economic Association*, Vol. 3(2-3).

Bassanini, A. and R. Duval (2006), "Employment Patterns in OECD Countries: Reassessing the Role of Policies and Institutions", *OECD Economics Department Working Papers*, No. 486, OECD Publishing.

Bouis, R. and J.-P. Renne (2006), "Caractéristiques des marchés du travail dans les pays de l'OCDE", *Diagnostics Prévisions et Analyses Économiques*, No. 111, Juin 2006, Direction Générale du Trésor et de la Politique Économique.

Boulhol, H., A. de Serres and M. Molnár (2008), "The Contribution of Economic Geography to GDP Per Capita", *OECD Journal: Economic Studies*, Vol. 2008/1, OECD Publishing.

Conway, P. *et al.* (2007), "Product Market Regulation and Productivity Convergence", *OECD Economic Studies*, Vol. 2006/2, OECD Publishing.

Elmeskov, J., J.P. Martin and S. Scarpetta (1998), "Key Lessons for Labour Market Reforms: Evidence from OECD Countries' Experiences", *Swedish Economic Policy Review*, Vol. 5, Issue 2, pp. 205-252, Social Science Research Network.

Guiso, L., L. Pistaferri and F. Schivardi (2005), "*Insurance within the Firm*", *Journal of Political Economy*, Vol. 113(5).

Kaplan, G. (2010), "Moving Back Home: Insurance Against Labor Market Risk", *Federal Reserve Bank of Minneapolis Working Paper*, No. 677.

OECD (2006), *OECD Employment Outlook 2006: Boosting Jobs and Incomes*, OECD Publishing.

OECD (2010), *OECD Employment Outlook 2010: Moving Beyond the Jobs Crisis*, OECD Publishing.

OECD (2011a), *How is Life? Measuring Well-being*, OECD Publishing.

OECD (2011b), *Divided We Stand: Why Inequality Keeps Rising*, OECD Publishing.

OECD (2011c), *Economic Policy Reforms 2011: Going for Growth*, OECD Publishing.

Reinhart, C. and K. Rogoff (2009), *This Time Is Different: Eight Centuries of Financial Folly*, Princeton University Press.

de Serres, A., F. Murtin and C. De la Maisonneuve (2012), "Policies to Facilitate the Return to Work", *OECD Economics Department Working Papers*, OECD Publishing, forthcoming.

Winters, L.A., N. McCulloch and A. McKay (2004), "*Trade Liberalization and Poverty: The Evidence So Far*", *Journal of Economic Literature*, American Economic Association, Vol. 42(1), pp. 72-115, March.

ORGANISATION FOR ECONOMIC CO-OPERATION AND DEVELOPMENT

The OECD is a unique forum where governments work together to address the economic, social and environmental challenges of globalisation. The OECD is also at the forefront of efforts to understand and to help governments respond to new developments and concerns, such as corporate governance, the information economy and the challenges of an ageing population. The Organisation provides a setting where governments can compare policy experiences, seek answers to common problems, identify good practice and work to co-ordinate domestic and international policies.

The OECD member countries are: Australia, Austria, Belgium, Canada, Chile, the Czech Republic, Denmark, Estonia, Finland, France, Germany, Greece, Hungary, Iceland, Ireland, Israel, Italy, Japan, Korea, Luxembourg, Mexico, the Netherlands, New Zealand, Norway, Poland, Portugal, the Slovak Republic, Slovenia, Spain, Sweden, Switzerland, Turkey, the United Kingdom and the United States. The European Union takes part in the work of the OECD.

OECD Publishing disseminates widely the results of the Organisation's statistics gathering and research on economic, social and environmental issues, as well as the conventions, guidelines and standards agreed by its members.

OECD PUBLISHING, 2, rue André-Pascal, 75775 PARIS CEDEX 16
(12 2012 03 1 P) ISBN 978-92-64-16825-1 – No. 59785 2012-02